Technology Now

Your Companion to SAM Computer Concepts

Corinne Hoisington

CENGAGE Learning

Australia • Brazil • Mexico • Singapore • United Kingdom • United States

Technology Now: Your Companion to SAM Computer Concepts
Corinne Hoisington

Product Director, Computing: Kathleen McMahon

Senior Product Team Manager: Lauren Murphy

Senior Product Manager: Marjorie Hunt

Associate Product Manager: Reed Curry

Product Development Manager: Leigh Hefferon

Senior Content Developer: Christina Kling Garrett

Product Assistant: Rachael Starbard

Digital Product Managers: Yvette Richey, Christina Brown

Marketing Director: Michele McTighe

Marketing Managers: Kristie Clark, Gretchen Swann

Marketing Coordinator: Elizabeth Murphy

Contributing Authors: Rachel Biheller Bunin, Barbara Clemens, Lisa Ruffolo

Developmental Editors: Rachel Biheller Bunin, Barbara Clemens, Lisa Ruffolo

Full Service Project Management: GEX Publishing Services

Proofreader: Harold Johnson

Indexer: Alexandra Nickerson

Intellectual Property Project Manager: Kathryn Kucharek

Cover Designer: GEX Publishing Services

Cover Photographer: ©Syda Productions/ Shutterstock

Composition: GEX Publishing Services

Manufacturing Planner: Fola Orekoya

Library of Congress Control Number: 2014938775
ISBN-13: 978-1-305-11014-4
ISBN-10: 1-305-11014-5

Cengage Learning
200 First Stamford Place, 4th Floor
Stamford, CT 06902
USA

Cengage Learning is a leading provider of customized learning solutions with office locations around the globe, including Singapore, the United Kingdom, Australia, Mexico, Brazil, and Japan. Locate your local office at: **www.cengage.com/global**

Cengage Learning products are represented in Canada by Nelson Education, Ltd.

For your course and learning solutions, visit **www.cengage.com**

Purchase any of our products at your local college store or at our preferred online store **www.cengagebrain.com**

Printed in the United States of America
1 2 3 4 5 6 7 18 17 16 15 14

Acknowledgements

This book is dedicated to Marjorie Hunt for her inspiration and vision in providing educational content to those who want to learn.

To my contributing authors, Lisa Ruffolo, Barbara Clemens, and Rachel Biheller Bunin, thank you for your collaboration at every turn, your passion for clarity, and your determination to turn an idea into reality.
Corinne Hoisington

Thank You, Advisory Board!

We thank our advisory board for providing insights and feedback that helped shape *Technology Now*:

- ➤ Melisa "Joey" Bryant (Forsyth Technical Community College)
- ➤ Mike Tetreault (McHenry County College)
- ➤ Wendy Postles (Wor-Wic Community College)
- ➤ Sandra Thomas (Troy University)
- ➤ Robert Salkin (Fulton-Montgomery Community College)
- ➤ Greg Pauley (Moberly Area Community College)

Contents

Chapter glossaries of all key terms are available for download on cengagebrain.com and on the Instructor Resource site.

Chapter glossaries of all key terms are available for download on cengagebrain.com and on the Instructor Resource site.

Enhance the learning experience with
Technology Now

Aligns perfectly with SAM Concepts tasks: *Technology Now* is adapted from the SAM Computer Concepts tasks to provide SAM users a stream-lined, consistent learning experience on important computer concepts topics.

Elevates learning with hands-on activities that engage and inspire: A wide variety of additional end-of-chapter hands-on activities, including critical thinking exercises, team projects, and ethics scenarios provide opportunities to engage and inspire in meaningful and relevant ways to reinforce key concepts and inspire the incorporation of technology at school, on the job, and in every day life.

Relevant content: Margin tips on emerging technologies ("Hot Technology Now"), Twitter-type message feed (#hashtag specific for each chapter), careers ("On the Job Now"), and relevant statistics ("By the Numbers Now") speak to current events in business and technology issues.

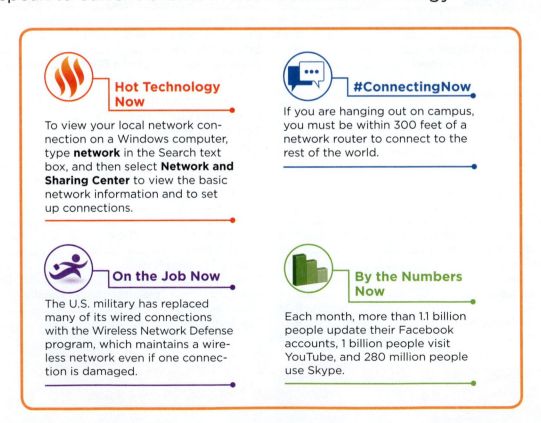

Hot Technology Now

To view your local network connection on a Windows computer, type **network** in the Search text box, and then select **Network and Sharing Center** to view the basic network information and to set up connections.

#ConnectingNow

If you are hanging out on campus, you must be within 300 feet of a network router to connect to the rest of the world.

On the Job Now

The U.S. military has replaced many of its wired connections with the Wireless Network Defense program, which maintains a wireless network even if one connection is damaged.

By the Numbers Now

Each month, more than 1.1 billion people update their Facebook accounts, 1 billion people visit YouTube, and 280 million people use Skype.

Follow the @SAMTechNow Twitter feed: Stay current with the latest trends and news in technology. Monitored and updated frequently by our technology experts, this feed will keep you engaged throughout the semester!

COURSECASTS **Learning on the Go. Always Available...Always Relevant.** Our fast-paced world is driven by technology. You know because you are an active participant—always on the go, always keeping up with technological trends, and always learning new ways to embrace technology to power your life. Let CourseCasts, hosted by Ken Baldauf of Florida State University, be your guide into weekly updates in this ever-changing space. These timely, relevant podcasts are produced weekly and are available for download at http://coursecasts.course.com or directly from iTunes (search by CourseCasts). CourseCasts are a perfect solution to getting students (and even instructors) to learn on the go!

WHAT MAKES
SAM 2013
GREAT?

Get workplace
ready with **SAM**

The market-leading assessment and training solution for Microsoft Office and computer concepts

SAM Exams

➤ Utilize exams with task and objective based questions to assess knowledge and skills.

SAM Training

➤ Training Assignments consist of task-based questions and activities to reinforce concepts.

SAM Projects

➤ Complete real-world projects using the actual Office applications to prepare you for future employment.

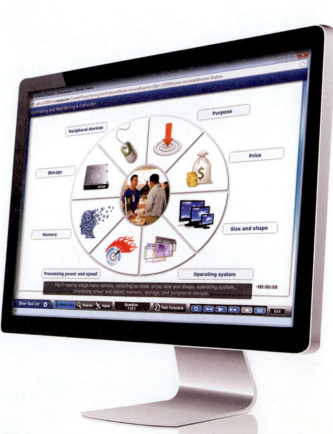

Getting Started

© Makenboluo/Shutterstock.com

Kiko is excited to use SAM so she can learn more about computers. She likes SAM because it's self-paced and personalized, allowing her to explore technology topics that are new to her and refresh information she already knows. SAM builds her confidence with engaging activities that prepare her for life after graduation.

Getting Started with Computing

computer | data | hardware | software | information | computer literacy | digital literacy | computer concepts | Microsoft Office | Microsoft Windows | Internet Explorer | Web | Internet | Web browser | home page

The Bottom Line

- Computer literacy is essential for acquiring a good job, contributing to global communications, and participating effectively in the modern world.
- This book and SAM help you achieve computer literacy.
- To get the most out of SAM, set up your computer and Web browser properly.

Throughout a typical day, you might use a computer to complete a course assignment, compare prices on a pair of headphones, exchange messages with a friend you're meeting for lunch, and listen to music as you walk to class. As you gain computer skills and knowledge, you enhance these experiences and prepare yourself for new ones. Learning and applying computer knowledge makes you computer literate, an essential qualification for a career in today's economy.

SAM (short for Skills Assessment Manager) is interactive software that helps you become computer literate as you learn and apply important computer skills and knowledge. The activities you perform in SAM are designed to complement your Cengage Learning textbooks on computer concepts, Microsoft Office, and Microsoft Windows.

Computer Literacy Basics

To be successful on the job and make the most of your personal life, you need to be comfortable using a computer. At the most basic level, a **computer** is an electronic device that receives data (input), processes and stores the data, and then produces a result (output). **Data** is a raw fact, such as text or numbers.

A computer includes hardware and software. **Hardware** is the device itself and its components, such as wires, switches, and electronic circuits. **Software** consists of programs that instruct the computer to perform tasks. Software processes data into meaningful **information**. See **Figure 1**.

Technology has changed rapidly since the computer was invented. To keep pace with these changes, you need to be computer literate. **Computer literacy** (also called **digital literacy**) is the knowledge you need to understand and use computers and related technology effectively. In general, this knowledge includes the basics of computer technology, known as **computer concepts**, and software skills. More specifically, you should be able to do the following:

Figure 1: Computers include hardware and software

Software

Hardware

© You can more/Shutterstock.com

- Identify the differences among types of computers, such as desktops, laptops, tablets, smartphones, and servers.
- Describe how to use electronic devices such as digital cameras, portable media players, and e-book readers.
- Identify types of input devices (such as keyboards, pointing devices, and cameras), output devices (such as displays, speakers, and printers), and storage devices (such as hard drives and USB drives).
- Explain the purpose of computer components such as the processor and memory.
- Define a network and explain the difference between the Internet and the Web.
- Describe how to use a browser to visit Web sites and open Web pages.
- Define system software and application software.
- Navigate an operating system and use it to manage files.
- Use productivity applications such as those in Microsoft Office.
- Identify risks in using computers and networks.
- Communicate using digital technology such as email, messaging, and social networks.
- Describe types of digital media such as graphics, video, and audio.

If any of this is new to you, you are in the right place. SAM helps you achieve computer literacy so you can succeed in a career, keep in touch with people around the world, and participate as an active, contributing member of contemporary society.

Achieving Computer Literacy with SAM

To improve your computer literacy, SAM offers training in computer concepts such as hardware, software, networks, and digital media. After you log into SAM, you start learning computer concepts by watching a brief video overview of a technology topic such as the Internet. Next, you watch a series of videos that expand on that topic. Finally, you respond to online activities that check your knowledge and provide immediate feedback to help you learn.

Depending on your course, SAM can also prepare you to use Microsoft Office, Windows, and Internet Explorer. **Microsoft Office** includes application software widely used in businesses and schools to produce professional-quality documents and other files. **Microsoft Windows** is a popular operating system that runs personal computers that includes **Internet Explorer**, Web-browsing software you use to access Web sites.

Using SAM on the Web

SAM is software provided on the **Web**, which is part of the **Internet**, a collection of millions of computers connected together throughout the world. To work in SAM, you use a **Web browser** (also called a browser for short), which is software for visiting Web sites. To visit a Web site, you enter the address of the Web site in the Address bar of the browser. (A Web address is also called a URL, or Uniform Resource Locator.) **Figure 2** shows the SAM Web address in the Address bar of Internet Explorer, though you can use any browser, including Mozilla Firefox, Apple Safari, and Google Chrome, to access SAM.

Figure 2: Entering the SAM Web address

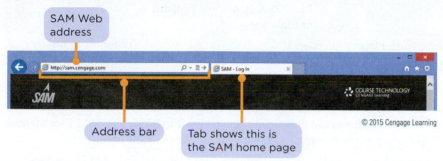

© 2015 Cengage Learning

To visit the SAM Web site, you enter the SAM Web address—sam.cengage.com—in the Address bar of your browser, and then press the Enter key to display the SAM home page. (A **home page** is the introductory page of a Web site.) Browsers insert the text http:// in the Address bar before Web addresses such as sam.cengage.com, so you don't need to enter http:// to visit the SAM Web site.

The name of the Web page is displayed on the tab next to the Address bar. For example, the name of the home page shown in Figure 2 is "SAM - Log In" because the page is designed to welcome you to SAM and allow you to log in (or sign in) by identifying yourself as a valid SAM user.

Setting Up Your Computer

If you are using a recent model of a desktop or laptop computer, you most likely have the hardware and software you need to use SAM.

If you are using an older computer, it should meet the minimum hardware requirements shown in **Table 1** on the next page. To display the window listed in the "Windows computer" and the "Mac computer" column, use the Help tool for your version of Windows or Mac OS X.

The software listed in **Table 2** on the next page should be installed on your computer.

Setting Up Your Browser

Before you can use your browser to access SAM, you must enable and disable the following settings in your browser so it can play videos without interruption:
- Enable JavaScript.
- Disable pop-up blocking for http://sam.cengage.com.
- Disable ad-blocking software for http://sam.cengage.com.

#getstarted

If you are using a tablet, it should have at least 512 MB of RAM.

Table 1: Hardware requirements

Requirement	Minimum	Recommended	Windows computer	Macintosh computer
Computer processor	Intel Pentium 4	Intel Centrino or equivalent multi-core processor	Control Panel, System window	About This Mac window
RAM (Memory)	512 MB	1 GB	Control Panel, System window	About This Mac window
Screen resolution	1024 × 768	1280 × 800	Control Panel, Screen Resolution window	Displays icon in the System Preferences window
Internet connection	56 K modem with persistent connection	Broadband (cable, DSL, T1, or ISDN)	Control Panel, Network and Sharing Center	Network icon in the System Preferences window
Available disk space	28.4 MB		This PC or Computer window	Finder window

© 2015 Cengage Learning

Table 2: Software requirements

Software	Minimum	Recommended
Operating system	• Windows 8.x • Windows 7 • Windows Vista SP1 • Windows XP SP3 • Mac OS X 10.6 Snow Leopard or higher	Any
Adobe Flash Player	Version 10.2	Version 11 or higher
Adobe Reader	Version 8	Version 9 or higher

© 2015 Cengage Learning

Details about selecting these settings in various browsers are provided in the SAM User Manual, which you can download after you log into SAM. The SAM User Manual is a step-by-step guide to using SAM that you can print or view online:

1. Open a browser and go to **sam.cengage.com** to display the SAM home page.
2. Log into SAM by providing a username and password.

   See "Accessing SAM" later in this chapter for complete instructions.
3. Click the **Help** link on the navigation bar to display a list of Help resources.
4. Click the **SAM User Manual** link to download the manual and display it in your browser.

Getting Started with SAM

As you learned earlier, SAM (Skills Assessment Manager) is software provided on the Web to help you increase your proficiency in technology. SAM uses interactive training, skill-based assessments, real-world projects, and personalized study tools to help you achieve computer literacy. Depending on your course, SAM might teach computer concepts, Microsoft Word, Excel, PowerPoint, Access, Outlook, Windows, or Internet Explorer.

Accessing SAM

If you are using SAM for the first time, want a refresher on accessing SAM, or are helping someone else access SAM, first make sure your computer is connected to the Internet. Start a Web browser, and then go to sam.cengage.com to display the SAM home page, where you log into SAM. See **Figure 3**.

You can log in as a first-time new user, as a first-time registered user, or as an existing user. See **Table 3**.

The Bottom Line
- SAM offers training, projects, readings, and exams to help you learn essential computer concepts and skills in Microsoft Office, Windows, and Internet Explorer.
- Because SAM is designed to complement your computer concepts course, you can use SAM to meet and master your course requirements.

#getstarted

If you are a new user, you can click the **how to log in to SAM** link to see step-by-step instructions for creating a SAM account.

Figure 3: SAM home page

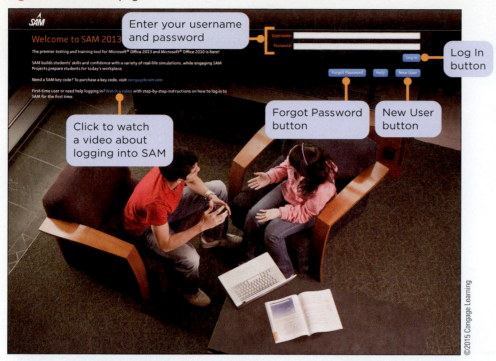

©2015 Cengage Learning

Table 3: Logging into SAM

	First-time new user	First-time registered user	Existing user
Description	This is the first time you are using SAM and you need to create an account because your instructor has not created one for you.	This is the first time you are using SAM with an account your instructor created for you.	You have already registered as a new user.

Steps	1. Click the **New User** button.
	2. Follow the onscreen instructions to create a SAM account by providing the following information:
	  • School's institution key
	  • Your key code, if necessary
	  • Personal profile information, including username (an email address), password, and secret question and answer
	3. Read and then accept the terms and conditions.
		1. Enter the username and password you received.
		2. Click the **Log In** button.
		3. Read and then accept the terms and conditions.
		4. Enter a secret question and answer.
		5. Enter and confirm a new password.
			1. Enter your username and password.
			2. Click the **Log In** button.

© 2015 Cengage Learning

If you cannot remember your password, click the **Forgot password?** button on the SAM home page. Enter your username, and then have SAM send your password to the email address listed in your profile or answer your secret question to reset your password.

Joining a Section

After you log in, the Activity Calendar opens, which is designed to display your SAM assignments for the month. However, before you can display your SAM assignments, you must join a section:

1. Click the **Sections** button on the navigation bar to display the Sections page, which lists the sections (or classes) you are enrolled in, if any. If the section you want to join is listed on this page with an "Accepted" status, you are all set—you are already enrolled in the section.

#getstarted

The username and password entered in your personal profile become your credentials for CengageBrain. If you already have a CengageBrain account, enter the username and password for that account.

2. To join a section, click the **Join a Section** button to list the sections you can join.
   - To display only sections offered by a single instructor, click the **Instructor** heading, and then click the instructor's name.
   - To display section details, including textbooks, click the section name.
3. Click the **Join Section** icon in the Join Section column for the section you want to join. Read and then close the results message. To join another section, click the **Join Section** icon for that section.
4. To confirm you are enrolled in the right sections, click the **My Sections** button, and then look for "Accepted" in the Status column. If the Status is displayed as "Wait Listed," you must wait for the instructor to enroll you.

Assignment Basics

After you join a section, you can access your SAM assignments on the Activity Calendar. If necessary, click the **Activities** button on the navigation bar, and then click the **Activity Calendar** button. **Figure 4** shows the Activity Calendar.

Figure 4: Activity calendar

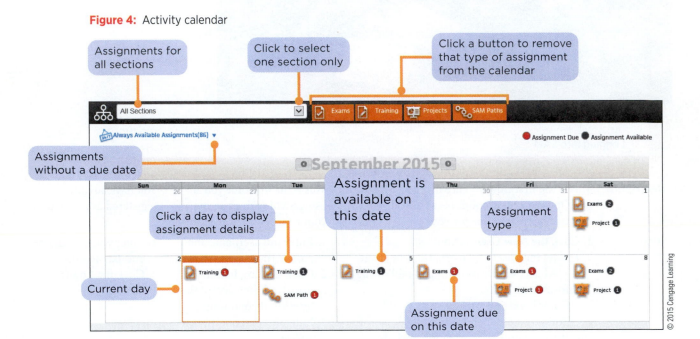

© 2015 Cengage Learning

A SAM assignment can be one of the types of activities described in **Table 4**.

Table 4: Types of SAM assignments

Name	Description
Training	Watch and respond to videos to increase your proficiency in computer concepts, or work in an environment that simulates Microsoft Office or Windows to improve your software skills.
Project	Use Microsoft Office to perform step-by-step instructions, and then submit the completed project for instant grading and immediate feedback.
Exam	Verify your knowledge of computer concepts and, if appropriate, Microsoft Office and Windows skills.
SAM Path	Complete a series of activities such as trainings and exams to master a particular skill or concept.
Reading	If your SAM account includes access to MindTap Reader, you can complete your reading assignments using an e-book that includes tools such as flash cards, narration, glossary, and more. Click the **Always Available Assignments** button to display a list of assignments with no due date, including readings.

© 2015 Cengage Learning

To display a list of all the activities for your sections, click the **Activities** button on the navigation bar, if necessary, and then click the **Activity List** button. See **Figure 5**. To remove a type of activity from the list, click an assignment button. For example, to remove projects from the Activity List, click the **Projects** button.

Figure 5: Activity list

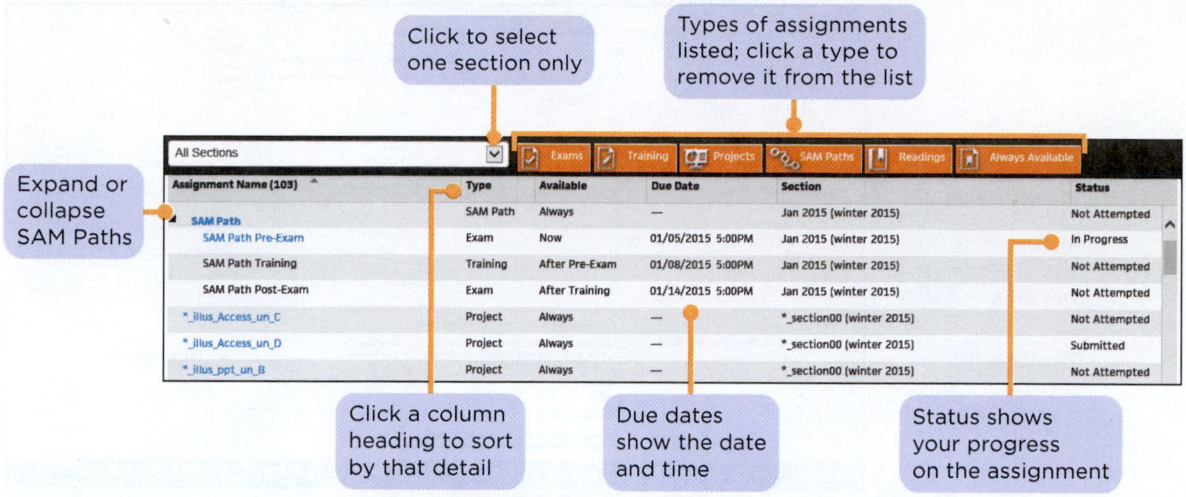

You can work on any assignment with an availability of "Always" or "Now." After an available assignment appears in the Activity Calendar or the Activity List, you can complete it at any time until the assignment is due. After the due date, the assignment name is removed from the list.

To begin an assignment:

1. Click a date to display a dialog box of assignments for that day, and then click the assignment you want to begin.

2. Read the information in the dialog box, and then click the **Start** button.

If an assignment's availability is "Inactive," you might need to enter a key code before you can begin the assignment:

1. In Activity list view, click the **Add Product** button on the Activity List page to open the Add Product window.

2. Enter the product's 18-digit key code. If you need to purchase a key code, visit cengagebrain.com.

Microsoft Office and Windows Training and Exams

If your course covers Microsoft Office and Windows, you can become proficient performing tasks with that software by completing SAM training assignments. Most instructors schedule training assignments so students can check their skills and knowledge before taking an exam, test, or quiz. SAM provides training in hundreds of Office and Windows tasks, with three or four training options for each task. Repeat each training option described in **Table 5** until you feel comfortable performing a task.

Table 5: Microsoft Office and Windows training options

Training type	Description
Intro	If you are using Microsoft Office 2013, read about the various ways to perform the task, such as using the ribbon, mini toolbar, shortcut menu, and keyboard combination. If you are accessing SAM 2013 on a Mac, hints are displayed for completing the task on a Mac if it differs from Windows.
Observe	Watch and listen to a brief video that guides you through the steps to complete a task.
Practice	Perform a task yourself with the help of guided audio and onscreen prompts.
Apply	Perform a task on your own without help.

After you start a training assignment from the Activity Calendar or the Activity List, the Content Player opens and displays a window describing the task. Read the description, and then click the **Continue** button. **Figure 6** shows a typical training assignment for a Microsoft Word 2013 task open in the Content Player.

Figure 6: Microsoft Word training assignment

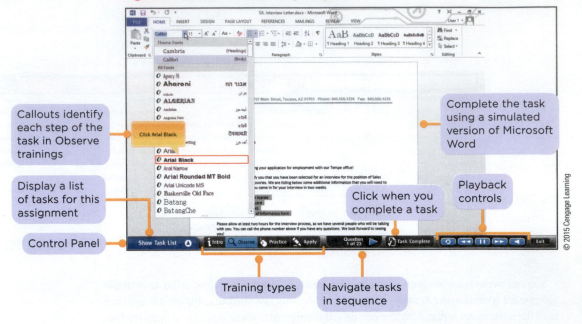

Callouts identify each step of the task in Observe trainings

Complete the task using a simulated version of Microsoft Word

Display a list of tasks for this assignment

Click when you complete a task

Playback controls

Control Panel

Training types

Navigate tasks in sequence

© 2015 Cengage Learning

To navigate assignments using the Content Player, perform the task, and then click the **Task Complete** button to receive credit for performing the task. (You do not receive credit if you exit by closing the browser window.)

- If you completed an Apply type of training, the Content Player displays the next task in the assignment.
- For any other type of training, the Content Player displays the next training type for the task. For example, when you complete the Observe training for a task, click the Task Complete button to perform the Practice training.

You can complete a training assignment as many times as the instructor allows.

Microsoft Office and Windows Exams

To prove your Microsoft Office and Windows skills and knowledge, you take SAM exams (also called tests and quizzes).

When you select an exam on the Activity Calendar or Activity List, be sure to read the exam description, which provides important details such as whether you can retake the exam, and if so, how many times. Click the **Start** button to display the first exam question in the Content Player, which is similar to the one used for training assignments except for the Control Panel. See **Figure 7**.

Figure 7: Control Panel for an exam

Display the tasks and questions in this exam

Navigate exam tasks and questions in sequence

Number of times you can answer the question or complete the task

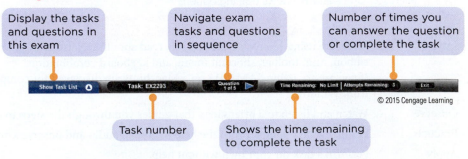

© 2015 Cengage Learning

Task number

Shows the time remaining to complete the task

A Microsoft Office or Windows exam can contain two types of questions, as described in **Table 6**.

© 2015 Cengage Learning

Table 6: Completing Microsoft Office and Windows exams

Type of question	Description	How to complete
Performance-based task	Tests your software skills using simulated versions of Windows or a Microsoft Office application	Read the onscreen instructions, and then perform the task they describe.
Objective question	Checks your knowledge using multiple choice, true/false, and fill-in-the-blank formats	Read the onscreen instructions, respond to the question, and then click the Submit button.

After you perform a task or respond to a question, SAM records your answer and displays the next question in the exam. If the exam allows you more than one attempt to respond correctly, you can try to perform the task or answer the question again.

Training and Exam Results

Training results include a report showing the progress you made in an assignment. The report indicates the percentage of completed tasks and describes the tasks you performed.

Exam results include a report containing your score and a study guide, which provides information such as the textbook pages, MindTap Reader sections, or SAM training tasks related to each exam question. Use the study guide to identify topics for further study if you want to achieve better scores on future exams.

To display training and exam results:

1. Click the **Activities** button on the navigation bar (if necessary), and then click the **Reports** button to display the results of your SAM assignments.

2. Click the **Report** icon for a training assignment. Click the **Report** icon or the **Study Guide** icon for an exam.

If your instructor has enabled the gradebook for your section, you can view your assignment scores. To display your assignment scores for a section:

1. Click the **Activities** button on the navigation bar (if necessary), and then click the **Gradebook** button.

2. Click the **Show All Items** arrow button, and then click a section. If your instructor has set up a gradebook for the section, your scores are displayed for each assignment.

Computer Concepts Training and Exams

To increase your computer literacy, you can complete SAM computer concepts training assignments. SAM provides training for hundreds of computer concepts tasks and topics, with three training options for each one. Repeat each training option described in **Table 7** until you feel you understand the concept thoroughly.

Table 7: Computer concepts training options

Training type	Description
Introduction	Watch and listen to a video providing an overview of the topics covered in the task.
Observe	Watch and listen to a series of videos that explore the fundamentals of computer concepts.
Apply	Perform assessment activities that give you immediate feedback on the material you just learned.

© 2015 Cengage Learning

After you start a computer concepts training assignment from the Activity Calendar or the Activity List, the Content Player opens and plays the Introduction video. When it's finished, click the **Task Complete** button to continue to the Observe training. The Content Player is similar to the one shown in Figure 6, except for the tools shown in **Figure 8** on the next page.

Figure 8: Observe training for computer concepts

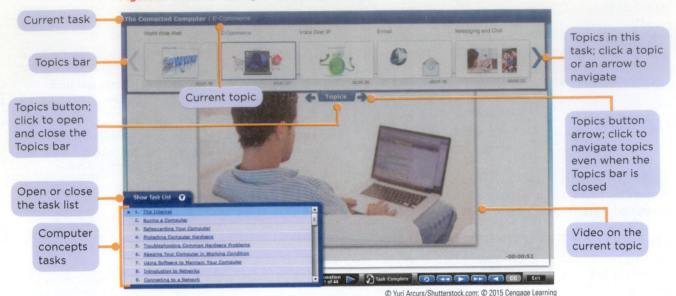

Current task

Topics bar

Topics button; click to open and close the Topics bar

Open or close the task list

Computer concepts tasks

Current topic

Topics in this task; click a topic or an arrow to navigate

Topics button arrow; click to navigate topics even when the Topics bar is closed

Video on the current topic

© Yuri Arcurs/Shutterstock.com; © 2015 Cengage Learning

When you complete the Observe training for a topic, you can continue to the next topic, or you can click the **Apply** button to take a short quiz on what you just learned. To complete an Apply training, read the instructions at the top of the window, and then perform the assessment activity as instructed. SAM provides feedback as you complete each part of the activity.

After you complete your training assignments, you can take SAM exams to prove your computer concepts knowledge. All of the questions in a computer concepts exam are objective questions, such as drag-and-drop or matching questions. Read the onscreen instructions, respond to a question, and then click the Submit button.

To see the results of training and exams, click the **Reports** button, and then click the **Report** icon or the **Study Guide** icon.

Microsoft Office Projects

SAM Projects give you the chance to work directly in Microsoft Office to reinforce application skills learned in your class, textbook, and SAM training assignments. Completing a SAM Project involves the following steps:

1. **Start the project and download files.**
   - Start a project the same way you start any SAM assignment—click the project in the Activity Calendar or the Activity List, read the instructions and details, and then click the **Start** button. The project dialog box opens. See **Figure 9**.
   - Download the instruction file, which contains the steps you follow to complete the project, and the start file, which you use to perform the project steps.
   - Download the support files, if any are listed. These are files you use in the project. Do not open any support files until a step in the instruction file specifically instructs you to do so.
   - Use the browser's tools to save the files on your computer.

2. **Perform the steps in the project.**
   - Use Microsoft Word to open the instruction file, which has a filename starting with "Assignment," read the Project Description and Getting Started sections, and then review the steps.
   - As instructed in the Getting Started section, open the start file, and then save it with a different name by changing the _1 to _2 in the filename. This is now your project file.
   - Using the project file, perform the steps in the instruction file. Compare your completed project to the final figure in the instruction file, make final adjustments as necessary, and then save and close your project file.

Figure 9: Project dialog box

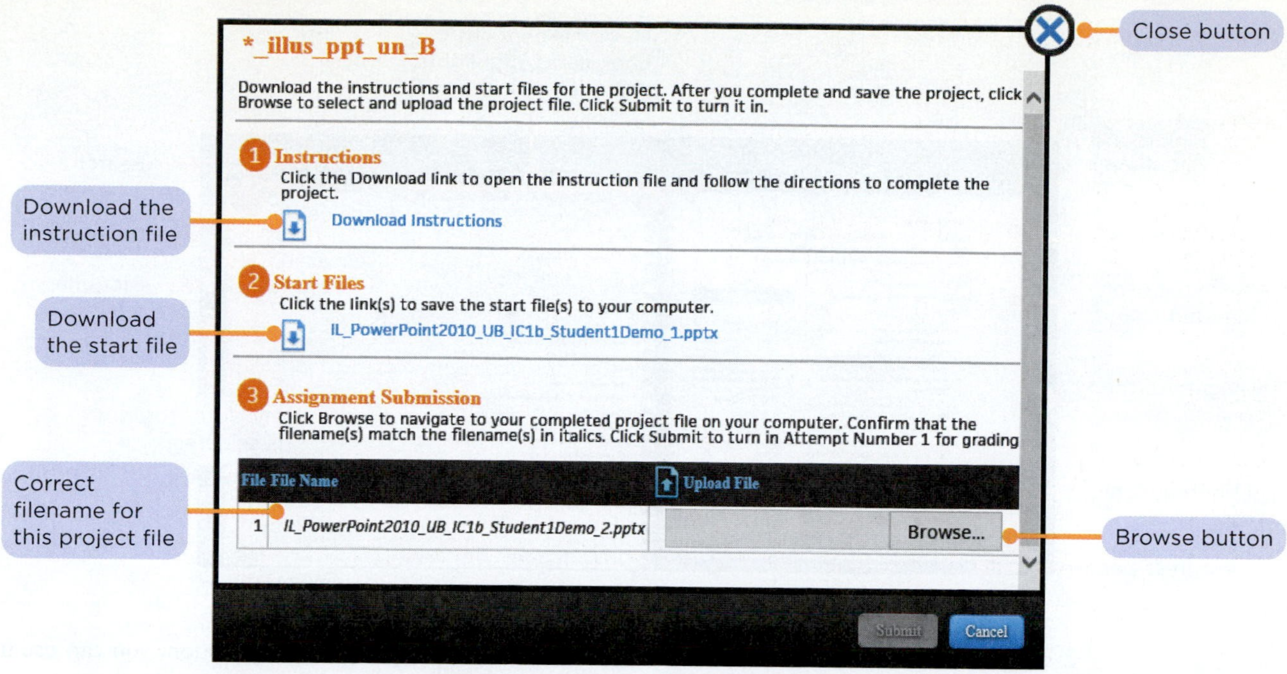

Close button

***_illus_ppt_un_B**

Download the instructions and start files for the project. After you complete and save the project, click Browse to select and upload the project file. Click Submit to turn it in.

1 Instructions
Click the Download link to open the instruction file and follow the directions to complete the project.
Download Instructions

Download the instruction file

2 Start Files
Click the link(s) to save the start file(s) to your computer.
IL_PowerPoint2010_UB_IC1b_Student1Demo_1.pptx

Download the start file

3 Assignment Submission
Click Browse to navigate to your completed project file on your computer. Confirm that the filename(s) match the filename(s) in italics. Click Submit to turn in Attempt Number 1 for grading

Correct filename for this project file

File File Name	Upload File	
1	IL_PowerPoint2010_UB_IC1b_Student1Demo_2.pptx	Browse...

Browse button

Submit Cancel

© 2015 Cengage Learning

3. **Submit the project to SAM for grading.**
   - If necessary, open the dialog box for the project again by clicking the project in the Activity Calendar or the Activity List, and then clicking the **Start** button.
   - Click the **Browse** button, and then navigate your computer to find and select your project file. Make sure its filename matches the one shown in the project dialog box; otherwise, SAM cannot accept the file.
   - Click the **Upload File** link. When SAM receives the project file, it begins to grade it immediately.
   - Close the project dialog box.

4. **Review the results.**
   - Click the **Reports** button on the Activities page.
   - Click the **Reports** icon for the project to download and save a graded version of your project file. Besides your score, SAM includes detailed information about how each step was graded, which skills were marked correct or incorrect, and whether a step received partial credit.
   - Click the **Study Guide** icon for the project to display information such as the textbook pages, MindTap Reader sections, or SAM training tasks related to each project step. Use this information to identify topics for further study.

Readings and Dropbox

Your instructor can assign readings from a Cengage e-book if one has been selected for your section. You complete reading assignments with MindTap, an online reading system that personalizes your learning with study tools including Read Speak, which narrates the text, and embedded videos. See **Figure 10** on the next page.

To start a reading assignment:

1. Select a reading the same way you select any SAM assignment—click the assignment in the Activity Calendar or the Activity List. If you are working with the Activity Calendar, click the Always Available Assignments button to display a list of reading assignments.

   If you haven't purchased the e-book yet, go to cengagebrain.com to purchase a keycode, and then enter the keycode.

2. If this is the first time you are accessing the e-book, read and then accept the MindTap Service Agreement.

Figure 10: Reading assignment in MindTap

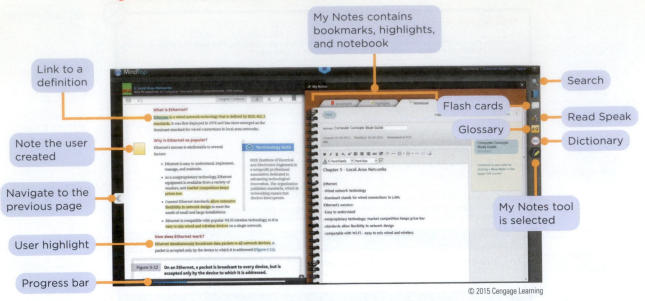

My Notes contains bookmarks, highlights, and notebook

Link to a definition

Note the user created

Navigate to the previous page

User highlight

Progress bar

Search

Flash cards

Read Speak

Glossary

Dictionary

My Notes tool is selected

© 2015 Cengage Learning

If your instructor chooses to use a SAM Dropbox for your section, you can use it as your instructor requests to post documents such as responses to e-book exercises. You can store up to 350 MB of files in the Dropbox. Your instructor might also include notes for you in the Dropbox.

The Dropbox is not for SAM project files. Be sure to submit SAM project files by uploading them using the project dialog box so SAM can grade the projects and assign credit to you for completing the assignments.

To copy a file to the SAM Dropbox:

1. Click the **Dropbox** button on the navigation bar to display the Dropbox page.

2. Click the **Section** arrow button, click the section for which you want to copy a file, and then click **OK** to display the Dropbox for the section.

   If your instructor left a note for you, it appears in the Note from Instructor section of the Dropbox window.

3. Click the **Submit New File** button to display the Submit File dialog box.

4. Click the **Browse** button, and then navigate to and select the file you want to copy to the Dropbox.

5. Click the **Save** button to save the file in the Dropbox.

Getting Help

To get help on using SAM, click the **Help** link on the navigation bar to display a list of SAM help resources. See **Figure 11**.

To download the Flash Player, click the **Flash Player** link. Adobe Flash Player must be installed on your computer so you can start an assignment.

To access the SAM User Manual, click the **SAM User Manual** link to download the manual as a PDF file you can save on your computer. Click the **Online Help** link to open the manual in your browser.

To access technical support:

1. Click the **Knowledge Base** link or the **Tech Support** link to open the Cengage Learning Customer Technical Page.

2. Sign in and then click **Select Product**, if necessary.

3. Click the **Search for Product** arrow button, and then click **SAM 2013** to display the technical support page for SAM 2013. Use this page to access help as follows:

Figure 11: SAM help resources

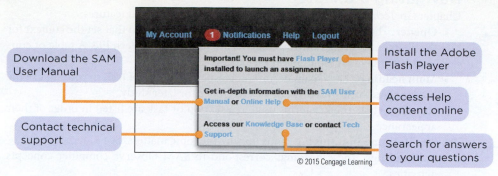

Download the SAM User Manual

Contact technical support

Install the Adobe Flash Player

Access Help content online

Search for answers to your questions

© 2015 Cengage Learning

- Select an article, file to download, or tutorial.
- Enter a key term in the Search box and then click the **Search** button to search for help information related to your key term.
- Click the **No, please create a new case** link to display a page where you can describe your problem and submit it to technical support. Follow the onscreen instructions to complete your case.

Getting Started with Technology Now

screenshot | tweet | follow | Timeline | hashtag

Technology Now: Your Companion to SAM Computer Concepts is designed as a printed or electronic book to accompany the online SAM computer concepts tasks. Each chapter in this book is devoted to a SAM task with the same name. For example, the material presented in the "Introduction to Networks" task in SAM corresponds to the "Introduction to Networks" topic in Chapter 7 in this book.

> **The Bottom Line**
> - Chapter topics align with SAM tasks to reinforce your understanding of computer concepts.
> - Chapters provide key terms, tips, and activities to enhance SAM content.

Figure 12: *Technology Now* and SAM computer concepts tasks

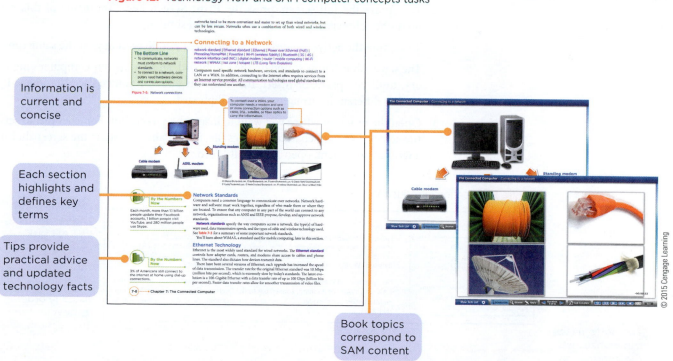

Information is current and concise

Each section highlights and defines key terms

Tips provide practical advice and updated technology facts

Book topics correspond to SAM content

© 2015 Cengage Learning

#ConnectingNow

Twitter-style messages provide practical information about the chapter topic. The titles vary depending on the chapter content. For example, the tip for Chapter 7, The Connected Computer, is titled #ConnectingNow.

Hot Technology Now

Hot Technology Now tips highlight emerging technologies.

On the Job Now

On the Job Now tips focus on careers in technology fields.

By the Numbers Now

By the Numbers Now tips summarize statistics in a meaningful way.

Navigating a Chapter

Chapters in *Technology Now* contain the following sections and features:

- **Opener**: The opening page displays a photo and a scenario that set the context for the chapter, showing how the contents are related to modern life. A table of contents lists the main topics in the chapter.
- **Main headings**: Each main heading corresponds to a SAM task so you can use the book as you work with SAM or as a reference for later study.
- **Key terms list**: The key terms used in a section or task are listed in order of their appearance.
- **The Bottom Line**: This box sums up why the topic matters. See **Figure 13**.
- **Subheadings**: These headings correspond to SAM Observe computer concepts activities.
- **Figures**: Figures illustrate the concepts being discussed; some are identical to images shown in SAM to reinforce your learning.
- **Tables**: Tables compare and condense chapter content.
- **Tips**: Four types of tips appear in the margins of each section.
- **End-of-chapter activities**: The Chapter Review poses questions that help you review what you've learned. Test Your Knowledge Now provides multiple-choice questions and a labeling exercise. Try This Now, Ethical Issues Now, Critical Thinking Now, and Team Up Now are hands-on activities and projects. A full list of key terms in alphabetic order appears at the end of each chapter.

Taking Screenshots

Some of the end-of-chapter activities guide you to explore new technologies and Web sites, and then ask you to take screenshots of what you explored. A **screenshot** is an image of a screen that you can save as a graphics file or insert in a document or other file. For example, if you visit a Web site, you can take a screenshot to capture an image of the first page you open. If an activity or your instructor asks you to take a screenshot, you can do so by completing the following steps:

1. Arrange the computer screen so it displays all the images you want to include in the screenshot.

2. To capture the full screen, press the **Print Screen** key. (The name of this key might be abbreviated to Prt Sc or something similar.)

   To capture the active window, press the **Alt+Print Screen** keys at the same time.

   The screenshot is now stored on the Clipboard, an area in your computer's memory, until you paste, or insert, the image in a file or you replace the image by storing different information on the Clipboard.

3. Open the program where you want to insert the screenshot. For example, to save the screenshot as a separate graphics file, open Paint. To insert the screenshot in a written document, open Microsoft Word.

Figure 13: Section introduction

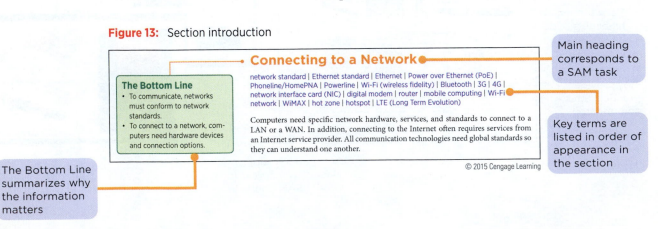

Main heading corresponds to a SAM task

Key terms are listed in order of appearance in the section

The Bottom Line summarizes why the information matters

Connecting to a Network

network standard | Ethernet standard | Ethernet | Power over Ethernet (PoE) | Phoneline/HomePNA | Powerline | Wi-Fi (wireless fidelity) | Bluetooth | 3G | 4G | network interface card (NIC) | digital modem | router | mobile computing | Wi-Fi network | WiMAX | hot zone | hotspot | LTE (Long Term Evolution)

Computers need specific network hardware, services, and standards to connect to a LAN or a WAN. In addition, connecting to the Internet often requires services from an Internet service provider. All communication technologies need global standards so they can understand one another.

The Bottom Line
- To communicate, networks must conform to network standards.
- To connect to a network, computers need hardware devices and connection options.

© 2015 Cengage Learning

4. Press and hold the **Ctrl** key and, while holding it down, press the **V** key to insert the screenshot in the open file.

5. Save the file containing the screenshot.

Using Twitter

You can use Twitter to communicate with others about the technology topics in this book. As you might know, Twitter is a social networking Web site that lets members communicate using messages of up to 140 characters. Many members simply read these messages, called **tweets**, while some also contribute tweets of their own.

To start using Twitter:

1. Sign up for an account.

   Go to twitter.com, enter your full name, email address, and a password in the sign up box, and then click **Sign up for Twitter**. Enter other requested information, such as your user name (the name that appears on your tweets), and then wait for Twitter to send you a confirmation email message. When you receive the message, respond to it as instructed in the message.

2. Find and follow interesting Twitter users.

   To **follow** Twitter users means that you subscribe to their tweets. You receive any message posted by someone you follow. One of the first users you should follow is @SAMTechNow. See "Following @SAMTechNow on Twitter" for details.

3. Read tweets in your Timeline.

   Your **Timeline** is the home page of your Twitter account. After you follow one or more Twitter users, their tweets appear in your Timeline soon after they are posted. Some tweets include links, which you can click to visit Web pages that might interest you. Tweets can also include keywords that begin with **hashtags**, such as #getstarted. You can click a keyword to find other tweets related to that topic.

4. Ask others to follow you.

   To set up a two-way conversation, ask a friend or two to follow you on Twitter. When you're ready to tweet, these followers will receive your messages.

5. Contribute to the conversation.

   Many users start contributing to Twitter by retweeting a message. You might retweet a message that you find significant or interesting. Click the Retweet link in a message to send the message to your followers. See **Figure 14**.

You can also click the Reply link to send a message to the author of a tweet. As you create tweets, you can mention other Twitter users by inserting their user name, as in "Learned something new about social networks from @SAMTechNow."

Following @SAMTechNow on Twitter

Corinne Hoisington, the author of this book, keeps up with trends and topics in contemporary technology, which can change rapidly. She tweets at the Twitter account for this book, which has the account name @SAMTechNow.

#getstarted

For complete information on using Twitter, see the Twitter Help Center at support.twitter.com.

Figure 14: Tweeting and retweeting

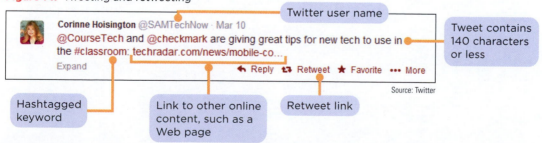

Twitter user name

Tweet contains 140 characters or less

Hashtagged keyword

Link to other online content, such as a Web page

Retweet link

Source: Twitter

To follow @SAMTechNow on Twitter:

1. Go to twitter.com and sign into your account.

2. In the search box at the top of your home page, enter **@SAMTechNow**.

3. Click **@SAMTechNow**, in the list below the search box, to display the @SAMTechNow home page.

4. Click the **Follow** button to start following @SAMTechNow.

5. Click the **Home** button on the navigation bar to return to your home page, and then click the **Following** link below your profile picture to verify that you are following @SAMTechNow.

Introduction to Computer Hardware

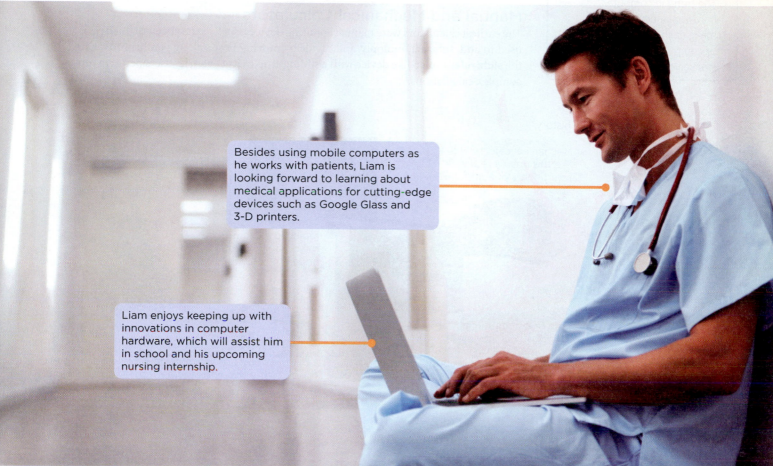

Besides using mobile computers as he works with patients, Liam is looking forward to learning about medical applications for cutting-edge devices such as Google Glass and 3-D printers.

Liam enjoys keeping up with innovations in computer hardware, which will assist him in school and his upcoming nursing internship.

© iStockphoto.com/GlobalStock

Liam Fix is interning in nursing next semester at the local hospital. During his internship orientation, the nursing instructor gave an overview of the computer hardware devices that the medical staff use throughout the hospital. Support staff access patient records on tablet computers. Surgeons in the operating room wear Google Glass for hands-free access to digital images during surgery. The hospital is also researching how to use 3D printers to create prosthetic limbs.

Microsoft® product screenshots used with permission from Microsoft® Corporation.

Computers in History

abacus | slide rule | vacuum tube | transistor | integrated circuit | microprocessor | personal computer (PC)

Humans have used tools and machines to count and manipulate numbers for thousands of years, ranging from the abacus in ancient times and the first computing machines in the mid-nineteenth century to handheld, powerful devices such as contemporary smartphones.

Manual and Mechanical Calculators

The earliest calculators were manual counting devices, such as the **abacus**, which people used to add, subtract, multiply, and divide by moving beads along parallel rods. Later, the **slide rule**, a ruler-like device with a sliding strip in its center, let users perform more complex calculations.

Figure 1-1: Computers in history

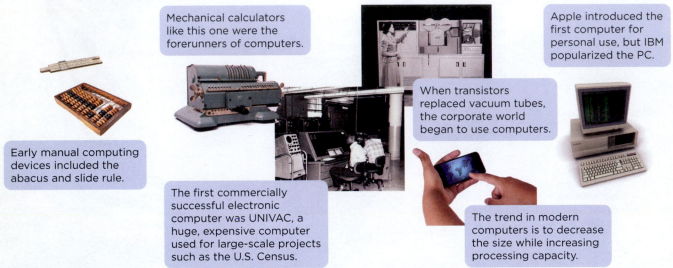

Mechanical calculators like this one were the forerunners of computers.

Apple introduced the first computer for personal use, but IBM popularized the PC.

When transistors replaced vacuum tubes, the corporate world began to use computers.

Early manual computing devices included the abacus and slide rule.

The first commercially successful electronic computer was UNIVAC, a huge, expensive computer used for large-scale projects such as the U.S. Census.

The trend in modern computers is to decrease the size while increasing processing capacity.

© Gyvafoto/Shutterstock.com, © slavapolo/Shutterstock.com, © Hintau Aliaksei/Shutterstock.com, UNIVAC courtesy of the U.S. Census Bureau, © Everett Collection/Shutterstock.com, © iStockphoto.com/Franck-Boston, © Luis Louro/Shutterstock.com

#introhardware

As early as 1623, German professor Wilhelm Schickard invented the first mechanical calculator, which performed calculations using levers and cranks. Computer historians sometimes refer to Schickard's machine as the first "automatic" calculator.

#introhardware

An exterminator sometimes serviced early computers because the vacuum tubes attracted bugs. Today we still use the term "bug" for a computer error.

Tabulating Machines

In 1834, English mathematics professor Charles Babbage designed a calculator called the Analytical Engine. Babbage thought that the repetitive capabilities of machines would work well with repetitive math calculations.

In the 1890s, Herman Hollerith designed a tabulating machine to speed up the time it took to count U.S. Census results. The machine used metal rods to read data cards and make calculations. Hollerith subsequently founded the Tabulating Machine Company in 1896, which later became International Business Machines (IBM).

The First Computers

In the 1940s, as the world went to war, governments developed the first generation of computers for code breaking and other strategic purposes. These first-generation computers used **vacuum tubes**, cylindrical glass tubes that controlled the flow of electrons, which can be set to one of two states: on or off. Vacuum tube computers were expensive and could perform only limited calculations. The vacuum tubes used a lot of power, were very hot, and wore out quickly.

The ENIAC was a vacuum tube computer developed to calculate the trajectory of World War II weaponry. The first commercially successful electronic computer was UNIVAC, created by the Remington Rand Corporation in the 1950s. It measured 14 feet long, 7 feet high, and 9 feet wide and cost $1 million.

Second Generation

In 1956, second-generation computers replaced vacuum tubes with **transistors**, which were smaller, cheaper, and more reliable. Computer manufacturers such as IBM, Burroughs, and Honeywell began selling computers to businesses, universities, and government entities. One of the most popular computers of the time was the IBM 1401, considered by some as the Model T of the computer industry.

Second-generation computers contained many components still in use today, including tape and disk storage, memory, operating systems, stored programs, and printers. They also stimulated new types of jobs, including those for programmers, computer analysts, and information technology experts.

Third and Fourth Generation

Third-generation computers were made possible in the 1960s with the development of **integrated circuits**, which packed the equivalent of thousands of vacuum tubes or transistors into a miniature silicon chip. In 1965, RCA and IBM released computers that used integrated circuits, and Digital Equipment Corporation (DEC) introduced the first minicomputer, which could run multiple programs for multiple users at the same time.

In 1971, Ted Hoff moved computer technology to the fourth generation by developing the **microprocessor**, which was even faster, smaller, and less expensive than earlier integrated circuits. See **Figure 1-2**. Because microprocessors are still a key component in all computers, today's computers are considered fourth-generation computers.

Figure 1-2: Early microprocessor

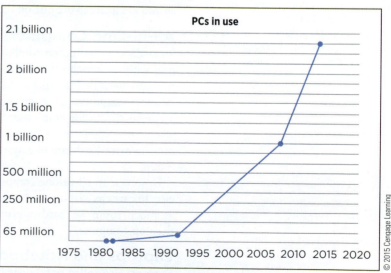

The first microprocessor, similar to the one shown here, was developed in 1971.

© Timothy Hodgkinson/Shutterstock.com

Rise of PCs

In the 1970s and 1980s, computers meant for personal use started to gain popularity. At first, computer enthusiasts and hobbyists built computers from kits. In 1978, Steve Jobs and Steve Wozniak of Apple Computer Corporation introduced the Apple II, a preassembled computer with color graphics and the popular spreadsheet software called VisiCalc.

IBM followed Apple's lead in 1981, introducing its own machine, dubbed a **personal computer (PC)**. Other manufacturers began making less expensive clones of IBM PCs to capture a share of the growing market. **Figure 1-3** shows the growth of personal computers since 1981.

Modern Computers

Modern computers are still based on microprocessors, which have become ever smaller in size

Figure 1-3: Number of personal computers in use

PCs in use

2.1 billion
2 billion
1.5 billion
1 billion
500 million
250 million
65 million

1975 1980 1985 1990 1995 2000 2005 2010 2015 2020

© 2015 Cengage Learning

but larger in processing capacity. Handheld tablets and smartphones have brought connectivity to the masses.

Present-day computers are a far cry from the simple counting tools and cumbersome devices of old. Today, you have thousands of times more computing power at a fraction of the cost in a device that fits into the palm of your hand.

Types of Computers

desktop computer | monitor | system unit | all-in-one desktop | laptop | notebook | subnotebook | Ultrabook | tablet | stylus | slate | convertible tablet | mobile device | smartphone

Computers are so much a part of our world that you might not even realize when you're using one. Chances are, though, that you use one every day.

Figure 1-4: Types of computers

Desktop computers are mainly used by office workers to perform business tasks.

When purchasing a computer today, most people choose a laptop or tablet.

Smartphones, portable music players, and e-book readers are types of modern computers.

© Goodluz/Shutterstock.com, © iStockphoto.com/Yuri_Arcurs, © leungchopan/Shutterstock.com, © Goodluz/Shutterstock.com, © iStockphoto.com/Alina555, © Ijansempoi/Shutterstock.com

By the Numbers Now

In past years, you would have been hard pressed to find a computer of decent quality even for $1500. Today you can find many computers below $500. These lower prices allow people everywhere to enjoy the benefits of computing without breaking the bank.

Desktop Computers

The first type of personal computer was the **desktop computer**, which consists of a system unit, a **monitor** (the display screen), a keyboard, and a mouse. The **system unit** contains most of the electronic circuitry in the computer and can lie flat on the desk or, if it's a tower unit, sit under the desk or on the floor.

Sales of desktop computers are declining, though they remain popular with serious gamers and business users. Schools and businesses still have many desktop computers, so you are likely to use one on the job or in a computer lab.

All-in-One Computers

Some desktop computers combine the system unit with the monitor to create an **all-in-one desktop**. Because they take up less space than desktop computers, all-in-one computers are a logical choice for home users and anyone else who wants to use a large monitor without the extra hardware of a system unit. See **Figure 1-5**.

However, an all-in-one computer is not as easy to carry as a laptop, and it does not allow as much room for hardware upgrades as a desktop computer.

Figure 1-5: All-in-one desktop computer

© iStockphoto.com/rustemgurler

The system unit is located behind the monitor in an all-in-one desktop.

Laptops and Notebooks

Laptops, also called **notebooks** if they weigh less than 6 pounds, are as powerful as many desktop computers. They are lightweight, small, and portable because they can run on a rechargeable battery. See **Figure 1-6**. Notebooks that weigh less than 4 pounds are called **subnotebooks**; those that include Intel processors are called **Ultrabooks**. The term "ultrabook" (with a lowercase "u") has become a common way to refer to a thin, lightweight, high-performance notebook. To reduce bulk and weight, ultrabooks do not have hardware such as optical drives or Ethernet ports.

You can attach a mouse to a laptop, but because laptops also include touchpads and other tracking devices that perform the same functions as a mouse, you often don't need an external mouse.

A laptop might include a CD or DVD drive, as well as one or more USB ports for connecting printers, cameras, and other devices. However, these extra drives are being phased out of many laptops, which include built-in cameras and microphones and depend on wireless connectivity for other functions. For example, you can connect to the Internet to back up files in the cloud.

Tablets

A **tablet** is a small, flat computer with a touch-sensitive screen that accepts input from a digital pen, a **stylus**, or your fingertips. You can use a tablet as a writing or drawing pad. A tablet is convenient for people who need to use their computers as they would a pad of paper or a sketch book and yet take advantage of the tablet's power to access data, perform calculations, and search the Web.

There are two types of tablet displays. The standard one-piece rigid tablet, also called a **slate**, has a display built into the top of the tablet case. The iPad and Samsung Galaxy Tab are popular slates. Slates often include a touch screen keyboard that lets you press the screen to type. The **convertible tablet** display is attached by a hinge and can be opened like a laptop or used flat like a slate, as in the Surface Pro. See **Figure 1-7**.

Figure 1-7: Slate and convertible tablet

Slate with touch screen keyboard

Surface Pro convertible tablet with snap-on keyboard

© Canadapanda/Shutterstock.com, © iStockphoto.com/pressureUA/Anatoliy Babiy

Mobile Devices

A **mobile device** is a portable computer that weighs up to 2 pounds. It often accepts input through your fingertips, a digital pen, or a stylus. Many mobile devices also accept voice commands and provide a keyboard for entering data. In addition, these devices have features that mobile users need, such as hardware for connecting to Wi-Fi networks, navigating with a GPS, and working with media files.

A mobile device has a mobile operating system, such as Android OS, iOS, or Windows Phone. It can also run application software called apps. Typical apps on mobile devices include those that provide access to the Web, take photos and videos, play music, find directions, and manage email, appointments, contacts, and other personal information. A **smartphone** includes these features plus phone capabilities. Other types of mobile devices include portable media players, e-book readers, and game consoles.

Figure 1-6: Laptop

All types of laptops, including notebooks and ultrabooks, contain the system unit, the monitor, and the keyboard in a foldable case.

Touchpad

© iStockphoto.com/SKrow

By the Numbers Now

Many laptop and tablet batteries provide 9–12 hours of power.

Hot Technology Now

You can use a free app and Web site named Glympse (glympse.com) to detect your location by using the closest cell phone tower. Many companies use Glympse to track the position of taxis, mail trucks, trash collection trucks, and delivery vans.

Input Devices

keyboard | mouse | scroll wheel | trackball | touchpad | pointing stick | stylus | digital pen | touch screen | gesture | Web cam | scanner | microphone | voice recognition software | MIDI | game controller | joystick | gamepad | voice input | speech recognition software | biometric technology | biometric input device | fingerprint reader | facial recognition system

Imagine that you receive a computer as a gift. You set it up, sit down at your desk, press the power button, and wait for something to happen. The computer starts up and displays the operating system on the display screen . . . and then what? Without an input device, you are stuck; you cannot do anything. You need an input device to put the computer to work—to communicate instructions or commands.

Figure 1-8: Input devices

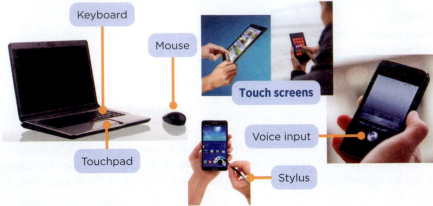

© Antonio Jorge Nunes/Shutterstock.com, © violetkaipa/Shutterstock.com, © Dirima/Shutterstock.com, © iStockphoto.com/pixelfit/Petar Chernaev, © iStockphoto.com/dem10

Figure 1-9: Backlit keyboard

© TACstock1/Shutterstock.com

A backlit keyboard makes it easy to work in a dimly lit place.

On the Job Now

Instead of using pointing devices or keyboards, doctors often enter medical orders and patient information as voice input that is immediately translated into text.

Keyboard

A **keyboard** is an input device you use by pressing keys for letters, numbers, and symbols to enter data into the computer. Most English keyboards are organized in the standard QWERTY layout, named for the letter keys on the second row. You enter commands directly by pressing specialized function keys. For example, the F1 function key opens a Help screen in most programs. Countries outside the United States use different keyboards configured to their alphabet and numerical systems.

Desktop and notebook computers generally use physical keyboards, some with special features such as backlighting. See **Figure 1-9**. Tablets and smartphones have keyboards as well, either built-in or onscreen. These virtual keyboards are software controlled and often use formats other than QWERTY to accommodate their smaller size and fewer keys.

Pointing Devices

A **mouse** is a pointing device that fits under your hand. As you move the mouse, its movements are mirrored by the pointer on the screen. You click a mouse button to enter a command. A mouse might also include a **scroll wheel** for scrolling the display.

A **trackball** is a pointing device with a ball anchored inside a casing. The trackball device is stationary, making it a good alternative to a mouse if you have limited desk space. You roll the ball with your fingers to move the pointer.

A **touchpad** is a flat surface often found on laptop computers. You glide your finger across the pad to move the pointer across the screen. You tap the pad to input commands. Two buttons near the touchpad work like mouse buttons.

A **pointing stick** is a pressure-sensitive pointing device the size and shape of a pencil eraser. Pointing sticks are embedded in the keyboard. You push the pointing stick with your finger in the direction you want the pointer to move. See **Figure 1-10**.

Figure 1-10: Pointing stick on a laptop keyboard

Use the pointing stick to move the onscreen pointer.

Pen Input Devices

You use a pen input device such as a stylus or digital pen to write, draw, or make selections on a touch screen or graphics tablet. A **stylus** is a small plastic or metal device shaped like a pen. You use a stylus to tap or press icons and buttons on a touch screen or type text by tapping an onscreen keyboard.

A **digital pen** is more powerful than a stylus because it can include an electronic eraser or programmable buttons. A digital pen lets you write or draw on a tablet by pressing and dragging the tip of the pen on the screen.

Touch Screens

A **touch screen** is a visual display that responds to the touch of your finger, hand, stylus, or digital pen to enter data and commands. Tablet computers, kiosks, and smartphones commonly use touch screens. You interact with a touch screen by making a motion, called a **gesture**, to issue a command. Most portable media players, such as iPods, have touch-sensitive pads that you manipulate with a fingertip to select songs, play video, or control volume and other settings.

Cameras and Scanners

Cameras and smartphones can be input devices when you use them to transfer their pictures or video to a computer. You can transfer digital video or image files directly from your camera wirelessly, via a USB port, or using a memory card slot to transfer images from the camera's memory card to a computer.

Most computers come with built-in digital video cameras called **Web cams**, which are used for video conferencing or chatting. They convert your image and the words you speak to digital format and enter the data as input to your system. That data becomes output on a display screen.

An input device called a **scanner** converts printed material into digital format. A scan head moves across the document to read and capture

Figure 1-11: Bar code scanner

Handheld scanner reads a bar code and enters it as input into a cash register's computer.

the information and then creates an image file. A scanner can be connected to a computer via a cable or USB port, or it can be wireless. The bar code reader that a cashier uses to record a purchase in a cash register is another kind of scanner. It reads the bar code and inputs item and price data into the cash register's computer. See **Figure 1-11**.

Microphones

You use a **microphone** to enter voice or sound data into a computer. A microphone is usually internal, though it can be connected to your computer wirelessly or via a wire or USB cable. Some Web cams include microphones you can use to chat.

When you speak into a microphone, software converts your voice into digital data, either by recording it as a sound file or by translating it into text on the screen. To translate your voice to text, you use **voice recognition software**. Many applications include this software as a built-in feature.

Hot Technology Now

The Dragon Dictation app for the iPad accepts the words you speak and instantly turns them into typed text.

Hot Technology Now

Use the iTalk Recorder app for the iPad to archive voice or instrument audio.

Hot Technology Now

To select voice recognition settings in Windows 8.x, search for Windows Speech Recognition.

You can input music and other sounds into a computer by connecting an external device, such as a guitar, into MIDI and other compatible computer ports. **MIDI**, short for Musical Instrument Digital Interface, is a system for creating and storing synthesized music, and includes a standard for connecting electronic musical devices to computers. Music production software lets you manipulate synthesized sounds to compose new music or edit existing music files.

Game Controllers

A **game controller** is another kind of input device. When you play a video game, you can use one of the following types of game controllers to control your actions on the screen:

- A **joystick** is a vertical stick or lever that pivots in a 360-degree range of motion.
- A **gamepad** is a handheld console with buttons and other input mechanisms you typically press with your thumbs to play a game. The popular Wii remote controller is a motion-sensing gamepad. You control game play with your arm and hand movements rather than buttons.
- You use a light gun to shoot targets on the screen.
- Steering wheel controllers simulate on-screen driving.

Voice Input

When you ask Siri for directions on an iPhone or speak to another type of device, you are providing **voice input**, a type of input that uses the human voice to give commands to a computer. The computer must have voice recognition or **speech recognition software** installed so it can accept the voice input and interpret it as computer commands. People prefer speaking to a computer rather than using other forms of input for the following reasons:

- People can talk about 3–5 times faster than they can type.
- They tend to provide more complete information when speaking commands or asking questions.
- They can use a computer even when the keyboard or pointing device is unavailable, difficult to see, or difficult to use.
- They can minimize the repetitive movements required to use a keyboard or pointing device.

#introhardware

Voice input is an important technology for mobile devices because it means users can issue commands without using their hands. For example, when wearing Google Glass, you can say, "Okay, Glass, get directions to the Whitney Museum," to display a map with directions.

Biometric Input

Biometric technology analyzes a person's unique physical characteristics, such as fingerprints or voice patterns, to confirm identity and grant access to restricted spaces or computer systems. A **biometric input device** is a data-collection machine that creates a digital imprint of a physical characteristic, and then transfers that information to a host system for review.

On the Job Now

If your job requires international travel, a program named Global Entry allows you to use automated check-in and arrival kiosks with retinal scanners to speed up your time in the security line.

Figure 1-12: iPhone 5s fingerprint scanner

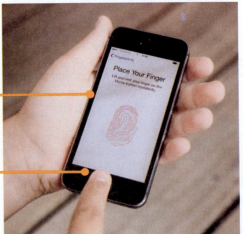

iPhone 5s introduced biometrics for smartphones.

Place your finger on the fingerprint scanner to identify yourself.

© iStockphoto.com/Mlenny

Fingerprint readers, also called fingerprint scanners, are the most common biometric device. They are relatively inexpensive, with some models costing less than $100. Businesses and consumers use them to restrict access to personal computers. See **Figure 1-12**.

Airport security and law enforcement officials use **facial recognition systems** to scan the faces of people trying to board airplanes or enter sensitive areas. They can compare these facial scans with database pictures of known criminals. Other biometric input devices create and transfer imprints of your hands, voice, eyes, or signature.

Using the Keyboard

typing keypad | navigation keypad | numeric keypad | function key | Internet control key | media control key

The keyboard is the most commonly used input device for a personal computer.

Parts of a Keyboard

Each section of a keyboard contains different kinds of keys:

- The **typing keypad** includes numbers, letters, punctuation marks, and symbols such as $ or %.
- The **navigation keypad** lets you move around a document and scroll up and down.
- When you press the NUMLOCK key on some keyboards, the navigation keypad functions as the **numeric keypad**, which includes keys for numbers and symbols for addition, subtraction, multiplication, and division.
- Many keyboards include **function keys** in a row above the typing keypad.
- The **Internet control keys** on some keyboards let you navigate through Web pages, open your list of favorite Web sites, check email, and display the home page.
- In addition, **media control keys** let you play, pause, stop, rewind, and fast forward through digital music or video.

Typing Keypad

The typing keypad has keys that you press to enter letters, numbers, symbols, and punctuation marks. The SPACEBAR inserts a space as you type. You use the BACKSPACE key to delete or remove characters to the left of the insertion point. BACKSPACE also deletes any selected text or objects.

The modifier keys are on the edges of the letter keys. You use the modifier keys like CTRL and ALT with other keys to issue a command. The two SHIFT keys let you type uppercase letters and the symbols that appear on the top half of the number and punctuation keys.

Navigation Keypad

The navigation keypad has arrow keys for moving the insertion point on the screen. It also has HOME, END, PAGE UP, and PAGE DOWN keys for moving to the beginning or end of a screen, document, or file. Some keyboards have two navigation keypads between the typing keypad and the number keypad that contain INSERT, HOME, PAGE UP, DELETE, END, and PAGE DOWN keys in the top section and the arrow keys in the bottom section.

You use the DELETE key to delete characters at the insertion point. You use the INSERT key to switch overtype mode on and off. Overtype mode types over characters in a document rather than inserting characters.

Numeric Keypad

If a keyboard has a numeric keypad, it contains the keys for numbers and basic mathematical functions. The NUMLOCK key turns the numeric keypad on or off. On many keyboards, the numeric keypad functions as a navigation keypad when the NUMLOCK key is off. If a computer does not have a built-in numeric keypad, you can use an external keypad that plugs into a USB port. See **Figure 1-13**.

Function Keys

Function keys are those having labels that start with "F," such as F1. The functions these keys perform vary from program to program. A function key may be used to print a document, close a window, or save a file. In many programs, pressing the F1 function key opens the Help system.

The ESCAPE (ESC) key is located at the left of the function keys on many keyboards. The ESC key will undo the last action in some programs or close a dialog box.

Hot Technology Now

Windows 8.x touch devices include an onscreen keyboard that you can switch to different layouts such as a thumb keyboard or handwriting keyboards, which you can use with a stylus or fingertip.

Figure 1-13: External USB keypad

© Regisser/Shutterstock.com

Connect an external keypad using a USB port.

#introhardware

On a Windows 8.x PC, the Windows key (with the flying window logo) provides quick access to the Start screen.

Internet and Media Controls

Some keyboards have specialized keys to control Internet and media functions. Internet control keys let you navigate the Internet without using the mouse. You can return to the previous Web page with the Back button or go forward a Web page, refresh a page, and go to the home page using these keys. Keyboards with media control keys let you play and pause music and videos. You can also fast-forward and rewind using these keys.

Typing on Keyboards

Besides using the keys displaying letters and numbers, you can use the SPACEBAR, the long bar below the letter keys on the keyboard, to insert a space. The ENTER key moves the insertion point down one line. In a word processing program, it starts a new paragraph. In a dialog box or message box, the ENTER key also works to tell the computer to perform a command.

To type an uppercase letter or a symbol, press and hold the SHIFT key while pressing a character key. You can also use CTRL and ALT with other keys. For example, in some programs, when you press and hold CTRL and then press P, the Print dialog box opens.

Mobile Device Keyboards

To use the touch screen keyboards of mobile devices, you press the image of a key with your finger, an electronic pen, or a stylus. Many of the keys have more than one purpose, providing similar functionality to standard keyboards. Some mobile devices show letters on the first keyboard screen and then, after you click a button, numbers and symbols on another screen. In this way, onscreen keyboards can provide a full range of characters used in computer input. **Figure 1-14** shows the onscreen keyboards in Windows 8.x.

Mobile devices can also have mini keyboards with real keys rather than touch screen keys. They have fewer keys and less functionality than the keyboard on a laptop or desktop computer. In either case, mobile device keyboards are not designed for document creation. Most people use these keyboards for short messaging and notes.

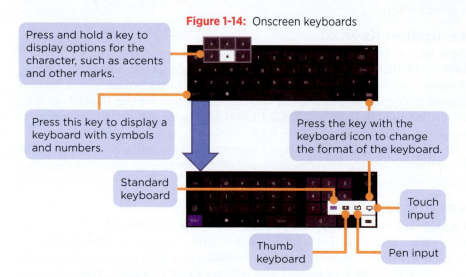

Figure 1-14: Onscreen keyboards

Press and hold a key to display options for the character, such as accents and other marks.

Press this key to display a keyboard with symbols and numbers.

Press the key with the keyboard icon to change the format of the keyboard.

Standard keyboard

Touch input

Thumb keyboard

Pen input

Using Pointing Devices

mechanical mouse | optical mouse | light-emitting diode (LED) | laser mouse | drag | gesture

You use a pointing device to move the pointer on a computer screen. A pointer can be in the shape of an arrow, an I-beam, a bar, or other shape or image.

The Mouse

A computer mouse can be wireless, or it can be connected to the computer via a wire or cable. Most wired mice connect through a USB port. Mice can also be mechanical or optical. A **mechanical mouse** has moving parts, such as a roller ball on the bottom. An **optical mouse** uses **light-emitting diodes (LEDs)** to detect movement. An LED is a light source that emits infrared or visible light when charged with an electric current. A **laser mouse** is an optical mouse that uses laser light. See **Figure 1-15**.

A typical mouse has a left button and a right button on the top or sides that you press to perform different actions. In addition, some mice have a scroll wheel between the buttons. When you move the wheel, you scroll the active window in the screen.

Figure 1-15: Types of computer mice

Scroll wheel

LED detects movement

Thumb buttons

Mechanical wired mouse   **Bottom of an optical mouse**   **Laser mouse**

© Tatiana Popova/Shutterstock.com, © iStockphoto.com/luismmolina, © Pedro Miguel Sousa/Shutterstock.com

Most mice require you to use them on a flat surface, but some newer mice, called gyroscopic mice or air mice, can actually be held in the air and can detect the motion of your hand as you move it in space.

Moving the Pointer

When you move a mouse, the rollerball or light-reflecting surface transfers signals as input to the computer so the software can respond to the actions of the mouse. The way the pointer moves mimics the hand motion. A pointing stick, joystick, touchpad, and trackball also let you move the pointer on the screen by directing the device with your hand.

Clicking and Double-clicking

To select an object such as an icon or menu command, you move the mouse pointer to the object and then press and release the left mouse button, or click. A pointing stick, joystick, touchpad, and trackball also have a left button that you can click. To issue a command, sometimes you have to double-click, which means you quickly press and release the left mouse button twice.

Dragging

Using a pointing device to move an object on the screen is called **dragging**. To drag an object with a mouse, place the pointer on the object, press and hold down the left button to select the object, and then continue to hold the button while moving the pointer. Using a touchpad is similar, except you press and hold the left button on the touchpad, and then drag a finger on the touchpad. The object moves across the screen with the pointer. When you reach the intended destination, release the mouse button to "drop" the object in its new place. Dragging to move or copy an object is sometimes called drag-and-drop.

You can also drag to highlight text in a word processing program or a range of cells in a spreadsheet application. Click at the beginning of the text or cells you want to select, and press and hold the left button. Keep pressing the button as you drag the mouse to complete the selection. When you have finished selecting what you want, release the button.

Right-clicking

To right-click, you press and release the right button on a mouse or touchpad. In many programs, right-clicking opens a shortcut menu that displays commands that are available to the current object, selection, or program area. If you are unsure about what you can do at any point in a program, right-clicking will often give you the common available options. For example, if you right-click the Windows desktop, the shortcut menu displays commands for changing the view, sorting desktop icons, and personalizing Windows.

Using Gestures

Touch screens let you use your fingers directly on the screen to select, move, and change the size of windows or objects. Any finger motion you perform is called a **gesture**. **Table 1-1** on the next page lists touch input gestures and describes them.

Hot Technology Now

A Windows 8.x app named BallStrike uses the camera on your device to detect gestures you make as you play an augmented reality fitness game.

#introhardware

Gestures can vary depending on the software and touch screen. For example, a tablet may use different gestures from a smartphone screen.

Table 1-1: Touch input gestures

Gesture	Description	Use it to
Tap	Touch and release an object quickly.	Select an object Press a button
Double-tap	Touch and release an object two times.	Start an application
Press and hold	Touch and hold an object.	Display a shortcut menu
Drag	Touch and hold an object and then move it with a fingertip.	Move an object
Swipe	Touch one side of the screen and then slide your fingertip horizontally or vertically.	Scroll Display the Charms bar (Windows 8.x) Close an application
Pinch	Move two fingers together.	Zoom out
Stretch	Move two fingers apart.	Zoom in

© 2015 Cengage Learning

Output Devices

liquid crystal display (LCD) | light-emitting diode (LED) | printer | ink-jet printer | laser printer | toner | multifunction device (MFD) | mobile printer | plotter | headphone | earbud | headset | projector | HDMI (high-definition multimedia interface) | voice synthesizer | text-to-speech technology | voice recognition software | closed caption

Without output devices, you wouldn't be able to see or hear anything on your computer or print anything from the computer.

Figure 1-16: Output devices

Desktop monitor

Laptop screen

Smartphone display screen

Tablet display screen

Color output from a printer

© iStockphoto.com/Nik_Merkulov, © Maksym Dykha/Shutterstock.com

On the Job Now

Medical surgeons using the eye-level screen in Google Glass can project patient information onto their retinas, instantly viewing relevant parts of a patient's chart and lab results.

Display Devices

All personal computers have a display device that shows text and images as computer output on a screen. These include touch screens, plasma screens, and LCD and LED displays. Some untraditional display devices are wearable glasses with the ability to display information in 3D. See **Figure 1-17**.

Most flat panel monitors use either **liquid crystal display (LCD)** or **light-emitting diode (LED)** technology. Many computer displays are capable of displaying images at very high resolutions. Display devices labeled 1080p or 1080i show images and video in high definition; they let you watch HDTV on your computer.

Figure 1-17: Google Glass

Google Glass is a wearable computer that displays output on a tiny screen so it appears full-size to the eye.

© Joe Seer/Shutterstock.com

Printers

A **printer** creates hard copy output on paper, film, photo paper, and other media. The most common printers are laser and ink-jet. Recent technology is 3D printing, which lets you

Figure 1-18: 3D printing

A 3D printer uses plastic to create objects based on computer models.

create objects based on computer models. These printers use special plastics to generate objects. See **Figure 1-18**.

Speed of traditional printers is measured in pages per minute (ppm). A printer can be connected to a computer or network by cable through a printer port, using a print server, through a USB port, or wirelessly using a Wi-Fi or Bluetooth network.

Ink-jet printers print by spraying small dots of colored ink onto paper. **Laser printers** use a laser beam and toner to print on paper and are faster than ink-jet printers. **Toner** is a fine powder that is sealed when heated on the page. Color laser printers can print a full range of colors. Other laser printers print only in black and shades of gray.

A **multifunction device (MFD)**, or all-in-one printer, can function as an input device by copying and scanning documents and as an output device by sending faxes and printing.

Mobile Printers

A **mobile printer** is a small, lightweight printer that you can attach to a mobile device for on-the-go printing. Many mobile printers work with Bluetooth wireless technology. Mobile printers are battery-powered and use ink-jet or thermal technology to print. Thermal technology either uses wax-based ink or burns dots onto coated paper to print.

Because a mobile printer is so small, it fits easily into the case of a mobile device. Their small size, however, prevents some mobile printers from using standard 8-1/2 × 11 inch paper; instead, they print on smaller, sometimes odd-sized, papers.

Large-Format Printers

A large-format printer is a special kind of printer that can print on very large sheets of paper. Some large-format printers called **plotters** use charged wires to produce high-quality drawings for professional applications such as architectural blueprints. Graphic artists and designers use large-format ink-jet printers to print large drawings, posters, and photographs.

Speakers

Audio output includes recorded music, spoken voice, sound tracks for movies or video, computer-generated music, or other sounds, such as the beeps a computer emits if you make an error. Speakers can be built into a computer, smartphone, or tablet. Wired or wireless external speakers can also be added to a system to enhance sound. Some speakers are small enough to fit into your pocket. See **Figure 1-19**.

If you want to listen to sound in a public space, **headphones** are an option for many devices. They can be connected via a USB or other cable, or can be wireless. Computers, mobile phones, and digital music players have jacks for headphones or **earbuds**, which are speakers small enough to place in your ears.

If you want to video chat or use your computer for telephone calls over the Web, a **headset** is a good option. Headsets include one or more headphones (for output) and a microphone (for input).

Projectors

Projectors, sometimes referred to as data or video projectors, let you display computer output on a wall or projection screen. Many projectors work with dual screens so you

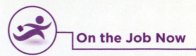

On the Job Now

Many companies require employees to cover their computer displays with a privacy screen to prevent others from viewing sensitive, confidential information.

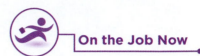

On the Job Now

3D printers are changing the manufacturing industry by creating engine parts, lightweight airplane parts, aerodynamic car bodies, and custom prosthetic devices.

Figure 1-19: Micro speaker

This micro speaker is only 23 mm in diameter.

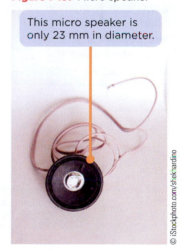

#introhardware

Noise-cancelling headphones tune out ambient noise to allow you to focus on your work or listen to music.

can view a slightly different output on your computer, such as a presentation with speaker notes, while your audience sees only the presentation.

Projectors can be connected to a computer wirelessly or via a cable. Many connect using HDMI cables to display output in high definition, and some work with 3D imagery to project holograms of 3D objects. **HDMI (high-definition multimedia interface)** cables transfer uncompressed video data and digital audio data among HDMI-compliant devices. Projectors can also include a dock so that you can share any video stored on a portable media device or smartphone with a wider audience. Newer projectors can be very small—even built into a smartphone, tablet, or laptop. They display the information from the mobile device on a large screen.

Voice Synthesis and Recognition

A **voice synthesizer** is an audio output device that converts text to speech. When you dial 411 for directory assistance, for example, the call is answered by a synthesized voice. **Text-to-speech technology** uses digitized voice files that can be interpreted by a computer.

Some operating systems have built-in voice synthesizers. For example, Windows has a tool called Narrator that can read screen contents. This feature narrates text displayed onscreen so that people with visual or cognitive impairments can use the computer.

Voice recognition software converts speech to text, which is especially helpful for those who have hearing impairments. Some voice recognition systems can even respond to commands with a synthesized voice. Many videos include the option to turn on subtitles, or **closed captions,** so that users can watch the action on the screen and read what is being said in the voice-over.

Central Processing Unit

central processing unit (CPU) | microprocessor | processor | integrated circuit | chip | motherboard | circuit board | core | multicore processor | control unit | arithmetic logic unit (ALU) | register | machine cycle | clock speed | megahertz (MHz) | gigahertz (GHz) | cycle | bus | data bus | address bus | bus width | word size | cache | processor cache | Level 1 (L1) cache | Level 2 (L2) cache | Level 3 (L3) cache | benchmark

Figure 1-20: Central processing units

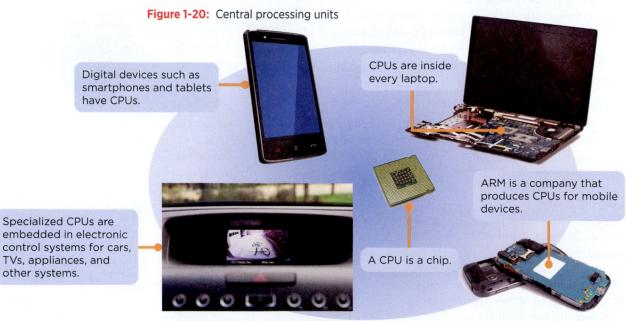

Digital devices such as smartphones and tablets have CPUs.

CPUs are inside every laptop.

Specialized CPUs are embedded in electronic control systems for cars, TVs, appliances, and other systems.

ARM is a company that produces CPUs for mobile devices.

A CPU is a chip.

© aarows/Shutterstock.com, © saginbay/Shutterstock.com, © CLS Design/Shutterstock.com, © Raw Group/Shutterstock.com, © NorGal/Shutterstock.com

The **central processing unit (CPU)** is the brain of a computer. The CPU is often called a **microprocessor** or a **processor**. It is an **integrated circuit**, or **chip**, and can contain millions of electronic parts and circuits. The CPU is built into the **motherboard**, which is the main **circuit board** that houses much of a computer's electronics.

Processor Cores

One of the most important factors to consider in purchasing a computer is CPU performance. The more powerful the processor, the faster and better the computer will make calculations, format pages, load and stream video, and more. Processor performance is determined in part by the number of **cores**, or processor units, on a CPU. The more cores, the more processing power. The first processors were single core, but processors today can be dual core (two cores) or multicore, such as quad-core processors (four cores).

A **multicore processor** generally is faster and more powerful than a single-core processor. Multicore processors are particularly valuable when you run multiple programs at once or work with programs that require a lot of power, such as games, graphics, and video applications. For example, three popular Intel processors are the i3, i5, and i7. The i3 is for the casual computer user or someone who uses a computer mainly to access the Internet. The i5 is good for the daily computer user or user of productivity apps. The powerful i7 is necessary for a heavy gamer.

Processor Logic

CPUs have different parts or functions. Two of the most important are the **control unit** and the **arithmetic logic unit (ALU)**. The control unit is like a traffic cop, directing the flow of instructions throughout the processor. The ALU performs arithmetic operations, such as addition and subtraction, and comparison operations such as comparing two numbers to see if they are the same. The ALU temporarily holds data, such as two numbers to add, in **registers**, or small storage locations within the CPU.

Every instruction to the computer goes through a four-step process in the CPU called the **machine cycle**: fetch, decode, execute, and store. Some parts of the machine cycle are performed by the control unit, and others are performed by the ALU. See **Figure 1-21**.

Clock Speed

The processor clock sets the speed at which the CPU executes instructions. **Clock speed** is measured in hertz. **Megahertz (MHz)** specifies millions of cycles per second, and **gigahertz (GHz)** specifies billions of cycles per second.

A **cycle** is the smallest unit of time a process can measure. Processors with faster clocks can execute more instructions per second than processors with slower clocks. If you are buying a computer, you can often find information about a processor's clock speed in the ad for the computer.

Bus Speed and Width

A **bus** is an electronic channel that allows the CPU and various devices inside or attached to a computer to communicate. A bus has two parts: the **data bus**, which transfers the data, and the **address bus**, which transfers the information about where the data exists in memory.

Bus width, measured in bits, determines the speed at which data travels. The wider the bus, the more data that can travel on it. For example, a 64-bit bus transfers data faster than a 32-bit bus. Bus width is also called **word size**.

Cache

Cache is a storage space for recently or frequently used data in a place that is quick and easy to access. You may have heard of browser cache or disk cache. A **processor cache**

#introhardware

Intel and AMD are popular CPU manufacturers for desktops, laptops, and servers.

Figure 1-21: Machine cycle

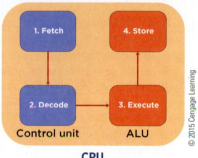

© 2015 Cengage Learning

On the Job Now

If your company builds a mobile app or Web site, the app should be validated with benchmark tests to confirm that it can handle heavy Internet traffic.

stores frequently used data and instructions next to the processor. It improves processor speed because it's easier and faster to retrieve information from the cache than from the processor itself.

There are several types of cache: **Level 1 (L1)**, **Level 2 (L2)**, and **Level 3 (L3)**. L1 and L2 cache are built into the processor chip. L3 cache resides on a separate chip. It takes a processor less time to retrieve data from L1 or L2 cache than from L3 cache.

Benchmarking

A **benchmark** is a test run by a laboratory or other organization to determine processor speed and other performance factors.

Although you can look at individual factors such as clock speed, bus speed, and cache level, many other factors determine the performance of a processor. It is best to do some research to see how various processors perform on benchmark tests. You can find this information on the Web and in articles published by computer magazines.

Digital Data Representation

binary number system | bit | byte | ASCII | Unicode | sampling | pixel

The **binary number system** consists of only two digits: 0 and 1. Computers are binary machines because they are electronic devices, and electricity has two states: on and off.

Figure 1-22: Digital data

The binary number system consists of only two digits: 0 and 1.

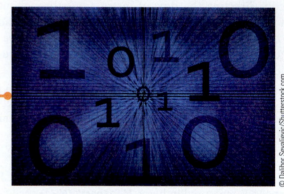

© Dalibor Sevaljevic/Shutterstock.com

Bits and Bytes

Bit is short for "binary digit," the smallest unit of information handled by a computer and the basis of today's computer processing. A bit can have the value of 0 or 1.

Bits appear in groups of 8. A group of 8 bits is called a **byte**. Bytes can represent letters, symbols, and numbers. Bytes are the basic building blocks of digitally representing sounds and colors.

Representing Text

When you press a key on your keyboard, the computer translates the character into bits and bytes using a text coding scheme. Text coding schemes use groups of bits to represent characters. **ASCII** is an 8-bit coding scheme, with different binary codes representing each uppercase letter, lowercase letter, mathematical operator, and logical operation. For example, **Figure 1-23** shows part of an ASCII table with the binary codes for the lowercase letters "d," "o," and "g."

Entering the binary code for "dog" requires quite a bit of typing. Your computer translates your keystrokes into binary digits, however, so you can simply type the three letters.

ASCII doesn't include characters for languages such as Chinese or Arabic. **Unicode**, a 16-bit coding scheme, is an extension of ASCII that can create over 65,000 symbols and characters in many languages.

The Bottom Line

- Computers are digital devices, meaning they can work only with separate, individual digits such as 0 and 1.
- When you digitize data, you convert it from human-recognizable forms to forms that computers and other digital devices can use.
- Groups of binary digits (bits) carry the instructions your computer needs to function and to represent all kinds of data, including text, pictures, music, and video.

Figure 1-23: Binary codes

Character	Binary
d	01100100
o	01101111
g	01100111

© 2015 Cengage Learning

Representing Sound

The human ear hears sound, such as music and speech, as sound waves that continually change. To digitize sound, a process called **sampling** takes samples of sound waves a specified number of times per second. Each sample is stored as a binary number. The more samples per second, the more accurate the representation of the sound. However, a higher sampling rate also requires a larger file to store the data.

Representing Images

Bits can also be used to represent images. Each color is assigned a binary number, such as 0000 for black and 1111 for white. To digitize an image, the image is treated as a series of colored dots, or **pixels**. To a computer, an image is a list of the color numbers for all the pixels it contains.

File Sizes

The amount of binary information in any file determines its file size. All files are measured in bytes, though the terms used to express file size vary to make it easier to describe the files. **Table 1-2** lists and defines terms for measuring file size. In the ASCII coding scheme, each character you type is 1 byte. In a plain text file, the word "dog" takes up 3 bytes of the total file size. When you add coding for formatting and graphics, the file size increases substantially. Sound and video files tend to be much larger than text files and take longer to download. A high-speed Internet connection is required to download movies and high-definition video.

Table 1-2: File size units

Term	Abbreviation	Approx. Number of bytes
Byte	B	1
Kilobyte	KB	1 thousand
Megabyte	MB	1 million
Gigabyte	GB	1 billion
Terabyte	TB	1 trillion

© 2015 Cengage Learning

Memory

random access memory (RAM) | memory chip | memory module | volatile | dynamic RAM (DRAM) | static RAM (SRAM) | magnetoresistive RAM (MRAM) | read-only memory (ROM) | BIOS | power-on self-test (POST) | firmware | boot | programmable read-only memory (PROM) | electrically erasable programmable memory (EEPROM) | flash memory | nonvolatile | virtual memory | swap file | page

Figure 1-24: Computer memory

RAM modules store temporary data.

ROM chip includes instructions needed to start the computer.

Programmable ROM is used in smartphones and other mobile devices.

Virtual memory is an area of the hard disk that stores overflow data from RAM.

Hot Technology Now

Streaming music is the continuous flow of music to a device without needing to store it on your hard drive. The most popular streaming music sites include Pandora, Spotify, Xbox Music, Grooveshark, Last.fm, and Slacker.

#introhardware

Many email service providers set a size limit such as 10 MB for files you attach to an email message. To avoid this limitation, you can share much larger files from your cloud storage.

The Bottom Line

- Some memory is volatile, which means that when the computer is shut down, the information in volatile memory is erased. Other memory is nonvolatile. It stores data even when a computer has been powered off.
- Memory types include random access memory (RAM), read-only memory (ROM), virtual memory, and programmable memory.

Computer memory holds data and programs as they are being processed by the CPU. Memory stores three kinds of information: instructions to be processed, data necessary to complete the instructions, and the results of the data processing operation.

RAM

Random access memory (RAM) is stored on a set of chips called a **memory chip** or a **memory module**, which is a small circuit board that slides into a slot on the motherboard.

When you start an application, its instructions are loaded from the hard drive, or internal storage, into RAM so that the application opens. When you interact with the application, such as by saving a file, you are copying it from RAM onto a disk or another permanent storage location.

Most RAM is **volatile**. That is, if your computer loses power, any data stored in RAM is lost. RAM capacity is measured in gigabytes. Today's PCs generally need 4–16 GB of RAM.

Other RAM

RAM comes in three basic types: **Dynamic RAM (DRAM)** chips need to be recharged constantly or they lose their data. This means that the slightest interruption of power results in data loss. However, DRAM chips are the least expensive of the three types.

Static RAM (SRAM) chips are faster, more reliable, and don't need to be recharged as frequently, but they are more expensive than DRAM chips. **Magnetoresistive RAM (MRAM)** chips use magnetic charges instead of electrical charges to store data. They have greater storage capacity and use less power. They also store data and instructions even after a computer has been turned off. In other words, they are nonvolatile—but more expensive.

ROM

Read-only memory (ROM) is the memory permanently installed on your system when your computer is manufactured. The ROM chip is attached to the motherboard (see **Figure 1-25**) and contains the **BIOS**, or basic input/output system. The BIOS includes the instructions for starting up your computer as it performs the **power-on self-test (POST)**, which tests the CPU, storage devices, and many other components. After ROM has tested the hardware on the system, it loads the operating system and provides the interface between the operating system and the hardware.

Figure 1-25: Replacing chips on a motherboard

CPU   ROM chips

© Andrii/Shutterstock.com

Instructions on a ROM chip are called **firmware**. Your computer's start-up, or **boot**, instructions are an example of firmware. They tell the CPU how to use the hardware in your system.

Programmable Memory

Programmable read-only memory (PROM), **electrically erasable programmable memory (EEPROM)**, and **flash memory** are types of programmable ROM. Like other

ROM, they are **nonvolatile**, meaning they keep their contents even if the computer is powered off.

A chip with PROM is a blank ROM chip on which a programmer can write code. Once a PROM chip is programmed, it cannot be changed. PROM is used in cell phones, video game consoles, RFID tags, and other electronics as a simple programming tool.

EEPROM is like PROM except it can be programmed more than once. Flash memory is a type of programmable memory that can be electrically erased and reprogrammed. Flash memory is faster and cheaper than traditional EEPROM. Most BIOS chips now use flash memory. Flash memory cards also store programs and data on many digital electronics devices.

Virtual Memory

When an operating system uses **virtual memory**, it swaps files between RAM and the hard disk to avoid running out of RAM. The part of the hard disk used by virtual memory is called a **swap file**. The amount of data and instructions that can be swapped at any given time is called a **page**.

Virtual memory is especially useful when you have many applications open at the same time. Information from an application you aren't currently using is swapped to the hard drive while you're working in another application. However, overuse of virtual memory can slow down your computer because retrieving data from a hard drive is much slower than getting it from RAM.

Storage

hard disk | hard drive | magnetic hard drive | platter | solid state drive (SSD) | external hard drive | optical media | solid state storage | cloud storage

Figure 1-26: Storage devices

Internal hard drive   **External hard drive**   **Memory cards**   **USB flash drive**

© Andy Pollard/Shutterstock.com, © iStockphoto.com/bedo, © aarrows/Shutterstock.com, © Mackey Creations/Shutterstock.com

Internal Hard Drives

The main storage medium on a personal computer is the **hard disk**, which is contained in a storage device called the hard disk drive or **hard drive**. See **Figure 1-27**. Most hard drives use magnetic storage, though some use solid state storage.

Most desktop and laptop hard drives use magnetic technology. A **magnetic hard drive** is made up of one or more disks called **platters** that spin on a spindle, and read/write heads that move over the surface of the disks to save and retrieve data. The disks and heads are stored in a protective case.

Platters use magnetized particles to store data as bits. Depending on its orientation, a particle represents either a 0 bit or a 1 bit. To change the data on a disk, the orientation of the particles is changed.

Hard drives offer fast access to your data and large storage capacity, making them a good option as the main storage device for a PC. Hard drive capacities today range from 160 GB to 2 TB or more. On the downside, magnetic hard drives are easily damaged by impact and foreign particles. You need to protect your hard drive from excessive movement and contaminants such as dust. **Solid state drives (SSDs)** are more durable than magnetic drives, so they are particularly useful for portable devices such as tablets.

Figure 1-27: Internal hard drive

A hard disk is a storage medium.

A hard drive is a storage device that contains a disk and other parts.

© Gregory Gerber/Shutterstock.com

External Hard Drives

You can add storage capacity to your computer relatively easily and inexpensively by attaching an **external hard drive** via either a USB cable or a Firewire cable. External hard drives are a great way to back up data so it is protected in the event your computer or internal hard drive fails. Because you can detach an external hard drive from your system and lock it away, your data is safe should your computer be hacked or damaged.

You can also use external hard drives to transfer large files from one system to another. To transfer data, you save it to the external hard drive, and then attach the drive to the computer to which you want to copy the data.

Tape Storage

Tape drives use magnetic storage technology. They are an older technology used by organizations for backing up large quantities of data. Data is stored on a tape cartridge inserted into a tape drive.

Access to the data stored on tapes is sequential—that is, you may need to forward or rewind a tape in order to access the data you need. Sequential access makes tape storage slower than hard drive or optical storage, which use random or direct access to move directly to where the data is stored on a drive. Even with its slower access time, tape was a relatively inexpensive and durable storage media suitable for high-volume data storage needs.

Optical Storage

Optical media include CDs, DVDs, and Blu-ray discs (BDs), though their use as storage media is declining. They store data as light and dark spots on a disc. When you store data on an optical disc, you "burn" the disc. Storage capacities for optical discs vary, with prices rising accordingly. CDs generally hold up to 1 GB of data, DVDs can store up to 17 GB of data, and more expensive BDs can store 100 GB of data.

Optical storage devices have two benefits over magnetic storage. First, they are easy to store and transport. Second, they are less susceptible to damage, although you do need to be careful to keep the discs free from scratches and dust.

Solid State Storage

Solid state storage uses nonmagnetic technology and can be removable, such as flash drives and memory cards, or contained in a device, such as a solid state hard drive. See **Figure 1-28**. Solid state devices store data as electrical charges.

Figure 1-28: Solid state hard drive

Solid state hard drives have no moving parts.

© Albert Lozano/Shutterstock.com

Unlike magnetic disk drives, solid state drives have no moving parts, so they aren't vulnerable to mechanical failure or damage if dropped. They also require less power than magnetic drives, and are not susceptible to data loss due to power interruptions. On the other hand, the storage capacity of solid state technology doesn't yet match that of magnetic drives, and it costs more per gigabyte of storage.

Cloud Storage

Cloud storage lets you store your data remotely over the Internet. Cloud storage providers save clients' information and programs on servers.

You might use cloud storage to add storage capacity to your system or to back up data, so that even if your system is damaged, your files will remain intact. People use cloud storage to access their data from Internet-connected devices wherever they are. For example, the Apple iCloud service allows you to access your media files from your phone, tablet, or computer.

With services such as Google Drive, Microsoft OneDrive, and Dropbox, you can also use cloud storage to collaborate on documents and projects with others all over the world.

Cloud storage has some disadvantages. If you lose power or your Internet connection, you cannot access your data. If your cloud provider goes out of business, you might lose your data. In addition, whenever your data is transferred to a third party, you need to consider privacy issues.

Hot Technology Now

Cloud storage services such as icloud.com or onedrive.com allow you to store contacts, calendars, photos, music, books, apps, and more in the cloud and access them on all your devices.

#introhardware

Go to twitter.com, search for **@SAMTechNow,** the book's Twitter account, and then follow @SAMTechNow to get tweets on your home page.

Chapter Review

Computers in History

1. Describe the general trend in computer hardware innovation.

2. How does a microprocessor compare to an integrated circuit?

Types of Computers

3. What are the five general categories of personal computers?

4. Describe the two types of tablet displays.

Input Devices

5. Name four types of pointing devices.

6. What is a biometric input device?

Using the Keyboard

7. What can you do if your computer does not have a built-in numeric keypad?

8. Describe how onscreen keyboards can provide a full range of characters used in computer input.

Using Pointing Devices

9. What is the difference between an optical mouse and a laser mouse?

10. Describe four touch input gestures and what each does.

Output Devices

11. Name four types of output devices.

12. What is a voice synthesizer?

Central Processing Unit

13. What role does the CPU play in a computer?

14. Name two factors to use when comparing CPUs.

Digital Data Representation

15. Why are computers considered binary machines?

16. Name five units for measuring computer data and explain what each means.

Memory

17. Describe the difference between volatile and nonvolatile memory.

18. How does a computer use virtual memory?

Storage

19. What are the advantages and disadvantages of using a magnetic hard drive to store data?

20. What are the advantages and disadvantages of using cloud storage?

Test Your Knowledge Now

1. Third-generation computers introduced _____, which packed the equivalent of thousands of vacuum tubes or transistors into a miniature silicon chip.
   a. slide rules
   b. the ENIAC
   c. integrated circuits
   d. solid state technology

2. When IBM introduced computers for personal use, it called them _____.
   a. personal computers (PCs)
   b. Apple computers (ACs)
   c. clones
   d. VisiCalcs

3. Some desktop computers combine the system unit with the monitor to create a(n) _____.
   a. system desktop
   c. tower
   b. ultra-desktop
   d. all-in-one desktop

4. A(n) _____ is a laptop computer that weighs less than 4 pounds and is manufactured according to the specs set by Intel.
   a. ultratop
   c. lightbook
   b. Ultrabook
   d. ultra laptop

5. You interact with a touch screen by making a motion called a _____ to issue a command.
   a. click
   c. flip
   b. gesture
   d. signal

6. A fingerprint reader is an example of a _____ device.
   a. biometric
   c. motion-detecting
   b. touch-sensitive
   d. biological

7. A(n) _____ is an input device for touch screens that is more powerful than a stylus because it can include an electronic eraser or programmable buttons.
   a. electronic stylus
   c. digital pen
   b. fingertip
   d. biometric scanner

8. Keyboards with _____ keys let you play, pause, fast-forward, and rewind music and videos.
   a. Web
   c. numeric
   b. navigation
   d. media control

9. A(n) _____ mouse uses light-emitting diodes (LEDs) to detect movement.
   a. mechanical
   c. gyroscopic
   b. optical
   d. magnetic

10. A(n) _____ printer prints by spraying small dots of colored ink onto paper.
   a. ink-jet
   c. laser
   b. optical
   d. dot matrix

11. To have a video chat, you can use a(n) _____, which includes one or more headphones and a microphone.
   a. earbud
   c. voice synthesizer
   b. micro headphones
   d. headset

12. The _____ is an integrated circuit, or chip, and is often called the brain of the computer.
   a. RAM module
   c. BIOS
   b. central processing unit (CPU)
   d. ROM chip

13. The CPU is built into _____, which is the main circuit board that houses much of a computer's electronics.
   a. the data bus
   c. nonvolatile memory
   b. volatile memory
   d. the motherboard

14. The number of _____ in a CPU determines the CPU's processing power.
   a. ALUs
   c. caches
   b. control units
   d. cores

15. A(n) _____ is the smallest unit of information handled by a computer and can have the value of 0 or 1.
   a. byte
   c. megabyte
   b. bit
   d. kilobyte

16. _____ is a 16-bit coding scheme, an extension of ASCII that can be used to create over 65,000 symbols and characters in many languages.
   a. ASCII plus
   c. Unicode
   b. Extended code
   d. ASCII 16

17. Most RAM is _____ because if your computer loses power, any data stored in RAM is lost.
   a. inaccessible
   c. volatile
   b. nonvolatile
   d. unnecessary

18. The _____ chip is attached to the motherboard and contains the BIOS, which includes the instructions for starting up your computer.
   a. RAM
   c. BIOS
   b. ROM
   d. POST

19. A magnetic hard drive is made up of one or more disks called _____ that spin on a spindle, and read/write heads that move over the surface of the disks to save and retrieve data.
   a. platters
   c. magnetos
   b. plotters
   d. spinners

20. _____ storage uses nonmagnetic technology, and it can be contained in a device or can be easily removed, such as flash drives and memory cards.
   a. Magnetic
   c. Cloud
   b. Optical
   d. Solid state

21. In the space next to each term below, write the letter of the phrase that defines it.
   a. provides a way to add storage capacity to your computer or to back up data
   b. nonvolatile memory
   c. 1 billion bytes of data
   d. the four-step process that every instruction to the computer goes through
   e. small, flat computer with a touch-sensitive screen that accepts input from your fingertips

   _____ gigabyte   _____ machine cycle

   _____ external hard drive   _____ ROM

   _____ tablet

Try This Now

1: Tablet or Laptop – The Business Decision

You serve on the technology committee at the local office of your company. You are a sales person who travels in the local region and occasionally takes longer trips by train or plane. The sales team uses various applications such as Outlook for email, Access to store product information in a database, and Excel for order forms. Your company has made the decision to purchase tablets or laptops for everyone on the sales team.

    a. Research popular laptops and tablets at CNET.com (an unbiased technology site). Create two tables with the specifications of the laptop and tablet that you would recommend.

    b. Research and document at least five advantages a tablet offers the sales team.

    c. Research and document at least five advantages a laptop offers the sales team.

    d. In your opinion, would you recommend a laptop or tablet? Explain why in one written paragraph.

2: 3D Printers Changing the Manufacturing World

The manufacturing world is quickly changing with the invention of the 3D printer. Research the use of 3D printers in manufacturing today and in the future.

    a. Write 100 words or more on at least five uses of 3D printers in manufacturing.

    b. Research and document the cost and specifications for a 3D home printer. Share the link of the 3D printer you researched.

    c. Name three types of media or materials used within the 3D printer to create products.

3D Printer

© iStockphoto.com/bluehill75

3: Using Voice Input on a Mobile Device

Note: This assignment requires a smartphone or computer with a microphone.

  A free Web site and app named Dictionary.com supports voice input so that when you speak any word in English, Dictionary.com displays the spelling and definition of that word. Open your browser on any computer, go to the Dictionary.com Web site, and then install the free app on your smartphone or other mobile device. Tap or click the microphone icon and then speak into your device's microphone as you read five technology terms and their definitions from Dictionary.com.

    a. Write a paragraph describing an example of how you could use voice-to-text technology in your future job.

    b. Which five terms did you read using Dictionary.com?

    c. Do you think voice and speech recognition technology can assist learners for whom English is a second language? Why or why not?

Critical Thinking Now

1: Investigate Cloud Storage Providers

After the hard drive of your older computer crashed recently, you are reconsidering the way you back up data. Investigate three cloud storage providers that provide home computer users with free storage space for backing up files such as documents, music, pictures, and videos. Write a paragraph on each of the cloud storage options, explaining which one would you select and why.

2: Touch Screen Options

You are considering buying a large display screen for your home computer for playing games, watching media, and performing general computing tasks. The display screen needs to work with your primary computing device. Research large touch screen monitors, select one that suits your needs, and then write two paragraphs about your findings. The first paragraph should discuss the specifications of the touch screen you would like, and the second paragraph should discuss the features and cost of the touch screen.

3: Email Attachments vs. Cloud File Sharing

When you send a file, you can attach it to your email message or share the file using cloud storage. Compare and contrast email attachments versus cloud file sharing in a Word document of 150 words or more. Be sure to use your own words, and share your opinion after your comparison.

Ethical Issues Now

You can use apps such as Glympse to recover lost or stolen smartphones by determining their GPS position. In fact, you can find the location of any phone as long as you have the permission of the owner.

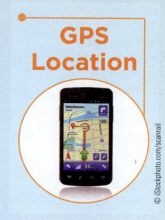

GPS Location

© iStockphoto.com/scanrail

a. If you were a parent, how would you feel about placing an app such as Glympse on your young teenager's phone for safety issues to determine his or her exact location? Write a paragraph stating your opinion.

b. Your best friend recently got engaged and seems concerned about the whereabouts of her fiancé at times. She asked you to install the Glympse app on a pay-as-you-go phone and place it in the trunk of the fiancé's vehicle to track his location. How would you handle this ethical dilemma? Write a paragraph stating your opinion.

c. Some governments use their citizens' cell phones to track those citizens when they leave their home country. Write a paragraph explaining whether your country should track you without your permission when you are abroad.

Team Up Now – Google Glass in Your Career

Google Glass can be used in a wide variety of jobs and fields, including the aviation industry. At one time, repairing airplanes required two mechanics: one to hold the manual displaying schematic drawings of airplane parts and another to actually fix or replace the part. Now a single airplane mechanic can use Google Glass to refer to a hands-free display of the schematics as he or she repairs the plane. As a team, research five other jobs that can use Google Glass to be more productive.

a. Create a combined document describing five jobs that could use Google Glass and explaining how the device would make people in those jobs more productive. Write a full paragraph for each job.

b. Create a bulleted list of 10 reasons Google Glass could be a security concern within business in general.

c. As a team, compile your own opinions of how Google Glass could be used by students in the classroom. List and explain four possibilities.

d. Identify three YouTube videos that describe the use of Google Glass.

Key Terms

abacus
address bus
all-in-one desktop
arithmetic logic unit (ALU)
ASCII
benchmark
binary number system
biometric input device
biometric technology
BIOS
bit
boot
bus
bus width
byte
cache
central processing unit (CPU)
chip
circuit board
clock speed
closed caption
cloud storage
control unit
convertible tablet

core
cycle
data bus
desktop computer
digital pen
drag
dynamic RAM (DRAM)
earbud
electrically erasable programmable memory (EEPROM)
external hard drive
facial recognition system
fingerprint reader
firmware
flash memory
function key
game controller
gamepad
gesture
gigahertz (GHz)
hard disk
hard drive
HDMI (high-definition multimedia interface)

headphone
headset
ink-jet printer
integrated circuit
Internet control key
joystick
keyboard
laptop
laser mouse
laser printer
Level 1 (L1) cache
Level 2 (L2) cache
Level 3 (L3) cache
light-emitting diode (LED)
liquid crystal display (LCD)
machine cycle
magnetic hard drive
magnetoresistive RAM (MRAM)
mechanical mouse
media control key
megahertz (MHz)
memory chip
memory module
microphone

microprocessor
MIDI
mobile device
mobile printer
monitor
motherboard
mouse
multicore processor
multifunction device (MFD)
navigation keypad
nonvolatile
notebook
numeric keypad
optical media
optical mouse
page
personal computer (PC)
pixel
platter
plotter
pointing stick

power-on self-test (POST)
printer
processor
processor cache
programmable read-only memory
  (PROM)
projector
random access memory (RAM)
read-only memory (ROM)
register
sampling
scanner
scroll wheel
slate
slide rule
smartphone
solid state drive (SSD)
solid state storage
speech recognition software
static RAM (SRAM)
stylus

subnotebook
swap file
system unit
tablet
text-to-speech technology
toner
touch screen
touchpad
trackball
transistor
typing keypad
Ultrabook
Unicode
vacuum tube
virtual memory
voice input
voice recognition software
voice synthesizer
volatile
Web cam
word size

Introduction to Software and Apps

Students in Madison's major of architecture and construction use apps to design plans, keep track of building materials and supplies, and track the progress of a construction project.

Madison is taking her first architecture class. She is learning how to construct floor plans using computer-aided design (CAD) software.

© iStockphoto.com/Yuri_Arcurs

Madison Eckstein has been assigned a project in her architecture class using CAD software to design an eco-friendly starter home. The project includes calculations for everything from how much concrete will be needed to how many hours a home will take to build.

Microsoft® product screenshots used with permission from Microsoft® Corporation.

What Is Software?

software program | program | app | system software | application software | software developer | programmer | programming language | software publisher | graphical user interface (GUI) | instructions | input | preinstalled software | operating system | utility program | productivity software | Web app | portable app | Software as a Service (SaaS) | load | uninstall | software update | patch | service pack | upgrade

The Bottom Line

- You use system and application software to interact with your computer and to perform tasks.
- Some software programs are preinstalled on your computer; others you install.
- You can update software to improve performance, and upgrade software to obtain new features.

Every time you click an icon on your desktop, press commands on a touch screen, or follow a link on your tablet, you are using software. Software is what makes computers so useful in our everyday lives. It interacts with computer hardware to turn machines into invaluable tools that help us perform tasks throughout the day.

Figure 2-1: Creating and using software

What Is Software?

Software, also called a **software program** or simply a **program**, is a set of instructions that tells a computer what to do, how to do it, and where to send the results, or output. The two types of software are system software and application software, or **apps**. See **Figure 2-2**.

Figure 2-2: System software and application software

Application software (also called an app) performs specific tasks.

System software controls a computer and its peripherals, such as its keyboard and mouse.

© Oleksiy Mark/Shutterstock.com, © tele52/Shutterstock.com

Software is written by **software developers**, or **programmers**, using computer-readable code, called a **programming language**. Software is produced and distributed by **software publishers**, who either sell it or give it away. Some well-known software publishers include Microsoft, Oracle, Apple, and Google. Most software uses a **graphical user interface (GUI)**, which lets users interact with the computer by tapping, clicking, or pressing buttons, menus, icons, and links, rather than typing commands.

How Software Works

Software interacts with computer hardware and other software in an organized chain of events; each link in the chain relays **instructions** along the chain until the job at hand is successfully completed.

When you type on a keyboard, select a menu option, press a button, or interact with a touch screen, you issue a command to the computer—you give it **input**. For example, when you click the Print button in a word processing program, you're entering the command to print the current document. Then a series of events occurs:

1. The word processing software tells the system software that you want to print.

2. The system software relays the command to the printer software.

3. The printer software instructs the hardware, or printer, to print the document.

4. Finally, the printer produces the printed document as output.

Preinstalled Software

Computers come with **preinstalled software**, software that is already on the machine. Most important is the system software that allows you to use the computer the first time you turn it on. Preinstalled software typically includes an **operating system** and **utility programs** that run and maintain the computer. **Figure 2-3** shows some preinstalled programs that come with Windows 8.x.

Increasingly, manufacturers preinstall additional programs, or **apps**, as part of marketing agreements with software companies. These might include games, more utility programs, and trial versions of **productivity software** that lets you create documents, such as Microsoft Office. Preinstalled programs also take up memory and storage space. Consider uninstalling any software you don't intend to use.

Installing Software

On a desktop or laptop computer, you typically install software on your computer's hard drive. On tablets and smartphones, you typically download applications or apps to your device from an online app store. To install software, you can download the software from an app store (see **Figure 2-4** on the next page) or Web site and follow any onscreen installation instructions.

For tablet and smartphone apps, you usually just click an Install button. In either case, you'll probably have to agree to the conditions of a software license to continue. On a laptop or desktop, you might be asked to choose between a standard or custom installation.

Increasingly, software publishers are creating **Web apps** and **portable apps** that you can use without installing them. Web apps are stored either on the Web or on a portable storage device. You can obtain many apps by paying a monthly subscription fee, instead of paying for the entire product all at once. This arrangement is known as **SaaS**, which stands for **Software as a Service**. For example, Microsoft Office 365 is the subscription version of Microsoft Office.

Running Software

Once software is installed, you run a program to make it work. Some software starts automatically when you start your computer; other software you need to start yourself. Most programs are represented by an icon on your desktop. You can also find programs by opening their folders on your hard drive. To start, or run, a program, click or double-click the program icon or filename.

When you run a program or app, your computer or mobile device **loads**, or reads and transfers it, into memory so that you can use it.

When you have finished working with a program, you should save any files you want to keep and then close the program to free up memory.

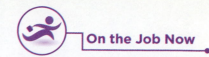

On the Job Now

The average pay for a software developer is around $79,000. A developer writes programming code to create mobile apps and other computer programs.

#introsoftware

Preinstalled software that takes up a lot of memory and disk space is called bloatware.

Figure 2-3: Some preinstalled Windows 8.x programs

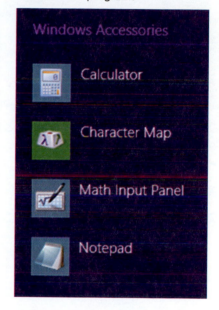

#introsoftware

Some Microsoft Office 365 licenses allow users to install multiple copies of the software on two to five personal computers and devices.

Figure 2-4: Downloading and installing an app from the Windows Store

Click the Install button

Uninstalling Software

If you no longer use certain software, or if your computer came with software you don't need, you can remove, or **uninstall**, the unwanted programs. Operating systems provide ways to safely remove software. In Windows, you use the Uninstall feature in the Control Panel or on the Start screen. In Mac OS X, you move the program icon from the Applications window to the Trash.

On smartphones and tablets, you may need to use different methods to uninstall a program. In any case, an uninstall program removes the unwanted software and all of its related files from your computer or device.

If you try to remove unwanted Windows software by dragging a program icon to the Recycle Bin, you may remove the file that runs the program, but not its associated files. Be sure to use the uninstall method appropriate for your computer or device.

Updating Software

Software publishers periodically update their programs to fix problems, enhance features, and improve performance. **Software updates** come in the form of **patches** (smaller fixes) and **service packs** (larger fixes), which replace small sections of existing code with the new, improved code. It's a good idea to install updates as they become available. In most cases, you check for updates and download them from the publisher's Web site. See **Figure 2-5**.

By the Numbers Now

Of the 10 most popular smartphone apps in the world in 2013, 5 are Google apps such as Google Maps and Google Search.

Figure 2-5: Downloading a software update in Windows

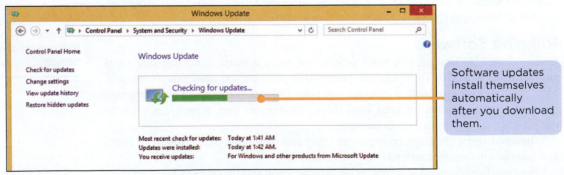

Software updates install themselves automatically after you download them.

In addition to updates, software publishers periodically introduce new versions, or **upgrades**, of their software products with new features. If you own the current version, you can upgrade to the newer version for less than it would cost to buy the software outright. Upgrades are less time sensitive than updates, so you can wait until you're sure you need the newer version.

Software Development

software development | programming | computer programmer | developer | algorithm | low-level language | high-level language | machine language | assembly language | source code | software development methodology | predictive methodology | agile | adaptive | extreme programming model | text editor | program editor | compiler | interpreter | assembler | debugger | code library | Integrated Development Environment (IDE) | Software Development Kit (SDK) | comment | debugging tool | beta | quality assurance (QA)

The process of creating software is called **software development** or **programming**. The people who write software programs are called **computer programmers** or **developers**. Software programs are based on **algorithms**, which are step-by-step procedures for solving specific problems. Programmers write coded instructions using special programming languages and program development tools.

Figure 2-6: Developing software

© Andrey_Popov/Shutterstock.com, © kimberrywood/Shutterstock.com, © Sashkin/Shutterstock.com

Development Overview

Many of the conveniences we have today are in some way the result of programmers doing their jobs. The software development process involves a series of steps, shown in **Figure 2-7** on the next page.

Programming Languages

Programmers use special languages that contain words, abbreviations, punctuation, and symbols to communicate specific instructions to the computer. Hundreds of programming languages exist today. **Figure 2-8** on the next page shows examples of machine, assembly, and high-level languages.

Low-level languages include machine and assembly languages. Low-level languages are fast and don't use a lot of computer memory, but they are technically difficult and time-consuming to write. **High-level languages** create source code using words and structures similar to spoken language.

High-level languages make programming easier; however, they must be translated from source code into machine code before a computer can read them.

Figure 2-7: Software development process

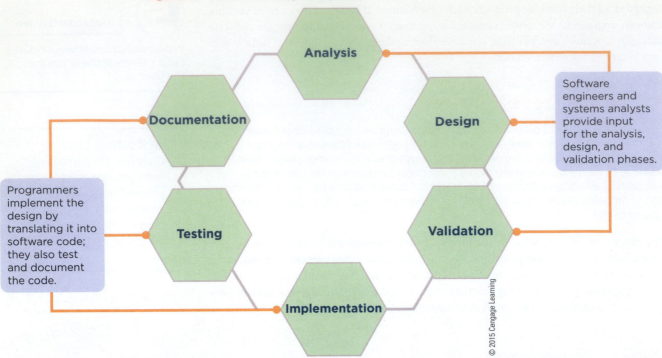

Software engineers and systems analysts provide input for the analysis, design, and validation phases.

Programmers implement the design by translating it into software code; they also test and document the code.

© 2015 Cengage Learning

Figure 2-8: Machine, assembly, and high-level languages

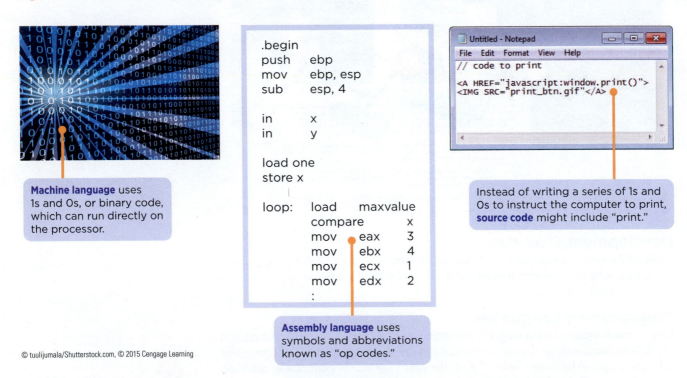

Machine language uses 1s and 0s, or binary code, which can run directly on the processor.

```
.begin
push      ebp
mov       ebp, esp
sub       esp, 4

in        x
in        y

load one
store x
    |
loop:     load      maxvalue
          compare          x
          mov       eax    3
          mov       ebx    4
          mov       ecx    1
          mov       edx    2
          :
```

Assembly language uses symbols and abbreviations known as "op codes."

```
Untitled - Notepad
File  Edit  Format  View  Help
// code to print

<A HREF="javascript:window.print()">
<IMG SRC="print_btn.gif"</A>
```

Instead of writing a series of 1s and 0s to instruct the computer to print, **source code** might include "print."

© tuulijumala/Shutterstock.com, © 2015 Cengage Learning

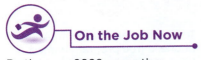

On the Job Now

By the year 2020, more than 1.5 million programming jobs will be available.

Most business and scientific applications are written in high-level languages such as C#, Visual Basic, PHP, and Java. Java is a popular high-level language for Web-based programming. For mobile apps, developers might use Objective-C, JavaScript, or HTML5.

Development Methodologies

A **software development methodology** provides a framework for designing, writing, and testing software. Two important methodologies are predictive and agile; each methodology has a number of different models. The **predictive methodology** focuses on planning and preparation to minimize changes later in the development process. Predictive programming is useful for large-scale development projects using many programmers across multiple locations.

For example, in the waterfall predictive model, development progresses sequentially from one phase to the next. Only when one phase is finished does the next phase begin.

The **agile**, or **adaptive**, programming methodology focuses on flexibility; program designs and specifications change and evolve as a project moves forward. Agile programming works well for projects with small development teams working closely together.

For example, the **extreme programming model** relies on short development cycles and continual feedback to drive design and coding. Changes can be made to the design and software code throughout the development process.

Programming Tools

Programming tools are applications that programmers use to write other software programs. Common programming tools are shown in **Table 2-1**.

Table 2-1: Programming tools

Programming tools	What they do
Text editors **Program editors**	Let programmers write code using a word processing-like interface that often includes features such as AutoCorrect and AutoComplete.
Compilers **Interpreters**	Translate source code from high-level languages into machine code so it can be understood by the processor.
Assemblers	Translate assembly language into machine code.
Debuggers	Examine software code line by line to identify errors or "bugs," such as incorrect formulas or logic errors.

© 2015 Cengage Learning

Code libraries contain modules of customizable code for common functions such as accessing files or issuing the Print command.

Most programmers today get their tools from **Integrated Development Environments (IDEs)** such as Visual Studio, or from **Software Development Kits (SDKs)**, which are collections of programming tools designed for specific types of applications or programming languages.

Testing and Documentation

Programmers document and test software before releasing it for distribution. When coding software, programmers write **comments** to give other programmers an overview of the program and identify the purpose of each section of code. See **Figure 2-9**.

Figure 2-9: Comment in code

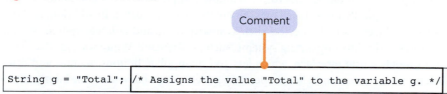

```
String g = "Total"; /* Assigns the value "Total" to the variable g. */
```

To test for errors, programmers use **debugging tools**; compilers and interpreters often identify coding errors as well. Programmers also run programs with test data to identify potential problems.

Software publishers often distribute **beta**, or test, versions of their software to selected users so they can help identify problems and even request new features before final software is released.

Finally, a **quality assurance (QA)** team usually tests an application thoroughly to confirm that it works as advertised. The QA process can involve back-and-forth communication between the QA testers and the programmers as bugs are found and then fixed.

Hot Technology Now

To create an iPad or iPhone app, you can use a language called Objective-C, a free development environment for building iOS apps.

#introsoftware

Some elementary schools are teaching an introductory programming language to third through fifth graders. Students learn how to create animations, computer games, and interactive projects using Scratch, a graphical programming language developed at the Massachusetts Institute of Technology.

Types of Software

computer software | system software | operating system (OS) software | platform | graphical user interface | command-line interface | utility software | widget | gadget | device driver | application software | mobile application | mobile app | native app | Web app | productivity software | vertical market software | horizontal market software | personal information management (PIM) | note-taking software | Web page authoring software | groupware | embedded software | Windows Embedded | Android @Home | malware | virus | worm | Trojan horse | keylogger | bot | spyware

Computer software manages the functions of computers and many other devices. Computers use several types of software, such as system software and application software. Other types of devices, such as refrigerators, cameras, and cars, use software to control their operation.

Figure 2-10: Four types of software

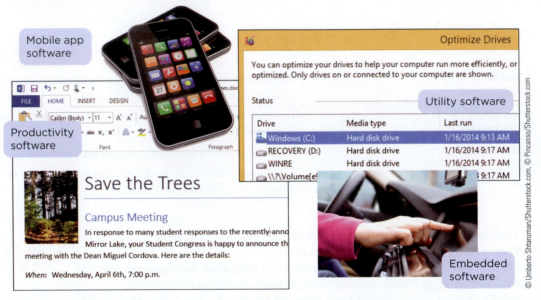

System Software

System software performs computer-related operations and maintenance. System software falls into two categories: operating system software and utility programs. **Operating system software**, also called **OS software** or a **platform**, manages computer hardware and software. For example, it allocates memory, launches applications, configures hardware devices, and establishes your Internet connection. The most common operating systems today are Microsoft Windows, Apple Mac OS X, and Linux.

An OS is typically preinstalled on your computer's hard drive. In addition, an OS is often embedded in smaller devices such as smartphones and in larger systems such as server networks. Most operating systems, such as Microsoft Windows and Mac OS X, use a **graphical user interface**, which lets you manipulate buttons, menus, and other objects to issue commands. Some operating systems use a **command-line interface** that requires users to type commands. See **Figure 2-11**.

Utility Software

Utility software is system software that performs maintenance-related tasks on computers, such as locating files, cleaning up or defragmenting (consolidating data on) disks, and compressing files. Many utility programs are built into the OS. You can buy or download additional utility programs, including antivirus, file management, and diagnostic programs.

Widgets or **gadgets** are utility programs that appear on the desktop and display small pieces of information. Examples include calendars, clocks, and weather stations.

Figure 2-11: Graphical user interface and command line interface

Graphical user interface

Command line interface

© Dmitry Melnikov/Shutterstock.com

A **device driver** is a utility program that controls a peripheral device such as a printer, keyboard, mouse, modem, or scanner. Some device drivers come with your computer's operating system, such as the driver that works with your keyboard. Others come with the peripheral device itself, usually on a CD or DVD. You can also download drivers from the manufacturer's Web site.

Unlike application software, which runs in a window on your desktop, device drivers usually run in the background whenever they're needed; you don't need to activate them.

Application Software

While system software gives you tools to interact with your computer, **application software** (also called an app) lets you perform specific tasks, such as writing a document, analyzing a set of numbers, or preparing a presentation. At work, you can use application software to automate complex, repetitive, or routine tasks. At home or at school, you can use application software for everything from creating documents to watching videos, doing research, and playing games. Some of the most popular types of applications are shown in **Table 2-2**.

#introsoftware

Mac operating systems use codenames such as Mavericks, Mountain Lion, Lion, Snow Leopard, Leopard, Tiger, Panther, Jaguar, Puma, Cheetah, and Kodiak.

Table 2-2: Types of application software

Application software type	Lets you create
Word processing	Letters, reports, memos, contracts, or any other text document
Spreadsheet	Budgets, data analyses, lists, forms, schedules, or any other document with numbers and text
Database	Large collections of data, including inventories, customer lists, and employee information
Presentation	Onscreen displays of text, graphics, sound, and video to show to a group
Graphics	Illustrations, drawings, flowcharts, layouts, and logos

© 2015 Cengage Learning

You can install some application software directly on your computer. Other programs reside on portable storage devices, mobile devices, or on the Web.

Mobile Applications

Mobile applications, also called **mobile apps**, are written specifically for mobile devices such as smartphones and tablets. **Native apps** are installed on a device, while **Web apps** are installed on a server and must be interpreted by the device's browser, so they run more slowly than native apps. **Figure 2-12** shows a mapping mobile app on a smartphone.

Like other application software, mobile apps perform tasks. Because they operate on the more limited operating systems and smaller screens of mobile devices, mobile apps tend to be narrower in scope and functionality. For example, you might use a mobile app to take notes in class, but probably not to write an entire research paper.

Figure 2-12: Smartphone mobile app

© Oleksiy Mark/Shutterstock.com

Thousands of mobile apps are available today. They do anything from mapping your current location to updating your status on Facebook to finding the best price on a pair of boots. Using mobile apps, you can stay connected and productive from almost anywhere at any time.

Productivity Software

Productivity software is application software that makes people more productive by automating common or repetitive tasks. Programs sold in productivity suites include word processing, spreadsheet, database, presentation, and graphics programs. **Figure 2-13** shows the Microsoft Office productivity suite.

Figure 2-13: Microsoft Office productivity suite

Hot Technology Now

A free mobile app named Duolingo is designed to teach languages including Spanish, French, and German. Duolingo offers extensive written lessons and dictation opportunities.

By the Numbers Now

Of the 20 distinct job skills requested in high-paying job postings, oral and written communication and a mastery of Microsoft Office software top the list.

Vertical market software is productivity software that is customized for specific industries. For example, schools use student information software to process course registrations, build class schedules, and track attendance and grades. **Horizontal market software** performs tasks that are common across industries. Examples include payroll processing, accounting, and project management. Other productivity software focuses on highly specialized applications that appeal to all types of users. See **Table 2-3** for examples.

Table 2-3: Specialized productivity software

Software type	What it does
Personal information management (PIM) software	Organizes calendars, schedules, address books, and more
Note-taking software	Converts and stores handwritten notes in digital form
Web page authoring software	Lets you create, manage, and maintain Web pages
Groupware	Allows multiple users with a network or Internet connection to collaborate on documents, and participate in online conferences or Webcasts

© 2015 Cengage Learning

Embedded Software

In addition to computers, software runs on many household appliances and consumer electronic devices, including washing machines, refrigerators, DVD players, ovens, radios, and even cars! **Embedded software** is typically stored on a computer chip inside the appliance.

Embedded software is generally limited in functionality. Often it is used to monitor the physical environment surrounding the appliance, such as measuring and regulating internal temperatures for refrigerators or external temperatures for thermostats. Embedded software in cars tends to be more sophisticated and includes monitoring as well as diagnostic applications. It can alert a driver to low tire pressure or provide complex directions to a destination.

Some embedded software uses simple graphics such as buttons or LED and LCD displays. More sophisticated embedded software might use touch screen technology. **Windows Embedded** is the Microsoft collection of embedded operating systems for household and industrial devices such as digital photo frames, medical devices, and ATMs. **Android @Home** is the Google initiative to expand the Android OS beyond smartphones and into the household appliance market.

Malware

While most software is helpful, some is not. **Malware**, short for malicious software, is written by hackers to intentionally damage computers by deleting files, erasing hard drives, stealing information, or slowing computer performance. You can unknowingly download malware by clicking an infected hyperlink or pop-up ad, or by opening an infected email attachment. A malware program may take effect immediately upon entering your computer, or it may wait for a specific condition to be met.

Malware comes in many forms. A **virus** installs itself on your computer and alters its operations. A **worm** is a self-replicating program that eats up system resources. **Trojan horses**, often used as **keyloggers** (short for keystroke logging) to steal passwords to online accounts, disguise themselves as useful programs, such as utilities.

A **bot** is software that takes control of your computer so it can be used by hackers to carry out further attacks. **Spyware** secretly gathers personal information.

#introsoftware

Criminals secretly install spyware and malware on computers to gather and report personal information about their users.

Purchasing Software

packaged software | download | app | custom software | Web app | open source software | Linux operating system | freeware | shareware | public domain software

You can purchase packaged software, download software from the Internet, or subscribe to a Web application. Many software applications are sold commercially, but others are free. Still others make their source code available to the public so users can customize it. Make sure the software you acquire meets your needs and your computer's system requirements.

Packaged Software

The term **packaged software** refers to software that is mass produced and appeals to a wide range of users. Packaged software is generally copyrighted and has many features. Popular packaged software programs include Microsoft Word and Adobe Photoshop.

You can purchase packaged software from retail stores, catalogs, or Web sites. Packaged software typically includes a card containing a key code, which lets you **download**, or electronically copy, the software from the Internet. The package may also contain instruction manuals, and any necessary registration information or certificates.

You can also download applications, or **apps**, directly from software publishers' Web sites or online stores, using your computer or mobile device. Three popular online stores are listed in **Table 2-4** on the next page.

The Bottom Line

- Purchased software can be packaged (see **Figure 2-14** on the next page), downloaded from the Internet, or obtained by subscriptions on the Web.
- Custom software is specially developed for a company's specific needs, but can be expensive.
- Proprietary software can be open source, shareware, or freeware.

By the Numbers Now

More than 1 million apps are available in the Apple App Store for devices running iOS, such as iPhones and iPads.

Figure 2-14: Packaged software

Custom Web app created in Microsoft Access can be shared with users who will access it using their browsers.

Download.com offers over 150,000 free downloadable software applications.

Packaged software purchased from a Web site uses Shopping Cart technology similar to this.

© Dmitri Mikitenko/Shutterstock.com, CBS Interactive Inc.

Table 2-4: Online stores

Online store	To open
Windows Store	Select the Store icon on the Start screen of a Windows device.
App Store	Select the App Store icon on an Apple device.
Google Play	Select the Play Store icon on the Apps screen of an Android device.

© 2015 Cengage Learning

Custom Software

Unlike packaged software, which is designed to meet the needs of many, **custom software** is designed to meet the unique needs of an organization or business. Companies either hire outside programmers to write custom software or use their own internal developers.

Acquiring custom software is more time consuming and expensive than purchasing packaged software, because developers must go through the entire development process: analyzing needs, creating a software design, and then developing, testing, and documenting that design before the software is ready to use. See **Figure 2-15**.

Figure 2-15: Developing custom software

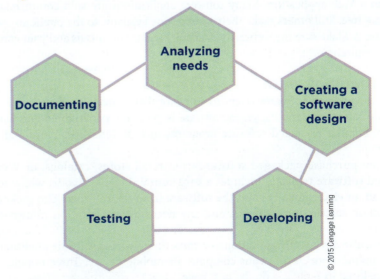

Analyzing needs

Documenting

Creating a software design

Testing

Developing

© 2015 Cengage Learning

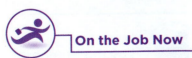

On the Job Now

A fast-growing field called informatics combines information technology with social science. Informatics uses computing to solve big problems in privacy, security, health care, education, poverty, and our environment.

On the other hand, custom software matches the users' needs exactly and can be modified if those needs change.

Web Apps

Web applications, or **Web apps**, are applications you access over the Internet using any computer or mobile device with an Internet connection. Web apps are available for common applications such as email, games, mapping, photo sharing, and more. With Web apps, you always have access to the most up-to-date version of the software without paying for an upgrade. Because Web apps reside on a host computer, you also save space on your hard drive.

Web apps, such as Yahoo! Mail (see **Figure 2-16**), Gmail, and the Microsoft Office Web apps, don't require users to install software on their own computers. Instead, the software runs on the host computer.

Figure 2-16: Yahoo! Mail Web app

Yahoo! Mail open in browser window

Some Web applications are free. Others require a one-time registration fee or a periodic subscription charge.

Web apps also have risks. If you lose your Internet connection, if the host computer is out of service, or if the Web app company fails, you lose access to the software and any data you haven't saved locally.

Open Source Software

Open source software is copyrighted software whose source code is "open" or available to the public. Users can copy, modify, and customize the software with certain restrictions. The concept of open source software was introduced in 1991 by Linus Torvalds, who created and then shared the **Linux operating system** with the world. Besides Linux, popular open source programs include Firefox, Audacity, and the OpenOffice productivity suite.

Open source software is typically distributed for free and requires less disk space and memory than many commercial programs. The software can be customized and has usually been tested by a wide range of programmers and users. A disadvantage to open source software is that it lacks the customer support you find with commercial software and can cause compatibility issues with other software.

Other Software

Other types of software include freeware, shareware, and public domain software. **Freeware** is software distributed free of charge, typically via the Internet. The developer retains the rights to the software; other developers cannot incorporate freeware into their own software. Many utility programs, device drivers, and games are distributed as freeware. For example, Microsoft Internet Explorer is a freeware program.

Shareware is copyrighted software distributed free of charge on a trial basis. Users then pay the developer on the honor system to keep using the software. Shareware users are encouraged to copy and share the software with colleagues; small developers often use the shareware model as a low-cost distribution method.

Ownership rights for **public domain software** are public property; such software is available at no cost. Although no one can apply for a copyright on public domain software, users are free to copy, modify, and resell the software.

Hot Technology Now

You can create a free Microsoft account at Outlook.com to use the free Microsoft Office Web apps. These touch-friendly Web applications let you create, edit, and share your Word, Excel, PowerPoint, and OneNote files from any browser.

Hot Technology Now

Download.com provides many paid, freeware, and shareware programs that can be installed to your local computer.

#introsoftware

57% of the apps at Google Play, the online store for Android apps, are free, which is the highest percentage of free apps of all the online stores.

Licensing Software

intellectual property | piracy | copyright | license | single-user license | end-user license agreement (EULA) | multiple-user license | site license | concurrent-use license | time-limited license | shrink wrap license | piracy | Digital Rights Management (DRM) | authentication | Certificate of Authenticity | encryption | encryption key | digital watermark | copy protection technology

Intellectual property is the legal term for ownership of intangible assets such as ideas, art, music, movies, and software. Many of these assets are easy to copy, making them vulnerable to unauthorized use, or **piracy**. Copyright protections and license agreements set rules for how intellectual property can be legally used, copied, and distributed, and by whom.

What Is a Copyright?

A **copyright** is the legal right to copy, distribute, modify, and sell an original work, including computer software. The copyright belongs exclusively to the creator of the work, such as the software developer or publisher. Without the permission of the copyright holder, no one else can legally copy, modify, or distribute the software, because it is the intellectual property of the creator.

Figure 2-17: Some methods of protecting intellectual property

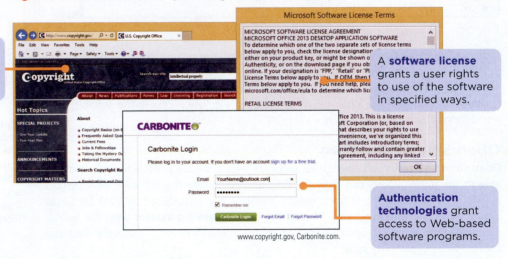

U.S. copyright law protects Intellectual property from illegal copying and distribution.

A **software license** grants a user rights to use of the software in specified ways.

Authentication technologies grant access to Web-based software programs.

www.copyright.gov, Carbonite.com.

On the Job Now

The growing field of patent law protects software code as an original work of authorship. Patent attorneys search for prior app patents that are similar to a new app idea.

A copyright is denoted either by the word "Copyright" or by a copyright symbol, which is the letter C inside a circle: ©. Even if there isn't a visible copyright notice, copyright protections automatically apply to software programs and other original works.

When you purchase copyrighted software, the copyright protection remains in effect. You have paid for the right to use the product, but all other rights remain with the copyright holder.

Software Licenses

When you purchase software, you are purchasing a **license** to use the software under the terms specified in the license agreement, which might include how many computers the software can be installed on and whether the license has an expiration date.

A **single-user license**, also called an **end-user license agreement (EULA)**, grants one user the right to use the software. Many students and home users buy single-user licenses. A **multiple-user license** lets many users use the software; the number of users and the price vary by license. Businesses and schools might purchase multiple-user licenses.

A **site license** allows an organization to install software on all computers at a site, either locally or through a network. Site licenses are generally priced at a flat rate per site. A **concurrent-use license** allows a specified number of copies of the software to be used at any given time within an organization. The license is typically priced per copy.

Finally, **time-limited licenses** grant usage rights for a fixed period of time. For example, a company might require additional software copies during its busiest months.

License Agreements

A software license is a contract between the software publisher and the user. Because users can't actually "sign" license agreements, publishers use other methods for validating them.

For packaged software, publishers use a **shrink wrap license**. Some packaged software comes in a box or envelope sealed with plastic shrink wrap. The license agreement is either written on the outside of the packaging or contained inside. By opening the software package, you automatically activate the shrink wrap license and agree to its terms.

For downloaded software from app stores or obtained via subscriptions, the details of the license usually appear on the screen during installation, and users must click "Agree" or "Accept" before the software is installed. See **Figure 2-18**. No matter what method you use to accept a license agreement, it is a legal contract, and you are bound by its terms.

Figure 2-18: End-user license agreement

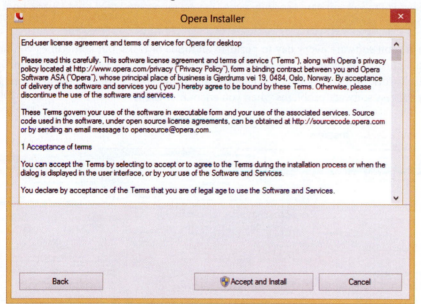

Pirated Software

Piracy, the illegal copying and distribution of copyrighted software, is a widespread problem for software publishers. Billions of dollars' worth of software is copied illegally worldwide. The United States has a piracy rate of 20 percent; China's is a staggering 80 percent!

Counterfeit software is often packaged to look like the real product and may be sold in retail stores or online. Consumers should be aware of warning signs that the software they are buying might be pirated. Pirated software often has no documentation, registration cards, license agreements, Certificates of Authenticity, or manuals. The labels on pirated software packages, jewel cases, or CD sleeves might look sloppy or unprofessional.

Software labels such as "Academic," "OEM," or "For Distribution with New PC Hardware" indicate that the software is not legally available for resale. If you buy a software disc that comes with an unconventional mix of programs, possibly from multiple software publishers, you are likely buying pirated software.

On the Job Now

Typically, companies require that their employees sign a computer usage policy, which restricts them from installing pirated software on company computers. The policy also limits personal usage of computers to reduce office distractions.

By the Numbers Now

71,060 jobs are lost in the United States every year due to online piracy.

Figure 2-19: Certificate of authenticity

Digital Rights Management

Increasingly, software publishers and trade groups use **Digital Rights Management (DRM)** technologies to fight software piracy and prevent unauthorized copying of digital content. DRM technologies include the following:

- **Authentication** technologies require users to log in with a valid user ID and password to access Web-based content such as software programs or e-books.
- Packaged software programs often include **Certificates of Authenticity** with validation codes that users must input during the installation process (see **Figure 2-19**).
- **Encryption** makes digital content unreadable unless viewed with a valid **encryption key** or authorized hardware device.
- A **digital watermark** is a hidden pattern or signal inserted into digital content to identify the copyright holder. Watermarks can also regulate and track who makes copies of the content and how often.
- **Copy protection technologies** prevent consumers from copying digital content or limit the number of copies they can make. For example, Apple limits the number of times you can copy a song that you purchase at the iTunes store.

Software Problems

application help | user manual | onscreen Help | Web-based Help | service pack | update | malware | security software | antivirus software | antispyware | antispam software | firewall software | security suite | crash | rebooting | cold boot | warm boot | backed up | replicate

You rely on software every day to perform all kinds of tasks, but sometimes you need help figuring out how to use your software more effectively. Other times software doesn't work properly. Software publishers and other sources offer tools that can help you address software problems when you encounter them

The Bottom Line
- To learn how to use software and to solve problems, you can use a user manual, onscreen help, or Web-based help (see **Figure 2-20**).
- Software publishers fix software bugs by issuing patches and service packs.
- You can protect your computer from malware using several types of security software.
- If your computer stops working, you can recover by rebooting it.

Figure 2-20: Onscreen help

When you start a program, onscreen messages can tell you if updates are available.

The Office Support Help screen lets you search for answers if you are having a problem using a program.

Onscreen alerts can tell you if a software subscription will expire soon.

#introsoftware

Unfortunately, 42% of the software running in the world has been illegally downloaded.

Using Application Help

Applications help you create reports, spreadsheets, presentations, and more. The more you know about an application, the more you can do with it. Most software applications include one or more forms of Help. **Application help** includes user manuals, onscreen Help, and Web-based resources.

- A **user manual** gives instructions on using the program's features and troubleshooting common problems. User manuals come with packaged software, or you can download manuals from the software publisher's Web site.
- **Onscreen Help** is an electronic user manual with additional benefits, such as being able to search for specific topics or click links to online resources. You can access onscreen Help from almost every window or dialog box in a program.

- **Web-based Help** can be found on a software publisher's Web site, blog, or another software-related site. You can chat with a customer support representative, step through a tutorial, watch a training video, or follow a discussion board.

Patches and Updates

Software publishers frequently update programs with patches that fix problems, enhance existing features, and provide additional security. Software patches are small sections of code, typically free of charge, that correct or enhance one area of concern, such as a single bug or security issue.

Software publishers number patches and other updates sequentially using decimal places. For example, a patch might change your software from version 3.0 to version 3.01. You can choose to automatically download and install patches as they become available, or you can periodically check for updates yourself and install only those patches you want.

Service Packs and Updates

Like patches, **service packs** (called **updates** in newer software products) fix bugs, enhance features, or improve security and are distributed over the Internet. Whereas a patch is a single fix, a service pack or update is a collection of patches or fixes bundled into a single release. Service packs are often issued for operating system software.

Many software publishers release service packs when they reach a predetermined number of patches for a program. Installing the service pack in one installation is easier than installing multiple patches. Some service packs are incremental and contain only changes that have not been issued in previous patches or packs. Other service packs are cumulative, containing all changes made to a program to date. Many newer software applications do not use service packs, instead using periodic online updates, which can deliver important patches and software updates more frequently.

Security Software

Malware, malicious software written by hackers, poses a significant threat to your computer and its contents. You can install several types of **security software** to protect your computer from harm.

- **Antivirus software** finds and removes viruses, Trojan horses, worms, and bots from your computer and scans incoming and outgoing email messages to identify threats. You should run antivirus software every time you start your computer, keep it running in the background at all times, and schedule periodic scans of your entire system. See **Figure 2-21**.

Figure 2-21: Running a security scan

- **Antispyware** prevents spyware from installing itself on your computer and removes any existing spyware.
- **Antispam software** blocks spam, or electronic junk mail, from your email inbox.
- **Firewall software** creates a personal security zone around your computer by monitoring all incoming and outgoing traffic and blocking any suspicious activity.

You can buy security software programs individually, but you can also find them bundled together in a security suite. **Security suites** typically contain antivirus, antispam, antispyware, and firewall software. Some offer additional features such as parental controls and network monitoring. Security suites cost less than standalone security programs and give you a consistent user interface. When you install a security suite, you need to uninstall any security software currently on your computer. As a general rule, you should update all security software regularly so you will be protected from current threats.

Program Crashes

When a computer program stops functioning properly—for example, if it freezes or won't start—it is said to **crash**. See **Table 2-5** for possible causes and solutions.

Restarting/Rebooting

Rebooting is the process of restarting your computer, either from a powered-down state (**cold boot**), or with the power on (**warm boot**).

Table 2-5: Program crash problems and solutions

Problem	Possible cause	Solution
Program won't launch	Incorrect installation	• Check validation codes • Contact Customer Service
Program freezes	Bug, virus, or corrupted files	• **Windows:** Press the CTRL, ALT, and DELETE keys together • **Mac:** Open Activity Monitor, select and close program • Shut down and restart computer • Install latest patches and service packs • Run security scan to check for viruses • Run disk cleanup and repair utilities

© 2015 Cengage Learning

You should reboot after installing new programs or updates or after encountering a problem that freezes your computer. A warm boot uses the operating system to restart your computer; processes and programs are closed properly, and most work is saved. To perform a warm boot, use the Restart command on your PC or Mac. (Newer computers may not have a Restart command.) With some computers, you can quickly press and release the power button to perform a warm boot.

If you are forced to shut your computer down completely after a crash, you have to perform a cold boot. First, turn off the computer, if necessary, by pressing and holding the power button, or unplugging the device from its power source. To reboot, reconnect the power source and press the power button.

Troubleshooting

You may experience a variety of software problems as you use your computer. You might see an error message on the screen, or the software might respond in unusual ways. If you have such a problem, you can perform some basic troubleshooting techniques to try and find a solution:

1. **Stop and think**: Remain calm and consider the situation. Randomly pressing keys or clicking could make matters worse. Taking a thoughtful, organized approach can help solve the problem.

2. **Save and back up**: Save any open documents if possible, and verify that your work is **backed up** (copied) to an external drive or online location.

3. **Gather information**: Write down the problem, including the exact text and numbers of any error messages. What were you doing when it occurred? Can you **replicate** (reproduce) it? What steps did you take to replicate it? Note the time and date, and any other programs that were running. Write down your computer model, operating system version, and application program versions.

4. **Research possible solutions:** Have you recently installed any software or hardware? Is your antivirus software up to date? Have you recently downloaded anything from the Internet that may have introduced a virus? Does a virus scan reveal any problems? Search the Internet using a short problem description. Check the software manufacturer's technical support Web site, as well as forums and newsgroups. Other people may have had the same problem. If you test possible solutions, try only one solution at a time, and write down what happens.

5. **Call for help:** If necessary, contact the manufacturer's Technical Support department, with your notes in front of you, so you can answer any questions they might ask. See **Figure 2-22**.

#introsoftware

Go to twitter.com, search for **@SAMTechNow,** the book's Twitter account, and then follow @SAMTechNow, to get tweets on your home page.

Figure 2-22: Getting technical support

Many companies have live support options so you can exchange text messages with support staff in real time.

A knowledgebase may contain solutions to many known issues.

Telephone support is often available to help solve problems.

Chapter Review

What Is Software?

1. What are the two main types of software?

2. What do you call apps that you can use without installing them?

3. Patches and service packs are two ways you can update your software. What is the main difference between patches and service packs?

Software Development

4. Describe an advantage of high-level programming languages, and give two examples.

5. What are the two important types of software development methodologies? Briefly describe each one.

6. Name three common tools that programmers use and briefly describe each one.

Types of Software

7. Briefly describe the function of operating system software, and name two common operating systems.

8. What is the purpose of utility software? Name two common types of utility programs.

9. Name and briefly describe three types of productivity software.

Purchasing Software

10. Name two popular online stores you might use to purchase software.

11. What is custom software? Name an advantage and a disadvantage of custom software.

12. Describe the purpose of open source software and give two examples.

Licensing Software

13. What is a copyright, and who owns the copyright to a product?

14. What are two types of software licenses? Briefly describe each one.

15. Name three types of authentication technologies that help protect against piracy, and briefly describe each one.

Software Problems

16. If you have a software problem, what are three kinds of application help that are available to you?

17. Name and briefly describe three types of security software.

18. Briefly describe the main steps you should perform to troubleshoot a software problem.

Test Your Knowledge Now

1. Software that lets users interact with the computer by tapping, clicking, or pressing buttons, menus, icons, and links has:
   a. preinstalled software.
   b. a compiler.
   c. a graphical user interface.
   d. a code library.

2. Software that you can pay for with a monthly subscription fee is called:
   a. a Web app.
   b. Software as a Service (SaaS).
   c. a portable app.
   d. productivity software.

3. The preinstalled software that runs your computer is called:
   a. an app.
   b. productivity software.
   c. a programming language.
   d. an operating system.

4. Which of the following translate source code from high-level languages into machine code?
   a. assemblers
   b. debuggers
   c. program editors
   d. compilers

5. Machine and assembly programming languages are examples of:
   a. high-level languages.
   b. low-level languages.
   c. debuggers.
   d. program editors.

6. The software development methodology that focuses on planning and preparation to minimize changes later on is called:
   a. extreme programming model.
   b. predictive methodology.
   c. adaptive methodology.
   d. agile methodology.

7. Which of the following allocates computer memory, launches application programs, and configures hardware devices?
   a. platform
   b. graphical user interface
   c. command-line interface
   d. application program

8. A widget is:
   a. a utility program that controls peripheral devices.
   b. a mobile application.
   c. an application that lets you create large collections of data.
   d. a utility program on the desktop that displays small pieces of information.

9. Which of the following is a form of malware that often uses keyloggers to steal passwords?
   a. a virus
   b. a worm
   c. a Trojan horse
   d. a mobile app

10. Mass-produced software that appeals to a wide range of users is called:
    a. custom software.
    b. Web apps.
    c. open source software.
    d. packaged software.

11. Web apps are:
    a. programs you access over the Internet with a computer or mobile device.
    b. designed to meet the unique needs of an organization or business.
    c. a form of packaged software.
    d. public domain software.

12. The Linux operating system is an example of:
    a. open source software.
    b. shareware.
    c. a Web app.
    d. custom software.

13. Copyright is intended to protect:
    a. encryption.
    b. end-user licenses.
    c. intellectual property.
    d. digital rights management.

14. The legal right to copy, distribute, modify, and sell an original work is called a:
    a. copyright.
    b. license.
    c. digital rights management.
    d. certificate of authenticity.

15. Which of the following DRM technologies makes digital content unreadable unless viewed with a valid key?
    a. digital watermark
    b. certificate of authenticity
    c. copy protection
    d. encryption

16. Which of the following is *not* a type of application help?
    a. a software publisher's Web site
    b. onscreen link
    c. user manual
    d. service pack

17. If a software company wants to issue a collection of software fixes, which of the following would they release?
    a. an update
    b. malware
    c. security software
    d. a patch

18. If you encounter a software problem, you should determine if you can _____ it.
    a. crash
    b. replicate
    c. patch
    d. reboot

19. In the space next to each image below, write the letter of the phrase that describes it.
    a. command line interface
    b. graphical user interface
    c. Microsoft Excel application software
    d. authentication
    e. Web app

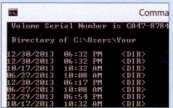

Try This Now

1: Microsoft Office Web Apps

Microsoft Office Web apps provide a free way to create, edit, and share Word, Excel, PowerPoint, and OneNote files from any browser. If necessary, create a free Microsoft account at outlook.com. Select the **OneDrive** option, and then select the **Create** button to use the PowerPoint presentation Web app.

    a. Create a five-slide presentation explaining the features of the Microsoft Office Web apps.

    b. Add appropriate images to each slide in the presentation.

    c. Save and share the presentation with your instructor using the Share feature.

2: Google Drive Web Apps

Google Drive is the home of Google Docs, a free office suite of productivity applications that offer collaborative editing on documents, spreadsheets, and presentations. If necessary, open a browser and create a Google free account at google.com. Sign in to your account, and then go to drive.google.com.

    a. Select the **Create** button and then select **Document**. Using the Google Docs word processor and the Google Drive Help feature, research using Google Drive for online storage, and then write at least 100 words describing this feature.

    b. Select **File** and then select **Share**. Invite your instructor to share this document by entering his or her email address.

3: Software Recommendations

Before you purchase software, you should read unbiased reviews, compare prices, and understand specifications to improve your purchasing experience. One of the most popular sites for software and hardware reviews is cnet.com.

Software Review

    a. Open the site cnet.com. Select **Reviews** on the navigation bar, select **Software**, and then select the **iOS** platform. Sort the listing of reviews by most popular. What are the 10 most popular iOS software packages? List the price for each one.

    b. Select one of the 10 iOS software packages. Cnet includes comments labeled "The good," "The bad," and "The bottom line." Copy this information about your selected software and paste it into a word processing document.

    c. For the iOS software you selected, summarize in one paragraph what the reviews stated.

Critical Thinking Now

1: Office 365 Subscription-Based Software

You are employed part time by a restaurant chain. Your duties include assisting with the bulk food orders and delivery for each restaurant location in your city. The chain uses Microsoft Office in their restaurants and business offices. Your boss requested that you research Office 365 subscriptions at office365.com.

    a. Which programs are available in the Office 365 subscription?

    b. How much would your business pay for each employee per month to use Office 365 installed on five of their home computers?

    c. What are the advantages of subscription-based software compared to traditional perpetual software? Name at least three advantages.

    d. What are the disadvantages of subscription based software in comparison to traditional perpetual software? Name at least three disadvantages.

2: Spyware Virus Protection

You recently purchased a Windows tablet, which comes equipped with free antivirus software called Windows Defender. Research and determine if this antivirus software provides enough coverage for personal usage. Write at least 150 words explaining your conclusions.

3: Android Tablet Apps

Your school has received a grant that provides all students with an Android tablet. In addition to your academic apps, you would like to see what popular apps are available. Open the page https://play.google.com. Find this week's Play Picks and read about the top five apps. Write a paragraph on the purpose and cost of each one, for a total of five paragraphs.

Ethical Issues Now

Subscription-based software such as Office 365 Home Premium or Student Advantage lets you install five personal copies of Office on your computers.

© iStockphoto.com/StockRocket

Subscription-Based Software

    a. Research the Office 365 Home Premium plan. Investigate OneDrive for storage and cloud-based access to all your email, calendars, and documents. What are the guidelines for sharing the five copies of Office and OneDrive storage?

    b. Write a paragraph on the guidelines for sharing your Office 365 Student Advantage subscription with two of your roommates. (All three of you live in the same apartment.)

    c. Would you prefer buying software outright or paying for a subscription plan? Write least 150 words on the pros and cons of purchasing software or paying for subscription.

Team Up Now – Google Drive VideoNotes Web App

Google Drive includes a Web app named VideoNotes, which is a tool for taking notes while watching videos. VideoNotes allows you to play any YouTube video on the left side of your screen as you make notes on a notepad on the right side of the screen. VideoNotes integrates with your Google Drive account. All the notes you type are synchronized with the video. Later, if you select a line in your notes, the video begins to play from the corresponding location. You'll use VideoNotes to interact with your team in this exercise.

    a. Research and identify three YouTube videos that describe different Web apps.

    b. Share the links of the three YouTube videos with each member of your team.

    c. Sign in to google.com, and then open the drive.google.com page. Select the **Create** button and then select **VideoNotes**. Each team member should open the three YouTube videos and take detailed notes as the video plays.

    d. Share your VideoNotes with each team member and your instructor using Google Drive.

Key Terms

adaptive	copy protection technology	Integrated Development
agile	copyright	Environment (IDE)
algorithm	crash	intellectual property
Android @Home	custom software	interpreter
antispam software	debugger	keylogger
antispyware	debugging tool	license
antivirus software	developer	Linux operating system
app	device driver	load
application Help	Digital Rights Management (DRM)	low-level language
application software	digital watermark	machine language
assembler	download	malware
assembly language	embedded software	mobile application
authentication	encryption	mobile app
backed up	encryption key	multiple-user license
beta	end-user license agreement (EULA)	native app
bot	extreme programming model	note-taking software
Certificate of Authenticity	firewall software	onscreen Help
code library	freeware	open source software
cold boot	gadget	operating system
command-line interface	graphical user interface (GUI)	operating system (OS) software
comment	groupware	packaged software
compiler	high-level language	patch
computer programmer	horizontal market software	personal information
computer software	input	management (PIM)
concurrent-use license	instructions	piracy

platform
portable app
predictive methodology
preinstalled software
productivity software
program
program editor
programmer
programming
programming language
public domain software
quality assurance (QA)
rebooting
replicate
security software
security suite
service pack

shareware
shrink wrap license
single-user license
site license
Software as a Service (SaaS)
software developer
software development
Software Development Kit (SDK)
software development methodology
software program
software publisher
software update
source code
spyware
system software
text editor
time-limited license

Trojan horse
uninstall
update
upgrade
user manual
utility program
utility software
vertical market software
virus
warm boot
Web app
Web page authoring software
Web-based Help
widget
Windows Embedded
worm

System Software

Alex loves his new tablet with the latest Windows system software. He can store his e-books, assignments, messages, and course information in folders and read them anywhere without being confined to a desk.

Alex taps tiles on his tablet to share files on his cloud computing drive, take photos, listen to music, get directions, and connect to friends.

© Dragon Images/Shutterstock.com

Alex Rivera is enjoying the park as he reads *Great Expectations* by Charles Dickens for his freshman English class. Because he uses Windows system software on his laptop, he can take notes, search for files and Web information, and back up everything in the cloud at the same time. System software is more powerful and flexible now that it includes built-in apps.

Microsoft® product screenshots used with permission from Microsoft® Corporation.

Introduction to System Software

system software | operating system (OS) | DOS | command-line interface | graphical user interface (GUI) | update | service pack

The Bottom Line
- System software is the software that runs a computer, and includes operating systems and utility programs.
- You need to keep your operating system up to date to keep your computer system running smoothly and to protect against security threats.

What makes computers so versatile and capable of performing so many tasks? Is it a blazing fast processor? Souped-up hard drive? Dazzling monitor? No, it's the system software. Without system software, a computer is just a bunch of electronic components in a case.

System Software

System software is the software that makes it possible for you to use a computer. The operating system and utility programs are system software that control behind-the-scene operations so you can use the computer productively. **Table 3-1** compares system software and application software.

Figure 3-1: System software

Microsoft Windows Start screen

Apple iOS on an iPad and iPhone

WinZip file compression program for iOS

Search utility built into Windows

Microsoft Windows desktop

© iStockphoto.com/hocus-focus, Courtesy of WinZip

Table 3-1: System software and application software

	System software	Application software
Purpose	Runs a computer	Lets you perform work or personal tasks
How it runs	Starts when you turn on the power to a computer, and then runs in the background	Starts at your request
Typical tasks	Keeps track of files, prints documents, connects to networks, manages hardware and other software	Provides tools for creating, editing, and viewing files such as documents and Web pages

© 2015 Cengage Learning

Operating Systems

The most critical piece of software on a computer is the **operating system (OS)**, a set of programs that manages and coordinates all the activities in a computer.

As system software, the OS runs mostly in the background as you perform other tasks. It determines whether you can run two programs at the same time, for example, or connect your computer to a network. Suppose you are writing a report and want to save the document on your hard drive. **Table 3-2** shows the role the operating system plays as you perform these tasks.

Table 3-2: System software and application software

Your task	Role of the operating system
Start a word processing program and then open the report document	• Starts the word processing program • Provides a way for you to access the report document
Add information to the report	• Manages memory so the program can run • Stores your unsaved work in temporary memory
Save the report on the hard drive	• Finds the hard drive on the computer • Makes sure the hard drive has enough space for the document • Saves the document on the hard drive • Stores the name and location of the saved document so you can find it later

© 2015 Cengage Learning

Brief History

Personal computer (PC) operating systems have been around since the 1980s. **DOS**, short for Disk Operating System (and pronounced *doss*, which rhymes with *toss*), was the first PC operating system. It uses a **command-line interface**, which displays only text. You type commands to interact with DOS. See **Figure 3-2**.

Figure 3-2: Command-line interface

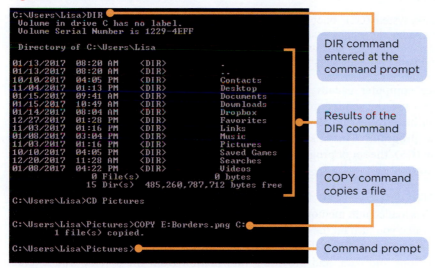

DIR command entered at the command prompt

Results of the DIR command

COPY command copies a file

Command prompt

Figure 3-3: Graphical user interface

Icons in a GUI

iTunes

© iStockphoto.com/bedo

In 1984, Apple introduced the Mac OS, which included a **graphical user interface (GUI)**. To interact with a GUI, you select icons, buttons, and other objects with a pointing device or your fingertip. See **Figure 3-3**.

Microsoft released Windows 1.0 shortly after the Macintosh debuted, though Windows did not become popular until version 3.1 was released in 1992.

Linux OS was introduced in the 1990s and continues to gain popularity. Linux is available in various forms, or distributions. Some distributions have command-line interfaces, while others use a GUI.

Windows, Mac OS, and Linux have continued to evolve into more powerful and easy-to-use operating systems such as Windows 7 and 8.x and Mac OS X Mountain Lion and Mavericks.

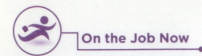
Versions and Updates

To completely identify an operating system, you state its name and version. For example, in Windows 8, Windows is the name of the OS and 8 is the version.

After releasing a major version, OS developers continue to work on the software to fix bugs, improve security, and enhance features. These OS changes are called **updates**. A collection of major updates is sometimes called a **service pack**.

Most operating systems include a feature that notifies you when updates are available for downloading. You can have the OS automatically download updates using an Internet connection and then install them, or you can do so yourself. Experts recommend that you let the OS install updates automatically to keep your system running smoothly and to protect against security threats.

Utility Software

Utility software performs a specific, limited task, usually related to managing or maintaining a computer system. Some utility programs are included with the operating system, such as the following:

- **File management programs** such as File Explorer (for Windows 8 and 8.1, collectively called Windows 8.x), Windows Explorer (for Windows 7), and Finder (for Mac OS X) let you copy, move, rename, and delete files and folders.
- **Search programs** help you find files stored on the computer.
- **Disk cleanup software** deletes unnecessary files.
- **File compression programs** reduce the size of files. Disk cleanup and file compression utilities work to free up disk space.

Other utility programs are available separate from the operating system. For example, you can install a collection of security utilities to protect your computer and its data.

Operating Systems

operating system (OS) | boot process | user interface | process | multitasking | multithreading | multiprocessing | parallel processing | random access memory (RAM) | virtual memory | page file | swap file | personal computer (PC) operating system | server OS | network OS | mobile OS | embedded OS | General Public License (GPL)

Is your computer usually reliable and quick to respond to your instructions? Can you use the same types of controls and tools in any program you start? Or do you have to learn a new way of working with software when you work with a new program? The answers to these questions depend on your **operating system (OS)**, the set of programs that manages and coordinates all the activities on your computer.

Operating System Functions

The OS is loaded into memory during the **boot process**, which is a series of events that begin when you turn on the computer.

After it starts, the OS is the go-between for you and the computer, accepting your instructions and data, and providing information from the system. You interact with the OS through the **user interface**, which controls how you enter and receive information.

The OS is also the go-between for software and hardware. For example, suppose you want to print a flyer you created in Microsoft Word. The OS completes this task in three steps:

1. When you select the Print command, Word sends the document to the OS for printing, and the OS accepts the document.

2. The OS sends the document to your printer and lets other software know the printer is busy.

3. Finally, the printer prints the flyer, and the OS signals that the printer is no longer busy.

Figure 3-4: Operating systems

Operating systems provide a user interface so you can interact with the computer.

Operating systems use the processor to handle requests from hardware and software.

Operating systems coordinate hardware tasks, such as printing.

Operating systems allocate memory to programs as needed, and then reclaim that memory when a program closes.

© Evgeny Karandaev/Shutterstock.com, © AGorohov/Shutterstock.com, © oksana2010/Shutterstock.com, © luchschen/Shutterstock.com

Processing Techniques

As you work with a computer, many activities, or **processes**, are competing for your computer's attention. Applications request action, the pointing device and keyboard send data, and Web pages arrive from your Internet connection and wait to be displayed on your screen.

In response, the OS uses one or more of the following processing techniques to handle and prioritize these requests efficiently and improve the performance of a computer:

- **Multitasking**: Most operating systems use multitasking to perform many tasks simultaneously, such as running two or more programs.
- **Multithreading**: The OS uses multithreading to process many parts, or threads, of a single program. Multithreading helps programs run faster and more efficiently.
- **Multiprocessing**: Most computers have multiple processors, such as dual-core or quad-core processors, which means the OS can use multiprocessing to split tasks among the processors.
- **Parallel processing**: Many operating systems also can use parallel processing to divide one task among many processors so that parts of the task are completed simultaneously, or in parallel.

Memory Management

One key task that operating systems perform is memory management, which involves using **random access memory (RAM)** efficiently.

Every program needs RAM to run, including the operating system. Each additional program you run or window you open requires RAM. The OS allocates RAM to a program as needed, and then reclaims that memory when the program closes.

To gain memory, operating systems take advantage of **virtual memory**, which uses part of the computer's hard drive as additional RAM. As the OS runs out of RAM for programs, it swaps data from RAM to the virtual memory area of the hard drive, which is also called the **page file** or **swap file**. This paging or swapping process continues until the program closes. See **Figure 3-5** on the next page.

Using virtual memory means the OS can access more memory than is physically available on your computer, but doing so is slower than just using RAM. Therefore, if you want programs to run faster, you probably should start with more RAM or add RAM to your computer.

Operating System Types

You can classify operating systems in different ways, such as by their user interface. Those with command-line interfaces require you to type text commands. Most operating systems have a graphical user interface (GUI) where you click objects such as icons to interact with the OS.

By the Numbers Now

New Windows computers typically have between 4 GB and 16 GB of RAM.

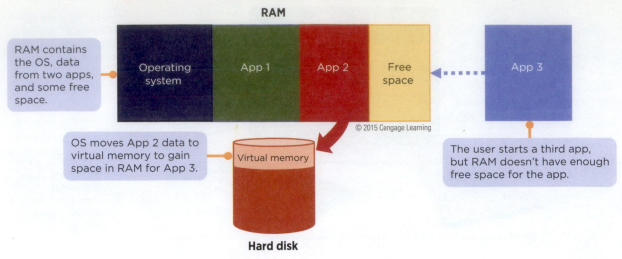

Figure 3-5: How an operating system manages memory

RAM

RAM contains the OS, data from two apps, and some free space.

Operating system | App 1 | App 2 | Free space

App 3

© 2015 Cengage Learning

OS moves App 2 data to virtual memory to gain space in RAM for App 3.

Virtual memory

The user starts a third app, but RAM doesn't have enough free space for the app.

Hard disk

Other types of operating systems include the following:

- Operating systems installed on a single computer are called **personal computer (PC) operating systems** or desktop operating systems. Most are single-user operating systems because one user interacts with the OS at a time.
- A **server OS** or **network OS** is a multiuser OS because it controls a single, centralized computer that supports many users on networked computers. It also controls access to network resources such as network printers.
- You use a **mobile OS** on a smartphone, tablet, or other mobile device.
- Motor vehicles and electronic devices, such as card readers, medical equipment, and robots, use **embedded OSs**.

Desktop Operating Systems

The PC operating system you prefer—for example, Windows, Mac OS X, or Linux—usually determines the type of PC you buy. The GPL encourages programmers to develop Linux utilities, applications, and enhancements. See **Table 3-3**.

Table 3-3: PC operating systems

OS	Type of computer	Notable features
Windows	Desktop computers, laptops, and some tablets	Provides two computing environments: a Start screen and a desktop with a taskbar
Mac OS X	Macintosh desktop computers and laptops	Desktop shows the Apple logo at the top with a Dock at the bottom
Linux	Desktop computers, laptops, and tablets	Distributed under the terms of a **General Public License (GPL)**, which allows you to copy the OS for your own use, to give to others, or to sell

© 2015 Cengage Learning

#syssoftware

The term "PC" once referred only to personal computers that ran Windows. Now "PC operating system" refers to the OS on a desktop computer or laptop, which is different from a mobile OS that runs on a tablet or smartphone.

Server Operating Systems

A server OS resides on a server computer and runs to manage a network. The following are three popular server operating systems:

- **Windows Server** is the server version of Windows. It includes advanced security tools and a set of programs called Internet Information Services. These programs manage Web applications and services.
- **Mac OS X Server**, like other server operating systems, supports all sizes of networks and servers. One unique feature is that it lets authorized users access servers using their iPhones or other Apple devices.

- **UNIX** is called a multipurpose OS because it can run on a desktop PC or a server. Many Web servers, which are the computers that deliver Web pages to your computer, use UNIX because it is a powerful, flexible OS.

UNIX is similar to Linux, which some servers use as their OS to provide network services such as email and Web access.

Mobile Operating Systems

A mobile device such as a tablet or smartphone uses a mobile OS, which has features similar to those of a PC OS, but is simpler and significantly smaller. A mobile OS works especially well with mobile device features such as touchscreens, voice recognition, and Wi-Fi networks.

Four popular mobile operating systems are iOS, Android OS, Windows Phone, and Windows RT. Each works with particular brands of handheld computers. See **Figure 3-6**.

By The Numbers Now

Apple Computer is focused on mobile devices and mobile operating systems because more than 70 percent of the company's revenue comes from sales of the iPhone and iPad.

Figure 3-6: Mobile operating systems

iOS is a version of Mac OS X written for Apple mobile devices.

Google developed Android to run on many types of smartphones and tablets.

Windows Phone is designed for smartphones, and Windows RT is designed for tablets.

© iStockphoto.com/hocus-focus, © iStockphoto.com/Mixmike, © iStockphoto.com/Moncherie, © iStockphoto.com/scanrail

Common Operating System Tasks

boot process | bootstrap program | ROM (read-only memory) | power-on self-test (POST) | RAM (random access memory) | kernel | resource | input | output | buffer | spooling | device driver | Plug and Play (PnP) | graphical user interface (GUI) | tile | icon | button

An operating system takes care of the technical tasks of running a computer while you work on school or professional projects, watch videos, connect with friends, or play games. To enhance your computer experience, the OS also lets you customize the user interface and set up hardware the way you like it.

Startup

To start an OS, you turn on the computer. Before you can interact with the OS, the computer must complete the **boot process** which is described below:

1. The computer receives power and distributes it to the computer circuitry.

2. The processor begins to run the **bootstrap program**, a special startup program built into a **ROM (read-only memory)** chip on the computer's motherboard.

3. The computer performs the **power-on self-test (POST)** to check crucial system components.

4. If the POST is successful, the computer identifies connected devices and checks their settings.

The Bottom Line
- The OS controls a computer from soon after you start it up until you shut it down.
- During that time, the OS manages resources including the processor, memory, storage space, and connected devices.
- The OS also provides the user interface so you can perform tasks.

Figure 3-7: Operating system tasks

Manages resources, including the processor, RAM, storage space, and connected devices

Provides a user interface

Shuts down the computer

Starts up the computer

Coordinates input and output

© AGorohov/Shutterstock.com, © oksana2010/Shutterstock.com, © luchschen/Shutterstock.com, © Gregory Gerber/Shutterstock.com, © PureSolution/Shutterstock.com,
© You can more/Shutterstock.com

#syssoftware

Windows 8.x computers typically take only a few seconds to start up and let you sign in with a picture password, which involves repeating three gestures on a picture.

5. The computer loads system files into **RAM (random access memory)**, including the **kernel**, or core, of the OS.

6. The OS completes setup tasks, such as requesting your username and password, and then it runs startup programs in the background and displays the main user interface.

Resources

An operating system controls your computer by managing its **resources**, which are components the OS requires to perform work, such as the processor, RAM, storage space, and connected devices. To manage RAM resources, an OS keeps track of the apps, processes, and other tasks the system is performing.

Microsoft Windows, for example, displays this information in the Windows Task Manager dialog box. See **Figure 3-8**.

Figure 3-8: Windows Task Manager

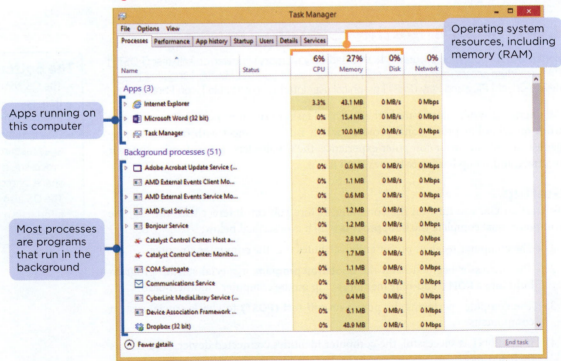

Operating system resources, including memory (RAM)

Apps running on this computer

Most processes are programs that run in the background

For example, the OS tracks the names and locations of your files so you can retrieve them from storage when necessary, and it logs empty areas in storage where you can save new files.

If the OS detects a resource problem, it notifies you and tries to correct the problem. If too many programs are open for the memory to handle, the OS displays a message and does not open additional programs. If a printer is not turned on when you try to print a document, the OS will send you a message to turn it on; if out of paper, you will get a message to add paper. If your hard drive has no more space, the OS will let you know that you do not have available space to save another file.

Input and Output

To keep the computer running smoothly, the OS manages input and output. For example, when you type text on the keyboard to provide **input**, the OS accepts and processes that data so the computer can display the text as **output** on the screen.

If a device is slow to provide input or output, the OS uses **buffers**, which are areas of memory that hold data from one device before it is transferred to another device. For example, by using a keyboard buffer, your computer doesn't miss any of your keystrokes, even if you type very quickly.

Placing data in a buffer so it can be retrieved later is called **spooling**. Print spooling allows the OS to send many documents to the printer and then print them in sequence while the computer is performing other tasks.

Hardware

The OS considers every device connected to the computer an input or output resource. For example, a microphone is an input resource and a speaker is an output resource, both for audio data.

To control a hardware resource, the OS communicates with a **device driver**, a small program that tells the OS how to interact with that device. Each device must have a driver. If you install new hardware, the OS usually recognizes the device right away or the next time you start the computer. The OS then tries to install the correct driver so you can use the new hardware immediately. This feature is called **Plug and Play (PnP)**. Most operating systems include drivers for common devices. If the OS can't find the correct driver on your computer, you can download it from the manufacturer's Web site.

User Interface

The main purpose of an OS is to control what happens behind the scenes. It provides a user interface so that you can interact with the OS and other programs.

Most operating systems use a **graphical user interface (GUI)**, which lets you select options and manipulate objects such as buttons and icons using a mouse or gesture. GUIs are based on graphical objects, where each object represents a computer task, command, or real-world object. See **Figure 3-9**.

- The Windows Start screen displays **tiles**, colorful rectangles that you use to start apps.
- An **icon** is a small picture that represents a program, file, or hardware device. When you double-click an icon in Windows, such as the Recycle Bin icon, a window opens to display related data.
- A **button** is a graphic that you click to make a selection. Buttons often appear together on a toolbar, taskbar, or Ribbon.

Typical Tasks

You interact directly with the OS to control parts of your computer and your computer experience:

- **Start programs**: You use GUI objects to start programs. For example, with Windows, you use tiles, buttons, icons, and the taskbar. On a Mac computer, you use icons and the Dock. See **Figure 3-10** on the next page.

Hot Technology Now

Windows 8.1 features Plug and Play support for 3D printing.

#syssoftware

On Windows 8.x computers, you can use the Devices charm to send information displayed on your screen to another device, such as a printer or second monitor.

Figure 3-9: Typical GUI objects

Tile   Icon

Buttons

Figure 3-10: Starting programs in Windows 7, Windows 8.x, and Mac OS X

Tile on the Start screen

Icons on the taskbar

Start button

Windows 7

Windows 8.x

People   Maps   SkyDrive

Photos   **skype**

Icons on the Dock

Mac OS X

Source: Apple

- **Manage files**: Most operating systems provide programs you use to manage files. For example, you can view a list of folders and files and move, copy, rename, or delete them.
- **Get help**: You also interact directly with the OS to get help. You can learn more about the OS and how to use commands and features.
- **Customize the user interface**: Typically, you can customize the user interface by selecting a theme, which includes a color scheme, a background graphic, sounds, and other elements.
- **Work with hardware**: Finally, you use the OS to set up hardware or change hardware settings.

Shut Down

Although you keep a computer running under most circumstances, you should shut it down if the power could be interrupted suddenly, as in the case of an impending thunderstorm. You should also shut it down if you aren't going to use it for a long time, to conserve energy.

Operating systems provide shut down options so you can close programs and processes in an orderly fashion. One option is a complete shut down, which closes all documents and programs and turns off the power to the computer.

Some operating systems have a Sleep or Hibernate option to use low power instead of shutting down. Both options store the current state of open programs and documents, saving you time when you resume work.

You can use the OS to set what happens when you press the power button or close the lid on a laptop. You can choose to shut down the computer, sleep, or hibernate.

Managing Your Computer's Windows

window | Minimize button | Maximize button | Close button | active window | program window | folder window | Snap

Many computer users start desktop applications until their screen is covered with programs and documents. Then they get frustrated when they can't find the information they want. Running full-screen Windows 8–style apps can make the interface even more confusing.

To avoid frustration and work more effectively, you can manage the windows on your desktop. In any operating system, a **window** is a rectangular area of the screen that displays the contents of a program, file, or folder.

Figure 3-11: Managing windows and apps

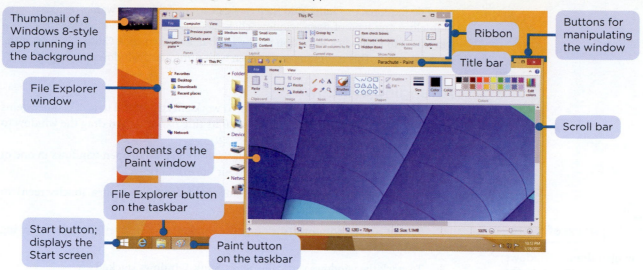

Thumbnail of a Windows 8-style app running in the background

File Explorer window

Contents of the Paint window

File Explorer button on the taskbar

Start button; displays the Start screen

Paint button on the taskbar

Ribbon

Buttons for manipulating the window

Title bar

Scroll bar

Defining a Window

After you turn on a Windows, Macintosh, or Linux computer, the desktop appears. When you open a desktop program, file, or folder, it appears on the desktop in a rectangular work area called a window.

Most windows share the same elements. **Figure 3-11** shows these elements in Windows 8.1:

- The center part of a window displays the contents.
- The title bar at the top of a window displays the name of the program, file, or folder shown in the window.
- The title bar also contains buttons for manipulating the window. The **Minimize button** reduces the window to a button on the taskbar. The **Maximize button** enlarges the window to fill the screen. The **Close button** closes the window. See **Figure 3-12**.
- Some windows include a Ribbon, toolbar, or menu bar, which contains text, icons, or images you select to perform actions and make selections.
- Windows can also include vertical and horizontal scroll bars so you can display contents currently out of view.

Switching Windows

You can have many windows and apps open at one time, each displaying a different document or program. The foreground window is the **active window**. Your next mouse or keyboard action applies to the active window. One way to make a different window active is to select its button on the taskbar.

You can use many keyboard shortcuts to manipulate windows. In Windows, you can press and hold the ALT key while you press TAB to cycle through thumbnails of the open windows. Release the ALT key to make the selected window active.

If you are using Aero in Windows 7, press and hold down the CTRL and WINDOWS keys, and then press the TAB key to display the windows in a 3D stack, an effect called Aero Flip 3D. Press TAB or use the mouse wheel to scroll the stack, and then click a window to make it active.

Opening a Window

You can use two types of windows on a desktop. A **program window** displays a running program. A **folder window** displays the objects in a folder, such as files and other folders.

- To open a program window in Windows 7, for example, click the **Start button**, and then click the **program name**. If a program icon appears on the Windows taskbar, you can select the icon to open a program window.

#syssoftware

If the Start screen appears when you start your Windows 8.x computer, use the Desktop tile to display the desktop.

Figure 3-12: Window-manipulation buttons

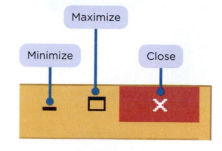

Maximize

Minimize

Close

Restore Down

#syssoftware

In Mac OS X, you select an icon on the Dock to make a window active.

Chapter 3: System Software • **3-11**

- To open a folder window, start a file management utility such as Windows Explorer, File Explorer, or Finder, and then navigate to the folder you want.

To close any type of open window, click its Close button. Another way to close a window is to right-click its button on the taskbar, and then click Close window on the shortcut menu. This technique works even with minimized windows.

Arranging Windows

You can arrange windows on the desktop to work effectively and to access other items on the desktop. To move a window, point to its title bar, and then drag the window to its new location.

In Windows 7 or 8.x, you can use the taskbar to display all open windows in one of three arrangements—cascading, vertically, or horizontally:

1. Right-click the **taskbar** (or press and hold the taskbar on a touchscreen) to display its shortcut menu.

2. Select **Cascade windows** to arrange the windows so they overlap while displaying each title bar.

3. To stack the windows vertically, select **Show windows stacked**.

4. Select **Show windows side by side** to arrange the windows horizontally across the desktop.

You can use **Snap** to arrange windows. Drag the title bar of a window to one side of the desktop until the outline of an expanded window appears.

Resizing a Window

You can resize windows to display more or less of their contents. The easiest way to make a window larger or smaller when working with any operating system is to point to a border or corner of the window until the resizing pointer appears. See **Figure 3-13**. Drag the border or corner to resize the window making it larger or smaller as needed.

In Windows 7 and 8.x, you can also use Snap to resize a window vertically. Point to the top or bottom border of the window until the resizing pointer appears. Drag the border to the top or bottom of the desktop. The height of the window expands to fit the height of the desktop.

To return the window to its original size, begin to drag the top or bottom border of the window. The window snaps to its original size without additional dragging.

Manipulating a Window

You can resize a window by maximizing or minimizing it. **Figure 3-14** shows useful buttons for manipulating windows in Mac OS X, Windows 8.x, and Windows 7.

- To make a window fill the desktop, click the Maximize button or double-click the title bar.
- In Windows 7 and 8.x, you can also use Snap to maximize a window. Drag the title bar upward until the window fills the desktop.
- To return a maximized window to its original size, click the Restore Down button or double-click the window's title bar.
- Click the Minimize button to reduce a window to a button on the taskbar. To display a minimized window, click its taskbar button.
- In Windows 7 and 8.x, you can use Shake to minimize all open windows except one. Point to a window's title bar and drag it left and right quickly to shake the window.
- To display the desktop, click the Show desktop button on the far right side of the taskbar.
- To peek at the desktop without minimizing any windows, point to the Show desktop button instead of clicking it.

#syssoftware

You can also drag a Windows 8-style app and snap it to the right or left side of the screen. The app is displayed in a panel as you work on the desktop or use another app.

Figure 3-13: Resizing a Mac window

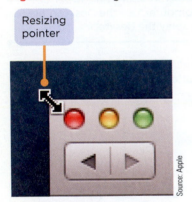

Resizing pointer

Source: Apple

Figure 3-14: Useful buttons

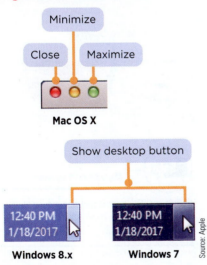

Minimize

Close   Maximize

Mac OS X

Show desktop button

12:40 PM
1/18/2017

12:40 PM
1/18/2017

Windows 8.x   Windows 7

Source: Apple

Common Operating System Features

desktop | taskbar | notification area | menu | submenu | dialog box | option button | check box | icon | Recycle Bin | disk cleanup utility | sector | defragmentation utility | file management utility | file compression utility | decompress

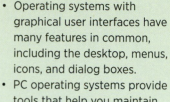

The Bottom Line
- Operating systems with graphical user interfaces have many features in common, including the desktop, menus, icons, and dialog boxes.
- PC operating systems provide tools that help you maintain computer disks and manage files.

Suppose you've always worked on a Windows computer but now you're visiting a friend who offers to let you use his Macintosh computer. Will you be able to get anything done on a different operating system?

The answer is yes, because PC operating systems share common features. When you become familiar with these features, you can use any personal computer to perform basic tasks and even keep the system in good working order.

Figure 3-15: Common features in PC operating systems

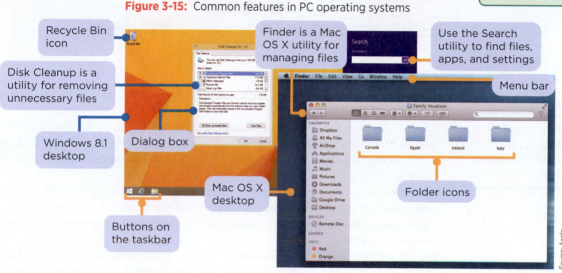

Recycle Bin icon

Disk Cleanup is a utility for removing unnecessary files

Windows 8.1 desktop

Dialog box

Buttons on the taskbar

Finder is a Mac OS X utility for managing files

Mac OS X desktop

Use the Search utility to find files, apps, and settings

Menu bar

Folder icons

Source: Apple

Desktops

Regardless of the brand of computer, the **desktop** is a main workspace for interacting with your computer. At the bottom of the Windows desktop is the **taskbar**, which contains buttons for running programs, viewing folders, and opening files. On the right of the Windows taskbar is the **notification area**, which displays the time and date plus shortcuts to utilities such as the volume control. Alerts for updating programs also appear in the notification area.

The Mac OS X desktop uses an area called the Dock for starting programs. Linux has bars on the top and bottom of its desktop. Chrome has the Shelf; like the Windows taskbar or Mac OS X Dock, the Shelf displays icons for starting programs.

Some desktops let you display gadgets or widgets such as a calendar, weather app, or sticky note. These small utilities usually start when the desktop appears and remain displayed until you shut down the computer.

Menus and Dialog Boxes

How do you make a computer do what you want it to do? One way is to use a **menu**, which displays a list of commands or options. You select the option you want from the list. See **Figure 3-16** on the next page.

To avoid displaying a very long list of options, many menus organize additional commands on a **submenu**. You can always identify a menu option that leads to a submenu or gallery because it has a triangle symbol. When you select a menu option with an ellipsis (three dots), a dialog box opens. A **dialog box** displays settings associated with a command. Dialog boxes contain controls that you use to select options and enter information to indicate exactly how you want the program to perform the command. For example, click a round **option button** to select one option from a group of options. Click one or more **check boxes** to identify selections you want from several options. Click the OK button to accept the settings in the dialog box.

#syssoftware

Most Windows programs use a Ribbon instead of a menu bar. Mac OS X, however, displays a menu bar for the active program at the top of the screen.

Figure 3-16: Common features in PC operating systems

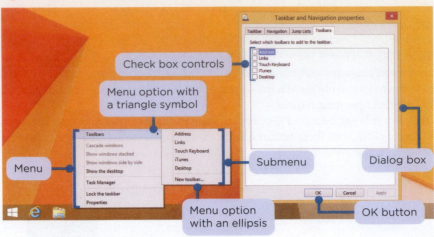

Icons and Buttons

Whether you use a Windows, Mac, or Linux operating system, you can use icons and buttons to interact with the computer.

- **Icons**: An **icon** is a graphic representing a program, file, or hardware device. Icons can appear on the desktop or in a window. Typically, you double-click an icon to start a program or display the contents of what the icon represents, such as a drive.
- **Buttons**: A button is also a graphic. Buttons are grouped together on a menu bar, toolbar, taskbar, or Ribbon interface. You tap or click a button to make a selection. If the button displays an arrow, a menu or gallery appears so you can select an option.

You can create icons for items like files and folders and arrange icons on the desktop or in a window by selecting sort settings. In contrast to icons, buttons are part of a program, so you typically can't create or rearrange them.

Disk Utilities

Regardless of the operating system you're using, if your computer starts to slow down, you probably need to use disk utilities to diagnose and repair problems on your hard disk.

To protect you from accidentally deleting a hard disk file, the OS stores the deleted file in a temporary location. In Windows, this location is the **Recycle Bin**. The file still takes up space on the disk, but does not appear in file listings. You then have the option of emptying the Recycle Bin to permanently delete the files. Files deleted from removable storage devices such as a flash drive do not get placed in the Recycle Bin. A **disk cleanup utility** finds and removes unnecessary files such as those stored in the Recycle Bin.

When you save data on a disk, the OS places it in an available storage area, or **sector**. Although the OS tries to place data in sectors that are next to each other, or contiguous, parts of files can be scattered over the disk. These fragmented files slow a computer's performance.

A **defragmentation utility** reorganizes the files on a hard disk so the OS accesses data more quickly. Although Windows users should defragment periodically to increase efficiency, Mac and Linux users might not need to. Follow the recommendations for your computer and operating system.

File Utilities

At some point, every computer user wastes time searching for files saved somewhere on the computer. To avoid these frustrating searches, you can use file utilities to manage your computer files. Following are examples of file utilities:

#syssoftware

The Windows 8.x Start screen uses tiles instead of icons because tiles are larger and easier to use in a touch-activated interface.

#syssoftware

To display a toolbar of buttons appropriate for your current task in a Windows 8-style app, right-click (or press and hold) a blank area of the screen.

#syssoftware

Windows 7 and 8.x automatically defragment (or optimize) the hard drive according to a schedule, which is once a week by default.

- **File management**: A **file management utility** gives you an overview of the files stored on your computer and lets you rename, delete, move, and copy files and folders. For example, in Windows 7, you use Windows Explorer. In Windows 8.x, you use File Explorer.
- **Search for files:** A search tool finds files that meet criteria you specify, such as characters in a filename.
- **File compression**: Use a **file compression utility** to reduce the size of a file so it takes up less storage space on a disk. Compressed files usually have a .zip extension. If you compress a file before attaching it to an email message, for example, the message travels more quickly to its recipient.
- You also use a file compression utility to **decompress**, or unzip, compressed files and restore them to their original size.

The Bottom Line
- Because an OS comes installed on new computers, you should know the strengths and weaknesses of the popular PC OSs.
- The OS determines how easy it is to use and upgrade your computer, so consider the user interface and flexibility as two of the most important criteria when comparing PC OSs.

Comparing PC Operating Systems

PC operating system | Windows | window | Mac OS X | Dock | Linux | distribution | General Public License (GPL) | Chrome OS | Web application

A **PC operating system** is developed to run on a desktop computer, a laptop, and in some cases, a tablet. Four popular PC operating systems are Windows, Mac OS X, Linux, and Chrome.

Figure 3-17: PC operating systems

Windows 8.1

Mac OS X Mavericks

Ubuntu Linux

Chrome OS

Source: Apple, Source: Ubuntu, Source: Google

Windows 7, 8, and 8.1

Windows is a PC operating system developed by Microsoft Corporation. Part of its graphical user interface features **windows**, which are rectangular areas of the screen devoted to a single program and its tools.

Three recent versions of Windows are Windows 7 (released in 2009), Windows 8 (released in 2012), and Windows 8.1 (released in 2013). The version number change from Windows 8 to 8.1 indicates that Windows 8.1 expands the features and functions of Windows 8 rather than offering a new design or technical foundation.

Windows 7, on the other hand, is significantly different from Windows 8 and Windows 8.1 (collectively called "Windows 8.x"). The major difference is that Windows 8.x is designed for computers with touchscreens, such as tablets and laptops with touch-activated display screens. Windows 8.x also runs on computers with traditional pointing devices such as a mouse or trackpad. **Table 3-4** on the next page compares two versions of Windows.

Table 3-4: Windows 7 and Windows 8.1

Feature or task	Windows 7	Windows 8.1
User interface	Desktop only	Start screen and desktop
Touch commands	Limited use of touch	Widespread use of touch
Initial view after startup	Desktop	Start screen or desktop
Start button	Use to start programs	Use to display the Start screen
Built-in programs	Accessories (such as Paint and WordPad) and gadgets (such as Clock)	Weather and Maps apps as well as expanded apps such as Skype
All installed programs	Start menu or All Programs menu	Apps screen
Utilities	Control Panel only	Control Panel or PC settings screen
File manager	Windows Explorer	File Explorer

#syssoftware

Apple is offering the most recent version of Mac OS X free of charge at the Apple App Store so that computers with older versions of the OS can be upgraded easily.

Mac OS X

Mac OS X is the PC operating system designed for Apple Macintosh computers. Like Windows, it has a graphical user interface with windows and a desktop. Its unique features include a menu bar at the top of the screen and the Dock at the bottom. The **Dock** contains icons for accessing files and apps. See **Figure 3-18**.

Mac OS X set the original standard for GUI operating systems, and continues to lead the computing industry in user interface design. The basic tools for using Mac OS X, such as the menu bar and the Dock, are similar in each version, easing the transition from one release of the OS to the next. Other strengths are that it is an easy-to-use, secure, and reliable OS. Weaknesses include a limited selection of hardware and productivity apps other than graphics software.

Figure 3-18: Mac OS X Mavericks

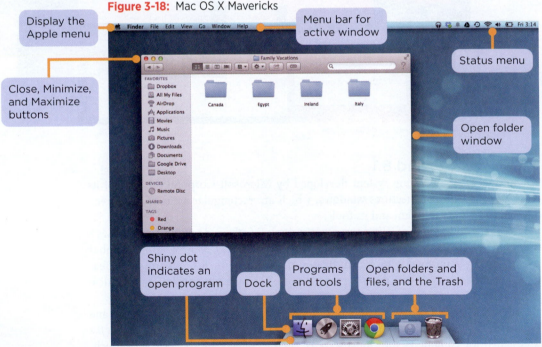

Source: Apple

Linux

Linux is a PC operating system related to UNIX, an OS first developed in the 1960s for large, special-purpose computers used by scientists, researchers, and system administrators. Linux is available in versions called **distributions**, including commercial distributions such as RedHat, openSUSE, and Ubuntu. Most distributions of Linux provide graphical user interfaces, though some, such as BSD, are better known for their command-line interfaces.

The main advantage of using Linux is its **General Public License (GPL)**, which makes the OS free to install and use. All distributions of Linux also run on any type of hardware and provide excellent security. The two main disadvantages are that installation and setup can be complicated and little commercial software is developed for Linux. (Plenty of open-source software is available, however.) Linux is the OS of choice for users who want flexibility and control over their computers and don't require commercial software.

Chrome OS

Chrome OS is a PC operating system developed by Google to work with Google Web applications. A **Web application** is software you access and use on the Web. The user interface is spare and simple, focusing on accessing the Internet and Web sites using the Chrome browser. Chrome OS is intended to run on secondary mobile computers such as Chromebooks, not on a user's primary computer. In addition to a browser, Chrome OS includes a file manager for viewing and manipulating files and a media player for viewing images and playing music. See **Figure 3-19**.

#syssoftware

Many operating systems, including Mac OS X and Android, are based on UNIX and Linux kernels (the cores of the operating systems).

#syssoftware

Unlike other operating systems, Chrome OS is available only on certain computers, such as Chromebooks, stripped-down, lightweight laptops designed mainly for accessing the Web.

Figure 3-19: Chrome OS on a Chromebook

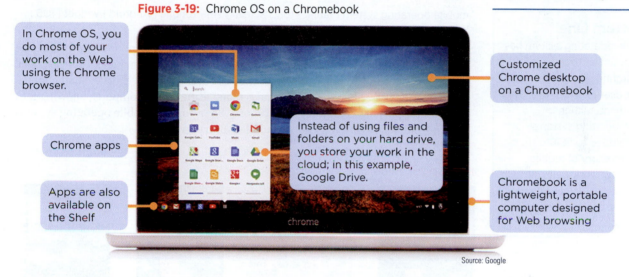

In Chrome OS, you do most of your work on the Web using the Chrome browser.

Chrome apps

Apps are also available on the Shelf

Customized Chrome desktop on a Chromebook

Instead of using files and folders on your hard drive, you store your work in the cloud; in this example, Google Drive.

Chromebook is a lightweight, portable computer designed for Web browsing

Source: Google

Which OS Is Right for You?

When selecting a PC operating system, most users consider ease of use (or the user interface) and flexibility as the two most important criteria. Other criteria include hardware support, software support, security, and availability. **Table 3-5** ranks the most recent versions of four PC operating systems—Windows, Mac OS X, Linux, and Chrome OS—according to these six criteria as 1 - Excellent, 2 - Good, or 3 - Needs improvement according to computer experts.

To select the right OS for you, determine which of the six criteria you consider the most important, and then choose the OS that ranks as 1 - Excellent in those criteria. The following summarizes the strengths and weaknesses of each OS:

- **Windows** works with a wide range of hardware and software. Its flexibility means you can customize it easily and use software developed for earlier versions. It comes preinstalled on most personal computers and is available for purchase and

By the Numbers Now

Among the current operating systems for PCs, Windows runs on 91 percent of the world's desktop computers, Mac OS X on 7.4 percent, and Linux on 1.7 percent.

Table 3-5: PC operating systems

OS	Ease of use	Hardware support	Software support	Flexibility	Security	Availability
Windows	2	1	1	1	2	1
Mac OS X	1	2	2	2	1	2
Linux	2	1	1 or 3	1	1	1
Chrome OS	1	3	3	2	1	3

upgrade on Microsoft Web sites, including the Windows Store. It is, however, the target of most malware. Using Windows 8.x also requires you to master two interfaces.

- **Mac OS X** offers a straightforward, consistent user interface with few security problems. It is provided only on Apple computers and works best with Apple hardware and software. While you can customize the interface easily, it is difficult to upgrade a Mac computer to run a new version of the OS.
- **Linux** distributions are available as free downloads and run on the computer of your choice. Although little commercial software is available for Linux (explaining its rank of 3), you can find many open-source applications to meet your needs (explaining its rank of 1).
- **Chrome OS** is designed for speed and simplicity on a secondary computer. However, it is available only on certain hardware such as Chromebooks and runs only Google Web applications.

Comparing Mobile Operating Systems

mobile operating system | tablet | touchscreen | smartphone | Android | widget | iOS | Windows Phone | tile | live tile | hub | BlackBerry | active frame

A **mobile operating system** is developed to run on a tablet, smartphone, or other mobile device. A **tablet** is a handheld mobile computer that typically includes a **touchscreen**, which is a screen you touch to interact with the user interface. Smaller than a tablet, a **smartphone** is a cell phone that includes many features of a computer, allowing it to run general-purpose computing applications. Four popular mobile operating systems are Android, iOS, Windows Phone, and BlackBerry.

Figure 3-20: Mobile operating systems

Android   iOS   Windows Phone   BlackBerry

© iStockphoto.com/Mixmike, iOS screenshot courtesy of Apple, © iStockphoto.com/scanrail, Source: BlackBerry

Android

Developed by Google, **Android** is a mobile OS based on Linux designed to run on many types of smartphones and tablets. Like Linux, Android is open-source software with a permissive license. This means that device manufacturers can modify the operating system to fit the needs of their hardware, and that independent developers can create apps to run on these devices.

Android uses a touch interface that centers on a home screen with rows of app icons. **Figure 3-21** shows the home screen on a Samsung tablet. Besides installing additional apps, you can install **widgets**, which display and update frequently changing information such as weather conditions.

Android's strengths include its personalization features, ability to run on a range of devices, and its apps. You can download Android apps from the Google Play Store, the primary Web site that provides games, media players, productivity apps, and other software, often free of charge.

The Bottom Line
- A mobile operating system has features similar to those of a PC operating system, but has a simpler user interface designed for touch interactions.
- Mobile operating systems are developed to fit into the limited memory of mobile devices and work well with mobile hardware features such as touchscreens and voice recognition.

Figure 3-21: Android home screen on a Samsung tablet

Apps are currently displayed

Switch the display to Widgets screen

App menu button

Status area

Toolbar

Source: Google

Weaknesses include a slower performance on some devices than that of other mobile operating systems, and frequent updates that device manufacturers control. Some manufacturers offer updates only to a limited selection of smartphones and tablets, leaving other users with outdated software.

iOS

Developed by Apple, **iOS** runs only on Apple mobile devices, including the iPhone, iPad, and iPod Touch, and is derived from Mac OS X. Like Android, iOS focuses on a touch interface. As shown in **Figure 3-22**, the home screen displays a transparent status bar at the top, icons for apps in the middle, and a dock at the bottom for icons such as email, phone, browser, and music. When you swipe to display another screen of icons for additional apps, the status bar and dock do not change.

Hot Technology Now

Android is the most widely used mobile OS in the world, running on more than 80 percent of smartphones.

Figure 3-22: iOS home screen

Transparent status bar

Icons for apps

Static dock

Like all mobile OSs, iOS includes voice recognition

Source: Apple

Strengths of iOS include its streamlined, fluid user experience, which comes from the ease and consistency of its interface. The quality and number of apps provided with iOS or available for installation are high. You can download and install iOS apps exclusively from the Apple App Store, which has strict standards for function and security. Apple also provides annual upgrades to iOS through direct download to all compatible devices.

One drawback of iOS is device selection—iOS is available only on Apple mobile devices, which are usually more expensive than other devices from other manufacturers. Another weakness is that personalization features are limited. For example, the home screen always displays rows of icons, though you can change the home screen background.

Figure 3-23: Start screen on Windows Phone

Each rectangle is a tile

Live tile changes frequently to update content

Tile for email app

Office hub integrates with Microsoft Office

Windows Phone

Windows Phone is the mobile OS from Microsoft intended to run on certain brands of smartphones, including Nokia, HTC, and Samsung. Windows Phone provides a touch interface similar to the Windows 8.x Start screen. In fact, the home screen in Windows Phone is called the Start screen. See **Figure 3-23**. It displays **tiles**, which are links to apps, tools, and items such as Web pages and contacts. They are called **live tiles** because they change depending on the status or changes to the app. For example, the tile for the email app displays the number of unread messages. A popular feature in Windows Phone is the ability to resize and move the tiles on the Start screen.

Integration among apps is a strength of Windows Phone, which shares content in locations called **hubs**. For example, the Pictures hub shows photos taken with the built-in camera and those posted on social networks including Facebook and Twitter. The Office hub coordinates mobile versions of Microsoft Office apps and their desktop counterparts, which is a big advantage for business users.

Drawbacks to Windows Phone are that it is available on only a handful of devices and currently offers far fewer apps than Android or iOS. However, the number of apps is growing. All are available at the Windows Phone Store.

BlackBerry

BlackBerry is a mobile operating system developed by BlackBerry Limited for the BlackBerry line of smartphones and tablets. Unlike earlier versions of operating systems for BlackBerry mobile devices, which relied on physical buttons and the keyboard built into each device, BlackBerry OS has a touch interface. Many models of BlackBerry devices still also include physical keyboards.

The BlackBerry interface uses **active frames**, which are similar to the live tiles in Windows Phone. Up to eight active frames are displayed in two groups, each showing up-to-date information from a recently used app. You scroll from one group of four active frames to the next group of four.

One notable strength of the BlackBerry OS is its universal inbox, which displays notices of phone calls, text messages, email messages, and social network updates in one place. The BlackBerry browser is also uncluttered, allowing for easy reading and browsing.

Weaknesses are the number of available apps (as of 2013, around 120,000 for BlackBerry OS compared to 900,000 for iOS) and the timing of upgrades. When BlackBerry 10 was released in 2013 as a major OS upgrade, some technology experts noted that it did not offer significant improvements to other available mobile operating systems.

Which Mobile OS Is Right for You?

When selecting a mobile operating system, most users consider five criteria: ease of use, performance, flexibility, range of devices, and number of apps. Performance refers to

Hot Technology Now

In late 2013, 3.6 percent of mobile devices ran Windows Phone. Experts claim this single-digit market share is due to the late entry of Windows Phone into the mobile OS market. It debuted in 2010, while iOS was released in 2007 and Android in 2008.

how reliably the OS performs tasks such as connecting phone calls and running apps. Flexibility refers to how much you can customize the OS. **Table 3-6** ranks the most recent versions of four mobile operating systems—Android, iOS, Windows Phone, and BlackBerry—according to these five criteria as 1 - Excellent, 2 - Good, or 3 - Needs improvement according to computer experts.

Table 3-6: Mobile operating systems

OS	Ease of use	Performance	Flexibility	Devices	Apps
Android	2	2	1	1	1
iOS	1	1	3	3	1
Windows Phone	1	1	2	2	3
BlackBerry	3	2	2	3	3

© 2015 Cengage Learning

To select the right mobile OS for you, determine which of the five criteria you consider the most important, and then choose the OS that ranks as 1 - Excellent in those criteria. The following summarizes the strengths and weaknesses of each OS:

- **Android** works with a wide range of hardware and provides many apps for every market in the Google Play Store. Its flexibility means you can customize it easily, though customizing the OS can make it more difficult to use.
- **iOS** is well designed, stylish, and easy to use. Its features are dependable and can be supplemented with secure apps from the Apple App Store. On the other hand, iOS runs only on Apple mobile devices and offers few personalization features.
- **Windows Phone** integrates Office apps with desktop applications, and allows more personalization than iOS (though less than Android). Not as many apps have been developed for Windows Phone as for Android and iOS.
- **BlackBerry** focuses on communication with its universal inbox. It is limited by the number of apps developed for the BlackBerry OS, which runs only on BlackBerry devices.

File Basics

file | executable file | data file | filenaming convention | extension | directory | path | kilobyte | megabyte | gigabyte | read-only file | file format | native format | Clipboard | source folder | destination folder | compress | extract | archive | backup

You've been working away on a screenplay that is sure to make a big splash as a hit movie. Now what do you do to preserve your creative work and send it off to a Hollywood agent? You save the screenplay as a file on your computer.

Figure 3-24: Working with files

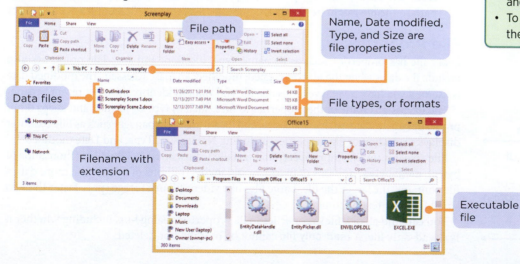

Chapter 3: System Software 3-21

Defining Files

What exactly is a computer file? It's a named collection of data on a storage medium such as a hard disk or USB flash drive. A **file** provides a compact way to store data, whether it's a document, photo, video, email message, computer program, or music.

Files can be divided into two categories. The first category is **executable files**, which are programs containing instructions that tell your computer how to perform, or execute, specific tasks. When you select a program to start, the computer runs the program's executable file.

The second category is **data files**, which contain data such as words, numbers, and pictures that you can manipulate. For example, a document you create or open using Word is a data file.

Naming Files

Every file on a computer has a name. When you save a file, you must give it a name that follows rules called **filenaming conventions**. See **Figure 3-25**.

Each OS has its own filenaming conventions. For example, Windows and Mac OS X filenames can contain up to 255 characters, including spaces and numbers. Windows does not allow filenames to contain some symbols like the asterisk or slash, while Mac OS X prohibits only the colon.

Most filenames include an **extension**, or short identifier separated from the main part of the filename by a dot, as in Screenplay Scene 1.docx. File extensions provide clues about a file's contents. For example, .docx files are Word documents. Windows .exe files and Mac OS X .app files are executable files containing computer programs. Applications automatically add the correct extension when you save a data file.

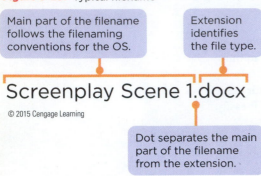

Figure 3-25: Typical filename

Main part of the filename follows the filenaming conventions for the OS.

Extension identifies the file type.

Dot separates the main part of the filename from the extension.

Screenplay Scene 1.docx

© 2015 Cengage Learning

Storing Files

To open or save a file, you must know the file's location, which is one of the storage devices on your computer.

- Windows and Linux identify each storage device by a device letter. For example, the main hard disk is usually drive C.
- Instead of using letters, Mac OS assigns a name to each storage device. For example, the main hard disk is called Macintosh HD.
- For each storage device on your computer, the OS maintains a list of files called a **directory**. The main directory is the root directory, which can be divided into smaller lists. Each list is called a subdirectory, or folder.
- To indicate a file's location, you use a file specification, or **path**. On a PC, a path includes the drive letter, one or more folder names, the filename, and the extension. The parts of the file path are separated by a backslash or an arrow. So, the path to the file might be C:/My Documents/Screenplays/Screenplay Scene 1.docx

File Properties

Every file has properties such as its name, type, location, and size. File properties also include the dates when the file was created, modified, and last accessed. The modified date is useful if you have several versions of a file and want to identify the most recent version.

The OS assigns some of the properties to files, such as type or format, and keeps other properties up-to-date, such as date, size, and location. A file manager such as File Explorer displays a selection of file properties, including Name, Size, Type, and Date modified.

File size is a significant property and usually is measured in **kilobytes** (thousands of bytes), **megabytes** (millions of bytes), or **gigabytes** (billions of bytes). The more data a file contains, the larger the file. Large files like videos fill up storage space faster than do small files like text documents.

You can find all of a file's properties in its Properties dialog box, including whether it is a read-only file. A **read-only file** cannot be modified or deleted.

#syssoftware

Every file has a different set of unique properties, which can vary depending on file type. For example, a song has a Contributing artists property, while a text document does not.

File Formats

File format refers to the organization and layout of data in the file. For example, text files have a file format different from those of graphics files. Graphics data can be stored in many file formats, such as JPEG or PNG. The file extension usually reflects the file format.

If you change a graphics file named Beach.jpg to Beach.docx, however, the file is still stored in the JPEG format, not the Word format. The data elements in the file are arranged in a way unique to JPEG files.

An application can always work with files in its **native format**, which is the format of files created in that application. An application might also work with other formats. For example, Word can work with doc files, docx files, and rtf files. An application typically lists these file formats in its Open dialog box. For example, **Figure 3-26** shows native file formats for Word.

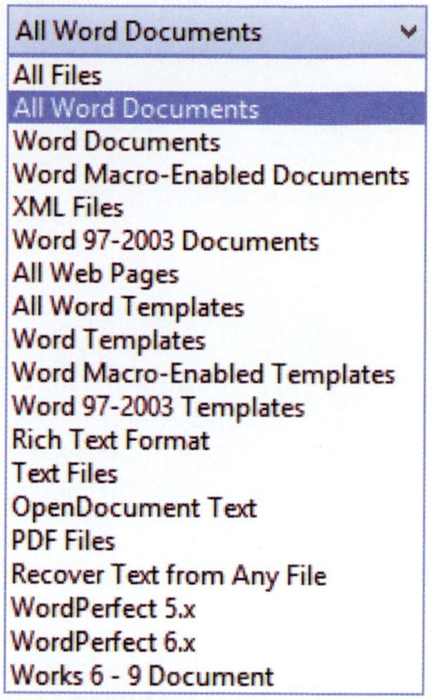

Selecting and Copying Files

If you want to copy or move more than one file from one location to another, you must first select the files. **Table 3-7** lists methods of selecting files using Windows 7 or Windows 8.x. If you select a group of files but want to remove one from the group, you can deselect, or clear the file's selection. The same methods work with folders.

After you select files, you can copy or move them using one of several methods. Some methods use the **Clipboard**, a temporary holding area for files and information that you copy or move from one place (the **source folder**) and plan to use somewhere else (the **destination folder**). **Table 3-8** lists the methods for copying and moving files in Windows 7 and Windows 8.x. The same methods apply to folders.

Figure 3-26: Microsoft Word file formats

All Word Documents ⌄
All Files
All Word Documents
Word Documents
Word Macro-Enabled Documents
XML Files
Word 97-2003 Documents
All Web Pages
All Word Templates
Word Templates
Word Macro-Enabled Templates
Word 97-2003 Templates
Rich Text Format
Text Files
OpenDocument Text
PDF Files
Recover Text from Any File
WordPerfect 5.x
WordPerfect 6.x
Works 6 - 9 Document

Table 3-7: Methods of selecting files

To select	Use this method
Files listed sequentially in a folder window	Click the first item, hold down the SHIFT key, click the last item, and then release the SHIFT key.
Files not listed sequentially in a folder window	Press and hold the CTRL key, click each item you want to select, and then release the CTRL key.
All files in a folder window	Click the **Select all** button in the Select group on the Home tab or press the CTRL+A keys.
To clear	**Use this method**
One file in a group of selected files	Press and hold the CTRL key, click each file you want to remove from the selection, and then release the CTRL key.
All files in a group of selected files	Click a blank area of the folder window.

Table 3-8: Methods of copying and moving files

Method	How to copy	How to move
Shortcut menu	Right-click a file, click Copy on the shortcut menu, right-click the destination folder, and then click Paste.	Right-click a file, click Cut on the shortcut menu, right-click the destination folder, and then click Paste.
Key combination	Click a file, press the CTRL+C keys, click the destination folder, and then press the CTRL+V keys.	Click a file, press the CTRL+X keys, click the destination folder, and then press the CTRL+V keys.
Drag	If the destination folder is on a different drive, drag a file to the destination folder; if on the same drive, press and hold CTRL while dragging.	If the destination folder is on the same drive, drag a file to the destination folder.
Right-drag	Using a mouse, point to a file, hold down the right mouse button, and then drag the file to a new location. Release the mouse button, and then click Copy here on the shortcut menu.	Using a mouse, point to a file, hold down the right mouse button, and then drag the file to a new location. Release the mouse button, and then click Move here on the shortcut menu.

© 2015 Cengage Learning

Compressing and Uncompressing Files

You can **compress** one or more files so they use less space when stored on a disk. You often need to compress files before you transfer them, such as when you attach files to an email message before sending it to someone else. Before you can open and edit a compressed file, you must uncompress it, or **extract** it.

PC operating systems include utilities for compressing files. Mobile operating systems often do not include file compression utilities, though you can install file compression apps such as PKZip and WinZip. A compressed file usually has a .zip extension and is called an **archive**.

To compress files in Windows, do the following:
- Select the files you want to compress.
- Right-click the selected files, point to **Send to** on the shortcut menu, and then click **Compressed (zipped) folder**.

The compressed file has the same name as the file you right-clicked, but uses a .zip extension.

To uncompress files in Windows, do the following:
- Double-click the compressed file (the one with a .zip extension).
- Select the files you want to extract, and then drag them to a folder.

Backing Up Files

#syssoftware

In Windows 8.x, the backup software is called File History. Once an hour by default, it creates backup copies of files you created or modified. The backup software in Mac OS X is called Time Machine, and it works in a similar way.

Have you ever deleted or copied over an important document? Have you lost files after a power failure or virus infection? Everyone has experienced these types of data disasters. You can't prevent all data disasters, so you need to create **backups**, or copies of files that you store in case the original files are damaged. A backup is a special type of file that allows you to restore data to the original storage location or a replacement device. Backup software can monitor the files on your hard disk, watch for changes, and then make the same changes to files in your backup, which is usually contained on an external hard drive or online server.

To protect your data, frequently back up all the folders containing data files using a backup utility provided by your operating system or a software vendor. To protect your entire system, occasionally create a full system backup.

Working with Folders and Libraries

library | folder

Managing files is an essential skill to master when you work with computers. It allows you to store important data, give files meaningful names, and find files quickly. You store files in folders and subfolders with descriptive names in much the same way you store paper documents in labeled folders in a file cabinet. Windows also includes **libraries**, which display folders and files from multiple locations.

Understanding Digital Folders

Imagine storing a list of your favorite musicians and movies, 25 video DVDs, 100 music CDs, and an entire music history book in a file folder. The amazing thing about storing files on a computer is that all of these items (or their digital equivalents) can be stored in a single **folder** on your computer's hard drive.

The easiest way to think of a digital folder is to consider the metaphor of a paper folder. You can move documents from one folder to another in a file cabinet, and you can move folders to different drawers. You can also rename folders by changing the name on the label. You can do all of this with digital folders as well.

Understanding Libraries

In Windows, libraries let you access files from different folders as if the files were all stored together. For example, you might store some music files in your private Music folder and others in a public folder that you share with your family. Your Music library displays files from both of those folders.

The Bottom Line
- You can store hundreds or even thousands of files on your computer's hard drive, online on a cloud storage site, or on another storage medium.
- You should master file management so that after you store, copy, move, and rename files, you can find them easily again.

Figure 3-27: Using folders and libraries

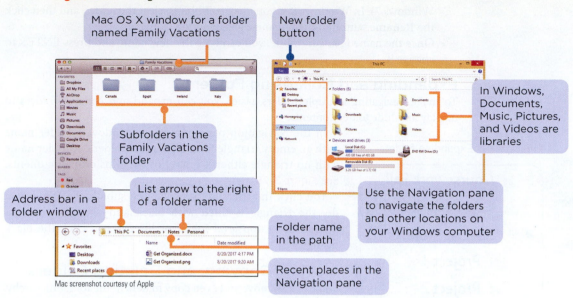

Mac OS X window for a folder named Family Vacations

New folder button

In Windows, Documents, Music, Pictures, and Videos are libraries

Subfolders in the Family Vacations folder

Use the Navigation pane to navigate the folders and other locations on your Windows computer

Address bar in a folder window

List arrow to the right of a folder name

Folder name in the path

Recent places in the Navigation pane

Mac screenshot courtesy of Apple

- By default, Windows includes libraries for Documents, Music, Pictures, and Videos; but you can also add your own libraries.
- You can see which folders are included in a library by clicking the library name in the Navigation pane of a folder window. When you look at the listing in the right pane, however, the different locations of the folders are transparent to you.

Navigating Folders

Folders let you store your documents in ways that make sense to you. You can customize folder names, folder hierarchy, and folder contents so that the organization of your data is logical and consistent with the way you work.

If you are taking courses at school, for example, you can store your documents for each semester in a folder, then for each course in separate folders within each semester. Each folder can have many subfolders, so for each course you can have folders for notes, papers, or whatever you want. You can navigate among folders using a few different methods:

- You can double-click a folder to open it.
- You can also click a folder name in the path shown in the Address bar to open the folder.
- Clicking a list arrow to the right of a folder name in the path displays a list of subfolders. You can click a subfolder name to open it.
- You can also select a folder name and click the **Open** button.
- You can type the path to the folder in the Address bar.

Imagine that you recently saw a file that you want to work with, but have forgotten where you stored it. You can use the Recent Places feature to find the file. To do so, click Recent Places under Favorites in the left pane.

Creating and Renaming Folders

You can create a new folder in a file management system such as Windows Explorer, File Explorer, or Finder. For example, you might want to add a folder to your Pictures library for photos you took during spring break.

Create a folder: In Windows, you click the **New folder** button to create a new folder. Windows gives the new folder the default name "New folder," but you can replace the default name with one that's more descriptive.

Rename a folder: You can also rename an existing folder in three ways:

- You can right-click the folder name and then click **Rename** on the shortcut menu.
- You can also click the folder name to select it and then click it again to make it editable.

#syssoftware

Windows and Mac OS X use "folder" as the term for a file container. Many distributions of Linux use the term "directory" instead.

- Finally, you can select the folder, click the **Organize** button, and click **Rename** (in Windows 7). In Windows 8.x, you use the Ribbon: select the folder, and then click the **Rename** button in the Organize group on the Home tab.
- Once the name is in edit mode, you can type the new name and press ENTER to change it.

Expanding and Collapsing Folders

To make navigating multiple folders easier, you can expand and collapse folders to display and hide folder contents.

In the Navigation pane of a folder window, a folder name with an empty triangle to its left has subfolders. A folder name with no triangle either is empty or contains only documents. See **Figure 3-28**.

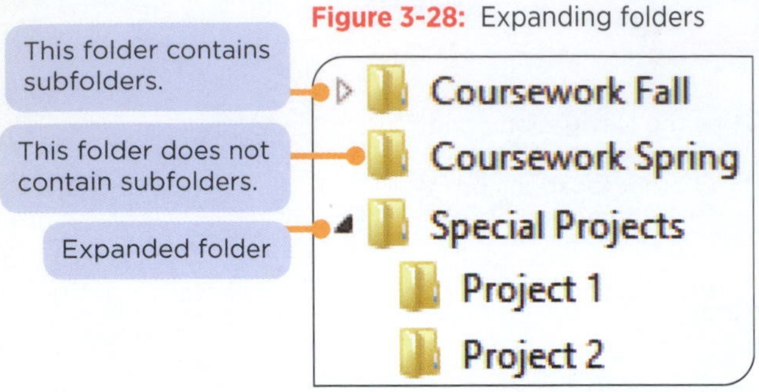

You click the triangle to display the subfolders. When you do, the triangle is filled with black and changes position. To collapse a top level folder or library, you click the black triangle.

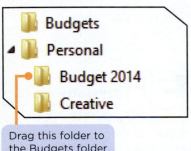

Figure 3-28: Expanding folders

This folder contains subfolders.

This folder does not contain subfolders.

Expanded folder

Moving, Copying, and Deleting Folders

You can also move and even copy folders in the folder hierarchy. Moving a folder moves its contents as well. Copying a folder also makes a copy of its contents.

For example, the Personal folder in **Figure 3-29** contains a subfolder called Budget 2014. You want to move that folder to the Budgets folder where it belongs.

- **Move a folder**: To move a folder, select it and then drag it over the name of the folder you want to move it to. As you drag, the words "Move to" appear in front of the name of the destination folder. If you move the folder by mistake, you can press CTRL+Z to move it back to its original location.
- **Copy a folder**: If you want to copy a folder and its contents instead of moving it, you can press the CTRL key as you drag. When you do, the words "Copy to" appear in front of the name of the destination folder.
- **Delete a folder**: You can delete folders in the folder hierarchy. Deleting a folder also deletes its contents.

The easiest way to delete a folder is to select the folder and then press the DELETE key. You can also right-click the folder name and click **Delete** on the shortcut menu; or you can click the folder name, click the **Organize** button, and then click **Delete** on the shortcut menu.

No matter which method you use to delete a folder, you will be prompted to confirm the deletion before the operation is complete. If you delete a folder by mistake, you can either undo the deletion by pressing CTRL+Z or restore the folder using the Recycle Bin.

Figure 3-29: Moving folders

Drag this folder to the Budgets folder to move it there.

File Management

Save command | Save As command | USB port | cloud | OneDrive

You often need to save files you receive from others, usually as attachments to email messages, or those you download from Web sites. If you are creating or editing a file, you should also save it frequently so you don't lose your work. File management rules apply to all types of files, whether they are spreadsheets, photographs, or documents.

Using Save and Save As

The first time you select a command to save a file on a PC, the operating system displays the Save As dialog box, which includes controls that let you specify where to store the file and what filename to use. **Figure 3-30** shows the Save As dialog box for Windows 8.1.

The Bottom Line
- Save your files on your hard drive, flash drive, or to the cloud so you can easily access them later.
- You should know how to navigate your computer so you can find and open files you've saved.

Figure 3-30: Save As dialog box

Suppose that after saving the file shown in Figure 3-30, which is a Word document, you open it and then make a few changes. Now you have two choices for saving the file:

- **Save command**: Use the Save command to save a document with the same name and in the same location. For example, in Word, you select the Save button on the Quick Access toolbar to save the document without changing its filename or storage location.

- **Save As command**: Use the Save As command to save the document using the Save As dialog box to specify a different name, file type, or storage location. In Word, you click the File tab to display the Save As command.

Saving a File to a Location on Your Hard Drive

The Save As dialog box is displayed when you save a file for the first time or when you select the Save As command. The Save As dialog box selects a storage location as follows:

- **New files**: By default, most operating systems save particular types of files in certain locations on your hard drive. For example, when you save a new document in Windows 8.1, the operating system presents the Documents folder as the storage location.

- **Existing files**: When you save an existing file, the operating system assumes you want to save the file in its current location. For example, if you open a document from the Projects folder in the Documents folder, and then select the Save As command to save the document, Windows displays the Projects folder as the storage location.

In either case, you can use the controls in the Save As dialog box to navigate to a different location. The following steps explain how to use the Windows 8.1 Save As dialog box to save a file in a folder on your hard drive.

1. **Open the Save As dialog box.**

   Use the Save command for new files or the Save As command for other files.

2. **Verify the current location.**

   The Address bar in the Save As dialog box shows the current folder. You can widen the dialog box to display the complete location in the Address bar. The Documents, Downloads, Music, Pictures, and Videos folders (and their subfolders) are on your hard drive and are good places to save your files.

3. **Navigate to the folder on your hard drive where you want to save the file**.

In the Navigation pane, click an expand icon next to a location such as the Documents folder to display the folders it contains. Continue clicking expand icons until the folder where you want to save the file is displayed in the Navigation pane.

4. **Select the folder where you want to save the file**.

In the Navigation pane, click the folder to select it. You can also double-click a folder in the right pane to select and open the folder.

5. **Save the file**.

Click the **Save** button in the Save As dialog box to save the file.

Saving a File to a Flash Drive

When you save a file to a flash drive, you are saving it in a location that is a storage device separate from your hard drive. The advantage of using a flash drive is that you can remove it from a computer and then use it on a different computer.

To save a file to a flash drive, first place the drive in a **USB port** on your computer. The USB port is a rectangular slot on your computer where you can attach a flash drive. You then open the Save As dialog box as you do for any other location: use the Save command to save a file for the first time and use the Save As command to save an existing file to a different location. The following steps explain how to save a file to a flash drive using Windows 8.1.

1. **Attach the flash drive to your computer, and then open the Save As dialog box**.

Insert the flash drive into a USB port on your computer, if necessary. Use the Save command for new files or the Save As command for other files.

2. **Verify the current location**.

The Address bar in the Save As dialog box shows the current folder. Unless you opened the file from the flash drive, the current folder is probably on the hard drive.

3. **Navigate to the flash drive**.

In the Navigation pane, click the expand icon next to This PC to display its locations, if necessary. The flash drive usually has a name similar to "Removable Disk" and a drive letter other than C. For example, your flash drive might appear as Removable Disk (E:).

4. **Select the folder where you want to save the file**.

Click the expand icon next to the flash drive name, and then click a folder on the flash drive to select it.

5. **Save the file**.

Type a filename, and then click the **Save** button in the Save As dialog box to save the file in the folder you selected.

Saving a File to OneDrive

Besides saving files on your hard drive or a flash drive attached to your computer, you can save them in the **cloud**, which is a storage location on a server. You can access files stored on the cloud from any device connected to the Internet. Microsoft Office applications can use OneDrive, a Microsoft product for saving files in the cloud. When you sign up for a Microsoft account, Microsoft creates a OneDrive for you and reserves space in it for your files. If you are using Windows 8.x on your own computer and use your email address as your username, you most likely have a Microsoft account. (You must have a Microsoft account to use OneDrive.)

The following steps explain how to save a Microsoft Office 2013 file to your OneDrive.

1. **Display the Save As options in Backstage view**.

Click the **FILE** tab, and then click **Save As** to display the Save As options. See **Figure 3-31**.

Hot Technology Now

If you don't have a Microsoft account, you can sign up for one by using your browser to go to outlook.com or to search for "Sign up for Microsoft account."

Figure 3-31: Saving a file to your OneDrive

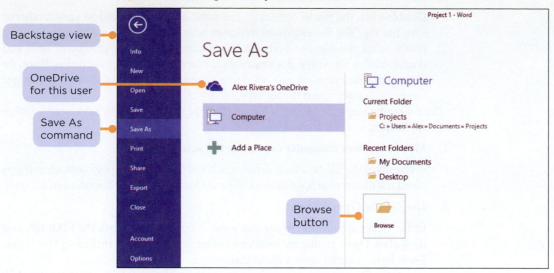

2. **Select your OneDrive**.

   Your OneDrive appears with your name in the Save As list, as in "Alex Rivera's OneDrive."

3. **Navigate to a folder on your OneDrive**.

   Click the **Browse** button to open the Save As dialog box, which displays folders on your OneDrive, including Documents, Favorites, and Public by default.

4. **Open the folder where you want to save the file**.

   Double-click the OneDrive folder where you want to save the file.

5. **Save the file**.

   Type a filename, and then click the **Save** button in the Save As dialog box to save the file.

Opening a Saved File

You open a saved file using the same techniques as when saving the file, except you use a different dialog box or window. In most PC operating systems, you can use a file manager such as File Explorer in Windows 8.x or the Finder in Mac OS X to open a saved file. If you are working in an application, you use the Open dialog box to open a file.

The following steps explain how to use the File Explorer in Windows 8.1 to open a file saved on your hard drive or flash drive.

1. **Make sure your computer can access the saved file**.

   If you saved the file on a flash drive, attach the flash drive to your computer. If you saved the file on your hard drive, your computer can access it.

2. **Open File Explorer**.

   Display the desktop, and then click the File Explorer icon on the taskbar to open a File Explorer window.

3. **Navigate to the location of the saved file**.

   In the Navigation pane, click the expand icon next to This PC to display its locations, including the flash drive. If you saved the file on a hard drive, click to expand icons as necessary to display the folder containing the file.

4. **Open the folder containing the saved file**.

   In the Navigation pane, click the folder containing the saved file to display the file in the right pane.

5. **Open the file.**

Double-click the file to open it in the same application used to create, edit, or save the file. The file extension indicates which application will start when you double-click the file. For example, Word files have a .docx extension, so if you double-click a file with a .docx extension, Word starts and opens the file. If you do not see the file extension, the operating system is hiding it by default. You might see icons that represent the file type.

The following steps explain how to use the Open dialog box in a Microsoft Office 2013 application to open a saved file.

1. **Make sure your computer can access the saved file.**

If you saved the file on a flash drive, attach the flash drive to your computer. If you saved the file on your hard drive or in your OneDrive, your computer can access it.

2. **Display the Open screen.**

In the Office application where you want to open the file, click the **FILE** tab, and then click **Open** to display locations containing your files, including OneDrive. From here, you can open a file in three ways:
- If the file you want to open appears in the list of recent files on the right, click the filename to open the file.
- If you saved the file in your OneDrive, select your OneDrive, which appears with your name in the Open list, as in "Alex Rivera's OneDrive," and then click the **Browse** button to display the Open dialog box.
- If you saved the file on a flash drive or hard drive, select **Computer**, and then click the **Browse** button to display the Open dialog box.

3. **Open the folder containing the saved file.**

Use the tools in the Open dialog box to open the folder containing the saved file. For example, double-click a OneDrive folder to display its contents or use the Navigation pane to display the contents of a folder on a flash drive.

4. **Open the file.**

Double-click the file to open it in the current application.

Customizing Microsoft Windows

default setting | shortcut icon | desktop theme | screen resolution | native resolution | screen saver | sound scheme | pinned item | user account | administrator account | standard account | guest account

When you start working with a new computer, you use its **default settings**—those the operating system sets during installation. The defaults are great, at first. As you learn your way around the computer, you'll probably want to change some settings to make your computer experience more pleasant and productive.

Figure 3-32: Customizing the Start screen and desktop

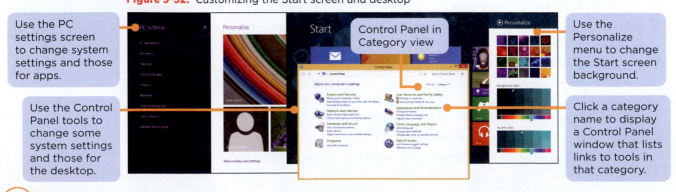

Use the PC settings screen to change system settings and those for apps.

Use the Control Panel tools to change some system settings and those for the desktop.

Control Panel in Category view

Use the Personalize menu to change the Start screen background.

Click a category name to display a Control Panel window that lists links to tools in that category.

Parts of the Desktop

You're ready to organize photos, watch videos, and play games on your new PC. Where do you start? The desktop. By default, the main area of the Windows desktop contains only the Recycle Bin icon. The Recycle Bin holds files selected for deletion.

You can use the Desktop Icon Settings dialog box to add icons to the desktop, such as the Computer icon, which you open to display the drives on your computer. See **Figure 3-33**.

Another type of icon you can add to the desktop is a **shortcut icon**, which is indicated by a small arrow next to an icon that illustrates the application or program. You double-click a shortcut icon to run a program or open a file.

One way to customize the desktop is to move the taskbar. You also can make the taskbar larger, add toolbars to it, and hide the taskbar when you're not using it.

Control Panel

When you're ready to fine-tune Windows so it looks and works the way you want it to, head for the Control Panel, a collection of tools for customizing Windows. You can use the Control Panel in the following ways:

- By default, the Control Panel appears in Category view, which organizes the tools into groups. You can click the arrow beside the View by button and then switch to Small icons or Large icons view to display the tools as icons.
- Click an icon to open a window or dialog box where you can customize Windows settings, such as security settings in the Action Center window.
- In Category view, click a category name to display a Control Panel window that lists links to tools in that category. You also can click a link within a category to open a window or dialog box to change settings.

Display Settings

If you want to set your Windows computer apart from other computers, you can start by customizing your desktop.

In the Appearance and Personalization category, the Control Panel provides options for changing the appearance of your desktop and windows. If you select the Personalization link, the Personalization window opens, shown in **Figure 3-34** on the next page.

A quick way to customize many settings at the same time is to select a **desktop theme**, which is a predefined set of elements such as background images and colors.

You also can adjust the screen resolution and color quality for up to two monitors. **Screen resolution** defines the number of pixels on a screen. If you set your screen resolution for more pixels, you can see more content on a screen without scrolling. Your monitor has an ideal setting, which is called its **native resolution**, but you can change it to suit your work style.

Screen Savers and Sounds

Fun and security don't usually go together, but you can have both in one tool: a **screen saver**, which plays animations on your computer screen and hides work in progress while you're away from your computer.

A screen saver is a set of animated images that appears after your computer is idle for a certain amount of time. When you move the mouse or press a key, the screen returns to its previous state. To secure a Windows computer, you can set the screen saver to request a password before it stops playing.

Another Windows setting you can personalize is the **sound scheme**, a set of sounds applied to Windows events, such as closing a program. Use the Sound dialog box to select a sound scheme or change individual sounds, such as the one that plays when you exit Windows.

Taskbar

The Windows taskbar contains the Start button, pinned items, program buttons, and the notification area. (Windows 8 does not have a Start button, though it does display a Start screen thumbnail when you point to the left edge of the taskbar.)

#syssoftware

Windows 8.x provides apps on the Start screen for organizing photos, watching videos, and playing games.

Figure 3-33: Desktop and shortcut icons

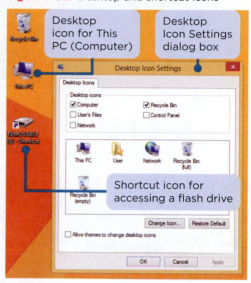

On the Job Now

Many businesses and schools use screen savers that promote new products or class offerings.

Figure 3-34: Personalization window

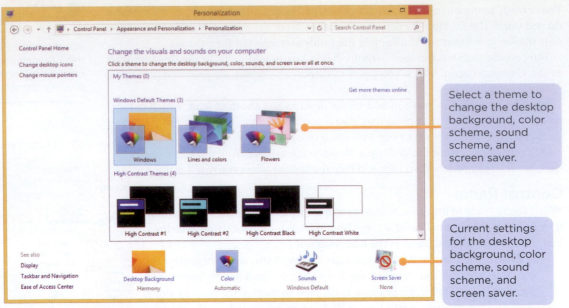

Select a theme to change the desktop background, color scheme, sound scheme, and screen saver.

Current settings for the desktop background, color scheme, sound scheme, and screen saver.

- **Pinned items**: By default, the Windows 7 taskbar includes three pinned items: program icons for Internet Explorer, Windows Explorer, and Windows Media Player. (Windows 8.x has two pinned items: icons for Internet Explorer and File Explorer.) A **pinned item** is an icon that always appears on the taskbar.
- **Window buttons**: Other taskbar buttons are for open windows. If you open two or more windows in a single program, the windows are grouped on one taskbar button. You can change this setting to display each window as a separate button. You can drag taskbar buttons, including pinned items, to rearrange them in the order you prefer.
- **Notification area**: To keep the notification area free from clutter, you can select the icons you want to display all the time. To display the other icons, click the Show hidden icons button.

Keyboard and Mouse

If you want to change how your keyboard responds to your keystrokes when working in Windows, click the Keyboard link in the Small icons or Large icons view of the Control Panel. This opens the Keyboard Properties dialog box, where you can change the following settings:

- **Repeat delay**: Change the Repeat delay, or how long you hold down a key before the computer starts displaying repeat characters. To make the repeated characters appear more quickly or slowly, change the Repeat rate.
- **Pointing device**: Click the Mouse link in the Control Panel to customize your pointing device, which might be a mouse, trackpad, or pointing stick.
- **Left and right mouse buttons**: If you're left-handed, you can reverse the mouse buttons so you use the right button to select items and the left button to display shortcut menus.
- **Pointer shapes**: On the Pointers tab, you can customize pointers that appear when you select objects, for example, or resize windows.

User Accounts

User accounts protect your computer against unauthorized access. A user account includes information such as a user name, or user ID, and a password. A user account also includes permissions that indicate which files and folders you can access and what changes you can make to the computer. Finally, a user account keeps track of your personal preferences, such as your desktop theme or screen saver.

Windows offers three types of user accounts: administrator, standard, and guest. The type of account determines how much control the user has over the computer. See **Figure 3-35**.

#syssoftware

Go to **twitter.com**, then search for **@SAMTechNow**, the book's Twitter account, and follow @SAMTechNow to get tweets on your home page.

Figure 3-35: Windows user accounts

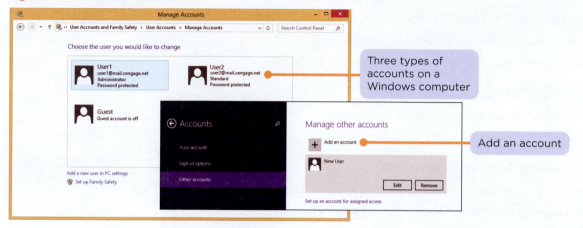

- **Administrator account:** The first account you set up on a new Windows computer is an administrator account, an account that has full access to the computer. For example, you use this account to add other user accounts.
- **Standard account:** This type of account is designed for everyday computing. It can protect your computer and data by preventing users from changing settings that affect all users. You can access the files and folders in your account, but not the files and folders of other users.
- **Guest account:** This type of account provides temporary access to a computer, but does not allow any changes to settings or software.

Chapter Review

Introduction to System Software

1. What is system software and what types of programs does it include?
2. What is the difference between system software and application software?

Operating Systems

3. How does an operating system manage memory?
4. What are the three main categories of operating systems?

Common Operating System Tasks

5. What are the four resources that an operating system manages?
6. What types of computer tasks does an operating system typically handle?

Managing Your Computer's Windows

7. Name three window elements that all operating systems have in common.
8. Explain how to switch windows in various operating systems.

Common Operating System Features

9. Name five features that operating systems with graphical user interfaces share.
10. What is the purpose of a disk utility? What is the purpose of a file utility?

Comparing PC Operating Systems

11. What are four popular PC operating systems in use today?
12. Compare the strengths and weaknesses of Windows with those of Mac OS X.

Comparing Mobile Operating Systems

13. What is a mobile operating system? What are the four popular mobile operating systems in use today?

File Basics

14. What is a file? What are the two main categories of files you use on a computer?
15. What is significant about file formats?

Working with Folders and Libraries

16. Describe two ways to open a folder in Windows operating system.

File Management

17. What is the main difference between the Save command and the Save As command?
18. Describe one way to open a file using an Office application.

Customizing Microsoft Windows

19. What tool do you use to customize the Windows desktop?
20. What is a desktop theme?

Test Your Knowledge Now

1. _____ software is the software that runs a computer.
   a. Application
   b. File management
   c. System
   d. GUI

2. _____ software performs a specific, limited task, usually related to managing or maintaining a computer system.
   a. Utility
   b. Management
   c. Background
   d. Backup

3. The _____ is the set of programs that manages and coordinates all the activities on your computer.
   a. file manager
   b. operating system
   c. disk cleanup software
   d. boot process

4. Most operating systems use _____ to perform many tasks simultaneously, such as running two or more programs.
   a. multiprocessing
   b. multitasking
   c. multithreading
   d. parallel processing

5. During startup, the computer performs the _____ to check crucial system components.
   a. power-on self-test (POST)
   b. read-only memory (ROM) test
   c. spooling check
   d. buffer verification

6. To control a hardware resource, the OS communicates with a(n) _____, a small program that tells the OS how to interact with that device.
   a. application
   b. hardware utility
   c. control program
   d. device driver

7. A _____ is a rectangular area on the screen that displays the contents of a program, file, or folder.
   a. button
   b. user interface
   c. menu
   d. window

8. _____ contain controls that you use to select options and enter information to indicate exactly how you want the program to perform the command.
   a. Dialog boxes
   b. Menus
   c. Option buttons
   d. Icons

9. A _____ utility reduces the size of a file so it takes up less storage space on a disk.
   a. disk cleanup
   b. file compression
   c. file management
   d. search

10. Four popular PC operating systems are Windows, Mac OS X, Linux, and _____.
    a. Chrome
    b. iOS
    c. Blackberry OS
    d. Android

11. Developed by Google, _____ is a mobile OS based on Linux and is designed to run on many types of smartphones and tablets.
    a. Android
    b. Windows Phone
    c. iOS
    d. Linux Mobile

12. The BlackBerry interface uses _____, which reflect the most recent changes to an app.
    a. updating tiles
    b. active frames
    c. live icons
    d. static symbols

13. When you save a file, you must give it a name that follows rules called _____.
    a. file protocols
    b. filenaming conventions
    c. file drivers
    d. naming syntax

14. _____ refers to the organization and layout of data in the file.
    a. File layout
    b. File sector
    c. Fragmentation
    d. File format

15. By default, Windows includes _____ for Documents, Music, Pictures, and Videos.
    a. libraries
    b. drives
    c. utilities
    d. bookshelves

16. In the Navigation pane of a folder window, a folder name with a(n) _____ to its left has subfolders.
    a. triangle
    b. square
    c. circle
    d. arrow

17. Use the _____ command to save the document with the same name and in the same location.
    a. Save
    b. Save As
    c. Back up
    d. Rename

18. Microsoft Office applications can use _____ as a location for saving files, which is a storage location on a Microsoft server.
    a. OneDrive
    b. Windows Phone
    c. Windows Drive
    d. StorageDrive

19. A desktop _____ is a predefined set of elements for the desktop, such as background images and colors.
    a. Control Panel
    b. window
    c. theme
    d. picture

20. The first account you set up on a new Windows computer is a(n) _____ account, which you use to add other user accounts.
    a. guest
    b. standard
    c. system
    d. administrator

21. In the space next to each term below, write the letter of the phrase that defines it:
    a. path
    b. compress
    c. executable file
    d. boot process
    e. virtual memory

    _____ What you can do to one or more files so they use less space on a disk

    _____ A specification that includes a drive letter, one or more folder names, a filename, and an extension

    _____ A series of events that begin when you turn on the computer

    _____ What the operating system uses to gain memory when RAM is full

    _____ A program containing instructions that tell your computer how to perform specific tasks

Try This Now

1: Windows Help and Support

Note: This assignment requires the use of Windows 7 or a later version of Windows.

Technology continues to change, but knowing how to get answers to your questions using Help is important in any system software. Using the Search tool in Windows, type Help and Support to find help on using Windows. Answer the following questions using Help and Support and identify your version of Windows.

    a. What does the F1 keyboard shortcut do?
    b. What are the steps to create a user account?
    c. What are the steps to create a new folder?
    d. What settings can you control in Family Safety?
    e. How do you open Windows Updates?

2: Mac OS X Support

Being versatile and switching from a Windows PC to a Mac is helpful in the business world. Using a Mac computer or the site apple.com, search for the OS X support Web pages, and then answer the following questions by searching the help topics. Also, if you are using a Mac, be sure to identify your version of Mac OS X.

    a. What does the F11 keyboard shortcut do?
    b. What are the steps to create a folder?
    c. Mac OS X includes VoiceOver, a built-in screen reader that describes aloud what appears on your screen and speaks the text in documents, Web pages, and windows. How do you turn on VoiceOver?

3: Mobile Operating Systems

The latest versions of Android, Apple, and Microsoft phones offer exciting new features in their latest mobile operating systems.

    a. Select one of the three major mobile smartphone platforms. If money were no object, which new phone model would you select today? What is the price of this phone?
    b. List eight new features of your select mobile OS.
    c. Write a paragraph on your favorite new feature.

Mobile OS

© iStockphoto.com/Carpe89

Critical Thinking Now

1: What's New in Windows?

A new generation of updated features is available in the latest operating system produced by Microsoft. Research the latest version of Windows and create a table with five of the latest features in the first column and an explanation of each feature in the second column.

2: What's New in Mac?

Cutting-edge technology is showcased within the newest Mac OS X. Research the latest version of the Mac OS X and create a table with five of the latest features in the first column and an explanation of each feature in the second column.

3: Mac and Microsoft Accessibility Features

Both Mac and Microsoft operating systems come standard with assistive technologies that help people with disabilities enjoy the power and simplicity of their computers. Mac OS X includes features such as VoiceOver, Zoom, and Dictation, while Microsoft includes the Ease of Access Center. These features are centerpieces for assistive OS technologies. Research these accessibility features and write a paper of 200 words or more about how these features are designed with a range of abilities in mind.

Ethical Issues Now

When smartphones first emerged in the workplace, businesses often provided the same smartphone model for every employee to use for work purposes. The Information Technology (IT) department could control these similar phones, but in recent years, bring-your-own-device (BYOD) adoption rates at companies are being driven upward by employees who want to cut the corporate desk phone cord and prefer using their favorite mobile operating system.

Mobile devices are turning into true business tools, but IT departments are very concerned with the increased risk the BYOD trend introduces. They don't want sensitive business information supporting critical functions being vulnerable to attacks on employees' smartphones and tablets.

a. Research the BYOD trend and write 150 words or more describing examples and issues of mobile security.

b. Research the advantages and disadvantages of having your smartphone or tablet with you anywhere, making any coffee shop into your office.

c. Write at least 150 words on these advantages and disadvantages.

Team Up Now – Wolfram Alpha Data Analysis

Wolfram Alpha is a data knowledge engine developed by Wolfram ResearchShare. Wolfram Alpha connects to online databases worldwide to answer your questions. Each team member should perform the following searches at the Wolfram Alpha Web site (wolframalpha.com).

a. What is the population of your birth city?

b. How common is your first name?

c. What is the median salary of a career field of interest?

d. Where was the strongest earthquake in the world in the last 24 hours? What was its magnitude?

e. Determine the number of calories in your most recent meal.

f. What was the weather in your birth city on the day you were born?

g. Locate the price of gas from a neighboring state or province and compare it to that from your state or province.

As a team, compare your responses. For each of the questions, locate the sources at the bottom of each of the results pages. List one of the sources for each of the responses. Submit the responses and sources of each of the team members to your instructor.

Key Terms

active frame	desktop	gigabyte
active window	desktop theme	graphical user interface (GUI)
administrator account	destination folder	guest account
Android	device driver	hub
archive	dialog box	icon
backup	directory	input
BlackBerry	disk cleanup utility	iOS
boot process	distribution	kernel
bootstrap program	Dock	kilobyte
buffer	DOS	library
button	embedded OS	Linux
check box	executable file	live tile
Chrome OS	extension	Mac OS X
Clipboard	extract	Maximize button
Close button	file	megabyte
cloud	file compression utility	menu
command-line interface	file format	Minimize button
compress	file management utility	mobile operating system (OS)
data file	filenaming convention	multiprocessing
decompress	folder	multitasking
default setting	folder window	multithreading
defragmentation utility	General Public License (GPL)	native format

native resolution
network OS
notification area
OneDrive
operating system (OS)
option button
output
page file
parallel processing
path
personal computer (PC) operating
   system
pinned item
Plug and Play (PnP)
power-on self-test (POST)
process
program window
RAM (random access memory)

read-only file
Recycle Bin
resource
ROM (read-only memory)
Save command
Save As command
screen resolution
screen saver
sector
server OS
service pack
shortcut icon
smartphone
Snap
sound scheme
source folder
spooling
standard account

submenu
swap file
system software
tablet
taskbar
tile
touchscreen
update
USB port
user account
user interface
virtual memory
Web application
widget
window
Windows
Windows Phone

Application Software

Willow is working on her chemistry lab using Microsoft Excel and Microsoft Word. She finds her lab instructions online using her school's class management software.

Using Excel spreadsheets, Willow is recording her findings using formulas and converting appropriate units. Part of the lab requires graphing her findings using a 3D clustered column chart.

Using a Word document, Willow summarizes her findings in an MLA cited report.

© iStockphoto.com/tetmc

Willow Tyrell is majoring in chemistry. She uses application software such as Microsoft Office to record, catalog, analyze, store, and report laboratory test data. Microsoft Excel spreadsheets can simplify sophisticated formulas and graphs.

Microsoft® product screenshots used with permission from Microsoft® Corporation.

Introduction to Application Software

application software program | software application | app | local application | portable application | Web-based application | mobile application | word processing | spreadsheet | presentation | database | graphics | mobile app | convergence

Whether you're listening to music, writing a paper, searching the Web, or checking your email on your mobile phone, chances are you are using application software. **Application software programs** (also called **software applications** or just **apps**) help you perform a task when you are using a computer or smartphone.

Figure 4-1: Applications cover a wide range of features and functions

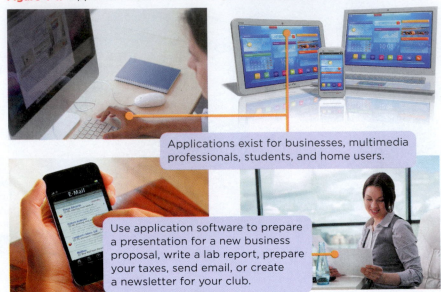

Applications exist for businesses, multimedia professionals, students, and home users.

Use application software to prepare a presentation for a new business proposal, write a lab report, prepare your taxes, send email, or create a newsletter for your club.

© auremar/Shutterstock.com, © Hasloo Group Production Studio/Shutterstock.com, pizuttipics/Fotolia, Scanrail/Fotolia

On the Job Now

While IT departments have traditionally viewed mobile device support as a separate topic from desktop support, the growing use of mobile devices in the workplace are requiring them to support multiple platforms, as the BYOD (bring your own device) trend continues.

Accessing Applications

Software applications can be categorized by how you access them or by the device on which you use them. **Local applications** are installed on your computer's hard drive. They tend to be programs with lots of features and functionality. Microsoft Office is a popular suite of applications for word processing, spreadsheets, databases, email, and presentations. It can be installed locally on a computer.

Portable applications are stored on and run from portable removable storage devices such as CDs, DVDs, or flash drives. You connect the storage device to a computer to run the application. Portable applications save valuable space on your computer. OpenOffice.org Portable is a portable application suite offering programs similar to Microsoft Office products.

Web-based applications are programs that you access over the Internet in a browser on your computer or as an app on your mobile device. Because they run off the Internet, Web-based apps often offer collaboration features that installed apps can't handle. The files you create are typically stored online along with the program. Google Docs, as well as Microsoft Office 365, are Web-based applications used for creating documents, spreadsheets, databases, and presentations. Unlike Microsoft Office, which you purchase and can use as long as you want, Microsoft Office 365 is a renewable subscription service with pricing options for different users. **Mobile applications** work on your smartphone or tablet. Though they can be limited in functionality, mobile apps give you on-the-go computing capabilities. See **Figure 4-2**.

#appsoftware

Google Drive provides 15GB of free online storage for the files that you create with your Web-based applications.

Common Features

Application software programs have many common features; they
- are usually represented on the desktop by an icon.
- can be started by double-click or tapping the icon.

- open in a window on your desktop.
- are identified by a title bar at the top of the program.
- have menu commands that you use to tell the computer what to do.
- have buttons you click or tap to issue commands or perform other actions.

Figure 4-2: Web-based applications

Mobile applications work on your smartphone or tablet.

You can access Web-based applications anywhere you have an Internet connection.

dny3d/Fotolia, mipan/Fotolia

To save your work, you create a file that stores the information and data from the program. You give each file a unique filename. The program might automatically add a dot (.) and a file extension to the name, which identifies the file type, such as .docx for a Word file or .xlsx for an Excel file or .jpeg for an image file. You might be familiar with PDF files; PDF stands for Portable Document Format; these files are readable in Adobe Reader, a free program.

Application Types

Some of the most popular application software programs include word processing, spreadsheet, database, graphics, and presentation software, as well as mobile apps. See **Table 4-1**.

#appsoftware

You can use Microsoft Office programs to save your files in the .pdf format so you can share your files with others who might not have the Office programs.

Table 4-1: Application types

Application type	Use to
Word processing	Create, edit, format, view, print, and publish documents.
Spreadsheet	Perform numerical analysis and enhance the appearance of data. Spreadsheet files can include numbers, charts, graphics, text blocks, and data tables.
Presentation	Create electronic slides for presentations. Presentation files can include pictures, charts, audio, video, and animation.
Database	Create and manage databases with a few items, or up to thousands, even millions, of items, such as customers or inventory items.
Graphics	Create, view, manipulate, and print digital images such as photos, drawings, clip art, and diagrams.
Mobile apps	Get directions, play games, browse the Web, create lists, manage calendars, send email, and communicate with others on mobile devices such as smartphones and tablets.

© 2015 Cengage Learning

Hot Technology Now

Most software designers build apps for all three platforms—Android, iOS, and Windows—to reach a larger mobile audience.

Future Applications

Convergence and mobility are key trends in application software. **Convergence** means that the distinction between "categories" of application software is becoming more blurred. Computing is also becoming increasingly mobile. Application software is moving from the hard drive to more portable devices and networks such as flash drives, smartphones, and the Web. See **Figure 4-3**.

Figure 4-3: Convergence of applications

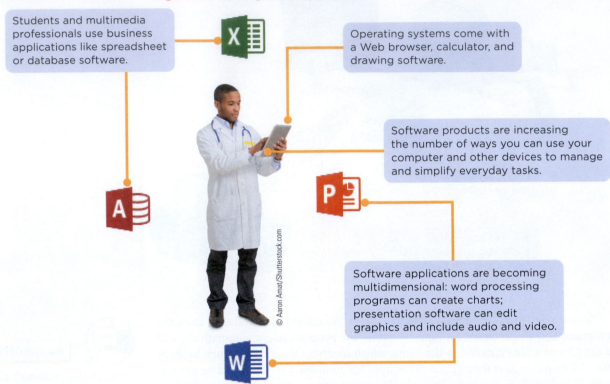

Students and multimedia professionals use business applications like spreadsheet or database software.

Operating systems come with a Web browser, calculator, and drawing software.

Software products are increasing the number of ways you can use your computer and other devices to manage and simplify everyday tasks.

Software applications are becoming multidimensional: word processing programs can create charts; presentation software can edit graphics and include audio and video.

© Aaron Amat/Shutterstock.com

The Bottom Line
- Creating documents electronically allows you to create, edit, format, and manage your work easily.
- Word processors have text and document formatting options as well as document management tools.

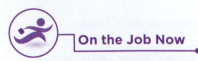

On the Job Now

Some of the most popular word processing programs used on the job today include Microsoft Word, Apple iWork Pages, Corel WordPerfect, and OpenOffice Writer.

Word Processing

word processing software | document | insertion point | document management tools | format | font type | font size | point | font style | font color | indent | tab | alignment | line spacing | paragraph spacing | margin | bullet | page break | page orientation | template | desktop publishing (DTP) software | Web development software | speech recognition software

Have you written a research paper lately? How about a letter? If yes, then chances are you used **word processing software**, one of the most widely used types of application software.

Key Features

Although the user interface and functionality of word processing programs may differ, all programs share some common key features. The files you create are called **documents**, which are organized into pages. When you start a word processing program, a blank document opens on the screen. The screen displays an **insertion point** to mark your place and a scrolling mechanism to navigate the screen. You have access to variety of commands and options you can use to create the document.

You use the keyboard to type letters and numbers, and the corresponding characters appear on the screen. Some programs also make it possible for you to speak into a microphone; the program translates your words into text to create a document. As you type, or enter text, the word processing software automatically "wraps" words onto a new line. When the text fills a page, new text automatically flows onto the next page.

Figure 4-4: Word processors can create many types of documents

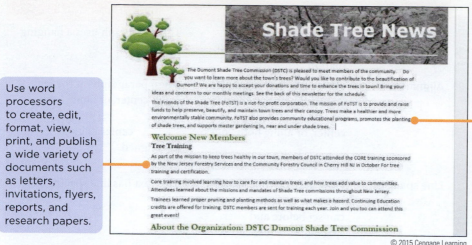

Use word processors to create, edit, format, view, print, and publish a wide variety of documents such as letters, invitations, flyers, reports, and research papers.

Businesses use word processing programs to create memos, contracts, invoices, and marketing brochures.

© 2015 Cengage Learning

Formatting features modify the appearance of a document. Editing, review, reference, and graphics capabilities enhance document content. **Document management tools** protect and organize files and let you collaborate with others.

Text Formatting

Formatting tools change the appearance of a document. You can highlight important information, make text easier to read, and add flair to your document.

You **format** text by changing the font type, size, style, color, and effects. Most programs provide a wide range of font types, styles, colors, and effects. See **Table 4-2**.

Table 4-2: Text formatting options

Format option	Description and use	Examples
Font type	Defines what characters look like. Some fonts have rounded letters; others are more angular. Some are formal; others are more casual.	Times New Roman Comic Sans MS ALGERIAN
Font size	Determines the size of the character, measured in **points**; each point is 1/72 of an inch; change the title font to be bigger than the rest of your text or use smaller fonts for footnotes or endnotes.	This text is 12 points This text is 18 points
Font style	Adds visual effects features to text; bolding text makes it stand out on the page, shadow gives it depth, underlining and italicizing text provide emphasis.	**bold** shadow underline *italics* highlighting
Font color	Determines the color of each character and adds interest; be sure to use font colors that show up well against the document background.	Red text Blue text Green text

© 2015 Cengage Learning

#appsoftware

You can add further interest with text effects such as reflection, strikethrough, shadowing, edges, and outlining.

Document Formatting

To give a document a cohesive appearance, you can apply styles and features to a whole document, or to paragraphs or sections of a document. Good formatting improves a document's appearance and readability by creating visual balance, controlling white space, and enhancing layouts. See **Table 4-3** on the next page.

Table 4-3: Document formatting options

Format option	Determines	Example/Description
Indent and **tab**	Where text begins on a line in relation to the left margin	This paragraph uses a hanging indent.

Alignment	How a line or paragraph is placed between the two margins on the page: right, center, or along both edges	Align paragraphs at the left, right, center, or along both edges:
		        center aligned
		left aligned
		              right aligned

Line spacing	How much "white space" between each line of text; can set before and after spacing; can be measured in points	This text has line spacing set to 2.0.
Paragraph spacing	How much "white space" between each paragraph; can set before and after spacing; measured in points; affects document length	These paragraphs have 6 points of line spacing after each one. These paragraphs have 6 points of line spacing after each one.
Margins	Where text begins from the left side of a page and where it begins to wrap on the right side of the page; you also set top and bottom margins	Narrow margins make a wider line, or more text on the page.
Bullets	The placement of a character before each line of text	This is a bulleted list: • Apples • Pears • Plums

© 2015 Cengage Learning

You can determine how the text is placed on the page. When creating a document, you can also insert manual **page breaks** to specify a specific location for a new page to begin. A manual page break will start a new page no matter how much text is on that page. **Page orientation** can be portrait or landscape. You can also insert borders around paragraphs and pages to create a specific style, for example for a document that is a menu or invitation.

You can forgo all formatting decisions by creating documents from pre-formatted templates. **Templates** are documents that contain document formatting such as margins, fonts, and page layouts that you use to create new documents. They are available for common types of documents such as letters, flyers, invitations, and legal contracts. Most word processing programs provide a collection of built-in templates; you can find even more on the Internet.

Advanced Features

Word processing programs provide tools to improve document content and appearance, making it easier for you to create documents. Some of these features are listed below:

- **Spelling- and grammar-checking tools** find and fix errors.
- **Research tools** help you find just the right word, search online to check facts, and provide topic-related information.
- **Language tools** translate passages and help create multi-lingual documents.
- **Tables** and **columns** organize data.

On the Job Now

You can create a professional document using built-in Microsoft Office templates such as a purchase order, press release, memo, bill of sale, sample proposal, meeting minutes, or invoice.

- **Graphics** such as photographs, clip art, logos, charts, and screenshots illustrate ideas and add visual appeal.
- **Headers** and **footers** display document information such as title, page number, date, and author on every page.
- **Reference features** follow standard style guidelines and add professionalism to reports with tables of contents, bibliographies, footnotes, citations, and index.
- **Hyperlinks** direct readers to related documents, email addresses, or Web sites.

Document Management

Word processing software offers document management tools that you use to edit, share, protect, and save your documents. Tools that make it easy to edit, delete, and rearrange text within a document are essential parts of any word processor. Even more useful are the tools that you can use to copy text and graphics from one document to another. See **Figure 4-5**.

Figure 4-5: Creating a document with text and graphics

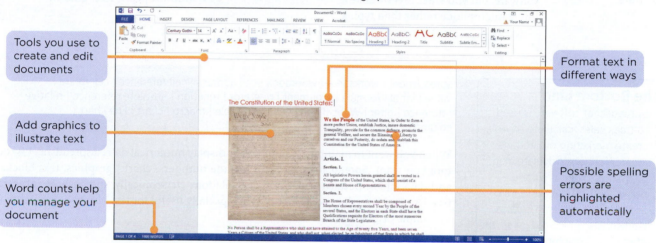

Tools you use to create and edit documents

Format text in different ways

Add graphics to illustrate text

Possible spelling errors are highlighted automatically

Word counts help you manage your document

When working collaboratively on documents, multiple users can read and edit a document simultaneously. Changes and edits can be tracked by the individual, compared between users, and merged into a final document. You can prevent unwanted changes by marking a document as "read-only" to disable editing. You can also restrict access by setting a password. When you are done working, save your file as a Word document, a text document, or in other formats such as Portable Document Format (PDF), a Web page, or in an earlier version of your word processing software if you need to share it with others.

Practical Applications

Who uses word processors? **Table 4-4** summarizes how word processing software is used by all types of people to create all sorts of documents.

#appsoftware

You can send documents as email attachments or share files using a cloud computing service.

Table 4-4: How word processors are used

Who uses word processing	For what purpose	To create
Businesses executives, office workers, medical professionals, politicians, and lawyers	Communications and documentation; mail merge for mass mailings	Agendas, memos, contracts, proposals, letters, reports, email, newsletters, personalized bulk mailings and labels
Personal	Daily activities	Letters, event flyers, and checklists
Students	Academic tasks	Essays, reports, stories, lab reports, and resumes
Conference promoters, personal event planners	Special events	Business cards, postcards, invitations, conference tent cards, name tags, gift tags, and stickers
Web designers	Convert documents to HTML	Documents to be published as Web pages

Related Programs

Some key features of word processing software are incorporated into related types of application software, such as desktop publishing, Web development software, and speech to text programs. See **Table 4-5**.

Table 4-5: Programs related to word processors

Related program	Function	Use to create	Examples of programs
Desktop publishing (DTP) software	Combines word processing with advanced graphics capabilities	Flyers, newsletters	QuarkXPress, Adobe InDesign, and Microsoft Publisher
Web development software	Allows non-technical users to create Web pages by automatically coding text with HTML tags	Web pages	iWeb, Adobe Dreamweaver, and Amaya
Speech recognition software	Has many features of word processing software, but you enter text by talking into a microphone rather than typing	Documents	Dragon Naturally Speaking and Windows Speech Recognition

© 2015 Cengage Learning

Spreadsheets

spreadsheet | worksheet | workbook | cell address | cell reference | cell range | value | label | formula | argument | operator | function | absolute reference | relative reference | filter | What-If analysis | pivot table | macro | chart | line chart | column chart

When you want to manipulate numbers or display numerical data, a spreadsheet is the tool you want. **Spreadsheet** files can include numbers, charts, graphics, text blocks, and data tables. Because it performs calculations electronically, spreadsheet software (see **Figure 4-6**) reduces data errors. It is especially useful for tasks involving repetitive or complex calculations.

Worksheet Basics

Spreadsheet software has many common features. See **Figure 4-7**.

A **cell range** is a group of cells. Cell ranges can be adjacent, with all cells touching, or nonadjacent, where not all cells are touching. To enter data in a worksheet, you click a cell to make it active and type the desired characters. You can also copy or import

Figure 4-6: Spreadsheet software

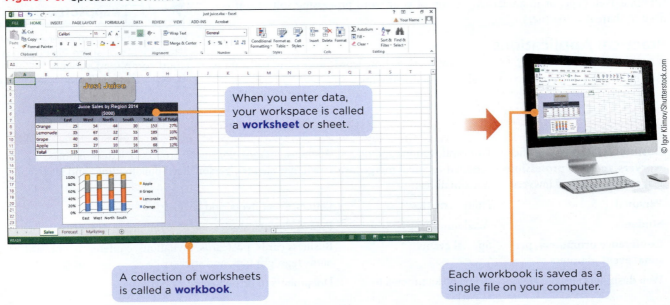

When you enter data, your workspace is called a **worksheet** or sheet.

A collection of worksheets is called a **workbook**.

Each workbook is saved as a single file on your computer.

© Igor Klimov/Shutterstock.com

Figure 4-7: Basic features of spreadsheet software

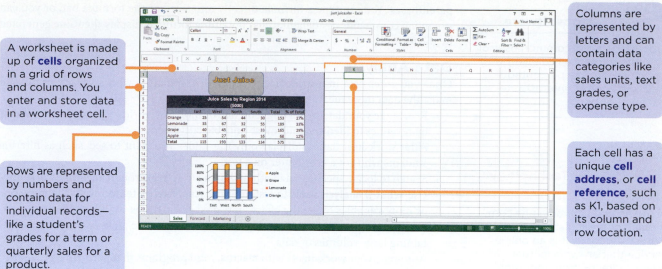

A worksheet is made up of **cells** organized in a grid of rows and columns. You enter and store data in a worksheet cell.

Rows are represented by numbers and contain data for individual records— like a student's grades for a term or quarterly sales for a product.

Columns are represented by letters and can contain data categories like sales units, text grades, or expense type.

Each cell has a unique **cell address**, or **cell reference**, such as K1, based on its column and row location.

data into a cell. You navigate a worksheet using scroll bars and arrows, move to other worksheets by clicking sheet tabs, and find formatting and data analysis commands on menus.

Key Features

You use spreadsheet software to create, edit, and format worksheets. To create a worksheet, you enter values, labels, and formulas into cells. A **value** is a number, a **label** is descriptive text, and a **formula** performs a calculation that generates a value. Editing tools let you modify worksheet data. You can change a cell value, move and copy cells, or delete cells. When you change a cell value, spreadsheet software typically recalculates the entire worksheet automatically. You can also insert or delete entire rows and columns.

Spreadsheet software often includes many additional features such as

- formatting tools to change a worksheet's appearance.
- page layout and view features to change the zoom level, divide a worksheet into panes, or freeze rows and columns to make large worksheets easier to read.
- file management features to control how you save, save files in other formats, and let multiple users share a workbook.
- printing features print a workbook let you control whether you print entire worksheets or parts of one.
- web capabilities to share workbooks online, insert hyperlinks, and save worksheets as Web pages.

Formulas and Functions

Spreadsheet software performs numerical analysis using formulas and functions. A formula contains a calculation, which specifies the operation to be performed, and **arguments**, which are the values involved in the calculation. To enter a calculation, you use mathematical **operators**, such as "+" or "−," or functions. Formulas can contain multiple mathematical operators and functions.

A **function** is a predefined calculation such as SUM or AVERAGE. Spreadsheet programs provide a wide variety of functions. For example, logical functions such as IF and AND test data conditions. Financial functions such as RATE and PMT calculate interest rates and loan payments.

Formula arguments can be values or cell references. An **absolute reference** refers to a fixed cell location that never changes. A **relative reference** identifies a cell by its location relative to other cells and changes when a formula is moved or copied.

Hot Technology Now

Popular spreadsheet programs include Microsoft Excel, Corel Quattro Pro, Apple Numbers, and OpenOffice Calc.

On the Job Now

Almost every occupation uses spreadsheets, including accountants, project managers, supervisors, business analysts, inventory specialists, and sales.

Formulas and functions begin with an equal sign (=); arguments are enclosed in parentheses. You can type a formula directly into a cell or the formula bar, or you can use menu commands. By default, cells containing formulas display the value generated by the formula.

Data Analysis

Once you enter data in a worksheet, you can manipulate it with a variety of tools to make the data more meaningful.

- Rearrange your data by sorting it on one or more categories; you might sort clients by revenues to identify your most valuable customers.
- **Filter** worksheet data to display only the values you want to see, such as filtering students who got a B or better on a test.
- Search to locate specific data without having to scroll through an entire worksheet.
- Use **What-If analysis** tools to test multiple scenarios by temporarily changing one or more variables to see the effect on related calculations.
- Use **pivot tables** to create meaningful data summaries to analyze worksheets containing large volumes of data.
- Automate your worksheets with **macros**, mini programs that perform a predefined action that you have to repeat frequently by just clicking a button.

Charting

Another important feature of spreadsheet software is the ability to create charts. **Charts** are graphical representations of data that visually illustrate relationships and patterns.

The most popular types of charts are line charts, column charts, and pie charts. Other chart types include scatter, radar, doughnut, stock, surface, area, and bubble. A **line chart** tracks trends over time. A **column chart** compares categories of data to one another, and a pie chart compares parts (or slices) to the whole. Each type of chart has multiple layout options. You can choose the chart type and layout that best suit your data. See **Figure 4-8**.

Figure 4-8: Charts in a spreadsheet

To create a chart, select a data range and choose a chart type, layout, and location.

When you modify any values in the data range for the chart, the chart updates automatically.

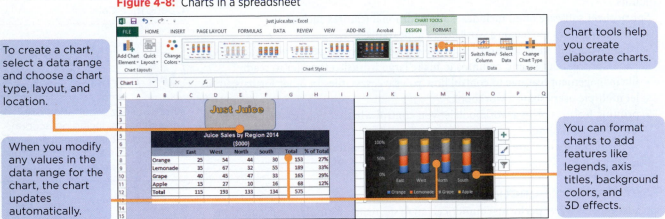

Chart tools help you create elaborate charts.

You can format charts to add features like legends, axis titles, background colors, and 3D effects.

Formatting

You can change how a worksheet looks using formatting features as well as by inserting elements, such as graphics. Formatting highlights important data and makes worksheets easier to read; elements enhance a worksheet. When you format a number, the underlying value remains the same even if its outward appearance changes. See **Table 4-6**.

Spreadsheet software has helpful features. You can create rules to automatically format cells based on their values. For example, you can specify that all cells with a value greater than 10% have a yellow fill color and bold text. Tables are specially formatted data ranges with built-in sorting and filtering capabilities. Most spreadsheet programs provide templates for common applications such as calendars, invoices, and budgets.

Table 4-6: Formatting a spreadsheet

Formatting option	Use to	Example
Currency	Identify currency value such as euros, pounds, or dollars	$4.50 or £4.50 or €4.50
Decimal places	Display additional level of accuracy	4.50 4.500, 4.5003
Font types, colors, styles, and effects	Emphasize text and numbers	4.50 4.500, *4.5003*
Alignment	Align text across cells for a title heading; center, or left- or right-align labels or values	Student Scores 75 80 95
Borders and shading	Enhance the worksheet	Student Scores 75 80 95
Cell height and width	Emphasize certain cells	Student Scores 75 80 95 88
Photographs, clip art, shapes, and other graphics	Illustrate a point; can format, reposition, and resize	☺ Student Scores 75 80 95 88
Headers and footers	Create professional reports	Bergen Data Analysis: Fall Report Page 3 of 5

Practical Applications

Spreadsheet software originated as an electronic alternative to paper spreadsheets used by bookkeepers and accountants to track sales and expenses. Use of the software expanded to other departments, and spreadsheet software remains popular with business users to this day. Spreadsheet software, originally used for accounting, has evolved to become popular with a wide range of users for a multitude of purposes.

- **Sales managers** use spreadsheet software to track sales by product, region, and salesperson.
- **Human resource managers** create time sheets, track hours, and calculate payroll.
- **Marketing managers** analyze buying behaviors and project future sales.

Spreadsheet software is also widely used outside of the business world.

- **Scientists, mathematicians, and economists** use spreadsheet software to model data and identify trends.
- **Home users** can make checklists, calculate loan payments, plan budgets, and maintain checking account registers.
- **Students and teachers** can create personal calendars and schedules and track and calculate grades.

Presentation Software

presentation software | thumbnail | slide master | animation | transition

Presentation software (see **Figure 4-9** on the next page) lets you create electronic slides for slide shows that can be viewed on a single computer, on a projection device, or over the Internet. You can share your ideas in person or on paper, or create a presentation that runs unattended in a kiosk, such as a booth at a trade show or airport.

Presentation Software Basics

You use presentation software to create a series of slides to visually display your messages or ideas. Each slide has a specific layout based on its content, and each layout contains placeholders for text and graphics.

The Bottom Line

- Slides in presentations contain graphics, text, video, and other media; slides are enhanced with transitions and animations.
- Presentation software is used to supplement lectures, classroom projects, and public meetings.
- Presentations are an essential tool for businesses and educators, and can create award certificates, calendars, cards, and invitations.

Figure 4-9: A presentation presents ideas

You can present your ideas in a concise multimedia format with pictures, charts, audio, video, animation, and even recorded narration.

© sita ram/Shutterstock.com, © Yganko/Shutterstock.com, © Pokomeda/Shutterstock.com, mostafa fawzy/Fotolia

As you work, you can display presentations in different views. Some views divide the program window into multiple panes, or sections, such as slide, outline, or notes panes. You click slide objects to select them. When you click a text box to edit text, an insertion point marks your place.

You navigate between slides using scroll bars or arrows. In some views, you can drag **thumbnails**, small versions of each slide, to change the order of slides in the presentation. Each program has a unique set of tools to format, edit, and enhance slides in the presentation.

Slide Content

Slides can contain text, graphics, and audio and video clips. See **Table 4-7**.

Table 4-7: Slide content

Slide content	How to enter	Provides
Text in a paragraph or bulleted list	Click a placeholder and type, or copy and paste text from another file.	Content; most programs offer a variety of bullet styles, including number and picture bullets
Graphics such as line art, photographs, clip art, drawn objects, diagrams, data tables, charts, and screenshots	Click a content placeholder, draw directly on the slide, or copy and paste a graphic from another file.	Illustrations to convey meaning and information for the slide content
Media clips, such as video and audio, including recorded narrations	Click a content placeholder and choose a file, or insert the file directly onto a slide by recording it.	Media content to enhance a slide show
Links	Click content placeholder, copy and paste links from a Web site or type the link directly.	Links to another slide, another document, or a Web page
Embedded objects	Click menu commands or a content placeholder.	External files in a slide

© 2015 Cengage Learning

Basic Formatting

In addition to content, slides include formatting, which is applied to text, objects, individual slides, or entire presentations.

- Text formatting options are similar to what you find in word processing software; choose font types, sizes, colors, and styles such as italics or bold.
- Change text direction, align text on a slide or within a text box, and add text effects such as shadows or reflections.
- Objects can be formatted by modifying fill colors and by adding styles, outlines, and effects.
- Graphics can be resized to make them larger or smaller; you can even rotate a graphic or change its shape.

- You can move objects to different locations on a slide and change their placement relative to other objects. You can modify alignment and join objects to form a group.

Designing and Presenting

When you create a slide presentation, there are several guidelines that you can follow to help you succeed at your task and create an effective presentation.

- **Be mindful of your target venue and audience:** Is your presentation going to be viewed in a large lecture hall? Over the Web by hundreds of people, in a kiosk? Answers to these questions can help you create slides to meet the needs. Web presentations should use graphics best designed for Web sites.
- **Limit your words:** Slides should supplement a presenter's lecture or speech and should have limited text. You want the audience to use the slides as a guideline and listen to the speaker. Many use the 6×6 rule as a guide; no more than six lines of text with no more than six words per line.
- **Use graphics wisely:** Be tasteful and careful in your selection of graphics. You don't want to overwhelm your audience with a barrage of meaningless pictures. Also consider the copyright and verify that you have permission to use any graphic that you didn't create yourself.
- **Don't overuse transitions and animations:** PowerPoint has a vast collection of visual motion effects called transitions and animations that you can use in a presentation. But you want the audience focusing on the content, not the elaborate effects on the screen. Pick one or two transitions and apply them to the entire presentation; use animations sparingly—only when they add to the content on the slides.
- **Consider accessibility factors:** Color blindness affects a portion of our population, so do not use red and green to distinguish content. Also, use large fonts to help readers with the text; fonts on slides should be no smaller that 20pt.
- **Use the Spelling and Grammar Feature:** No matter how much effort you put into a presentation, if your slides have spelling and grammar errors, your content will lose credibility. PowerPoint comes with a built-in grammar and spelling checker—use it before releasing your slides.

Advanced Formatting

You can format an individual slide or an entire presentation. Adding headers and footers lets you display the presentation title, slide number, date, or other information on a single slide or all slides automatically.

You can choose your own formatting options with slide masters. A **slide master** automatically applies any new formatting to all slides in your presentation that use that master. You can change slide orientation or modify slide dimensions. See **Figure 4-10**.

By The Numbers Now

Based on an IDC study, Microsoft PowerPoint and Microsoft Word rank in the top ten job skills most in demand for the top high-growth, high-salary jobs of the future.

Figure 4-10: Advanced formatting

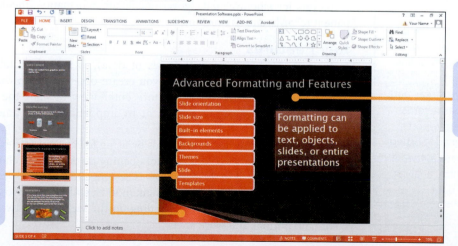

Built-in themes coordinate colors, fonts, and effects to give consistency and polish to a presentation.

Slide background designs enhance the look and feel of your presentation.

You can also use built-in templates for common slide designs such as diagrams, calendars, business and academic presentations, awards, and more.

Animations

To liven up your presentation, you might try **animation**—adding movement to an object or text. Most programs offer a variety of animations, such as entrance, exit, and emphasis, each with a number of options. A photograph can "fade in" as you display a slide, or an object can "fly in" from the side.

You can set animations to start manually when you click the mouse or automatically when you advance a slide. You can also set the duration of an animation effect. Animations can move horizontally, vertically, or diagonally across the slide. You can set the order for multiple animations. For example, you can animate an entire bulleted list to appear at once or you can animate bullets to appear one at a time.

Transitions

Transitions are actions that occur as you move from slide to slide in a presentation. For example, you can make your new slide appear to fade in with a "ripple" effect, or "push" the existing slide off the screen as it comes into view.

Transitions have several options you can control. You can change the direction, set the duration, and add sound effects; you can apply a transition to all slides or just selected slides in the presentation. Like animations, you can set transitions to start with a mouse click or after a set amount of time.

Display Options

The purpose of a presentation is to show it to other people. You can share and display your presentation in a variety of formats. Slide shows can be presented on a computer screen or projected onto a larger screen for an audience. You can run slide shows manually, with the presenter controlling slide order and advancement. Or you can set up a self-running slide show that runs automatically in a kiosk at a trade show or convention. You can print paper copies of your slides, such as handouts that show multiple slides per page, and include notes or comments.

Most presentation programs have Web capabilities that let you post and share presentations online. Colleagues or classmates can view a presentation remotely and collaborate on its design.

Databases

database | record | table | form | query | report | view | field | field name | data type | property | relational database | sort | filter | server

A **database** is a collection of data, organized and stored electronically. Database software lets you create and manage databases. Databases are used by businesses for inventories, employers for employee data, governments for information, medical professionals for patient records, and so much more.

Key Features

Data, organized into **records** (rows of data), is stored in tables in a database. When you use database software, you create objects, which can be **tables**, **forms**, **queries**, or **reports** that you use to store, enter, view, or share the data. You can enter data manually, a record at a time, or by importing larger amounts of data from external files.

You input data and navigate records by using forms. You retrieve data using queries and print reports to view results. After opening an object, you choose a view, depending on what you need to do. Each **view** is designed to perform specific tasks. You enter and edit data in some views. You design, modify, and format layouts of reports, forms, tables, and queries in others. Depending on the view, the software displays different command options and work areas.

The Bottom Line

- Personal computer database software is designed for small businesses and individuals, and some database software programs are designed for large, commercial databases, such as online retail sites or airline reservation systems.
- Database software stores data in tables in fields as records.
- Forms, queries, and reports, as well as filtering and sorting features in database software, are used to organize, analyze, access, and view data.

Figure 4-11: Databases

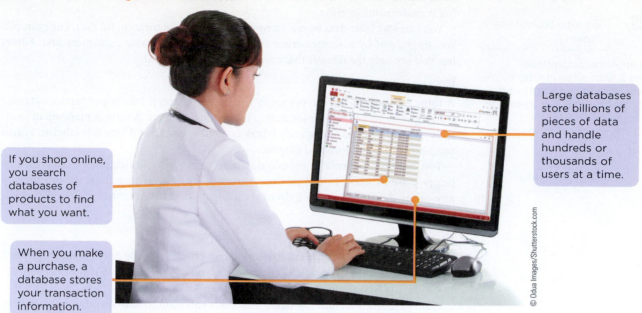

Large databases store billions of pieces of data and handle hundreds or thousands of users at a time.

If you shop online, you search databases of products to find what you want.

When you make a purchase, a database stores your transaction information.

© Odua Images/Shutterstock.com

Fields and Records

To understand databases, you need to understand how data is stored and organized. Each piece of data in a database is entered and stored in an area called a **field**, which is assigned a **field name**. Fields are defined by their **data type**, such as text, date, or number. The text data type stores data as characters that cannot be used in mathematical calculations. Logical data types store yes/no or true/false values. Hyperlinks store data as URL addresses. See **Figure 4-12**.

Hot Technology Now

Some of the most popular databases include Microsoft Access, Microsoft SQL Server, Oracle, and SAP databases.

Figure 4-12: Fields and records

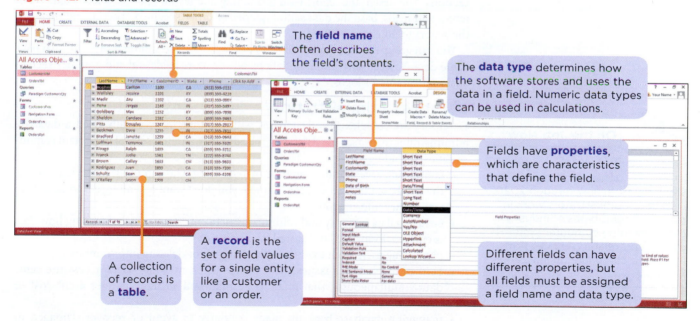

The **field name** often describes the field's contents.

The **data type** determines how the software stores and uses the data in a field. Numeric data types can be used in calculations.

Fields have **properties**, which are characteristics that define the field.

A **record** is the set of field values for a single entity like a customer or an order.

A collection of records is a **table**.

Different fields can have different properties, but all fields must be assigned a field name and data type.

Tables

Tables are organized in grids of rows and columns, much like worksheets. Tables store data for the database. Columns contain fields; rows contain records. A database can contain a single table or a collection of tables. Most database programs create **relational databases**, where two or more tables are related (connected). Relational

By the Numbers Now

When an Access database reaches 2 gigabytes in size, a business should consider using a larger database such as Microsoft SQL Server or Oracle.

databases link tables with common fields so that data doesn't have to be repeated, making it more prone to error.

You can **sort** table data by one or more fields to create meaningful lists. For example, you might sort by customer order amount to view high-value customers first. **Filters** lets you see only the records that contain criteria you specify.

Forms

A **form** is a database screen primarily used for data entry. Like paper forms, database forms guide users to fill in information in specified formats. A form is made up of "controls" or placeholders that specify where content is placed and how it is labeled. Forms can also contain buttons and graphics.

You can use controls to reduce data entry errors by limiting user choices. List boxes prompt users to choose items from a list, preventing them from entering any other data. Forms also help users navigate database records and find specific information.

Queries

A **query** extracts data from a database based on criteria that the query creator specifies. Criteria are conditions for a field. For example, you can use a query to find all customers in California who placed an order of more than $1000.

Query elements include the tables and fields you want to search and the parameters, or pieces of information, you want to find. You can use text criteria or logical operators to specify parameters. The query displays results in a datasheet, which you can view onscreen or print. You can save queries to run later; query results are updated using the current data in the tables each time you run the query.

Reports

A **report** is a user-designed layout of database content. Like forms, reports have label controls to describe data and other controls that contain values. You might prepare a monthly sales report listing top deals and agents or an inventory report to identify low-stock items. Most database programs provide tools to create reports. Report elements include the data set along with design elements such as headers, footers, titles, and sections. You design the report with formatting and layout options, select a data set of tables and fields, base the data set on queries or other specified criteria, and then run the report to populate it with data.

You can group data into categories and display totals and subtotals on fields that have value data. You can sort and filter data by one or more fields and add graphics such as charts, diagrams, or logos.

Database Administration

Databases are complex files. Databases with multiple users usually need a database administrator to oversee the database. The administrator has several important responsibilities, including

On the Job Now

Employment of database administrators is projected to grow substantially from now through 2020. Database administrators work in many different types of industries, including computer systems design and related services firms, insurance companies, banks, and hospitals.

- controlling access to the database by regulating who can use it and what parts of the database they can see; for example you don't want all employees to be able to view salary information.
- ensuring data integrity and minimizing data entry errors by controlling how data is entered, formatted, and stored.
- preventing users from inadvertently changing or deleting important data.
- controlling versions issues, which arise when multiple users access the same data simultaneously, that need to be managed so that changes aren't lost or overwritten.
- managing database back-up plans regularly to avoid or recover damaged or lost files.
- establishing and maintaining strict database security to protect susceptible data from attacks from hackers.

Using Databases

Databases have very significant roles in our world.

- Individuals might use database software on a personal computer to keep track of contacts, schedules, possessions, or collections.
- Small businesses might use database software to process orders, track inventory, maintain customer lists, or manage employee records.

Databases frequently acquire and share data from other sources. Because multiple users need access to the database, and databases can be quite large, the software generally runs on a shared computer called a **server**. Data can be exported data from a database into other programs, such as spreadsheets or word processors. You can convert database data to other formats, including HTML to publish it to the Web. In fact, Web-based databases are increasingly popular; even Facebook uses database software.

Although you may never need to create a database as large as the ones YouTube, Facebook, or iTunes use, database software is helpful for performing personal and professional data-related tasks.

#appsoftware

"Big data" refers to data collections so large and complex that it is difficult to process using traditional data applications. An example is how Amazon determines products that you might like based on your shopping patterns.

Graphics Software

bitmap | vector | pixel | red eye | filter | cropping

When you edit digital photos or create an image with a paint program, you're using graphics software. You can create, view, manipulate, and print many types of digital images using graphics software programs.

Figure 4-13: Using graphics software with bitmap or vector graphics

Bitmap image   Photo editing software   Vector graphic

Paint software

© 2015 Cengage Learning, © 2015 Cengage Learning, Photo courtesy of Rachel Bunin, dhipadas/Fotolia, Andrija Markovic/Fotolia

The Bottom Line

- Digital images can include photographs, drawings, clip art, diagrams, icons, and other graphics.
- Graphics software creates banners, flyers, newsletters, and company logos and includes paint software, drawing programs, and photo editing software.
- Graphics software tools include filters, cropping tools, paint brushes, and color palettes to change the size, color, shape, effects, and rotation of an image.

Image Formats

There are two kinds of digital images: **bitmap** and **vector**. Bitmap images are based on **pixels**—short for "picture elements." A bitmap assigns a color value to each pixel in a graphic. Together, the colored pixels give the illusion of continuity and result in a realistic-looking image. See **Figure 4-14**. A high-resolution photo can contain thousands of pixels, so bitmap files can be large and difficult to modify. Resizing a bitmap image can distort the image and decrease its resolution by decreasing the number of pixels per inch.

Vector graphics tend to be simple images such as shapes, lines, and diagrams. Clip art images are typically stored as vector graphics. Vector graphics use mathematical formulas instead of pixels to define their appearance.

Figure 4-14: Comparing bitmap to vector images

While not as detail-rich as bitmap images, vector graphic files are smaller and can be enlarged without losing image quality.

© RetroClipArt/Shutterstock.com, © Vitaly Korovin/Shutterstock.com, © Vitaly Korovin/Shutterstock.com

Some image-editing programs let you combine bitmap graphics and vector graphics in a single composition. A file containing both bitmap and vector graphics is called a metafile.

Key Features

Graphics software programs use a variety of drawing and editing tools to create, modify and enhance images. Image files include many formats. Common image formats are JPG, GIF, and PNG. You can use tools to change the size, color, shape, and rotation angle of a graphic. See **Table 4-8** for a summary of common graphics program features.

Paint Programs

You use paint software to create graphics by drawing or "painting" images on the screen. Most paint programs have limited capabilities and produce fairly simple bitmap images. Some programs also provide templates for adding graphics to popular documents such as greeting cards, labels, and business cards. See **Figure 4-15**.

By the Numbers Now

The JPG file format support 16 million colors and is best suited for photographs and complex graphics.

Table 4-8: Key features of graphics software programs

Feature	Description	Example
Freehand drawing	Use your mouse or a stylus to draw pictures on the screen; for example, choose a crayon, calligraphy pen, or airbrush style.	
Shape tools	Create straight lines and shapes.	
Color graphics	Use color palettes to fill shapes with color or create color brushstrokes, lines, and borders.	
Filters and effects	Add visual interest to graphics; add shadows, glowing edges, reflections, and textures.	Photo: Used with permission: Rachel Bunin
Text tools	Add explanatory or creative text to graphics; use interesting font types, colors, sizes, and styles.	Tools

© 2015 Cengage Learning

Figure 4-15: Paint program tools

Paint programs feature freehand drawing tools like pens, pencils, brushes, paints, and colors, as well as tools to draw or insert shapes and lines.

Editing tools add effects like shadows and glows, modify the color palette, create animations, and change borders, backgrounds, and fill colors. You can even change and create color palettes.

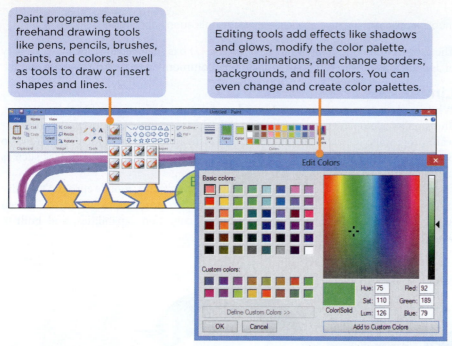

Drawing Programs

Drawing programs let you create simple images. Graphics created with drawing programs tend to look flat and almost cartoon-like. In contrast to paint software, drawing programs generally create vector graphics. One major advantage is that you can modify and resize them without changing image quality. Some drawing programs can layer graphics one on top of the other to create more complex graphics, or collages of images.

Drawing programs feature freehand drawing tools such as pens and brushes, as well as simple tools such as lines, shapes, and colors. You can use drawing programs to create original art, logos, diagrams, schematics, blueprints, business cards, and flyers.

Photo Editing Software

Photo editing software lets you edit, enhance, and customize digital photographs. Professional photographers, engineers, scientists, and just about any professional that works with photographs use photo editing software. Photo editing software brings out creativity in people and can be used for personal projects. In addition to sharing many of the features of other graphics software programs, photo editing software contains tools unique to manipulating photographs.

You can fix poor-quality photos by modifying individual pixels to correct discoloration, "erase" creases, or delete spots. You can retouch skin tones by erasing blemishes. See **Figure 4-16**. You can use tools to remove **red eye**, an effect that can happen when the flash from a camera is used on light-eyed people and makes them appear to have red eyes. You can adjust picture contrast, brightness, and sharpness to improve a photo's appearance. You can even turn color photos into black and white images or create a sepia-toned effect.

Photo editing software usually includes a wide range of unique **filters** and effects, such as the ability to make a picture look blurred, texturized, or distorted. **Cropping** lets you remove parts of the image deleting unwanted objects or people from your photo. You can also insert objects into your photo or rearrange a picture's composition.

Figure 4-16: Photo editing enhances photographs

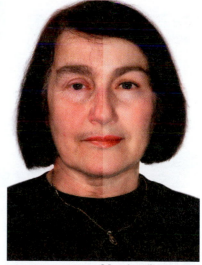

© Dreamframer/Shutterstock.com

Mobile Applications

mobile application | native application | Web application | app store

The growth of mobile computing (see **Figure 4-17**) has spawned a whole new category
of application software—**mobile applications**, commonly referred to as **mobile apps**.

Limitations

While mobile apps are very popular and useful, they do have significant limitations. The small-scale operating systems of mobile devices cannot support full-scale software programs such as Microsoft Word or Excel. Consequently, mobile apps tend to be limited in functionality and scope; each app usually focuses on a single task such as mapping, note taking, or scheduling. See **Figure 4-18**.

Keyboard and touch screen space is another limiting factor; mobile apps can't require heavy data or text input from users. When input is required, apps include on-screen keyboards, autocorrect features, handwriting recognition capabilities, and built-in word and phrase lists.

The Bottom Line

- Mobile apps let you use your mobile device as an extension of your desktop computer—without being tied to your desk.
- Mobile apps are software programs that run on mobile devices such as smartphones and tablets.
- Mobile apps can be native or Web based; each type has its features and drawbacks.

Figure 4-17: Using mobile apps

As you walk down the street to a job interview, you check your smartphone for directions.

You browse the company's Web site to familiarize yourself with its products.

An alarm rings to let you know you have 15 minutes until the appointment.

You pull up your calendar to double-check the date and you check your contact list to confirm your contact's name.

#appsoftware

If you are opening a document on your smartphone that has content that is not supported in Word Mobile, you can still open the document. The unsupported content will not be displayed though, and you might not be able to edit the document on your phone.

Key Features

Limitations aside, mobile apps are tremendously useful. The ability to access the Internet is a key feature shared by most mobile apps. Connectivity is crucial to today's mobile user; people want to stay connected to their office, home, and friends at any given time, no matter where they are.

Although mobile devices cannot run full-scale versions of desktop software programs, some mobile apps are compatible with these programs so you can transfer files between your desktop and mobile devices.

Most mobile apps are platform-specific; an app designed for an Apple iPhone will not work on an Android phone, and vice versa.

Figure 4-18: Using mobile apps with small screens

When you download a mobile app, the installation program installs an icon for the app on your screen.

Mobile apps must be compact and efficient in design to work within limited screen space.

© cobalt88/Shutterstock.com

Native Apps vs. Web Apps

A **native application (native app)** is a program that has been designed to run on a specific operating system such as Android, IOs, or Windows. Tablets, for example, each use a specific operating system based on the manufacturer. Native apps that have been designed for an Apple iPad running iOs, for example, will be optimized for that device and must be installed from the Apple store in order to run on that device. A **Web application (Web app)** is not installed on a user's device; instead, it resides on a server on the Internet, and it is run by a user through a Web browser. Web apps are not device specific.

There are benefits and disadvantages to both systems, and some companies, such as Facebook and Google, provide both a native app and a Web app to reach the broadest group of users possible. Native apps and Web apps differ in functionality and user interface. Often, a native app can take advantage of the features of a specific device, such as the camera, whereas the Web app, working through the browser, cannot.

Standard Apps

Mobile apps were originally developed as productivity tools based on desktop PC tools such as email, contact databases, and calendars. Mobile devices typically come with these apps pre-installed, as well as Web browsers, media players, and mapping apps. **Table 4-9** lists some common mobile apps.

Table 4-9: Common applications for mobile devices

Type of app	Lets you
Email	Send and receive emails from your mobile device
Contact management	Organize your address book
Calendar or scheduling	Track daily appointments and set reminders; sync your mobile calendar with your desktop calendar or share your calendar with colleagues or family members
Web browsing	Find articles, research products or companies, or find any information on the Web apps
News	Stay up to date on current affairs
Video or media player	Watch the latest YouTube video or listen to songs
GPS and mapping apps	Find directions, locate the nearest coffee shop, or even avoid traffic jams
Location-sharing	Share your whereabouts with friends and family

© 2015 Cengage Learning

More Apps

In addition to standard apps, you can choose from thousands of others. Some apps are practical; others are fun; see **Table 4-10** for some examples.

App Stores

While some apps come pre-installed on mobile devices, the majority are downloaded by users from manufacturer or third-party Web sites, sometimes called **app stores**. Some apps are free; those that are not free usually cost less than $5.

Mobile apps are written by the mobile device or operating system manufacturer, or more commonly, by third-party programmers. In recent years, the number of third-party app developers has expanded exponentially, fueling the tremendous growth in the number and variety of mobile apps. Most app stores specialize in apps for a particular type of smartphone or platform.

Table 4-10: Fun and useful applications for mobile devices

Type of app	Lets you
Social media	Stay connected with family and friends; for example, post a Facebook status update from your smartphone or "tweet" your thoughts via Twitter
Organizational	Take notes, set reminders, and make checklists; you can transfer files between devices using cloud (Internet) storage; jot down notes from a client meeting and forward the file to your office computer
Voice recognition	Search the Internet using your voice or make hands-free calls while driving
Travel	Book airline, hotel, and restaurant reservations, and read and post reviews
Language and translation	Facilitate foreign travel; interpret content in languages you don't speak or understand
Fitness	Set weight-loss goals, track your workouts, find a gym, and count calories
File sharing and storage	Collaborate with co-workers, organize your documents, and share photos and other files online
Banking	Manage your money and pay bills; even file your taxes

© 2015 Cengage Learning

Chapter Review

Introduction to Application Software

1. Define convergence and give one specific example of a program that has this feature.
2. List three common features of application software programs.
3. Explain the two ways in which you might obtain Web-based applications.

Word Processing

4. List and describe three common key features of word processing programs.
5. Explain how you might use three document formatting options, then list and explain how you might use three features of a word processor to improve the content in a document.
6. List and describe five text formatting features and explain how you might use them in a document.

Spreadsheets

7. Describe the basic structure of a workbook using the following terms: column, row, cell, cell range, worksheet, and tab.
8. Define and give an example of each of the following spreadsheet terms: label, value, formula, function, and cell range.
9. Give three examples of how you can analyze data using spreadsheet software.

Presentation Software

10. List and then describe three different elements you can place on a slide.
11. Explain how animations and transitions enhance a slide show.
12. How does the slide master affect the appearance of a presentation?

Databases

13. Briefly describe each of the following database objects: table, form, query, and report.
14. Explain how basic data is stored in a database; use the terms field, data type, and record in your explanation.
15. Describe what type of information you might store in a database, give an example of one record that might be in that database.

Graphics Software

16. List and explain three common key features often part graphics software programs.
17. Explain the difference between bitmap digital images and vector digital images.

Mobile Applications

18. List and describe the uses of three common applications for mobile devices.
19. Explain two ways to enter text data in most mobile apps.
20. What are the common ways you get mobile applications on your digital device?

Test Your Knowledge Now

1. Programs that you access over the Internet using your computer's browser, or as an app on your mobile device, are _____ applications.
   a. Web-based
   b. portable
   c. local
   d. browser

2. The blending of distinctions between categories of software is known as _____.
   a. mobile computing
   b. convergence
   c. applications
   d. transitions

3. Which of the following methods is not a feature of a software application program?
   a. double-click or tap the icon to start
   b. opens in a window
   c. adapts to any environment—mobile or Web or local automatically
   d. has menu commands and buttons you click or tap to issue commands

4. Which of the following is a text formatting feature of word processing?
   a. spell check
   b. margins
   c. bold style
   d. tab

5. If you wanted the same text to appear at the top and bottom of every page of your document, you would use the word processor's _____ to complete the task.
   a. research tools
   b. language tools
   c. tables and columns
   d. headers and footers

6. _____ determine where text begins on a line from the left margin.
   a. Indents and tabs
   b. Research tools
   c. Headers and footers
   d. Text formatting tools

7. A _____ is a number, a _____ is descriptive text, and a _____ performs a calculation in a spreadsheet.
   a. label, value, formula
   b. value, label, formula
   c. formula, label, value
   d. value, formula, label

8. Formula arguments can be _____ or cell references.
   a. labels
   b. cell ranges
   c. values
   d. absolute references

9. An absolute reference refers to _____ .
   a. a fixed cell location that never changes even when a formula is moved or copied
   b. a cell identified by its location relative to other cells and changes when a formula is moved or copied
   c. a group of cells that are contiguous
   d. a group of cells that share common formulas

10. A slide _____ automatically applies any new formatting to all slides that use it in your presentation.
    a. transition
    b. animation
    c. master
    d. layout

11. Actions that occur as you move from slide to slide in a presentation are called _____ .
    a. animations
    b. video
    c. transitions
    d. masters

12. Actions that define the movement of an object or text are called _____ .
    a. animations
    b. video
    c. transitions
    d. masters

13. You enter data in a database manually by entering one _____ at a time.
    a. table
    b. form
    c. query
    d. record

14. Most database programs create _____ databases, where two or more tables are linked tables with common fields so that data doesn't have to be repeated, making it more prone to error.
    a. absolute
    b. relational
    c. integrated
    d. query

15. A _____ is a database object primarily used for data entry.
    a. query
    b. table
    c. form
    d. record

16. A _____ extracts data from a database based on criteria that the creator specifies.
    a. query
    b. table
    c. form
    d. record

17. Bitmap images are based on _____ ; a color value is assigned to each one in a graphic.
    a. queries
    b. pixels
    c. forms
    d. records

18. There are two kinds of digital images: bitmap and _____ .
    a. pixel
    b. graphic
    c. vector
    d. web

19. A _____ application is a program that has been designed to run on a specific operating system, rather than residing on a server in the Internet.
    a. native
    b. Web-based
    c. mobile
    d. local

20. If you are traveling in unfamiliar places and need directions and maps, your device should have _____ apps to give directions, locate the nearest shops, or even help you avoid traffic jams.
    a. URL
    b. ISP
    c. GPS
    d. FTP

21. Identify each of the following terms by writing the matching letter on the line in the figure below with the word processing feature used:
    a. highlighting
    b. Font color
    c. header
    d. Font style
    e. Spell checker

Try This Now

1: Artistic Effects for Graphics in Microsoft Word

Note: This assignment requires the use of Microsoft Word 2010 or 2013.

Microsoft Word lets you apply artistic effects to a picture to make it look more like a sketch, drawing, or painting.

    a. Open Microsoft Word and select the Insert tab. In the Illustrations group, select Pictures.

    b. Insert a picture of yourself into the Word document.

    c. In the Word document, leave the inserted picture of yourself as the original picture.

    d. Copy and paste the original picture five times in the Word document. Under Picture Tools on the Format tab in the Adjust group, select Artistic Effects on each of the picture copies and select five different artistic effects. Label each picture with the name of the artistic effect.

    e. Save the document and submit it to your instructor.

2: PowerPoint Animation

Note: This assignment requires the use of Microsoft PowerPoint 2010 or 2013.

Using PowerPoint, you can animate an object on your PowerPoint slide to do something special such as move a logo from the bottom to the top of a slide for more visibility.

    a. Open Microsoft PowerPoint. Create a blank presentation. Select the Insert tab. In the Images group, select Clip Art on PowerPoint 2010 or Online Pictures on PowerPoint 2013. Insert a clip art image of a balloon on the first slide. If necessary, resize the balloon image to about one inch by one inch size.

    b. Select the balloon image. On the Animations tab, use the Add Animation button to apply an effect to the object that you clicked. Add any Entrance animation. Select Add Animation to add any two Emphasis animations. Lastly add any Exit animation.

    c. To view the animations, select the Preview button.

    d. Save and submit the PowerPoint file to your instructor.

3: Creating Graphics with Sumo Paint

Sumo Paint is a full-featured drawing and photo editing application that works in your favorite Web browser.

    a. Open the site Youtube.com and search Sumo Paint for tutorials on how to create a graphic using Sumo Paint. Watch at least a few minutes of the videos to get the basic idea of how to use Sumo Paint.

    b. Open the site sumopaint.com and select the use for free Web-browser version. Select New blank canvas.

    c. Draw a graphic using several tools of Sumo Paint based on the tutorials that you watched at YouTube.

    d. Select File and Save to My Computer and submit your graphic art to your instructor.

© iStockphoto.com/spxChrome

Digital Painting

Critical Thinking Now

1: Spreadsheet Usage In Your Career

Spreadsheets such as Microsoft Excel are used in a variety of careers. Research detailed uses of spreadsheets used in business activities and varied industries. Create a list of ten specific job titles with how each position would use Excel.

2: Office 365 Home Premium

Your family is considering purchasing a subscription to Office 365, the Home Premium version. Research the Office 365 Home Premium subscription and write at least 150 words about this subscription.

3: Comparing Google Drive to Office Web Apps

Both Google and Microsoft offer free lightweight online versions that include word processing, spreadsheet, and presentation programs. Write at least 200 words comparing the features of Google Drive and Microsoft Office Web Apps. In your opinion, which one comes out on top for you?

Ethical Issues Now

Intellectual property is the protection of ideas which includes the name, designs, inventions, images and symbols that a company uses. The success of a business largely depends on its assets. Information technology has enabled other businesses or companies to imitate or copy ideas from others and use it as their own.

a. Your boss has asked you to create a sales flyer using a word processor that will be emailed to customers. You need images for the sales flyer and your boss has told you to "just copy them off our competitor's Web site." Write a paragraph about the ethical situation that you are facing.

b. Research the legal penalties you and your company may face for using another companies intellectual property without permission. Write a paragraph about these penalties.

Team Up Now – Wolfram Alpha Data Analysis

Wolfram Alpha is a data knowledge engine developed by Wolfram ResearchShare. Wolfram Alpha connects to online databases worldwide to answer your questions. Each of the team members should perform each of these searches at Wolfram Alpha.

a. What is the population of your birth city?

b. How common is your first name?

c. What is the median salary of a career field of interest?

d. Where was the strongest earthquake in the world in the last 24 hours? What was its magnitude?

e. Determine the number of calories from your most recent meal.

f. What was the weather on the day you were born in your birth city?

g. Locate the price of gas from a neighboring state/province and compare it to your state/province.

As a team compare your responses. For each of the questions, locate the sources at the bottom of each of the results page. List one of the sources for each of the responses. Submit the responses and sources of each of the team members to your instructor.

Key Terms

absolute reference	font type	record
alignment	form	red eye
animation	format	relational database
app	formula	relative reference
app store	function	report
application software program	graphics	server
argument	indent	slide master
bitmap	insertion point	software application
bullet	label	sort
cell	line chart	speech recognition
cell address	line spacing	software
cell range	local application	spreadsheet
cell reference	macro	tab
chart	margin	table
column chart	mobile app	template
convergence	mobile application	thumbnail
cropping	native application	transition
data type	operator	value
database	page break	vector
desktop publishing (DTP) software	page orientation	view
document	paragraph spacing	Web application
document management tools	pivot table	Web-based application
field	pixel	Web development software
field name	point	What-if analysis
filter	portable application	word processing
font color	presentation	word processing software
font size	presentation software	workbook
font style	query	worksheet

The World Wide Web

Kye uses the Web throughout the day on his tablet to work on his classes, add updates to his blog, engage with education Web sites, read sports and news articles, and check his social networks such as Facebook and Twitter.

This semester Kye is taking Introduction to Business Law online. His entire course uses MindTap (a personalized online learning platform) for his readings, multimedia, activities, and assessments.

© Alexander Image/Shutterstock.com

Connecting to the cloud to store and retrieve files, Kye leverages the Web as a power user. Kye uses his favorite browser, Mozilla Firefox, with multiple tabs open to simultaneously check his grades in his online classes, read a new business law article for his business class, and watch a required video class lecture on YouTube.

Microsoft® product screenshots used with permission from Microsoft® Corporation.

What Is the Web?

Internet | Web | World Wide Web | command-line user interface | graphical user interface (GUI) | Web page | Hypertext Markup Language (HTML) | HTML tag | Web site | World Wide Web Consortium (W3C) | podcast | RSS feed | social networking | Multimedia Message Service (MMS) | streaming video | online games

Since the early days of its development, the World Wide Web has changed the way we get information, conduct business transactions, and communicate. Today, more than 2.5 billion people use the Internet and the World Wide Web, which is commonly referred to as "the Web."

The Early Internet

The United States government took the first step in bringing us the Web. In the 1960s, government researchers and scientists wanted to connect their computers so they could share data. Sending computer information via regular "snail" mail or by phone was slow, and they wanted a computer network that would not be disrupted if one part of the network were destroyed.

So, in 1969 the Department of Defense connected four computers to create a network called ARPANET. The DOD sketched out their idea, and it became a part of history. ARPANET's first job was to send email, which was much faster than using telephones or sending letters. The benefits of email became readily apparent, and soon other universities and government agencies wanted to connect their computers to the new network, too. Around 1973, users began to refer to the new interconnected network as the "Internet."

Essential Inventions

Between 1969 and 1989, the young Internet worked well for scientists and universities. But the user interface, which required that users type commands, was too hard for the general public to use. In addition, personal computers were not widely available. In 1968, Douglas Engelbart demonstrated several experimental technologies to the public, including the mouse, video conferencing, word processing, and a hypertext interface.

By the Numbers Now

Of those 2.5 billion people who use the Internet, 70 percent use the Internet every day.

Figure 5-1: The Internet and the World Wide Web

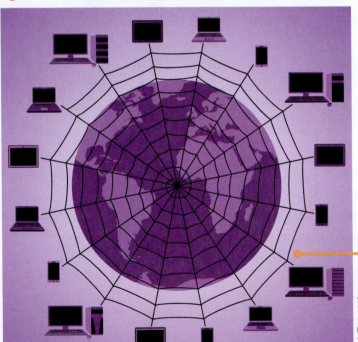

Although some people use the terms "Internet" and "Web" interchangeably, the Web is only part of the Internet.

© Strels/Shutterstock.com

Engelbart patented the first mouse in 1970, constructed from wood and metal wheels. It was named the "mouse" because of the tail that came out of one end. The mouse has evolved from this first design, but early mice had two or three buttons and a "tail." See **Figure 5-2**.

In 1989, researcher Tim Berners-Lee proposed that the Internet be organized into "pages" of related information. He wanted to link the pages using clickable text and images. He called this design the **World Wide Web**. Web page addresses that start with "www" indicate that they are part of the World Wide Web.

The introduction of the World Wide Web was a milestone, but until affordable computer hardware became commercially available, it was out of the general public's reach. In the early 1980s, companies began marketing personal microcomputers as household items. In 1982, more than three million personal computers were sold. Other hardware and software innovations followed in rapid succession, fueling the development of the Web into what we know today—rich with video, graphics, and sound.

The First Browser

As the Web became more popular, programmers developed more ways to use and access the Web. In 1993, the University of Illinois released the first Web browser, named Mosaic. See **Figure 5-3**. Mosaic was much easier to use than the command-line user interface of the early Internet. **Command-line user interfaces** required that a user use a keyboard to type a command or series of commands to interact with a computer. With a **graphical user interface (GUI)**, such as Mosaic, you didn't have to know the command you needed; you could simply select an item to get what you wanted.

Figure 5-2: Early computer mouse

© Natalia Siverina/Shutterstock.com

#worldwideweb

The computer companies HP, Google, Microsoft, and Apple have one thing in common: they were all started in someone's garage.

Figure 5-3: Mosaic was the first graphical browser

The mouse made it possible to click to select items off a menu.

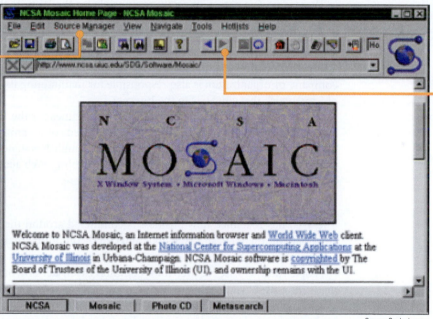

Mosaic distinguished itself from other early browsers with icons, bookmarks, pictures, and other graphical features.

Source: Geekwire.com

As computers became common devices in schools, homes, and businesses, the Web became an essential tool for teachers, students, home users, and people in business. As the Web grew, so did software application development.

Web Pages

What exactly is a Web page? A **Web page** is a **Hypertext Markup Language (HTML)** document. This means that each Web page is a text document containing embedded HTML tags. **HTML tags** are codes that define the Web page. Tags determine how text and graphics will appear on pages. See **Figure 5-4** on the next page.

HTML identifies each item in the document with specific information on where and how the image, video, paragraph, or any element should appear on the Web page.

By the Numbers Now

The number of Internet users has grown 566 percent since the year 2000.

Figure 5-4: HTML pages make up the Web

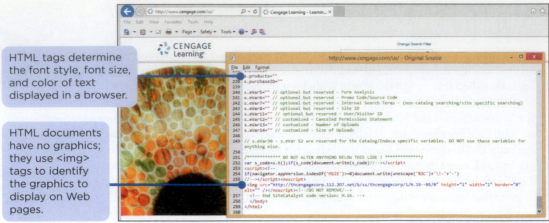

HTML tags determine the font style, font size, and color of text displayed in a browser.

HTML documents have no graphics; they use <img> tags to identify the graphics to display on Web pages.

© 2015 Cengage Learning

A collection of Web pages makes up a Web site. A **Web site** is usually created and maintained by a company, organization, or group, or even individuals. Web sites generally focus on a specific topic, business, or purpose. Trillions of Web sites make up the Web, and the Web is only part of the Internet.

Managing the Web

Have you ever wondered who is in charge of the Web or the Internet? Have you questioned who maintains the Web pages? Have you ever thought about who coordinates the individual networks around the globe?

There is no one person or group responsible for the Web. That would be impossible. The majority of Web sites are maintained by the person, group, company, or organization that establishes the site. For example, a university is responsible for maintaining its Web site and making sure the information is current for students and faculty. A travel agency makes sure that the airline and hotel links on its Web site are accurate. Each company or organization is also responsible for maintaining its hardware and the part of its network that connects to the Internet.

One of the leading organizations that set guidelines for the Web is the **World Wide Web Consortium (W3C)**, which consists of hundreds of organizations and experts that work together to write Web standards. The W3C publishes standards on topics ranging from building Web pages, to technologies for enabling Web access from any device, to browser and search engine design—and much more.

Web Uses

The Web has redefined how business is conducted around the world. Businesses can store data on the Web, and Web apps and cloud computing make it possible for people in different locations to work on the same files simultaneously.

People routinely use the Web for e-commerce transactions, buying products and services. You can buy tangible products such as clothes as well as digital products such as music and movies. You can make travel arrangements or make a doctor's appointment. Online ticket and reservation systems let us book travel reservations as well as concert and event tickets. Tangible products are shipped to physical destinations; digital products are delivered through your computer or even a smartphone or tablet.

The Web delivers information; you can use the Web to take courses online and even get a college degree. You can listen to **podcasts**, which are prerecorded audio files, to keep up with your favorite topics such as news, health, or politics. You can subscribe to **RSS feeds**, which deliver text, video, or graphics content you specify to your phone or desktop.

You don't need to be an established business to buy or sell products through the Internet. The Internet can function like a global garage or tag sale. You can buy and sell from other individuals through online auction sites such as eBay and uBid, or online classified ads on sites such as Craigslist or Freecycle.

The Web is used to trade stocks and conduct online investment activities and services as well as engage in financial transactions. Online banking is offered by most banks, so you can check account balances and pay bills directly from any digital device with an Internet connection.

The Web is essential for the employment market and finding jobs. Employers post job openings, job-seekers post resumes, and search sites try to match them.

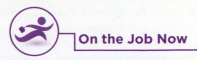
Entertainment and Social Networking

Web sites are available for socializing, communicating, and entertainment. Regardless of the device you use or whether you access the Web with or without wires, the Web provides valuable tools for interactions and entertainment, which let you do the following:

- Participate in **social networking** using sites such as Facebook, Instagram, and Twitter to communicate and share your ideas, announcements, videos, photos, and music, and links to Web sites.
- Send and receive real-time messages using instant messaging (IM) programs. Text messages contain fewer than 160 characters. **Multimedia Message Service (MMS)** is available on most cellular phones so you can add video, picture, and sound.
- Watch television programs using **streaming video**, a technology that transfers a segment of a video file from the Web to your computer, which plays while the next segment is sent.
- Play **online games** with others around the world. Many gaming sites offer multi-player gaming, which is another aspect of social networking.
- Promote business using Facebook, Twitter, or Pinterest to get the word out and share events and significant product or service announcements.
- Use LinkedIn to expand your professional network, find jobs, and find potential employees.

The Browser

browser | home page | start page | hyperlink | uniform resource locator (URL) | address bar | navigation bar | favorite | bookmark | tabbed browsing | history list | pop-up blocking | private browsing | phishing | pharming | hacked | App Tab | sync feature | Site Identity button | VoiceOver | Privacy pane | microbrowser | virtual keyboard | pinch-to-zoom | gesture | plug-in | add-on

To access the World Wide Web, or "the Web," you open a browser. A **browser** is an application that helps you communicate, access, and share information on the Web. The first graphical Web browser, Mosaic, used hyperlinked text and graphics to navigate between Web pages and was instrumental in the development of the Web as we know it today.

Navigation

Browsers have tools to make navigating the Web, or moving from one page to another, easy and fun. The page that appears when you open a browser is called the **home page**, or **start page**. Browsers come with many buttons and menus to help with navigation. You can always click the Home button to return to the Home page.

Web pages have **hyperlinks**, which are clickable words or graphics that you can use to move from one page to another or from one part of a Web page to another.

Each Web page has a **uniform resource locator (URL)**, which is a Web page address that identifies that page on the Web. Each time you click a hyperlink, you go to another Web page and the URL in the Address bar changes. All browsers have an **address bar** to let you know where you are on the Web. You can also type the URL of the Web page you want to go to. Regardless of your navigation method, the Web page loads, or appears, in the browser window. The **navigation bar** on a browser typically has Back, Forward, Refresh, and Stop buttons. **Table 5-1** on the next page lists some typical navigation features found in many browsers.

The Bottom Line
- Browsers let you view, or browse, Web pages and navigate Web sites using controls and menus.
- Browsers, such as Internet Explorer, Chrome, Firefox, and Safari, have many common features including tabs, search bars, and other tools to help you find information on the Web.
- Microbrowsers are browsers designed for mobile devices such as smartphones.

Table 5-1: Navigation features found on most browsers

Button or feature	Lets you
Back and Forward buttons	Once you visit a Web page during the current session, navigate between current and previous pages
Address bar	View, type, or paste the URL of a Web page you want to visit to go to the page
Refresh	Reload the page you are currently viewing
Stop button	Stop a Web page from loading
Search box	Type a phrase or Web address to display a page or list of pages matching the criteria
Home	Display the Home page

© 2015 Cengage Learning

By the Numbers Now

You can open a hundred tabs in the latest version of Internet Explorer in Windows 8.x.

Common Features

Most Web browsers include common features, so if you have used one browser, you won't have trouble learning another. Some of these features are as follows:

- **Favorites**, or **bookmarks**, which are saved shortcuts to Web pages.
- **Tabbed browsing** to access several Web pages in the same browser window.
- A **history list** of the Web pages you visit for a day, a week, a month, and so on.
- **Pop-up blocking** in your browser to prevent pop-up ads, or advertisements that appear in separate windows when you connect to a Web page.
- **Private browsing** mode, which lets you surf the Web without leaving history, temporary Internet files, or small text files called "cookies" that Web pages store on your computer's hard drive to identify you when you visit their site.

Security and Privacy

Many Web browsers have built-in security features that let you block spyware and pop-up ads, as well as protect you from other hazards on the Web. For example, **phishing** is the use of emails that look legitimate—but aren't—to get sensitive data. Such emails usually contain links that take you to fake Web sites. Once you are at the Web site, any personal information you add can be used to steal your identity.

You should never click links to a Web site that come in an email. If your bank needs to contact you and sends you a message, open a new browser window and type in the bank's URL to begin contacting the bank. **Pharming** is a scam in which a server is hacked and used to re-route traffic to a fake Web site to obtain personal information. **Hacked** means a computer has been taken over by an unauthorized user.

Although you must always be vigilant for fraud and other hazards when you visit Web sites, your browser can help protect you from some pitfalls. Some browsers such as Internet Explorer warn you of unsafe Web sites. However, even with that, when you conduct financial transactions on the Internet, such as banking, shopping, or investing, you should use a secure connection. See **Figure 5-5.**

IE and Chrome

Two popular browsers are Internet Explorer (IE) and Google Chrome, which can enhance your search or browsing experience by allowing you to do the following:

- Select a word on a Web page, click the button or menu that opens, and select services such as mapping, translation, and searching.
- Receive warnings of suspected phishing or malware while you browse.
- Remove unnecessary security warnings for downloads from reputable sites using an Application Reputation feature (Internet Explorer).
- Connect to your cloud storage using the browser.
- Use a combined search and Address bar, where you can type in searches as well as Web addresses.
- Translate a Web page to a different language in the browser itself, without plug-ins.
- Use enhanced tab features, such as the ability to pin Websites to the taskbar or Start screen for one-click navigation.
- View multiple Web sites simultaneously.

Figure 5-5: Secure page

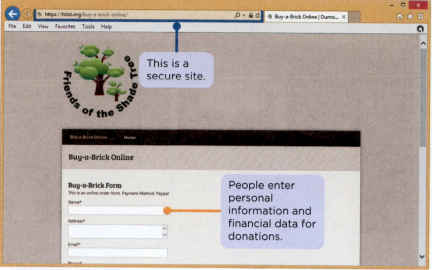

Courtesy of Friends of the Shade Tree

Firefox

Another popular browser, Mozilla Firefox, also offers helpful features:

- An **App Tab**, which lets you pin any Web site's icon so the Web site is always available. The App Tab displays a blue highlight when the corresponding site changes. App Tabs have no Close button, so you cannot accidentally close them. When you reopen Firefox, App Tabs open automatically for convenience.
- A **sync feature** connects your desktop and mobile Firefox devices so you can access your browsing history, passwords, and bookmarks on all your devices.
- An orange button, instead of a menu bar, contains common functions such as history and private browsing for quick access.
- Screen features that provide additional help for URLs you can't remember. As you type a site name, the feature locates possible matches from your history, bookmarks, and open tabs.
- A **Site Identity button** whose color tells you how much identity information is available for the site.

Safari

Safari, the default browser for Mac and iOs, is the first browser to comply with all standards from the W3C (World Wide Web Consortium), the leading organization for setting Web standards. Safari features include the following:

- Built-in support for Apple's **VoiceOver** screen reader. VoiceOver describes aloud what appears on the screen and reads the text and links of Websites, making the Web accessible to people with visual impairments.
- Enhanced keyboard navigation for navigating the Web without a mouse, as well as multi-touch gestures—such as double-tapping the trackpad with two fingers to magnify part of a Web page.
- A **Privacy pane**, which displays information such as tracking data left by Web sites you visit so you can remove the data and protect your privacy.

Microbrowser Challenges

You can access Web pages on your mobile computing device using a mobile browser, or **microbrowser**, which is specially designed for small screens. Popular microbrowsers include Opera, Google Android, Windows Mobile, Firefox Mobile, Dolphin, and Safari Mobile. See **Figure 5-6** on the next page.

Hot Technology Now

The Mozilla organization's mission statement is: "Our mission is to promote openness, innovation & opportunity on the Web."

Figure 5-6: Microbrowser on mobile devices

Text wrapping lets you read text on pages that were designed for large screens.

© iStockphoto.com/adventtr

Microbrowsers must display content on small screens. Some microbrowsers, such as Opera and Safari Mobile for iPhone, render Web pages as they would appear on your computer. Microbrowsers need to accommodate the low memory capacity and low bandwidth of wireless handheld devices.

Microbrowser Features

To help you view Web pages on the go, most microbrowsers also do the following:
- Provide **virtual keyboards**, in addition to touchscreen keyboards, and let you enter text without leaving the page you are viewing.
- Offer a **pinch-to-zoom** feature that capitalizes on mobile device touch screens: they let you use two fingers to adjust the screen size by pinching your fingers together to shrink a page.
- Let you draw shapes, called **gestures**, to issue instructions that your mobile device can execute.
- Let you sync your mobile device with your desktop computer to transfer history, passwords, and bookmarks.

Plug-ins

A **plug-in** (also called an **add-on**) is software that is added on to an existing application to provide additional features to that program. Common Web browser plug-ins add new features such as Web page language translation or the ability to identify harmful pages. Other plug-ins make it possible to play a video that might have been created in a new video format. Well-known browser plug-ins include the following:
- Adobe Flash Player, to play animations created in Flash.
- QuickTime Player, to play some sound and video files.
- Java plug-in, to run applets written in the Java programming language.
- Photon Flash Player for Android, to support video streaming and gaming on Android devices.

If your browser does not have the ability to play a file without the plug-in, you will often be prompted to install it. See **Figure 5-7**.

There's a trend to get away from using plug-ins in more modern apps, and most mobile browsers don't support the use of plug-ins such as Flash, opting for Web pages built in HTML5 and other modern technologies instead.

Hot Technology Now

Gestures are possible because of sensor hardware and touch screen technologies, which continue to develop and improve.

Figure 5-7: Downloading a plugin

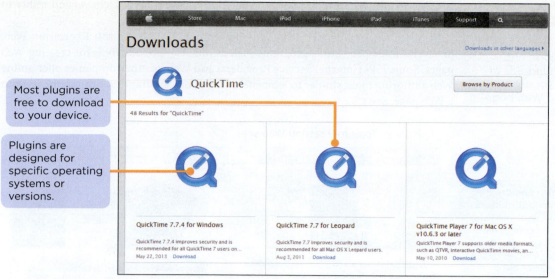

Most plugins are free to download to your device.

Plugins are designed for specific operating systems or versions.

Source: Apple

Web Page Development

Hypertext Transfer Protocol (HTTP) | uniform resource locator (URL) | scripting | Hypertext Markup Language (HTML) | HTML tag | XML (eXtensible Markup Language) | database | static Web publishing | dynamic Web publishing | script | HTML script | server-side script | dynamic Web page | client-side script

Have you thought about creating a Web page, but don't know where to start? Believe it or not, there are just three basic technologies involved in creating even the most dynamic multimedia Web pages.

HTML Basics

A Web page is a document that contains **HTML (Hypertext Markup Language)** tags. HTML has had several versions; the current version is HTML5. **HTML tags** are pieces of code that control how the document is displayed on the Web page—the text size, where a graphic is placed, and so on. There are several options for creating HTML tags. You can manually add HTML tags to a text document using a simple text editor such

The Bottom Line
- **Hypertext Transfer Protocol (HTTP)** is a communications protocol that transports data over the Web.
- **Uniform resource locators (URLs)** create a unique address for each Web page so it can be found by any browser on the Internet.
- **Scripting** furthers enhances the Web experience with small programs that work across several Web pages in the same way.

Figure 5-8: Creating HTML tags

```
<form action="#" method="post">
    <div>
        <label for="name">Text Input:</label>
        <input type="text" name="name" id="name" value="" tabindex="1" />
    </div>

    <div>
        <h4>Radio Button Choice</h4>

        <label for="radio-choice-1">
        <input type="radio"
value="choice-1" />

        <label for="radio-choice-2">
        <input type="radio" value="choice
    </div>

    <div>
        <label for="select-choice">Select Dropdown Choice:</label>
        <select name="select-choice" id="select-choice">
        <option value="Choice 1">Choice 1</option>
        <option value="Choice 2">Choice 2</option>
        <option value="Choice 3">Choice 3</option>
        </select>
    </div>

    <div>
        <label for="textarea">Textarea:</label>
        <textarea cols="40" rows="8" name="textarea" id="textarea"></textarea>
    </div>

    <div>
        <label for="checkbox">Checkbox:</label>
        <input type="checkbox" name="checkbox" id="checkbox" />
    </div>

    <div>
        <input type="submit" value="Submit" />
    </div>
</form>
```

Hypertext Markup Language (HTML) provides a structure for creating and formatting Web pages.

© PixDeluxe/Shutterstock.com

as Notepad, a program that comes with the Windows operating system, although this is tedious and not recommended. You could also use an HTML conversion utility to generate tags from existing documents.

Web authoring software, such as Adobe Dreamweaver, Microsoft Expression Web, or several free open source programs such as Bluefish, provide tools for creating Web pages. Some ISPs (Internet Service Providers) and Web hosting companies offer online Web authoring tools, similar to templates, where you can drag and drop elements onto a Web page. See **Figure 5-9**.

Figure 5-9: Tools for creating Web sites

You can create navigation bars, drop-down lists, and other features by using premade templates available online.

Templates and tools help you create tabs and buttons for your Web page.

XML

While HTML provides a way to format a Web page, **XML (eXtensible Markup Language)** provides a way to classify the contents of the Web page, making it easier to organize.

XML lets a Web page developer customize HTML tags to organize components of the page into different files. XML files give the pages a uniform look by defining how each element looks. For example, one file could define elements for name, address, contact information, etc. Another file might contain the actual content, such as product information; and a third file might identify the format, such as an HTML document.

Organizations such as news companies use this kind of structured system to identify and change the content of their Web pages, without having to work with the layout or format. So, when you visit the page, you recognize the colors, graphics, and the way the text is placed on the page, but each day, new content is shown to you.

XML can also help you conduct more efficient online searches. When you visit sites that sell items such as music recordings, for example, XML enables cataloging by title, artist, genre, and many other ways to help you find just what you're looking for.

Web Databases

When you use Web sites to make travel arrangements, post to social media sites, or shop, the content you see is data. The data for Web sites is stored in **databases**, which are organized collections of data. Accessing a database on the Web requires a browser.

One way to display data from a Web database is to use the database's report utility to convert a database report into an HTML document that a browser can display. This is called **static Web publishing** because the HTML document is a snapshot of the data—it's fixed and cannot be changed. Another way to display data from a Web database is to create Web pages on demand, retrieving the most current data at the

moment you request it. This is called **dynamic Web publishing**. When you shop at a home goods store, for example, the Web page will show you only the inventory in stock, or available to order. There could be hundreds of people shopping at once, so the database must be continuously updated to offer customers the best information for available products.

Script Basics

Have you ever wondered how a Web page fills in your delivery address after you've typed your billing address? Scripts make this possible. A **script**, often called an **HTML script**, is a set of program instructions that make Web pages interactive. A script can be embedded in the text of an HTML document or placed in a file that is referenced in the HTML document. Scripts make e-commerce sites interactive by doing the following:

- Using fill-in forms
- Verifying credit card data
- Collecting input for product orders

The data you enter is stored in your computer's memory. When you click the Submit button, your browser collects the data and sends it to a specified script on an HTTP server to be processed. Some browsers won't allow scripts to run due to security risks. If a Web site is using a secure connection, however, it is usually safe to run scripts on that site.

Client and Server Scripts

There are two types of scripts. One is a **server-side script** because it runs on a server rather than on your computer. A server-side script accepts data from fill-in forms, and then processes the data and generates a custom HTML document for the browser to display as a Web page. These Web pages are called **dynamic Web pages**. Web page developers write server-side scripts using languages such as Perl, PHP, C, C++, C#, and Java.

The other type of script is a **client-side script**, which runs on your local computer. Your browser executes the script, which means the browser must be able to use the programming language in which the script is written. VBScript and JavaScript are two popular languages for writing client-side scripts. See **Figure 5-10**.

Figure 5-10: Scripts

Scripts can be client-side scripts or server-side scripts.

© wongwean/Shutterstock.com

Using the Web to Find Information

search engine technology | search engine | Web crawler | spider | indexing utility | query processor | keyword | search phrase | hit | wildcard character | Boolean operator | Web master | search engine optimization | meta keywords | keyword stuffing

You can find virtually any information you want on the Internet; all you need to do is to search for it. **Search engine technology** makes finding the information you want easier by letting you enter search criteria and then doing the legwork for you.

Search Sites

Search sites are Web sites designed specifically to help you find information on the Web. Popular search sites include www.google.com, www.bing.com, and www.yahoo.com. Search sites use software programs called **search engines** to locate relevant Web pages. A search engine creates a simple query based on your search criteria and stores the collected data in a search database.

Some search sites such as Google, see **Figure 5-11** on the next page, use their own search engine, while others use third-party technology. For example, AltaVista and AlltheWeb use the Yahoo! search engine technology. Regardless of whether you use a search site or enter your criteria in a search box on a Web page, you'll be using a search engine to find information.

Search Engines

Search engine technology has four components: a Web crawler, an indexer, a database, and a query processor. See **Table 5-2** on the next page.

The Bottom Line
- You can enter criteria on a search site to perform your search or simply enter keywords into the search box found on most Web pages.
- When you perform a search, a search engine returns a list of results, typically with excerpts from each Web site that meets your criteria.
- You can then click any item in the results list to view that Web page.

Figure 5-11: Google home page

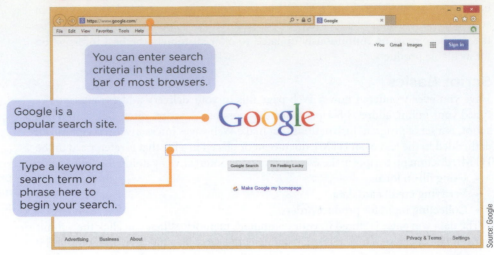

Table 5-2: Search engine components

Component	Description
Web crawler or **spider** program	An automated program that uses hyperlinks to jump between Web pages, collecting data about each page as it goes; Web crawlers can reach millions of Web pages each day.
Indexing utility	Receives data from a Web crawler and then compiles the collected data into an organized list of key words and URLs.
Query processor	Looks for your search criteria in the indexed database and then displays the list of results as URLs with corresponding descriptive information.

Search Basics

To conduct a Web search, you can type keywords into a search site or into the search box found on most Web pages. **Keywords** are one or more words that describe what you're looking for. Multiple keywords are called a **search phrase**.

The search engine uses your keywords to return a list of **hits**, or links to Web pages that match your criteria. See **Table 5-3** for some examples of search phrases and keywords to search for information on buying used Android smartphones.

If your search returns too many hits, continue adding additional words to narrow your search. You can also use a **wildcard character** such as the asterisk to search for derivations of a word. For example, if you want to search for all forms of words related to chlorine, you can search for *chlori* to get Web sites about chlorine, sodium chloride, chlorination, and so forth.

Table 5-3: Examples of search phrases

Keyword or phrase	Possible results	Suggested change
Looking for a used smartphone	A list of all used phones; returns too many hits	Add the word "Android."
Looking for a used Android smartphone	Still too many hits	Remove or omit common words such as "the" and "an"; remove verb.
Used Android smartphone	Too many hits; results still includes other smartphones	Search for an exact phrase by entering it in quotation marks.
Used "Android smartphone"	List of used Android smartphones	

Boolean Searches

You can create better search criteria by using a search operator, also called a **Boolean operator**. A Boolean operator is a word or symbol that identifies the relationship between keywords. See **Table 5-4**.

Table 5-4: Examples of Boolean searches

Boolean operator	Example	Results	Explanation
AND	Android smartphones AND tablets	Devices that are Android smartphones and tablets	The AND operator indicates that both (or all) terms in the criteria must appear on a Web page for it to be included in the results. Some engines use the plus symbol instead of the word AND. AND Results are inclusive of all possibilities using the key terms or phrase.
OR	Smartphones new OR used	All smartphones whether they are new or used	Either (or any one) of the search terms must appear on a Web page for it to be included as a search result.
NOT	Android smartphones NOT apps	Only smartphones, not Android apps	The search term must not appear on a Web page for it to be included as a search result. Some engines use the minus sign instead of the word.

Advanced Searches

You may be unable to narrow the list of results for your search by simply entering keywords or Boolean operators. Some search engines provide forms to help simplify your search. Such forms are available via the advanced search link on the main page of a search engine's Web site. **Figure 5-12** shows a Yahoo! advanced search form. With a little practice, you can create efficient Web searches whether you use additional keywords, wildcard characters, Boolean operators, or an advanced search form.

Figure 5-12: Advanced search page

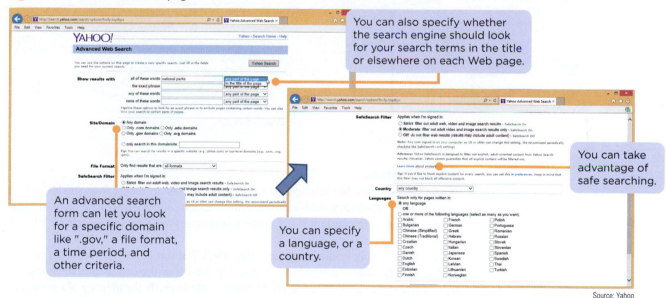

You can also specify whether the search engine should look for your search terms in the title or elsewhere on each Web page.

An advanced search form can let you look for a specific domain like ".gov," a file format, a time period, and other criteria.

You can specify a language, or a country.

You can take advantage of safe searching.

Source: Yahoo

Ranking Search Results

Although Web crawlers discover millions of Web sites each day, a **Web master**, the person who maintains a Web site, can manually submit URLs to a search engine. A Web master can submit URLs for paid placement or as banner or pop-up ads, for which merchants are charged only if the ad is clicked.

The order in which search results appear depends on the relevance of keyword matches and link popularity. Legitimate **search engine optimization** techniques are often used to improve page ranking. Link popularity means that pages with links to popular Web sites get higher ratings. Some Web site operators push their sites to the top of result lists by manipulating **meta keywords**, or words entered into the header section of the Web page when it's created. This is an unethical practice called **keyword stuffing**. Socially responsible search sites have procedures to override attempts at keyword stuffing and post their policies on paid placements.

Web Site Structure

uniform resource locator (URL) | encryption | Secure Hypertext Transfer Protocol | digital certificate | link | bitmap graphic | vector graphic | streaming | banner ad | pop-up ad | click-through rate | cookie | helper application | plug-in | add-on | script | animation

Suppose you want to find a book published by Cengage Learning. You go to the Cengage Web site. Like any Web site, it has many components and specific structures to help deliver its content to you.

URLs

Each **uniform resource locator (URL)** identifies a unique Web page on the Internet. Every page has a URL. The URL identifies the Web page as a unique page on the Internet and provides information about the page's location, type, and security. See **Figure 5-13**.

Some URLs will display file extensions, such as .html or .htm, to help identify the type of Web page. "HTML" stands for Hypertext Markup Language, which uses tags to specify how components of the page should appear in the browser.

Figure 5-13: Cengage Web site

The most common protocols are http for regular Web pages, https for secure pages, and ftp for transferring files.

URLs use forward slashes—not backward slashes—and they cannot contain spaces. Instead of a space, use a hyphen or underscore character.

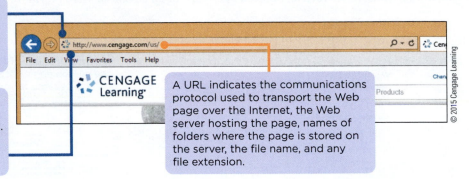

A URL indicates the communications protocol used to transport the Web page over the Internet, the Web server hosting the page, names of folders where the page is stored on the server, the file name, and any file extension.

© 2015 Cengage Learning

Secure Sites

Secure Web sites are essential to protecting sensitive data. A secure Web site is one that uses encryption to safeguard transmitted information. A Web site can be secured using several methods. **Encryption** is the process of temporarily scrambling data so it is not readable until it is decrypted.

The "https" prefix stands for **Secure Hypertext Transfer Protocol**. Web sites such as banks and retail stores use the https protocol to make a secure connection to your computer. Secure Web sites often use a **digital certificate** to verify the identity of a person or an organization. See **Figure 5-14**.

Web Page Components

Buttons and text boxes let you make choices and enter information. And without components such as links and graphics, Web pages would be incredibly dull and not very useful. Web graphics are either bitmap or vector.

- **Links** let you jump from page to page by clicking, following your interests. A link contains the URL of a Web page and can be text, such as an underlined word or phrase, or a graphic.

- **Bitmap graphics** consist of pixels, meaning that they lose quality when enlarged. JPG files compress bitmap graphics to save space and download time.
- **Vector graphics** use mathematical formulas instead of pixels and are widely used on Web pages because they maintain the same quality on all screens and have small file sizes.

Figure 5-14: A secure connection

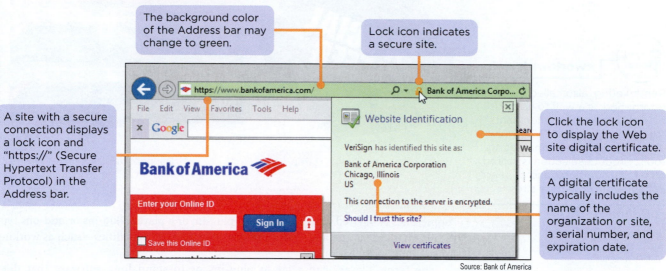

The background color of the Address bar may change to green.

Lock icon indicates a secure site.

A site with a secure connection displays a lock icon and "https://" (Secure Hypertext Transfer Protocol) in the Address bar.

Click the lock icon to display the Web site digital certificate.

A digital certificate typically includes the name of the organization or site, a serial number, and expiration date.

Source: Bank of America

Video and Audio

Many Web sites use video, which consists of images displayed in motion and usually accompanied by audio. When you click a link to download a video, it is downloaded from a Web server, where it is stored, to your computer.

A server can transmit an entire video file before it begins to play on your computer. But more commonly now, videos are also transmitted using **streaming**, where a small segment of the file is transmitted and begins to play while the server sends the next segment. This is a more efficient way to view videos on the Internet.

Web pages can also contain audio—speech, music, or other sounds—which can be part of a video or played as background music. Most operating systems include special software to play media files on computers, such as Windows Media Player, QuickTime, and iTunes. You can also download specialized players.

Pop-ups and Banners

Web sites, especially e-commerce sites, generate revenue by renting advertising space. When you tap or click a pop-up or a banner ad, your browser connects directly to the advertiser's site. A **banner ad** is an advertisement that appears in a Web page, typically near the top or at the side or bottom margins. A **pop-up ad** is an advertisement that appears in a separate window when you access a Web page. See **Figure 5-15** on the next page.

A Web site that hosts an ad earns a small fee based on the **click-through rate**, which is the number of times that visitors click the ad to connect to the advertiser's site. A disadvantage to pop-up and banner ads is that they sometimes install a **cookie** (a small data file) on your computer to track your spending and browsing patterns, which can be a privacy concern.

Helper Applications

Your browser may be able to handle HTML files but not multimedia files. If your browser cannot display a graphic or play an audio or video file, a message directs you to download the necessary software. Such software is called a **helper application** and

On the Job Now

Many businesses market their products using social media. Since Facebook users sometimes fill in a lot of information about themselves—starting with basic information such as where they live, their gender, and their age—an advertiser can be quite specific when deciding the Facebook target audience.

Figure 5-15: Pop-up and banner ads

Pop-up ad   Banner ads

#worldwideweb

Remarketing, also called retargeting, is a way to advertise by displaying visited merchants' stores in banner ads. When visiting a site using remarketing tools, product selection is stored on a local computer and appears in banner ads on other sites.

sometimes is referred to as an add-on, a plug-in, or a player. **Plug-ins** or **add-ons** typically refer to software added to a browser to extend its capabilities—such as working with additional file formats.

The term "player" can refer to plug-ins or to standalone software that does not need a host program to run. For example, Adobe Flash Player lets you view animations created in Adobe Flash. Once installed, your browser automatically runs helper applications when needed—such as when you click a link to play a Flash video. For Web sites programmed in the latest version of HTML, which is HTML5, helper applications to play media files are not necessary and are not supported.

Scripts

Scripts allow Web pages to be interactive. For instance, scripts help your browser fill in your username and password on some Web sites, allow e-commerce sites to verify credit card data, and let you complete online forms.

A **script** is a series of program instructions that can be embedded directly into the HTML code for a Web page or in a file referenced in the HTML code. Depending on the type of script, the server or the browser runs the script when you visit the Web page. A disadvantage to scripts is that they can pose a security risk, and some browsers do not allow them to run. You can generally run scripts safely if you are using a secure connection.

Animation

Animation is the process of creating the appearance of motion by displaying a sequence of still images, each with small changes from the previous image. Animation can draw attention to an important element of a Web page. Some Web sites use animated text that scrolls across the screen to display stock or sports updates, as well as weather and news.

GIF and Flash animations are two popular options for adding animation. Flash is a software animation technology developed by Macromedia and marketed by Adobe. Flash animations are stored in files with the .swf extension. An animated GIF is a series of bitmap images, with slight changes to each, placed in sequence to create animation.

#worldwideweb

Browsers that cannot support Flash display the error message, "You need to upgrade your Flash Player." Many companies no longer build Web sites using Flash.

Types of Web Sites

domain name | IP address | top-level domain (TLD) | Domain Name System (DNS) | domain name server | content aggregator | wiki | blog | social networking | file-sharing sites

With millions of sites on the World Wide Web (or simply the Web), how can you efficiently find the information or product you want? Understanding Web site categories can help. The types include portal, news, informational, business, blog, wiki, social networking, educational, entertainment, advocacy, Web application, content aggregator, and personal.

Domain Names

What is a domain name? A **domain name** is related to a Web site's Internet Protocol (IP) address, which you can enter in the Address bar of your browser to display the Web site. **IP addresses** are allocated to each network on the Internet to ensure that no two computers have same IP address. IP addresses can be hard to remember if you're not a computer, so computers also use text-based domain names. See **Figure 5-16**.

Figure 5-16: IP addresses and domain names

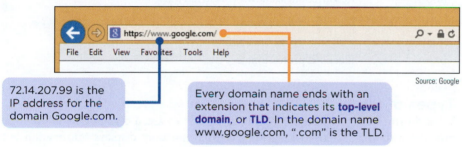

Source: Google

72.14.207.99 is the IP address for the domain Google.com.

Every domain name ends with an extension that indicates its **top-level domain**, or **TLD**. In the domain name www.google.com, ".com" is the TLD.

Naming Domains

Although it's hard to imagine, every domain name and its corresponding IP address have been entered into the **Domain Name System (DNS)**, which is a world-wide database. Rather than storing it in a single location, many Internet servers host part of the DNS to keep it secure. These servers are called **domain name servers**, or DNS servers, and typically are associated with Internet Service Providers (ISPs). When you're using a browser and request a Web site by its common domain name, such as cengage.com, a DNS server looks up the IP address so your browser can display the correct page.

Who issues domain names? The Internet Corporation for Assigned Names and Numbers (ICANN) coordinates Internet addresses around the world. ICANN supervises several for-profit accredited domain registrars, such as DreamHost and GoDaddy, and these organizations handle domain name requests.

Original TLDs

As you visit Web sites, you might notice some that have **top-level domains (TLDs)** other than .com. Originally, the United States had the seven TLDs, shown in **Table 5-5** on the next page, although recently TLDs have started to blur their meaning,

Newer TLDs

As Internet activity increases, ICANN continues to add new domains to the original seven TLDs, along with two-letter codes for countries such as .au (Australia), .ca (Canada), . de (Germany), and .jp (Japan). See **Table 5-6** on the next page.

The Bottom Line
- Every Web site has a unique IP address and a corresponding unique domain name. The domain name helps identify the type of Web site.
- Top-level domains (TLDs) help identify the type of Web site.
- Web sites with user-supplied content comprise a large part of the Web.

#worldwideweb

An IP address is similar to a postal address for each and every Internet-connected device.

Hot Technology Now

Thinglink.com helps you create interactive images with hotspots linked to YouTube videos, Web pages, text, and other content.

By the Numbers Now

In February 2011, the world officially ran out of the 4.3 billion available IPv4 addresses. IPv6 provides enough addresses for everyone's various devices.

Table 5-5: Traditional original TLDs and sites they represent

TLD	Generally used for
.com	Most commercial sites that sell products and services
.edu	Academic and research sites such as schools and universities
.gov	U. S. government organizations
.int	International treaty organizations
.mil	Military organizations
.net	Network providers, ISPs, and other Internet administrative organizations
.org	Organizations such as political or not for profit. Any Web site can have the .org TLD but, traditionally, only professional and nonprofit organizations such as churches and humanitarian groups use it.

© 2015 Cengage Learning

Hot Technology Now

Academicearth.org offers a comprehensive collection of free online college lectures from the world's top universities such as Cornell and Yale.

Table 5-6: More recent TLDs and sites they represent

TLD	Generally used for
.aero	The aviation industry
.biz	Unrestricted use, but usually identifies businesses, along with the .co and .com TLD
.info	Resource sites; allows unrestricted use
.jobs	Employment sites
.mobi	Sites optimized for mobile devices
.pro	Licensed professionals

© 2015 Cengage Learning

On the Job Now

For a career in the United States Army, view more information on the site www.army.mil. Notice the .mil file extension.

By the Numbers Now

English is the most used language on Web sites, but other top languages include Russian, German, Spanish, Chinese, French, Japanese, Arabic, and Portuguese.

Hot Technology Now

Websites such as join.me and bit.ly have purchased TLDs to make their domain names easier to remember.

Types of Sites

What do you want to do on the Web today? Chances are, a certain type of Web site provides just what you're looking for. The Web not only displays information but also lets you interact with it. You can contribute thoughts and images to the ongoing "conversation" through public forum sites, blogs, and chat rooms.

Using search sites and portals such as Google and Yahoo!, you need to remember only one URL to access a variety of services such as maps, shopping, and news. On entertainment Web sites, you can view or discuss activities ranging from sports to videos. For example, you can cast a vote on a topic for a television show.

A **content aggregator** site such as mDigger or Google News gathers, organizes, and then distributes Web content. Subscribers choose the type of content they want, and updates are downloaded to them automatically. News is an example of distributed content.

Webmail and Web Applications

Another type of Web site is a Webmail site. Instead of using an email program installed on your computer such as Outlook, you can use a Webmail service such as Gmail or Outlook.com to send and receive email. A Webmail service provides a Web page for your email, which you access using a browser. You can access your account from any computer or device with an Internet connection, even computers at a public location such as a library.

Web application sites include online tax preparation and document storage. You can also use Web applications such as Office 365 and Google Drive to create and manage documents and presentations. You'll learn more about Web applications in the next section.

User-Supplied Content

The Web is interactive—it allows you to both view and contribute information. You can contribute comments and opinions to informational sites such as news sites, blogs, and wikis. A **wiki** is a collaborative Web site where you and your colleagues can modify content on a Web page, and then publish it just by clicking a button. Wikis are great for group projects. A **blog**, short for "Web log," is a Web page listing journal entries in chronological order. One person usually creates a blog to reflect his or her point of view. **Social networking** sites such as Facebook and Google+ let participants share personal information, upload photos and other media, and make new friends. **File-sharing sites** such as YouTube and Flickr let you post and share photos, music, and other media.

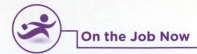

On the Job Now

Companies often communicate with their customers with the use of a blog, as in this example from Whole Foods Grocery Store: www.wholefoodsmarket.com/blog/whole-story.

Web Applications

Web application (Web app) | application service provider (ASP) | Software as a Service (SaaS) | cloud storage | online storage

Do you ever need to check your email or consult a map from home, work, and school? You can do that, and perform many other tasks, using a **Web application**, or **Web app**. Web apps are applications that reside on a server on the Internet, rather than a user's device, and are run by a user through a Web browser.

Structure and Design

A Web app runs in any browser that supports basic Web technologies such as HTML and JavaScript. Web apps are popular because most devices have a browser as basic software and therefore can access and run the Web app. Some Web apps are free, others charge only for enhanced features or services, and some require ongoing usage fees.

    Application service providers, or **ASPs**, provide software-based services over the Internet, whereas Internet service providers, or ISPs, provide access to the Internet. Running software directly from the Internet is called **Software as a Service**, or **SaaS**. Google Drive is an example of SaaS. Web apps often incorporate other reusable Web apps, such as an interactive calendar, calculator, or currency converter for online shopping or auctions.

Online Cloud Storage

As more applications are becoming Web-based and consumers want to access their files from anywhere using multiple devices, online or cloud storage is increasingly important. Some Web sites provide storage, some provide Web apps, and some do both. See **Figure 5-17** on the next page.

    Windows OneDrive is a host site that provides Microsoft Office Web apps and cloud storage, allowing you to create and store data on Microsoft servers. Files can be private or you can share them with others by granting access. Privacy and security is often provided through password protection at cloud storage sites that provide Web apps.

    Cloud storage services vary among providers and may be restricted to specific types of files. For example, you can store only photos on Flickr. The primary goal of some cloud storage sites, such as box.net, is to provide online storage, but they don't let you change or work with files. Online and cloud storage sites are usually password-protected, and you can specify whether your files are private or shared.

Productivity Applications

Productivity applications help you accomplish specific tasks such as creating a document or presentation. Google Drive offers productivity applications such as word processing, spreadsheet, presentation, and database software along with cloud storage. You can use online presentation sites such as Prezi to create and share presentations.

    Microsoft Office Web Apps and Google Drive offer simplified versions of productivity applications and are ideal for individual users who want to collaborate with others. Microsoft Office 365 is the online version of Microsoft Office Professional Plus, designed primarily for businesses or large groups of users. It also includes Microsoft server products and Office Web Apps—the browser-based versions of Excel, Word, PowerPoint, and OneNote.

The Bottom Line
- Web apps run in a browser, so they are accessible from most any device with Internet access.
- Web apps are not typically stored on your computer or other device, though some host Web sites such as Google Earth may require you to download additional software.
- Web app advantages include being able to access files and features while on the go and sharing information seamlessly with others; disadvantages include needing Internet access to get at your files and programs.

Hot Technology Now

Google Hangouts (www.google.com/+/learnmore/hangouts) supports video calls with up to 10 friends.

Other Web Applications

There are many Web apps that provide you with the tools you can use for daily activities as well as help you manage your finances and business needs. See **Table 5-7**.

Figure 5-17: Web apps in the cloud

© SCOTTCHAN/Shutterstock.com

The terms **cloud storage** and **online storage** are often used interchangeably to describe remote storage on the Internet.

Table 5-7: Some other Web apps

Web app	Function category	Notes and description
Britannica Dictionary.com IMDB.com	Online reference software	Look up information and facts on specific topics such as synonyms, definitions, and movie and TV trivia.
YouTube Pinterest Tumblr	Media sharing	Share graphics and video.
Kayak Expedia Yelp	Travel	Make travel arrangements, find local hotels and restaurants, read and contribute traveler reviews.
Photoshop Express Picnik Flickr	Online photo editing and sharing	Extra storage and features cost money.
Gmail Outlook.com Yahoo! Mail	Email programs	Create, send, and manage email messages.
Turbo Tax Online TaxACT Online	Tax preparation	Some tax preparation programs let you prepare your return for free, but may charge for printing or electronic filing.
Google Earth Google Maps MapQuest	Mapping applications	Require software download; Google and MapQuest offer part of Web app free, but charge for advanced features.

© 2015 Cengage Learning

Advantages and Disadvantages

You should weigh the advantages and disadvantages of using Web apps and decide what best suits your needs. The advantages of using Web apps are as follows:

- You can collaborate on projects with coworkers in multiple locations, even if you have different work schedules.
- You can access your work from any location because data is stored on the app's Web site.
- You save storage space on your computer.
- You don't have to install updates, since the newest version is always available on the app's Web site.
- You can access Web apps from any device with a browser and Internet connection, including computers, smartphones, or even enhanced media players.

The disadvantages of using Web apps are as follows:

- If a cloud computing provider has technical problems, Web apps and related data could become unavailable.
- If a provider goes out of business, you can lose functionality and files.
- Some Web apps offer fewer features and may run more slowly than installed applications.

Electronic Commerce

e-commerce | business-to-consumer (B2C) | cookie | consumer-to-consumer (C2C) | business-to-business (B2B) | Secure Electronic Transaction (SET) | Secure Sockets Layer (SSL) | Transport Layer Security (TLS) | S-HTTP | electronic wallet | digital wallet | online investing | aggregate site | digital gift certificate | digital gift card | digital coupon

E-commerce refers to the purchase of physical products such as clothing and computers, intangible products such as music, and services such as education, over the Internet. Some businesses offer shopping both in the store and online. Both businesses and consumers use e-commerce to enhance their organizations and private lives. E-commerce is divided into business models, shown in **Figure 5-18** on the next page, based on the type of buyer and seller.

Business-to-Consumer

In the **business-to-consumer (B2C)** e-commerce model, businesses provide goods and services to consumers. The most widespread example of this is online shopping. To shop online, you can visit the Web site of a store, browse pictures and descriptions of items you want to purchase, and then follow directions for payment.

Single merchants typically operate B2C sites. A B2C store keeps its inventory information in a database. As you browse through the merchandise, the merchant's Web server and database work together to create a Web page for the item that you select. Businesses typically ship physical goods to your front door via the postal service or a commercial delivery service.

The site tracks your selected items using cookies. A **cookie** is a small file generated by a Web server that acts like a storage bin for the items you place in your shopping cart. Cookies store shopping cart item numbers, credit card numbers, and other information.

Consumer to Consumer

One common example of C2C transactions are online classified ads such as those found on Craigslist.com. Online auctions are another example of the **consumer-to-consumer (C2C)** business model. An online auction works much like a real-life auction or yard sale.

C2C sites have multiple sellers, with different sellers for different items, rather than a single merchant hosting a B2C site. To sell a collection of DVDs, for example, you could post an ad on an Internet auction site such as eBay or Yahoo! Auctions, and potential buyers could bid on the collection. The auction site coordinates the bidding process and the transactions between buyer and seller, but does not handle the actual merchandise. Many C2C sites use email forwarding, which hides real email identities, to connect buyer with seller and still protect everybody's privacy. You pay a small fee to the auction site if you sell the item.

Hot Technology Now

Amazon, the world's largest e-commerce company, is experimenting with a delivery system called Amazon Prime Air to get packages into customers' hands in 30 minutes using unmanned aerial vehicle drones.

On the Job Now

Many B2Bs use RFID (Radio Frequency Identification) to identify products. Its advantages are that it requires no human intervention; tags can usually be read even when they are not facing a reader antenna for inventory and location.

Figure 5-18: Common e-commerce business models

Business-to-consumer (B2C)

Consumer-to-consumer (C2C)

Business-to-business (B2B)

© Scott Maxwell / LuMaxArt/Shutterstock.com

E-commerce is divided into business models based on the type of buyer and seller.

Business-to-Business

The **business-to-business (B2B)** e-commerce model involves the transfer of goods, services, or information between businesses. In fact, most e-commerce is actually between businesses. Services that businesses provide to each other include advertising, credit, recruiting, sales and marketing, technical support, and training. Businesses also use B2B e-commerce to purchase raw materials, tools and machinery, office furnishings and equipment, and transportation services in a global market.

E-commerce Payments

When you shop or bank online, be sure the Web site uses a secure connection. The prefix "https" and a locked padlock icon should appear in the Address bar, and the background should turn green. **Secure Electronic Transaction (SET)** is a standard protocol for securing credit card transactions over the Internet. SET uses both encryption and digital certificates. See **Figure 5-19**.

E-commerce sites also use **Secure Sockets Layer (SSL)**, **Transport Layer Security (TLS)**, and **S-HTTP** technologies to encrypt data. This helps protect consumers and businesses from fraud and identity theft when conducting commerce on the Internet.

One payment method is to submit your credit card number directly at a merchant's Web site. You might find a form that asks for the number and your personal information when you check out. Some sites offer to store this information for you. You can also make a person-to-person online payment, especially on auction sites. PayPal and Google Checkout are two such services, in which you open an account and deposit money from your bank or provide your credit card number.

Another option is an **electronic wallet**, also called a **digital wallet**, which is software that stores the payment information you enter when you finalize an online purchase. You also can pay using a one-time-use or virtual account number, which lets you make a single online payment without revealing your actual account number. These numbers are good only at the time of the transaction; so, if they are stolen, they are worthless to the thieves.

Online Banking and Investing

The number of consumers who bank online is growing rapidly. You can check account balances, transfer funds among accounts, pay bills electronically, and perform other transactions without leaving your home. Online banking is not only convenient for the consumer but also useful in reducing costs for the bank.

You can also manage your stocks and other securities online. These activities are called **online investing**. You typically can view stock quotes on search and news Web sites, but you need an online broker for investment activities. Online investing services let you buy and sell stocks, view performance histories, and set up an online portfolio to display the status of your investments.

Comparison Shopping

Web sites such as BizRate, NexTag, and PriceGrabber are called **aggregate sites** because they specialize in collecting and organizing data from other consumer Web sites. They save you time and money by letting you compare prices from multiple vendors.

Digital technology has changed the way the travel industry does business. You can make reservations and purchase your own tickets and accommodations online. You can even write reviews about your experiences for other consumers to read. Some e-commerce sites such as Orbitz, Travelocity, and Kayak consolidate travel information on flights, hotel reservations, and rental cars. You can use this collected information to find the best deals and discounts and research destinations.

Hot Technology Now

Yelp.com operates an "online urban guide" and business review site that is helpful to find highly rated restaurants and other local services.

Advertising

E-commerce sites often contain a great deal of advertising. The sites generate income by selling space for banner ads and pop-up ads; the ad revenue helps support the sites and reduces costs to consumers.

When you click an ad on a Web site, your browser connects to the advertiser's Web site. This activity is called a click-through. The host merchant receives a small fee based on the click-through rate. Sometimes, clicking a pop-up or banner ad installs a cookie on your computer. Some consumers do not want cookies installed on their computer, so browsers contain settings allowing users to block them. If you set your browser to limit cookies, you may find that some features of e-commerce do not work as well.

When e-commerce first became popular, people were learning how to buy and sell on the Internet and often would click ads. Over time, however, click-through rates have declined because consumers often ignore ads or install software to block them.

Deals and Discounts

Although using an online payment service is the most common way of exchanging digital cash, e-commerce also uses **digital gift certificates**, **digital gift cards**, and **digital coupons**. Digital coupons consist of codes that you enter when you check out and pay for online purchases. You can print and use digital gift certificates and digital gift cards at restaurants or other businesses. Groupon, Google Offers, and LivingSocial are examples of deal-of-the-day Web sites. Rules and restrictions vary among the sites. See **Figure 5-20**.

Figure 5-19: Business transactions on the Web

© Jmiks/Shutterstock.com

Some MasterCard and Visa credit card companies provide corporations with Web-based transaction capabilities.

Hot Technology Now

Sites such as CouponCabin.com and CouponMom.com provide coupon codes, printable coupons, and local coupons for discounts.

Figure 5-20: Digital coupons and gift cards promote shopping

Redemption rates are high with mobile phones because consumers typically have their phones with them when they shop.

Some Web sites specialize in collecting and offering deals or coupons, often daily, and often via email or mobile phone.

© DelMosz/Shutterstock.com

The Internet of Things

barcode | QR code | Near Field Communication (NFC) | Radio Frequency Identification (RFID) | Internet of Things (IoT)

The Internet is not only people using keyboards and screens to access and share information and commerce. Objects also use the Internet. Several technologies exist that transmit data to and from computers through the Internet automatically, without any human intervention. The Internet of Things is possible because all digital devices in an office or home are connected and can share data.

Barcodes and QR codes

Barcodes have been in use for many years. **Barcodes**, printed codes that look like a series of stacked bars, are used in stores and supermarkets to code items for pricing and inventory. Each bar has a number value. Barcode readers are used to scan the code to tie into a database that contains the specific product. Barcodes are not unique: a code in one store might identify a bar of soap, but can identify a chair or other product in another. See **Figure 5-21**.

QR codes look like squares with square pattern blocks inside the main square object. See **Figure 5-22**. QR codes can be found in magazines, on billboards, in packaging, on tags for products, and in digital form on Web sites. There are several Web sites that you can use to generate a QR code free of charge. Each QR code is unique and may be used to open a browser to view a URL, save a contact to the address book, or compose text messages.

Both QR code and barcode readers are available on mobile devices such as tablets and smartphones. Use a smartphone to scan a QR code in a magazine, bulletin board, or on a sign in a public place. QR codes can be used to connect to a Web site to get more information about a product or service. Scanners are generally free apps, so you can access the information for a product directly from your mobile device as long as you are on the Internet.

Figure 5-21: Barcodes

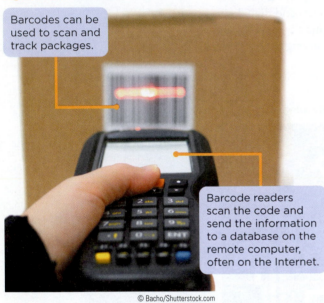

Barcodes can be used to scan and track packages.

Barcode readers scan the code and send the information to a database on the remote computer, often on the Internet.

© Bacho/Shutterstock.com

Figure 5-22: QR codes

© RedKoala/Shutterstock.com

RFID and NFC

We live in a world where wireless transmissions are commonplace. Two wireless technologies used for tagging and tracking are **NFC** or **near field communication**, and **RFID** or **radio frequency identification**. Both use radio signals for tagging and tracking, sometimes replacing barcodes. NFC is a newer technology.

RFID tags
- contain an antenna for transmitting data and a memory chip that stores data;
- are a one-way system and work at distances of many feet and even at high speeds;
- have been in used by businesses for product tracking and loss prevention as well as in employee ID badges;
- provide security access to secure areas for selected people; and
- are used by pet owners who chip their pets to identify them in case they are lost; by transportation departments on car tags to collect tolls; by airlines, to track and control commercial shipping baggage; in "smart passports" and credit cards; and in identification badges that let employees access secure areas.

NFC chips
- are similar to RFID but go beyond RFID capabilities;
- work with NFC readers installed on smartphones to provide two-way communication at very short ranges (about 10 centimeters) or by touching two devices;

- can be used by organizations, medical professionals, and businesses to collect and transmit information, so that users with readers installed on smartphones can get data about events or products and share back information; and
- support applications such as digital wallet and contactless payment systems that can be used from a smartphone.

Tagging and Tracking Objects

The **Internet of Things (IoT)** is a school of thought that developed in 2009. Its basic premise is that all objects can be tagged, tracked, and monitored through a local network, or across the Internet. In this way, we can tag and therefore know where people, products, and other objects are, and their relationship to each other, at any given time.

IoT is based on RFID and NFC technologies, which allow tagging, tracking, and communication between objects, and facilitate mobile payments for products and services. Companies such as Google are investing heavily into devices with NFC technology to be able to cash in on the markets for and benefits of IoT.

Use in Inventory and Tracking

As a business owner, you want to have a supply of products when customers arrive in your store or order online. However, how can you know the right amount of product to buy, stock, and warehouse? The Internet of Things can help you manage and plan for warehousing and shipping.

Through RFID and NFC tracking, products can indicate where they are. Why ship a bicycle from California to New York, when there is one located much closer in New Jersey? By creating smart communities and smart products, we can reduce shipping time, reduce costs, and make business more efficient. See **Figure 5-23**.

Other Uses

The Internet of Things has the potential to enhance our daily lives in ways we cannot even imagine. Some possible uses for tagging things to the Internet include the following:
- Payment systems for transportation systems such as urban buses and subways and for toll roads
- Traffic monitoring and management
- Medical management for patients in remote locations to reduce office visits
- Crowd management at large events
- Home monitoring systems for heat, water, and light to save energy

Advances in wireless communications and the Internet can join forces to further enhance our daily lives.

Figure 5-23: NFC—Near field communication, mobile payment

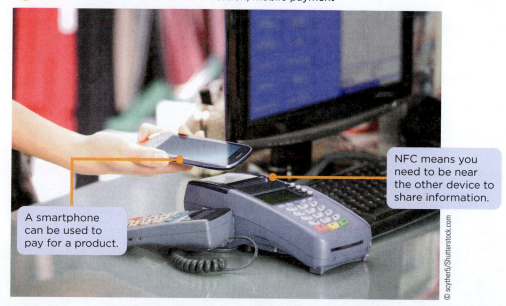

A smartphone can be used to pay for a product.

NFC means you need to be near the other device to share information.

© scyther5/Shutterstock.com

Hot Technology Now

The iPhone can make mobile payments using an app called Passbook. Passbook also allows users to store coupons, boarding passes, tickets, and promotional cards.

#worldwideweb

Go to twitter.com, search for @SAMTechNow, the book's Twitter account, and then follow @SAMTechNow to get tweets on your home page.

Chapter Review

What Is the Web?

1. List three early inventions that led to the development of the World Wide Web.

2. For what purposes did scientists and universities start using the early Web?

The Browser

3. List four common features of all browsers.

4. Name three current browsers and describe one feature of each browser.

5. List and explain two of the challenges of microbrowsers.

Web Page Development

6. Explain why a URL is important and how it is used in Web page development.

7. Give an example of how you can identify a secure Web site and what types of sites might be secured.

Using the Web to Find Information

8. What is the difference between a search engine and a search site?

9. Describe the functions of a Web crawler, an indexing utility, and a query processor. Explain how they work together to provide search results.

10. Create two different search criteria for finding information about your town using Boolean operators. Explain the type of results you can expect from each search.

Web Site Structure

11. What is a link and what is its function in a Web page?

12. How are videos transmitted from a Web site to your computer?

Types of Web Sites

13. Define the terms "domain name" and "Internet Protocol (IP) address." Explain how they are related and how you use either one to display a Web site.

14. List three TLDs, explain what they mean, and give an example of each.

Web Applications

15. Define and explain the term "Web app."

16. What are three advantages and three disadvantages of working in the cloud?

Electronic Commerce

17. Define the term "e-commerce" and explain how it is used in our daily lives.

18. Name three ways you can pay for a service or product you purchase online.

The Internet of Things

19. Define "RFID" and "NFC."

20. Explain three ways in which RFID technology is used today and three ways in which NFC technology is used today.

Test Your Knowledge Now

1. The Department of Defense connected four computers in 1969 to create a network called the _____.
   a. HTML
   b. Internet
   c. ARPANET
   d. World Wide Web

2. The first browser, Mosaic, was easier to use than previous interfaces because it had _____.
   a. a graphical user interface
   b. a command-line interface
   c. video streaming
   d. RFID technology

3. A Web page is a text document with _____ tags.
   a. Hypertext Protocol
   b. Hypertext Markup Language (HTML)
   c. graphic
   d. W3C standard

4. Web pages include _____ that direct you to other Web pages.
   a. graphics
   b. hyperlinks
   c. URLs
   d. address bars

5. Which of the following is part of every Web site?
   a. QR code
   b. Forward button
   c. banner ad
   d. home page

6. The use of emails that look legitimate but are designed to capture sensitive information is called
   a. pharming.
   b. phishing.
   c. browsing.
   d. spam.

7. Which of the following is not a Web browser?
   a. OneDrive
   b. Firefox
   c. Chrome
   d. Safari

8. _____ is the name of the communications protocol that transports data over the Web.
   a. Uniform resource locator (URL)
   b. Hypertext Markup Language (HTML)
   c. Scripting
   d. Hypertext Transfer Protocol (HTTP)

9. The way to display data from a Web database for on-demand Web pages is to use _____ publishing.
   a. static Web
   b. XML tag
   c. dynamic Web
   d. streaming Web

10. The two types of scripts used to enhance HTML pages are _____ side scripts.
   a. client- and dynamic-
   b. client- and server-
   c. XML- and HTML-
   d. URL- and HTTP-

11. Google, Bing, and Yahoo! are examples of popular _____ sites.
   a. search
   b. query
   c. email
   d. technology

12. Search engine technology has four components: a Web crawler, an indexer, a(n) _____, and a query processor.
   a. site
   b. database
   c. engine
   d. utility

13. Which of the following is an example of a Boolean search query?
   a. "What street is the farm on?"
   b. "Find all farms that are not in Dumont"
   c. "When does the farm open"
   d. "Where can I buy a smartphone?"

14. Web site operators who push their sites to the top of results lists by manipulating meta keywords are practicing _____, which is unethical.
   a. keyword stuffing
   b. Boolean searching
   c. indexing
   d. Web crawling

15. _____ is the process of temporarily scrambling data so it is not readable until it is decoded.
   a. Certification
   b. Encryption
   c. Coding
   d. Securing

16. Web pages use _____ graphics, which use mathematical formulas instead of pixels, to maintain the same quality on all screens and have small file sizes.
   a. bitmap
   b. vector
   c. video
   d. JPG

17. A _____ is a series of program instructions that can be embedded directly into the HTML code for a Web page or in a file referenced in the HTML code.
   a. vector
   b. script
   c. bitmap
   d. Flash GIF

18. _____ addresses are allocated to each network on the Internet to ensure that no two computers have the same address.
   a. HTML
   b. HTTP
   c. URL
   d. IP

19. The three letters that follow a "dot," as in .edu, .org, or .mil, are called _____.
   a. top-level domains
   b. domain name servers
   c. domain name systems
   d. suffixed domains

20. A _____ is a Web page listing journal entries, in chronological order, that usually reflect an author's point of view.
   a. wiki
   b. blog
   c. page
   d. social network

21. In the space next to each image below, write the letter of the technology it represents.
   a. QR code
   b. URL
   c. scanner
   d. barcode
   e. HTML

http://www.cengage.com/us/

55555 5

File Edit Format
1 <!DOCTYPE html >
2 <html lang="en" i
3 <head>
4 <meta http-equiv=

© Bacho/Shutterstock.com, © RedKoala/Shutterstock.com, © Bacho/Shutterstock.com,
© 2015 Cengage Learning, barcode photo courtesy of Barbara Clemens

Try This Now

1: Advanced Power Search with Google

When searching for information on the Internet, finding up-to-date, precise information is vital. The Google advanced search feature provides options for exact words, Boolean operators, numeric ranges, specific language, reading level, and last update date. Open a browser and go to the site www.google.com/advanced_search to view the Google Advanced Search form.

    a. In the exact word or phrase text box of the advanced Google Search, type "wearable computers." The quotes are necessary to search for the exact phrase with the words in that specific order.

    b. In the language text box of the advanced Google Search, select English.

    c. In the last update text box of the advanced Google Search, select in the past week to locate current information.

    d. Select the Advanced Search button. Open the first non-ad result site on the results page.

    e. Read the site and write at least 100 words about the wearable computers mentioned on this site.

2: Comparing Career Search Sites

Locating an easy-to-use, powerful career search site with positions in your career field is an important step in finding your dream job. Whether you are looking for a summer job or a full-time position, online career search sites are the first place to begin a successful job search.

    a. Using your favorite search engine, search for three career search sites. Using each job search site, type in a possible career field to search for the number of openings.

    b. Write a paragraph about each of the three different career search sites (list the URL of the site) comparing the ease-of-use of each site and how successful you were in locating possible employment options.

3: Consumer Web Reviews Using Yelp

Yelp.com has given a voice to the consumer to share reviews of their experiences at local eateries and other businesses such as nail salons and car repair shops. Open a browser and open yelp.com. Search for a large city that you would like to visit.

    a. Search for the top five rated restaurants in the selected city using Yelp. List the five restaurants with the highest rating, and for each one, list the type of food and address. Copy and paste a review from each of the restaurants into a Word document.

    b. Research and write at least 100 words about how some businesses try to manipulate their reviews on a site such as Yelp.

    c. Save the document and submit it to your instructor.

Critical Thinking Now

1: The Best Web Browser

Everyone wants a browser that is fast, secure, and easy to use. Select three current browsers (desktop or mobile) and research the features of each one. Write at least 200 words that compare the three browsers and recommend the browser that is best in your opinion.

2: Google Scholar Search Engine

Google provides an academic search engine at scholar.google.com for articles, books, online repositories, and college theses. Search for the topic of biometrics at google.com and at scholar.google.com. Write at least 150 words about the sources that appear in the results page for each search.

3: Advertising Online with Personalized Remarketing

Remarketing

Remarketing is the way sellers, in trying to market products, repeatedly show you products you have researched. By reminding you of products you have searched for online, by placing them in personalized ads on other Web sites you visit, you are reminded and perhaps persuaded to buy a previously viewed product from a retailer's Web site. For example, if you have been researching a new smartphone online, that same model of smartphone may reappear in banner ads over the next few weeks on other unrelated Web sites that you frequent.

Research how effective remarketing is with online shoppers. Write at least 150 words about your impressions of personalized remarketing and its effectiveness.

Ethical Issues Now

Mobile wallets can offer many services that include payment functionality and organizational capability.

    a. Research the safety of using credit cards in face-to-face transactions compared to using mobile wallet payments. Be sure to include recent advances in RFID and NFC technologies. Write at least 150 words on the advantages and disadvantages of using each.

    b. If you could save money by using discounts that have been applied to your personal mobile wallet payment account, would you consider using Google Wallet or Apple Passbook? Why?

    c. How could you use mobile wallets to organize store loyalty cards?

Team Up Now – Remote Collaboration with Google Hangouts

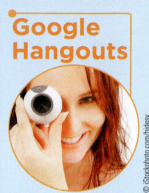

Google Hangouts

© iStockphoto.com/hidesy

Note: This assignment requires the use of a Web cam.

    Company employees and student teams connect daily using remote Web conferencing and Web applications. Discuss a date and time that you can meet online with your classmate team using Google Hangouts. One person on the team must be designated to initiate the hangout and invite the other team members. Each of the team members must first create a free Google account. Read about setting up a Google Hangout at www.google.com/+/learnmore/hangouts.

    a. When everyone on the team has arrived in the Google Hangout, take a screen shot with all the team members' names listed.

    b. Collaborate with your team members to determine how Google Hangouts could be used for business teams. Create a short 150+ word document about your ideas.

    c. Submit the combined screen shot and paragraph to your instructor.

Key Terms

add-on	digital wallet	keyword
address bar	domain name	keyword stuffing
aggregate site	domain name server	link
animation	Domain Name System (DNS)	meta keywords
App Tab	dynamic Web page	microbrowser
application service provider (ASP)	dynamic Web publishing	Multimedia Message Service (MMS)
banner ad	e-commerce	navigation bar
barcode	electronic wallet	Near Field Communication (NFC)
bitmap graphic	encryption	online games
blog	favorite	online investing
bookmark	file-sharing sites	online storage
Boolean operator	gesture	pharming
browser	graphical user interface (GUI)	phishing
business-to-business (B2B)	hacked	pinch-to-zoom
business-to-consumer (B2C)	helper application	plug-in
click-through rate	history list	podcast
client-side script	hit	pop-up ad
cloud storage	home page	pop-up blocking
command-line user interface	HTML script	Privacy pane
consumer-to-consumer (C2C)	HTML tag	private browsing
content aggregator	hyperlink	QR code
cookie	Hypertext Markup Language (HTML)	query processor
database	Hypertext Transfer Protocol (HTTP)	Radio Frequency Identification (RFID)
digital certificate	indexing utility	RSS feed
digital coupon	Internet	script
digital gift card	Internet of Things (IoT)	scripting
digital gift certificate	IP Address	search engine

search engine optimization
search engine technology
search phrase
Secure Electronic Transaction (SET)
Secure Hypertext Transfer Protocol
Secure Sockets Layer (SSL)
server-side script
S-HTTP
Site Identity button
social networking
Software as a Service (SaaS)
spider

start page
static Web publishing
streaming
streaming video
sync feature
tabbed browsing
top-level domain (TLD)
Transport Layer Security (TLS)
uniform resource locator (URL)
vector graphic
virtual keyboard
VoiceOver

Web
Web application (Web app)
Web crawler
Web master
Web page
Web site
wiki
wildcard character
World Wide Web
World Wide Web Consortium (W3C)
XML (eXtensible Markup Language)

Purchasing and Maintaining a Computer

Understanding computer specifications can be confusing unless you understand what all those numbers represent.

Eric is shopping for a new computer. With so many choices including ultrabooks, tablets, and all-in-one computers with brand names such as Samsung, Apple, Asus, Dell, and more, he needs information to make the right decision.

© iStockphoto.com/Yuri

Eric Tirrell understands that deciding which computer to buy is not easy because there are so many choices. He intends to bring his computer to class, so battery life, weight, and a keyboard are important factors. He knows that getting the most features while staying within his budget is the key goal in his computer search.

Microsoft® product screenshots used with permission from Microsoft® Corporation.

Buying a Computer

The Bottom Line

- The computer you buy needs to be within your budget, and it must support the computing tasks you expect to perform.
- Before buying a computer you'll need to weigh many options, including purpose, price, size and shape, operating system, processing power and speed, memory, storage, and peripheral devices.

form factor | desktop | all-in-one | ultrabook | laptop | notebook | convertible | tablet | mobile device | operating system | platform | processor | central processing unit (CPU) | random access memory (RAM) | gigabyte (GB) | storage device | byte | terabyte (TB) | internal hard drive | external hard drive | solid state drive (SSD) | service plan | extended warranty

Computers are part of your daily life. If you don't already own a computer, you've probably used one in a computer lab or a library, or perhaps you've borrowed one from a friend. At some point, you'll probably need to buy a computer. Computers can be expensive, so you want to make an informed purchasing decision. What is your intended use? Do you need only to send email, or do you plan to create and track the budget for a small business? Will you be creating soundtracks, videos, or presentations? Do you plan on storing hundreds or even thousands of mp3 files and photographs? Will you store files locally or in the cloud? The answers to these questions will help determine your choice.

Figure 6-1: Weighing purchasing options

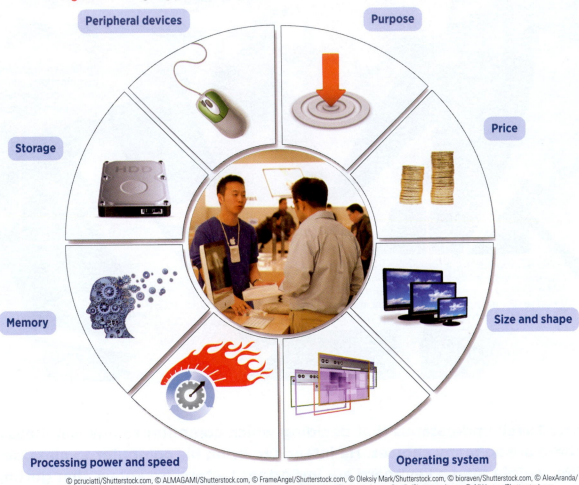

© pcruciatti/Shutterstock.com, © ALMAGAMI/Shutterstock.com, © FrameAngel/Shutterstock.com, © Oleksiy Mark/Shutterstock.com, © bioraven/Shutterstock.com, © AlexAranda/Shutterstock.com, © zsooofija/Shutterstock.com, © Lightspring/Shutterstock.com, © Cowpland/Shutterstock.com, © urfin/Shutterstock.com, © All Vectors/Shutterstock.com

By the Numbers Now

New Windows OS computers start around $400 for a basic ultrabook. A Chromebook computer, which is designed specifically for Web-based tasks, typically costs between $250 and $300.

Budget

How much money do you have to spend on a computer? Once you determine your budget, you can narrow your search to look for the best computer that fits your budget.

Can you afford to buy everything you want all at once? Maybe you can buy the basic computer now and add peripherals such as a scanner, camera, or printer later. If you have a restricted budget, buy a computer with a more powerful processor and less memory—you can add more memory to it later.

Intended Uses

Before you buy a computer, think about why you need it and how you intend to use it. Consider the following questions:

- Are you going to use the computer for school or work, to write reports and other documents?
- Do you plan to use the computer primarily to read e-books, check email, and surf the Web?
- Are you planning on using the computer to store and play an extensive music collection?
- Are you going to use the computer while traveling? Do you work in remote areas or harsh environments?
- Will you be viewing video on the Internet?
- Are you an artist or engineer working with complicated graphics?
- Do you want to play high-end computer games?

The answers to these questions will help you decide the size and shape, operating system, hardware specs, and peripherals to look for in a computer.

#buyacomputer

If you need Microsoft Office or other installed programs, keep in mind that not all tablets can run traditional programs.

Form Factor

Once you've determined the tasks you want to perform and your budget, you can decide the **form factor**, or size and shape of the computer, that will work best for you. See **Figure 6-2**.

Figure 6-2: Some form factor options

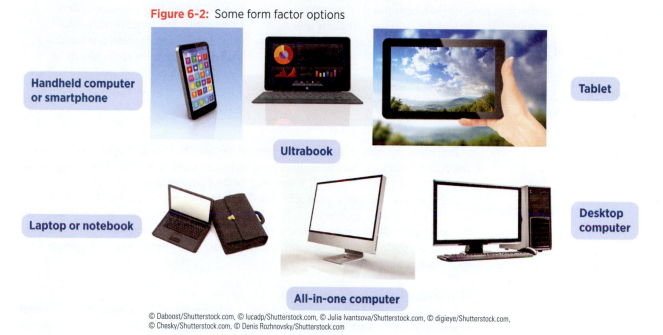

Handheld computer or smartphone

Ultrabook

Tablet

Laptop or notebook

Desktop computer

All-in-one computer

© Daboost/Shutterstock.com, © lucadp/Shutterstock.com, © Julia Ivantsova/Shutterstock.com, © digieye/Shutterstock.com, © Chesky/Shutterstock.com, © Denis Rozhnovsky/Shutterstock.com

The basic computer types can be further organized into a number of form factors to help with your purchasing options. Your choices include desktop, all-in-one, ultrabook, laptop or notebook, convertible, tablet, and mobile device such as a smartphone. Each form factor has unique strengths and weaknesses. You want to be sure to get the most processing speed and memory for your money in the form that best meets your needs. **Table 6-1** on the next page explains some of the options.

The ultrabook form factor represents a thin, light, powerful portable computer, built using a particular Intel specification. Although the term Ultrabook is a registered trademark of the Intel Corporation, the technology industry uses "ultrabook" to represent computers from various manufacturers with similar form factors.

By the Numbers Now

The longest battery life of a tablet on a single charge is around 14 hours.

Operating System

Once you determine the form factor for your computer, the next decision you need to make is what operating system you will use. The **operating system**, or **platform**, coordinates the functions of various hardware components and determines the types and brands of application software you can use.

Table 6-1: Comparing form factors

Form factor	Advantages	Disadvantages
Desktop	Less expensive than comparable laptops, ultrabooks, tablets, or notebooks; can be powerful; often used by businesses.	Box is larger; takes up a significant amount of space and is difficult to move.
All-in-one	Internal system components and electronics are integrated into the back of the monitor, so the computer is one unit; powerful alternative to desktop unit.	Can be expensive; not very portable; have limited upgrade options.
Ultrabook	High-end performance notebook that is thin and light; uses solid state drives; has good battery life; solid box construction ranging from 13 to 20 inches and from about 3 to 18 pounds; excellent portability.	Prices vary, but can be expensive.
Laptop or **notebook**	Lighter and portable; most can run in wireless, battery-powered mode for hours; many have built-in Web cams.	Can cost more than comparably equipped desktop computers and are more easily damaged.
Convertible	Provides a detachable keyboard base that has extra ports or drives; converts to a tablet for mobility when keyboard is not wanted and can use a virtual keyboard instead.	Added cost; user has to manage not to lose the parts.
Tablet	Smaller and cheaper than laptop and notebook computers; can be laid flat, and most fit easily into a purse or backpack; useful for online applications such as Web browsing or email.	Less powerful; fewer features; offers significantly less functionality than other types of computers; not suitable for creating complex spreadsheets or performing application-intensive tasks.
Mobile device	Small and portable; often includes phone and text capabilities.	Less powerful, fewer features, small screen

© 2015 Cengage Learning

The main operating systems for computers are Windows, Apple, and Chrome. Tablet computers and mobile devices have various operating systems depending on the manufacturer, such as Android, Windows Mobile, Chrome, and Apple iOS.

Some people choose a platform based on its user interface, or "look and feel," which controls how information appears on the screen and how you interact with the computer. Others may choose a platform based on the software they anticipate running on their machine. Make sure the software you want to run will operate with your chosen platform.

Hardware Requirements

You should also examine your hardware requirements. The **processor**, or **central processing unit (CPU)**, controls the computer's operations. Faster, more powerful processors provide more computing power. Get the fastest processor, most memory, and largest amount of storage you can afford.

You should take the time to review the specifications and recommendations for the following processors: Intel Core i7, i5 and i3 processors, Intel Pentium, Celeron, Xeon, Intel Mac, AMD Phenom, AMD Athlon, and ARM Cortex. Computers with the Intel i7 processors are best for gamers and heavy technical users, while i5 computers are designed for programmers, Web designers, and other users. i3 processors are best for light use such as Microsoft Office, Web research, and email, and are common on student computers. Most widely available computers offer sufficient processing power for the average home or student user. Professional users or heavy gamers will require more powerful processors.

Random access memory (RAM) is temporary storage used to store data and operate programs while the computer is running. The amount of RAM you need depends on what programs you intend to run. RAM is measured in **gigabytes (GB)**. In general, 4–16 GB is recommended for most users.

Hot Technology Now

To read unbiased reviews and comparisons on tech products, check out CNET (cnet.com).

Storage devices store files permanently so you can retrieve them later. For example, you can write a paper, save it to a storage device, and then open it later to print it. Storage capacity is measured in bytes; some built-in hard drives now boast over a terabyte (TB), which is 1 trillion bytes, of storage. Most computer storage devices can store between 500 GB and 1 TB of information, although tablets and mobile devices store considerably less. Most computers have an internal hard drive that can be supplemented with an external hard drive or portable hard drive that connects through a USB port. A solid state drive (SSD) is a hard drive with no moving parts and therefore more durable and suitable for portable computers. SSDs tend to be more expensive than magnetic hard drives with the same storage capacity.

Add-on Devices

Depending on your budget and needs, you may decide to purchase add-on devices, or peripherals, to enhance your computer. These might include a printer, a scanner, a keyboard and mouse (for laptops or tablets,), a Web cam (for a desktop), an external hard drive, a touch screen, or other devices.

Desktop, laptop, and notebook computers provide flexibility by letting you add devices that plug into USB ports. For example, flash drives and external hard drives are external USB devices that provide extra storage. You might also want to attach a mouse and a camera. Consider a computer with multiple USB ports to accommodate such add-on devices.

Because wires can get tangled, many add-on devices can connect wirelessly using Bluetooth technology. For example, you can connect a wireless mouse, printer, or keyboard to your computer.

Making the Purchase

Once you've determined the kind of computer you need, research your purchasing options to narrow your choices; then you're ready to go shopping. Where do you begin? Here are some tips:

- Consult knowledgeable salespeople at electronics retailers, get expert opinions by reading computer and consumer magazines, and look online for reviews and comparisons of different computer types, brands, and models.
- Organize your findings in a spreadsheet or chart.
- Look for the options that best fit your needs and budget while offering the most power and functionality.
- You might prefer to buy your computer at a local retailer, or you could purchase it online directly from the vendor or an online retailer. Many people buy a computer online for the best price and have the computer delivered to their doorsteps.
- Another decision you will have to make is whether to purchase an extended warranty or service plan. Service plans and extended warranties are useful if you are not familiar with computers, or if you feel your computer might need replacement parts due to wear and tear. Before purchasing a plan or extended warranty, read through it from start to finish to see if it is right for you.

No matter where you purchase your computer, thoughtful research will help you get the best computer for your needs and your budget.

Protecting Computer Hardware

uninterruptible power supply (UPS) | power fluctuation | power spike | power surge | surge suppressor

We protect and maintain equipment and devices that we value, such as our car or cell phone. Computers are made of sensitive electronic components that are easily damaged, but we often fail to take even simple steps to protect and maintain them.

Extreme Temperatures

Computers are made of both electronic and mechanical parts that are designed to function in regulated environments, with controlled temperature and humidity levels. Heat is bad for electronics, so computers have built-in cooling systems to keep components

Figure 6-3: Use common sense

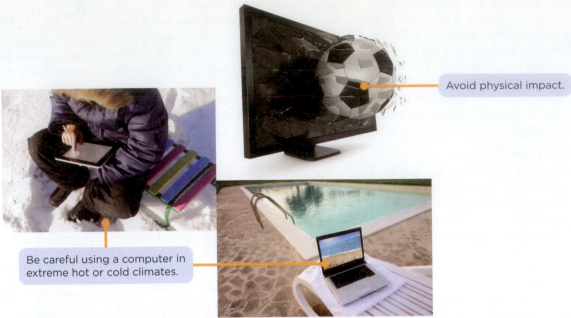

Avoid physical impact.

Be careful using a computer in extreme hot or cold climates.

© Chepko Danil Vitalevich/Shutterstock.com, zentilia/Fotolia, © ollyy/Shutterstock.com

#buyacomputer

Do not leave your phone in a hot car because condensation can gather under the screen and ruin the display. The mobile battery can overheat and possibly explode or never hold a charge again.

Figure 6-4: Use a special tote to carry your computer when traveling

© photomak/Shutterstock.com

from overheating. Keep your computer in a well-ventilated area; never place it near a radiator or leave it in the sun, where it could be damaged beyond repair.

Freezing conditions can also seriously damage your computer's mechanical and electronic components, so never leave your laptop in your car on a cold day, or outside overnight. As a rule of thumb, if you feel comfortable, your computer will be comfortable as well.

Physical Impact

Computers, components, and peripheral devices are not made to withstand significant physical impact. Be aware of the objects in use near your computer equipment, and take care when moving objects nearby.

Portable computers are designed for mobility and need to be protected during transport. See **Figure 6-4**. Pack your device in a specially designed, padded case during transport to cushion it from any impact or other jarring motions.

If your work requires a lot of physical movement, or if you work outside in extreme weather conditions, consider using a weatherized or ruggedized laptop or mobile computer.

Liquids

Computers run on electricity or battery power; neither should come into contact with liquids. Always keep beverages and other liquids at a safe distance from your computer to prevent short-circuiting its components in the case of a spill. When using your smartphone or other computer equipment outside, keep it out of the rain.

If you must take your computer near a beach or lake, put it in a waterproof carrier for protection against water and other hazards.

Magnetic Fields

Hard drive storage uses magnetic technology to arrange particles on the disk, representing the data you need for files and programs. Keep strong magnets away from your computer and storage devices. This is especially true for desktop, laptop, and notebook computers that use magnetic storage technology.

Magnets do not affect solid state storage devices, such as some hard drives, memory sticks, thumb drives, and flash drives. Solid state storage devices use low-power chips with no moving parts and are almost impervious to magnetic fields, vibration, or even extreme temperatures.

Dust and Sand

Keep dust, dirt, and sand away from your computer. If dirt or sand particles get into the keyboard or system unit, they'll damage the computer components. If dirt gets in the fan of the power supply, it can cause the fan to stop working and your computer will overheat.

Keep a can of compressed air near your work area and use it regularly to remove dust particles from vents, ports, keyboards, and fan components.

Power Fluctuations

Computers and other digital devices need power to work. Power is supplied by either AC current from a wall outlet or from a battery. If the power goes off, or your battery runs out of power, the device will shut down. Loss of power won't damage your equipment, but it may cause you to lose unsaved files. You can avoid data loss by installing an **uninterruptible power supply (UPS)** to prevent power loss to your computer.

More damaging than power outages are **power fluctuations**. **Power spikes**, or **power surges**, can occur before and after outages. Small surges can damage your computer over time, but the large power surges from lightning can wipe out your computer. To prevent power fluctuations from damaging electronic components, you should always use a **surge suppressor** with your computer. See **Figure 6-5**.

Hot Technology Now

Some touch tablets and smartphones have a special glass called Gorilla Glass. The composition of this glass creates a stronger surface that rarely scratches or shatters.

On the Job Now

When you travel with your computer, extend your computer's battery life by dimming the screen, closing programs running in the background, and turning off Wi-Fi.

Figure 6-5: Devices to help with power problems

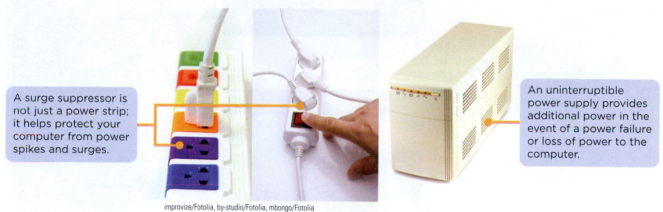

A surge suppressor is not just a power strip; it helps protect your computer from power spikes and surges.

An uninterruptible power supply provides additional power in the event of a power failure or loss of power to the computer.

improvize/Fotolia, by-studio/Fotolia, mbongo/Fotolia

Safeguarding Your Computer

global positioning system (GPS) | real-time location system | radio-frequency identification (RFID) tag | cloud backup | password | personal identification number (PIN) | username | firewall | data encryption | full data encryption (FDE) | Encrypting File System (EFS)

Your computer is valuable, not just for its resale value, but for its contents. Often, the data on a computer is worth more than the computer itself, because the time you spend in creating or acquiring data has value. If you spent weeks writing a research paper and your laptop is then stolen or destroyed, you would have to invest considerable time and effort to recreate the paper. In addition, your computer contains a wealth of data about you, your friends and colleagues, and perhaps your company. You wouldn't want your Social Security or credit card numbers falling into the hands of a thief.

Secure Devices

Because computers are valuable, they are often targeted by thieves. If you use your computer in a public space, such as a coffee shop or library, do not leave it unattended. When you are not using your computer, you should store it in a secure place away from public view.

But you cannot stand guard over your computer all the time. If you leave your computer in an unsecured location from time to time, such as a dorm or open office, you

The Bottom Line

- Software programs, documents, photographs, music, and video files stored on your computer have value in both time and money.
- Because you have so much value tied up in your computer, you want to take steps to keep your computer and the data it contains safe and secure.
- Safeguard data by using secure devices, backing up your data, using passwords, building a firewall, and encrypting your data.

Cable lock

Hot Technology Now

Store your documents, pictures, videos, and music using cloud computing technologies such as OneDrive, iCloud, DropBox, or Google Drive.

The tracking system sends out a signal when activated. An online service that you must subscribe to traces the signal and pinpoints the location of the device.

#buyacomputer

Many phone makers are adding a smartphone "kill switch" that prohibits a stolen device from unauthorized use.

Hot Technology Now

Some great apps to track your lost phone are Where's My Droid (Android), Find my iPhone/iPad, and Find my Phone (Windows).

need to protect it from theft. Use a cable lock to secure the computer to a table or desk. If possible, lock up your peripherals as well. See **Figure 6-6**.

Recover Stolen Devices

If your computer does get lost or stolen, you can use innovative tracking technology to get it back.

Using **global positioning system (GPS)** technology and **real-time location systems** such as **radio-frequency identification (RFID) tags**, you can install computer-tracking software and equipment on your laptop or smartphone. See **Figure 6-7**.

Other technologies, such as LoJack for Laptops and Find My iPhone, go one step further by letting you remotely lock and/or delete sensitive data from your computer, or any iOS device, before thieves can access it.

Figure 6-7: Tracking devices through RFID and GPS technology

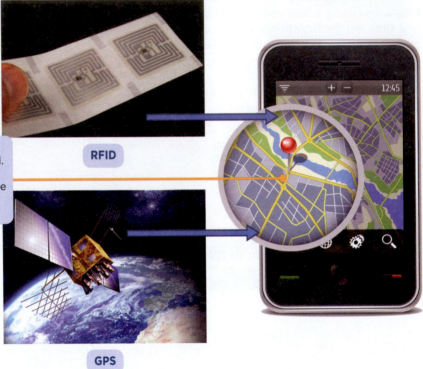

RFID

GPS

Back Up Data

The files on your computer contain valuable information and represent hours of work. Some files, such as photos or videos, may be irreplaceable. So you need to make sure you never lose them. Your best protection is to back up your files to an external storage location and then store these backups in a safe place. Consider off-site locations to prevent loss from fire or flooding.

You can use personal storage devices such as external hard drives, flash drives, or CDs and DVDs to back up your files. See **Figure 6-8**.

You can also back up your files to remote servers over the Internet, called **cloud backup** or cloud storage. With cloud backup (see **Figure 6-9**), you can retrieve your data anytime from anywhere in the world. You can also configure your system to run backups automatically on a regular basis.

Some disadvantages of cloud backup and storage are the following:

- The unpredictability associated with relying on an outside vendor—for example, if the servers go down periodically, you may have to wait to access your data.
- If your cloud provider suddenly goes out of business, you may not have access to your data.

- If your Internet connection fails, you may have to manage for a length of time without access to your files.
- Potential for security breaches.

Make sure you have contingency plans in case these events occur.

Figure 6-8: Back up your data

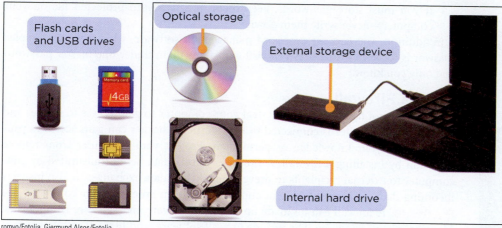

romvo/Fotolia, Gjermund Alsos/Fotolia

Figure 6-9: Cloud storage

Beboy/Fotolia

Use Passwords

Passwords, personal identification numbers (PINs), and usernames are the keys to your digital world. You need these keys to access your personal accounts with online retailers, banks, and social sites. **Passwords** are short words or phrases kept secret by a person and used to gain access to a site or data. Passwords often combine letters, numbers, and characters to prevent unauthorized users from getting them and using them for illicit activities. **Personal identification numbers**, often called **PINs**, are short number sequences, also kept secret and frequently used by banks, used to access accounts. **Usernames** are words determined by users to identify themselves in the digital world, such as on Web sites or blogs. Your computer should be password

Hot Technology Now

File History is the backup and restore feature on a Windows 8.X computer. File History regularly backs up versions of your files in the Documents, Music, Pictures, Videos, and Desktop folders on your PC.

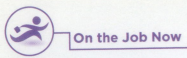
Figure 6-10: An illustration of a firewall

© Tonis Pan/Shutterstock.com

protected as well. If it is ever lost or stolen, no one can access your files without first entering the correct password.

Follow these rules for creating good, also called strong, passwords:

- Use passwords that are at least eight characters with a combination of upper- and lowercase letters, numbers, and symbols.
- Never use dictionary words, birthdays, names, or information specific to your family.
- Use a different password for sensitive activities such as banking.
- If you must store passwords, keep them in a password-protected file on your computer—never write them down.

In addition, you can use password management software, which creates complex passwords for each of the sites you visit and stores them under one master password that only you know.

Build a Firewall

A thief does not have to physically steal your computer to gain access to its files and data. If your computer is connected to the Internet, a hacker can gain access to your files without your knowledge or permission. Protect your computer from remote intrusion by installing a firewall. A **firewall** inspects data being transmitted by your computer to external recipients to prevent unsolicited data exchanges. It also inspects incoming data for harmful content and blocks it from entering your computer. See **Figure 6-10**. A firewall can be made up of both hardware and software components. Many routers provided by ISPs include firewall software, and firewall software is part of most operating systems.

As an added precaution, you should shut down your computer or disconnect it from the Internet if you are not using it for extended periods of time.

Encrypt Data

If your computer contains sensitive data, you can add an additional layer of protection beyond passwords and firewalls by using data encryption. **Data encryption** "scrambles" or encodes data so that even if unauthorized users somehow gain access to your files, they will not be able to read or understand what is in them. **Full data encryption (FDE)** automatically protects all of the data on your computer. You can also choose to encrypt specific files and folders using the **Encrypting File System (EFS)** in Windows or File-Vault for Mac OS.

As with most hazards, prevention is the best medicine. Keep your computer safe by keeping it in sight, locking it up when unattended, installing tracking software, setting passwords, using a firewall, and encrypting sensitive data. And always back up your data to an off-site location.

Troubleshooting Common Hardware Problems

head crash | RAM (random access memory) | virtual memory | disk defragmentation utility | disk optimization utility | video card | optical storage technology

You press the power switch. The computer does not respond, no lights come on—nothing happens. Did the power supply fail? Did your hard drive crash? Is your display broken? Computers are notoriously prone to problems. You should be able to troubleshoot some common hardware problems without incurring the time and expense of professional repairs.

Hard Drive Crash

You store documents, photographs, software, and other files on your computer's hard drive. Magnetic hard drives, mostly found in older desktop computers, are fragile and susceptible to damage from motion and outside elements like dirt and dust. They are usually built inside airtight enclosures.

Figure 6-11: Common problems

Storage hard drive failure

Power problems

Other electronic parts failure

Display problems because of broken screen or video card problems

If you boot up your computer and it doesn't get past the startup screen, the problem might be with the hard drive. Magnetic hard drives operate with a read/write head hovering about two-millionths of an inch over the disk platter. See **Figure 6-12**.

If the head touches the platter, or if dirt gets on the disk, you can have a hard drive crash or **head crash**. You won't be able to access files or run programs. A head crash most likely means you need to replace the drive. Solid state storage devices, which are much less susceptible to damage and failure, do not have any moving parts, so if you have problems with the hard drive, it's probably had some other electronic problem. You might not be able to prevent a head crash, but you can make sure your files and programs aren't lost by regularly backing them up to an external drive or cloud storage.

Disk Space

Your hard drive has limited storage space. If you don't have enough free space, you won't be able to save any more files and you'll also have trouble running your programs. When a program needs more **RAM (random access memory)**, the temporary storage used while the computer is running, than is currently available on the computer, it calls on the hard drive to create **virtual memory**, which is temporary space on the disk. If your hard drive is too full, the program won't run.

You should always have at least 200 MB of free space on your hard drive. To find out how much disk space you have if you use Windows, from the desktop, locate and select your hard drive on the computer and then select the Properties command. For Mac users, you can determine the amount of free space by selecting About This Mac from the Apple menu; in the window that opens, select More Info, select Storage, and then you can review the storage used and available in the window that appears.

What can you do if your hard drive is too full? Here are some helpful tips:

• Free up space by uninstalling unused programs and deleting old files; be sure you back up any old but needed files before deleting them.

• Run a disk cleanup utility to identify and remove other extraneous files you might have overlooked.

Figure 6-12: Hard disk drive read/write head on platter

Chapter 6: Purchasing and Maintaining a Computer ● 6-11

#buyacomputer

Windows 8.X computers are set by default to optimize drives weekly.

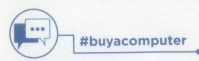

- Optimize the way your remaining files are stored by running a **disk defragmentation utility**, also called a **disk optimization utility**. Defragmenting reorganizes your hard drive to maximize free space.

Display Problems

If your system unit works properly, but the monitor doesn't, you won't be able to operate the computer. A damaged screen on a laptop or tablet is not easy to remedy, so if you determine you need to repair your laptop or tablet screen, take the entire computer to an authorized repair shop.

However, if a desktop computer's screen remains blank after you turn on the computer, and the indicator lights on the monitor don't illuminate, your monitor may be the problem. You can follow these simple steps to troubleshoot the problem:

1. First, for a standalone monitor, check to see that it is plugged into the power source.
2. If you have power, but still don't see any images, verify that the monitor is connected to the computer.
3. If that checks out, you may have a hardware failure. Plug a different monitor into your computer. If it works, the problem is with your first monitor and not your computer.
4. If the second monitor is blank, you may have a damaged **video card**. This is a circuit board that processes image signals. In either case, you'll need to take the monitor or computer to a technician for repair.

Hot Technology Now

Most tablets communicate with their keyboards using Bluetooth for a wireless connection. Bluetooth keyboards are available in standard, portable, mini, and foldable form factors.

Keyboard Problems

What if your keyboard isn't working? If your computer uses an external keyboard, check to make sure the keyboard is plugged into the correct port. If your keyboard is wireless, be sure the batteries are not out of power, and make sure there is nothing blocking the signal to the computer.

Prevent other keyboard problems by taking some simple precautions. Don't eat or drink while typing. Food particles can make keys stick, and liquids can short out electrical connections. Keep dust and dirt away with regular cleaning using compressed air and a vacuum cleaner designed for electronic devices.

Pointing Device Problems

If you turn on your computer, and you don't see a pointer on the screen, you might have problems with your pointing device. If you are using an attached mouse, make sure the cable that attaches your device to your computer is plugged in. A wireless pointing device has a number of parts that need to work together. See **Figure 6-13**.

Figure 6-13: Wireless mice have many parts

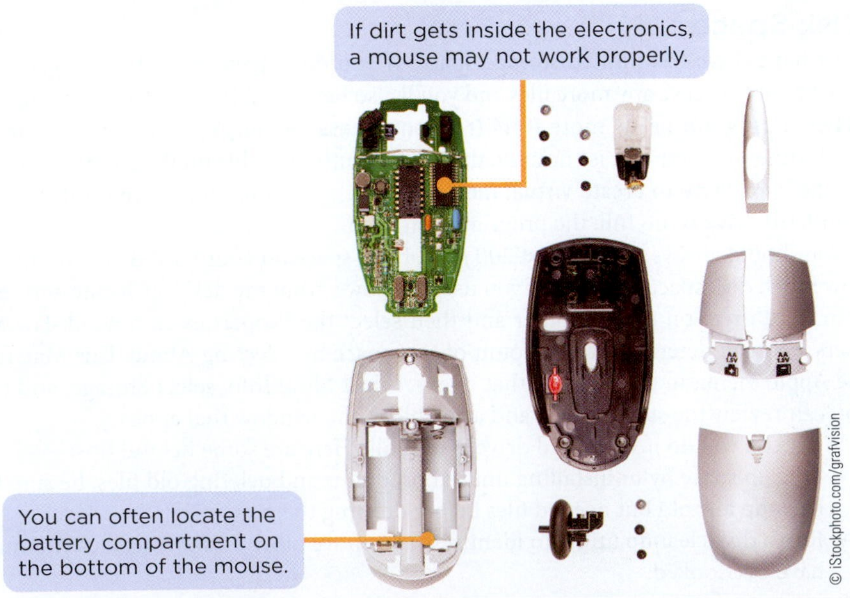

If dirt gets inside the electronics, a mouse may not work properly.
You can often locate the battery compartment on the bottom of the mouse.
© iStockphoto.com/grafvision

First, check the batteries; install fresh batteries on a regular basis. If your wireless pointing device uses a USB transmitter/receiver, check that the transmitter is inserted correctly in the USB port and make sure that it properly connects the device to the computer. As with any electronic device, make sure it's not dirty and ensure that the table or mouse pad is clean.

If your touchpad isn't responding, it may be disabled. Detach all USB devices, turn the computer off, and then restart the computer and see if that fixes the problem. If your computer is running Windows, check the Control Panel and Device Manager for any signs of trouble with the device. If all these don't yield positive results, you may have to take the computer to an authorized repair shop.

Printer Problems

If you click Print and nothing happens, you can follow these simple steps to trouble-shoot printer problems:

1. **Power**: First, check to see that the printer is plugged in.

2. **Connectivity**: Is the printer properly attached to the computer? For wireless printers, this will not be an issue.

3. **Toner or ink**: Look to see if the computer's operating system is sending you any messages—the printer might have low toner or ink. Most systems will guide you through the replacement process.

4. **Paper**: Maybe the printer is out of paper, or maybe there's a paper jam. Most printers allow for easy access to the paper feeding mechanisms, so if there's a jam, you can open the panel and gently dislodge the crumpled paper.

Checking connections and replacing paper, toner, and ink are fairly simple tasks. But if there is a broken part, such as a belt or power supply, you'll have to contact a computer technician or buy a new printer.

Power Problems

If you press the computer's power button and you don't get any response, you may have a power problem. You can follow these simple steps to troubleshoot power problems:

1. If the computer is using wall current, check to see that it's plugged in, that power is going to the outlet or power strip, and that you have all cables connected.

2. If all that is working properly, the power supply may have failed, and you'll need to take the computer to a computer technician for repair.

3. Portable computers and external peripherals may have an AC adapter as an external power supply. Check to see that the power supply on the cable is not damaged. You can purchase a new adapter at most computer stores or online.

What if you can't connect to the Internet or other network? Make sure your router and modem have power and are connected properly to your computer. Are all the lights on and flashing? Try resetting either device by turning it off, then on again, with the power switch.

Other Problems

Are you having trouble getting your computer to recognize a storage device when you try to retrieve or open files? Learning how to troubleshoot and fix common problems can save you a lot of time, frustration, and money.

If you are using optical storage technology, maybe your computer can't recognize or read your DVD or CD. **Optical storage technology** uses light in the form of a low-power laser beam to record and read an optical disk, so the disk must be clean. Take the disk out and look for scratches or dirt. Disk cleaning cloths may salvage a dirty disk.

If your storage device is not working, perhaps there's dirt inside it, or perhaps it was damaged by liquid or extreme temperatures. If you insert a disc in an optical drive

#buyacomputer

Universal chargers fit many devices, but be careful that the voltage, input, and output are identical to your specifications.

and the device tries to read it without success, the device may be damaged. Damage or dirt on solid state storage devices, such as cards and drives, is less obvious. You can try cleaning the connection points with compressed air.

Keeping Your Computer in Working Condition

magnetic hard drive | head crash | solid state drive (SSD) | flash drive | memory card

Buying a computer is a significant investment for many people. Just as you should care for your car with regular oil changes and checkups, you should care for your computer with regular maintenance routines. You can take advantage of some well-known tips on how to care for your computer and peripheral devices. If your digital devices are kept in good working condition, they will work properly and last longer, giving you better value for your money.

Hard Drive

A **magnetic hard drive** is a sensitive device. Potential hazards abound that could cause a **head crash**, rendering the drive useless. If your data is not backed up, you will most likely lose of all your files. How can you avoid such a disaster?

Figure 6-14: Proper maintenance will protect your investment

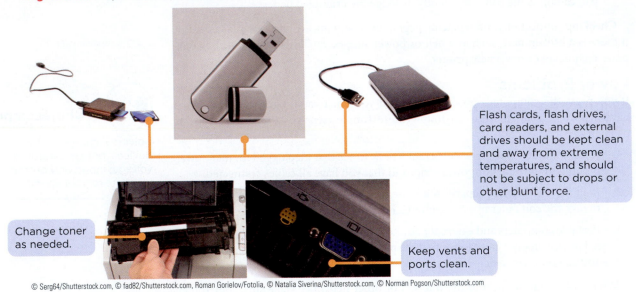

Flash cards, flash drives, card readers, and external drives should be kept clean and away from extreme temperatures, and should not be subject to drops or other blunt force.

Change toner as needed.

Keep vents and ports clean.

© Serg64/Shutterstock.com, © fad82/Shutterstock.com, Roman Gorielov/Fotolia, © Natalia Siverina/Shutterstock.com, © Norman Pogson/Shutterstock.com

First, back up your data on a regular basis so you will be protected in the event your hard drive does crash. To help prevent the hard drive from crashing, you should keep the computer in a dust- and dirt-free environment. Never bump into a computer while it is accessing the drive. Don't place the computer in extreme temperatures.

Solid state drives (SSDs), which have no moving parts, are less susceptible to dirt and impact but should still be treated with care.

Removable Media

Like hard drives, portable media devices can be fragile. A **flash drive**, for example, is a small portable solid state storage device that plugs into a USB port. It is often thrown into a purse or pocket, or attached to a key ring as an accessory. It is better to keep all media away from dust, dirt, and other hazards. Some helpful hints for caring for your removable storage media include the following:

- If your flash drive has a protective case or cover, use it to keep dust and dirt away from the USB plug.
- Store the **memory cards** from your digital camera in their cases when not in the camera.
- If you use DVDs and other optical media to back up your hard drive files, store the backup disks in sleeves or protective cases to keep them safe from scratches and dirt.
- Use a felt-tip marker to clearly label all portable media; and then store everything in a temperature-controlled, clean, safe place.

Screens

A display device is not like a window that you can just spray and wash. The membrane covering many screens is delicate and can be easily damaged. Touch screens in particular get dirty from being touched so often. Some helpful hints for caring for your computer or tablet display include the following:

- Before cleaning, always turn off your display device.
- Use cleaning products specifically meant for computer screens. You can also use a 50/50 solution of water and alcohol, but do not use ammonia-based products.
- Spray the cleaner on a lint-free, soft cloth, rather than directly on the screen. Wipe the cloth gently over the screen area. See **Figure 6-15**.
- Apply a screen protector to most tablets and smartphones to add fingerprint resistance and reduce glare.

If you clean your screen regularly, you will see more clearly and reduce eye strain when you use the computer.

Keyboards

Your fingers are constantly touching the keyboard. Even if you wash your hands before typing, a habit that is difficult to maintain, your keyboard is going to get dirty. Grime, hair, dust, and food will also likely coat the keys and fill in the spaces between the keys of a well-used keyboard. Some helpful hints for caring for your removable storage media include the following:

- Clean your keyboard regularly to keep keys from sticking or becoming unresponsive.
- Gently turn the keyboard upside down to release large particles.
- Use a special keyboard vacuum, not a regular household vacuum cleaner, to get rid of smaller particles. See **Figure 6-16**. Strong suction can dislodge the keys.
- Wipe the keys periodically with a soft cloth. Do not spray cleaners directly onto the keys.
- Keep a can of compressed air handy to spray over the keyboard now and then to keep dust and dirt away.

Pointing Devices

Like keyboards, pointing devices are subject to heavy physical contact. As your hands rest on the mouse or track ball, residue from your hands can transfer to the device. If you use a mouse pad on a well-used surface, dust from the pad will get on the mouse. Some helpful hints for caring for your pointing device include the following:

- Because most mice no longer have open bottoms, you can wipe the optical surface with a soft cloth.
- To keep the buttons in working order, use a vacuum designed for electronic devices. You can also gently shake and then blow on the mouse to remove dust. See **Figure 6-17**.
- Replace batteries regularly on wireless mice.
- If you use a laptop with a touch pad, keep your hands and fingers clean to keep residue off the pad.

On the Job Now

Many companies require screen filters to ensure privacy. For example, if you are seated next to someone on a train, the plastic privacy filter helps to mask confidential information.

Figure 6-15: Cleaning a computer screen

© cunaplus/Shutterstock.com

Figure 6-16: Cleaning a keyboard

© Venus Angel/Shutterstock.com

Figure 6-17: Cleaning a mouse

© anaken2012/Shutterstock.com

Printers

Maintain your printer not only by caring for the device itself but also by being mindful of the key consumables you use with it: ink or toner, and paper. Some helpful hints for caring for your printer include the following:

- Be sure to use the specific ink or toner recommended by the printer manufacturer.
- Toner can leave reside in the printer. To prolong the useful life of your printer, use your printer's cleaning cycles on a regular basis to reduce or eliminate this residue. To run a cleaning cycle, locate and press the proper button on your printer or computer, and then follow the given instructions.
- Store your paper in a dry area—humidity can cause the paper to stick and then jam during printing. If the paper jams, follow the instructions on your printer for gently removing the paper.
- To clean the inside of your printer, open the printer and use a can of compressed air to blow out any paper residue or dust. Use cloths or swabs to wipe surfaces with special cleaning fluids.

A Clean Computer

A clean computer works better than a dirty one. Sometimes, lack of care and maintenance can cause a computer to stop working altogether, so treat your computer kindly. Here are some helpful hints and tips:

- If your computer opens easily, clean both the interior and exterior regularly. Wipe down the exterior with lint-free antistatic wipes. Blow compressed air around openings, such as ports and vents, to clear dust.
- If you have a computer that requires a case to be opened, you can have a professional technician perform a cleaning service if you are not comfortable opening it yourself.
- If you do choose to clean the interior yourself, first check with the computer manufacturer to make sure you don't void the warranty by opening the case. Then be sure the computer is unplugged before starting. Wear an antistatic wristband to protect the components from static electricity. Use a special vacuum to clear away as much dust as possible, and then blow the interior with compressed air to get rid of particles the vacuum couldn't get.
- Clean any computer on a flat, stable surface such as a table to avoid dropping any part of it.

Proper maintenance of your computer and peripherals will keep them running smoothly and trouble-free.

Using Software to Maintain Your Computer

disk cleanup utility | disk defragmentation utility | disk optimization utility | device driver | computer virus | spyware | adware

You turn on your computer. It takes a while to boot up, even more time for the hour glass or spinning disk to stop whirling, and even longer for all the icons on your desktop to load. Perhaps you can't print from your printer, run your scanner, or save the photos from your camera. What's going on? Chances are you need to do some computer maintenance.

Disk Cleanup

A **disk cleanup utility**, available on many operating systems, removes unused files from your hard drive so the computer doesn't search through unneeded files. Unnecessary files can be anywhere on your hard drive. For example, when you place items in the Recycle Bin and don't empty it, those files remain on your computer, taking up space. When you browse the Internet, your computer stores multiple temporary Internet files.

Hot Technology Now

To print to a remote wireless printer, try the AirPrint app for iPads or PrinterShare app for Android devices.

The Bottom Line
- Utility programs can help return your computer to better working condition by scanning for viruses and spyware.
- Be sure that your computer updates drivers, and frequently run the programs that clean up and optimize your hard drive.

The Windows Disk Cleanup utility can identify files such as these and others that can be safely removed. The utility also indicates how much space you will gain by removing the unnecessary files. See **Figure 6-18**.

To start the Disk Cleanup utility in Windows, enter the keywords "Disk Cleanup" in the Search box, select Settings if necessary, and then select Free up disk space by deleting unnecessary files in the search results (note that different versions of Windows may have variations on this search result). Select the drive you want to clean up and click OK. Disk Cleanup scans your computer to find files to delete. You can see a brief description of each type of file before completing the cleanup. If you have any concerns, you can choose to keep any file.

Optimize Drives

A **disk defragmentation utility** or **disk optimization utility**, available on many operating systems, reorganizes the data on a magnetic hard drive so that you can access files more quickly. In Windows, search for the Optimize Drives utility from the Search bar by searching on the keyword "optimize." You can set the utility so that it runs at scheduled intervals to keep your computer working well.

The Disk Defragmention utility or Optimize Drives window displays the Disk Defragmenter or optimization schedule, noting the last time it ran and when it's scheduled to run next. See **Figure 6-19**.

Refer to your computer's user and technical manuals or online help for recommendations on how frequently you should defragment or optimize.

Device Drivers

A **device driver** is software that helps peripheral devices—such as printers, monitors, storage devices, pointing devices, and scanners—communicate with a computer. When you

Figure 6-18: Disk Cleanup for Windows

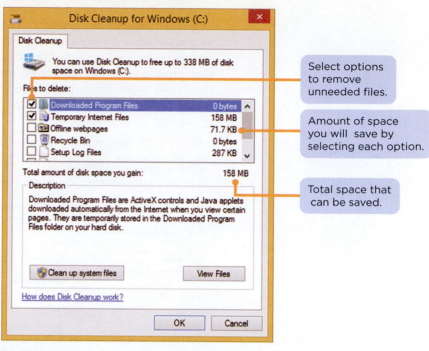

Figure 6-19: Optimize Drives utility

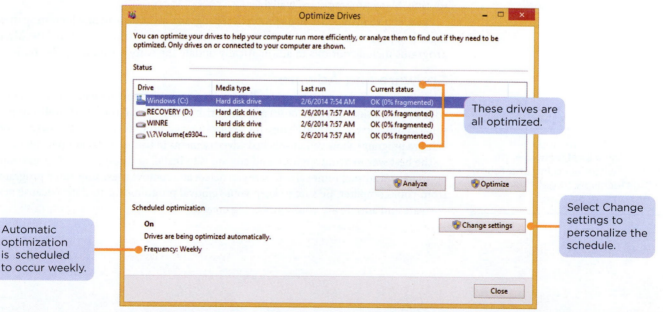

install a new peripheral device, it typically installs the drivers and software necessary to operate the device. Device drivers run only when needed, often to alert you to a problem.

But over time, the drivers may become out of date and stop working; your operating system may display a message to this effect. To update drivers, you can usually download the latest versions from the manufacturer's Web site. Operating systems often provide automatic updates for installed programs that include device drivers. You should update software when prompted. Be sure to periodically check the Action Center to see if anything is needed. See **Figure 6-20**.

Figure 6-20: System and Security Action Center

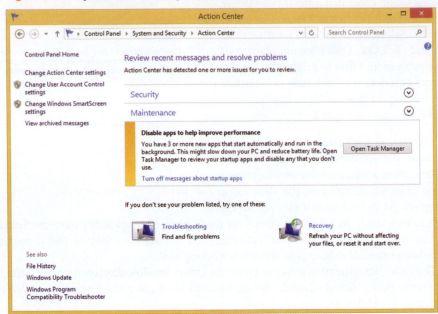

Virus Protection

A **computer virus** is malicious software that infects your computer without your knowledge or permission. A virus can wreak havoc on your computer by stealing data, wiping out files or entire hard drives, and slowing down performance. Viruses infect computers via email, Web downloads, and visits to Internet sites. Protect your computer from viruses by installing and running virus protection software as part of your maintenance routine. Many programs are available.

Once you've installed a virus protection program, set it to scan any incoming messages and programs to protect your computer, and be sure to keep it up to date. Many programs include options to automatically update the software on a regular basis.

Spyware and Adware

#buyacomputer

Go to twitter.com, and then search for **@SAMTechNow,** the book's Twitter account, and follow @SAMTechNow to get tweets on your home page.

Like viruses, spyware and adware install themselves on your computer without your knowledge or permission. **Spyware** poses a security risk because it can track and steal your personal information. It can also change the settings on your browser without your permission. **Adware** programs show you unsolicited advertisements in banners or pop-up windows.

The best way to avoid spyware and adware is to install and run prevention software. Spyware and adware removal software can detect and remove these unwanted programs from your computer. Be sure to keep your removal programs up-to-date, because new spyware and adware are constantly being created.

Chapter Review

Buying a Computer

1. What is the definition of "form factor"? List two form factors. How does form factor affect your buying decisions?

2. Name five important considerations when buying a computer.

3. Name two of the main options you have for operating systems.

4. List five questions you should ask yourself before you prepare a budget for your computer purchase.

Protecting Computer Hardware

5. Name three hazards you should avoid to keep your hardware safe.

6. What is the danger of dust and liquid to a computer system?

7. Explain the difference between a UPS and a surge suppressor.

Safeguarding Your Computer

8. Name two ways you can prevent your computer from being stolen.

9. Name two ways you can prevent your data from being stolen.

10. List four good habits to practice when creating a password, and give an example of a strong password.

Troubleshooting Common Hardware Problems

11. Explain the symptoms of a hard drive crash.

12. Describe what can go wrong with your display. What steps can you take to isolate the problem?

13. What are two symptoms of power problems?

14. List three steps you can you follow to troubleshoot printer problems.

Keeping Your Computer in Working Condition

15. Describe how you can work to keep your hard drive working properly.

16. Explain the best way to clean a display screen and keyboard.

17. What are two steps you can take to make sure your wireless mouse and keyboard function properly?

Using Software to Maintain Your Computer

18. Explain what a disk cleanup utility does to help you maintain your computer.

19. Explain what disk optimization does to help you maintain your computer.

20. Explain the difference between spyware and adware and why you want to prevent either from getting on your computer.

Test Your Knowledge Now

1. _____ is a form factor that is not a portable computer.
   a. Tablet
   b. Desktop
   c. Laptop
   d. Smartphone

2. Before buying a computer, you should first determine your _____.
   a. hardware
   b. CPU
   c. budget
   d. software

3. A _____ is a portable computer with a removable keyboard.
   a. tablet
   b. desktop
   c. laptop
   d. convertible

4. A(n) _____ computer is a high-end performance notebook that is very light, uses solid state drives, and has good battery life.
   a. ultrabook
   b. tablet
   c. laptop
   d. notebook

5. When you are buying a computer, you should consider getting the best _____ you can afford at the time because it is the most important component in a computer.
   a. printer
   b. RAM
   c. CPU
   d. display

6. A typical computer should have _____ of random access memory.
   a. 1–2 GB
   b. 100–200 GB
   c. 4–16 GB
   d. 400–1600 TB

7. Most computers have between _____ of built-in storage.
   a. 10 and 20 TB
   b. 100 and 200 MB
   c. 4 and 16 MB
   d. 500 GB and 1 TB

8. The major advantage of a tablet is _____.
   a. storage capacity
   b. expandability
   c. portability
   d. more features

9. If you want to protect yourself from a power failure if the power goes out, you should buy a _____ so you can still use your computer.
   a. battery
   b. UPS
   c. surge suppressor
   d. GPS

10. Buy a _____ to protect your computer from power fluctuations.
    a. battery
    b. UPS
    c. surge suppressor
    d. GPS

11. If your computer doesn't have enough RAM, it can use _____ to help with the shortfall.
    a. battery supply
    b. virtual memory
    c. power supply
    d. USB ports

12. Which of the following is most likely to help you locate a stolen computer?
    a. UPS
    b. RAM
    c. CPU
    d. RFID

13. To best protect your data and have access to it from anywhere in the world, you can use _____ storage technology.
    a. cloud
    b. solid
    c. internal
    d. random

14. The advantage that solid state drives (SSDs) have over magnetic hard drives is that they _____.
    a. work faster
    b. provide more storage
    c. have no moving parts
    d. can tolerate liquids

15. The main disadvantage of cloud storage is that _____; therefore, you might not be able to get your files.
    a. the devices are fragile
    b. the servers may be unreliable
    c. access is available only from tablets
    d. unreliable providers may go out of business

16. To free up space on your drive by removing unnecessary files, use the _____ utility.
    a. Disk Defragmenter
    b. Disk Cleanup
    c. Disk Optimizer
    d. Spyware

17. Which of the following can track and steal your personal information and change your browser settings without your permission?
    a. antivirus software
    b. adware
    c. spyware
    d. utilities

18. The first thing you should check when your wireless keyboard stops working is _____.
    a. batteries
    b. cables
    c. ports
    d. plugs

19. Which of the following does *not* belong in your toolkit to keep your computer clean?
    a. can of compressed air
    b. soft cloth
    c. ammonia
    d. small electronics vacuum

20. _____ programs show you unsolicited advertisements in banners or pop-up windows.
    a. Spyware
    b. Adware
    c. Virus
    d. Optimization

21. In the space next to each image below, write the letter of the term that describes each form factor.
    a. tablet
    b. smartphone
    c. desktop
    d. laptop

© Daboost/Shutterstock.com

Try This Now

1: Shop for an Ultrabook

Investigate the purchase of an ultrabook for school that is powerful, versatile, and affordable.

    a. Open the site amazon.com and search for an Asus ultrabook. Select an ultrabook that is reasonably priced, current, and powerful using the criteria that you read about in the chapter. Take a screenshot of your selection that shows an image of the computer as well as its price and specifications.

    b. Open the site newegg.com and search for a Samsung ultrabook. Select an ultrabook that is reasonably priced, current, and powerful using the criteria that you read about in the chapter. Take a screenshot of your selection that shows an image of the computer as well as its price and specifications.

    c. Open the site bestbuy.com and search for a Lenovo ultrabook. Select an ultrabook that is reasonably priced, current, and powerful using the criteria that you read about in the chapter. Take a screenshot of your selection that shows an image of the computer as well as its price and specifications.

    d. Place the three screenshots in a single Word document, and add your answers to the following: Which of the three sites was easiest to search? Which one of the three ultrabooks would you prefer? Why?

2: Shop for a Tablet

Investigate the purchase of a tablet for school that is powerful, versatile, current, and affordable. Search for a full-size tablet with a diagonal screen measurement that is more than 9 inches.

    a. Open the site bestbuy.com and search for the latest iPad. Select an iPad that is reasonably priced, current, and powerful using the criteria that you read about in the chapter. Take a screenshot your of selection that shows an image of the computer as well as its price and specifications.

    b. Open the site dell.com and search for a Dell tablet. Select a tablet that is reasonably priced, current, and powerful using the criteria that you read about in the chapter. Take a screenshot of your selection that shows an image of the computer as well as its price and specifications.

    c. Open the site frys.com and search for a Lenovo tablet. Select a tablet that is reasonably priced, current, and powerful using the criteria that you read about in the chapter. Take a screenshot of your selection that shows an image of the computer as well as its price and specifications.

    d. Place the three screenshots in a single Word document, and add your answers to the following: Which of the three sites was easiest to search? Which one of the three tablets would you prefer? Why? Which of the tablets included a keyboard?

3: Shop for an All-in-One Computer

Investigate the purchase of an all-in-one computer for your home that is powerful, versatile, and current. Search for a large all-in-one computer with a diagonal screen measurement that is more than 26 inches.

All-in-One Computers

© Glovatskiy/Shutterstock.com

    a. Open the site hp.com and search for an HP all-in-one computer. Select an all-in-one computer that is current and powerful using the criteria that you read about in the chapter. Take a screenshot of your selection that shows an image of the computer as well as its price and specifications.

    b. Open the site staples.com and search for any all-in-one computer. Select an all-in-one computer that is current and powerful using the criteria that you read about in the chapter. Take a screenshot of your selection that shows an image of the computer as well as its price and specifications.

    c. Open the site costco.com and search for any all-in-one computer. Select an all-in-one computer that is current and powerful using the criteria that you read about in the chapter. Take a screenshot of your selection that shows an image of the computer as well as its price and specifications.

    d. Place the three screenshots in a single Word document, and add your answers to the following: Which of the three sites was easiest to search? Which one of the three all-in-one computers would you prefer? Why? What were the screen sizes of each one? Were the keyboards wireless?

Critical Thinking Now

1: CNET Unbiased Reviews

When you research buying a computer online, finding unbiased information on a retail site can be challenging. The site cnet.com publishes objective reviews and news on the latest technology products. Using CNET, search the reviews for the best tablets. Read through the five top choices and watch the videos, if available. Write at least 100 words on which tablet you would select based on CNET's recommendations. Provide details such as name, price, and the bottom line from the review.

2: Lost iPhone

Your friend lives in a college dorm and she seems to misplace her iPhone weekly. After reading this chapter, you suggest that she download the Find My iPhone app. Research how the tracking app works and write at least 100 words to explain the process.

3: Touch Screen Monitor

People who use the smaller ultrabooks for their desk areas at home often prefer having a second, larger touch screen monitor. Research a large touch screen monitor that you could connect to an ultrabook. Write a list of the specifications and price of the touch screen that you select.

Ethical Issues Now

As an employee of a major smartphone company, you have been issued a prototype smartphone for testing purposes that has not been released to the public. You are under strict orders not to let the phone out of your sight. Today you had lunch at a local restaurant and left the phone behind on the table. After realizing the loss, you returned to the restaurant an hour later, but the prototype phone was gone.

Smartphone of the Future

© Norph/Shutterstock.com

  a. Knowing that you will be fired if the press is shown your prototype phone, should you tell your boss? Why or why not?
  b. Research a similar news story and write a synopsis of at least 100 words of what actually happened in the real-life story.

Team Up Now – Computer Maintenance Checklist

Based on the computer's operating system in your school's computer lab, work together as a team to create a computer maintenance checklist that contains text and video tutorial links.

  a. Research preventative maintenance tasks to keep your school's computer running smoothly.
  b. Create a checklist of five tasks that your team determines as critical to maintaining the computer.
  c. Search for a correlating video that provides a tutorial for each of the five tasks on the checklist and add the links to the checklist.
  d. Submit the checklist and video links to your instructor.

Key Terms

adware	form factor	power surge
all-in-one	full data encryption (FDE)	processor
byte	gigabyte (GB)	radio-frequency identification (RFID) tag
central processing unit (CPU)	global positioning system (GPS)	random access memory (RAM)
cloud backup	head crash	real-time location system
computer virus	internal hard drive	service plan
convertible	laptop	solid state drive (SSD)
data encryption	magnetic hard drive	spyware
desktop	memory card	storage device
device driver	mobile device	surge suppressor
disk cleanup utility	notebook	tablet
disk defragmentation utility	operating system	terabyte (TB)
disk optimization utility	optical storage technology	ultrabook
Encrypting File System (EFS)	password	uninterruptible power supply (UPS)
extended warranty	personal identification number (PIN)	username
external hard drive	platform	video card
firewall	power fluctuation	virtual memory
flash drive	power spike	

CHAPTER 7

The Connected Computer

Taylor is calm, knowing that her school's network security software is keeping her data safe from intruders.

Taylor's laptop is connected to her school's wireless LAN, so she can access the Internet to do research right outdoors.

Taylor and her lab partner are editing a draft of their project together—even though they are in different locations—using cloud computing.

© arek_malang/Shutterstock.com

Taylor Peterson is working on a project for her biology class. Thanks to networking technologies, Taylor can connect to the Internet to do research, exchange text messages with her lab partner, and use email to send questions to her professor, all while enjoying the fresh air.

Microsoft® product screenshots used with permission from Microsoft® Corporation.

Introduction to Networks

network | network interface card (NIC) | hub | switch | router | network architecture | peer-to-peer network | client/server network | server | client | local area network (LAN) | wireless access point | broadband modem | node | wide area network (WAN) | Internet | Internet backbone | network service provider (NSP) | Internet service provider (ISP) | Web | personal area network (PAN) | Bluetooth | wired network | wireless network

The Bottom Line

- Networks can be simple or complex, and network components can interact in different ways.
- Networks can span limited areas the size of your home office or school, or they can be as large as a town or a country.
- The Internet, a collection of personal, local, regional, national, and international computer networks, is the largest network in the world.

Networks let people share resources, devices, information, software, and data. A **network** is a system of two or more computers and communications devices linked by wires, cables, or a telecommunications system. Networks can connect devices over large or small areas.

Figure 7-1: Networks connect people

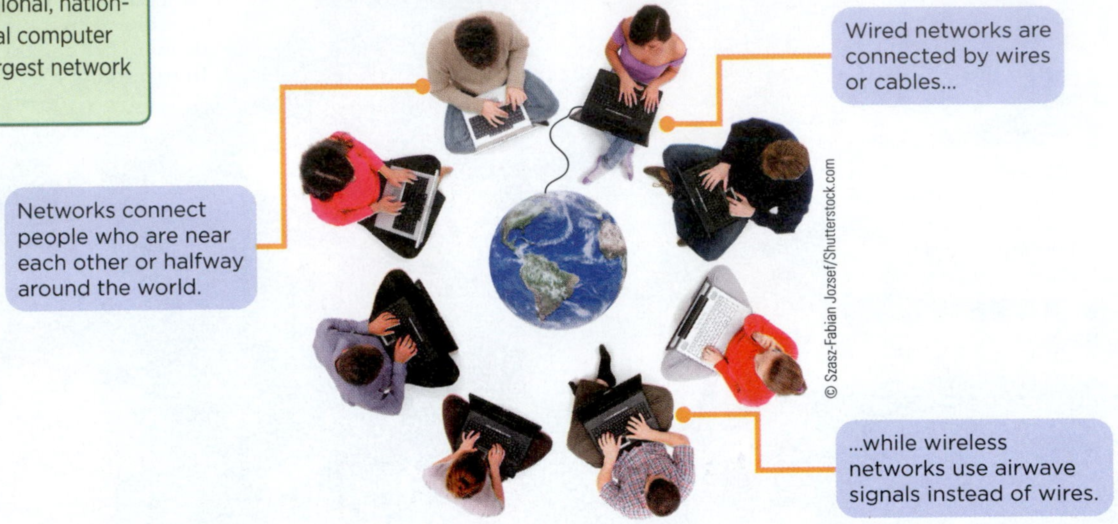

Wired networks are connected by wires or cables...
Networks connect people who are near each other or halfway around the world.
...while wireless networks use airwave signals instead of wires.
© Szasz-Fabian Jozsef/Shutterstock.com

Network Hardware and Software

How do networks make connections? They use both hardware and software.

- Simple networks, such as those you find in a home, often use the networking features of the home PC's operating system.
- Larger and more complex networks require more sophisticated network software. Networks that connect to other networks use special types of communications devices.

For hardware, networked computers need the components shown in **Table 7-1**.

Table 7-1: Network components

Component	Looks like this	Purpose
Network interface card (NIC)	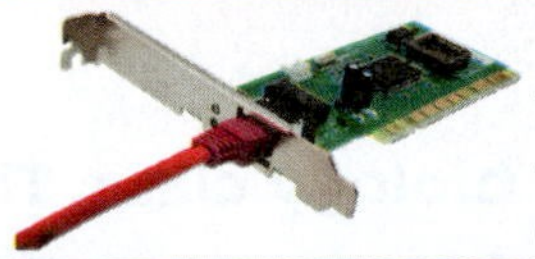 © moritorus/Shutterstock.com	A circuit board with special electronic circuits that connects a computer to a network.
Hub or **switch**	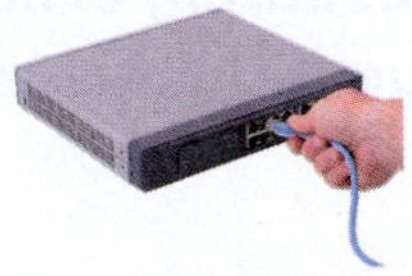 © Rob Hyrons/Shutterstock.com 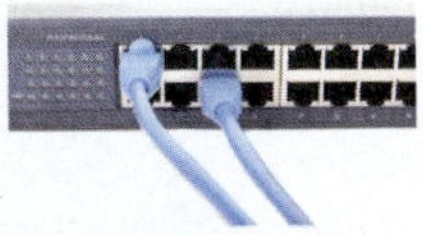 © Darryl Brooks/Shutterstock.com	A device that provides a central point for cables in a network. Hubs are less common as they transfer all data to all devices. Most networks now use switches, which transfer data only to the intended recipient.
Router	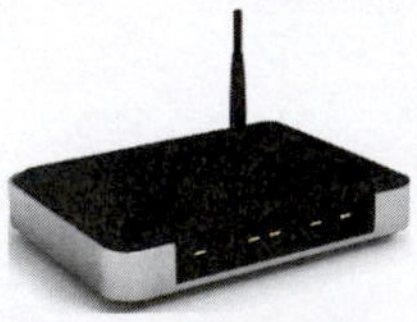 © Sashkin/Shutterstock.com	A device that connects two or more networks and directs, or routes, the flow of information along the networks.

© 2015 Cengage Learning

Network Architecture

Network architecture determines how networked computers interact with one another. Networks commonly use one of two architectural models: peer-to-peer or client/server.

A **peer-to-peer network** is best suited for networks of 10 or fewer computers, like those found in homes or small offices. Each computer maintains its own files and software. All computers have the same capabilities and responsibilities, but share resources and peripherals such as printers.

In a **client/server network**, one central computer, called the **server**, controls access to network resources. The other computers or devices are called **clients**. The clients request services from the server. For example, a client computer might ask the server for access to a software program, a customer database, the Internet, or a printer.

Home Network

If you have a computer at home, you probably use it with peripheral devices such as a printer, scanner, or external hard drive. If you have more than one computer, it makes sense for all computers to share the same devices. You probably also want your computers to connect to the Internet.

To connect your home computers to peripheral devices and to the Internet or other network, you can create a **local area network (LAN)**, which connects computers within a small geographic area. Your home LAN can be wired, wireless, or a combination of both.

For hardware, you may need to install a number of devices, such as those shown in **Table 7-2**.

Table 7-2: Network devices

Network device	Purpose
Wireless access point	Lets wireless devices connect to a wired network
Router	Sends data between networked computers
Broadband modem	Connects a computer to the Internet

© 2015 Cengage Learning

You only need a modem if you are connecting your network to one outside your home. Routers and modems are relatively inexpensive and easy to install. See **Figure 7-2** on the next page for a typical home network setup.

For software, most current operating systems, such as Windows and Mac OS X, have controls that let you set up and run home LANs.

Local Area Networks

A local area network (LAN) connects computers and devices in a limited area, such as a home, a school, or an office complex. Each computer or device on the network is called a **node**. Many LANs are designed as client/server networks. The network server is a centralized location for common files and software.

Organizations use LANs so people can share files and software, send and receive email, use high-speed printers, access the Internet, video-conference with satellite offices, and more.

Networks can save organizations money by allowing users to share resources. For example, most software developers sell special versions of their software for use on networks. Organizations pay a license fee per user rather than installing a program on each machine. The per-user license fee is generally less than the cost of each installation.

Wide Area Networks

A **wide area network (WAN)** covers a large geographic region. A WAN is appropriate for a state, country, or other large area where data needs to be transmitted over long distances. See **Figure 7-3** on page 7-5.

#ConnectingNow

If you are hanging out on campus, you must be within 300 feet of a network router to connect to the rest of the world.

On the Job Now

As hospitals and other healthcare organizations increase their use of information technology, they will need more network administrators to manage the growing systems and networks. Employment of network and computer systems administrators in general is expected to grow 28 percent from now to 2020, faster than the average for all occupations.

#ConnectingNow

Change the preset password on your home router to a strong password, which is long and uses numbers, letters, and symbols.

Hot Technology Now

To view your local network connection on a Windows computer, type **network** in the Search text box, and then select **Network and Sharing Center** to view the basic network information and to set up connections.

Figure 7-2: Typical home network setup

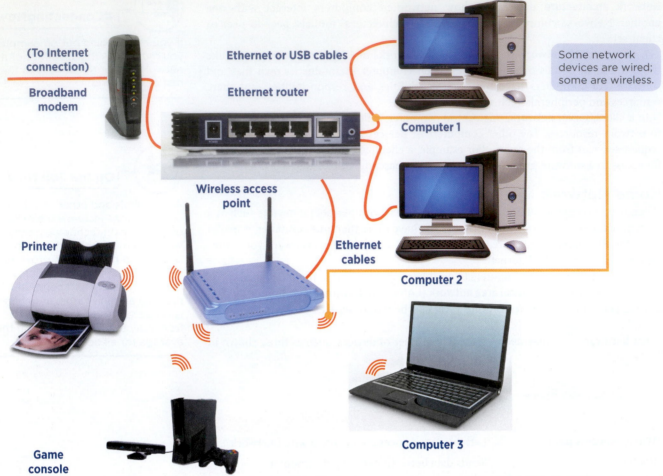

(To Internet connection)

Broadband modem

Ethernet or USB cables

Ethernet router

Wireless access point

Printer

Ethernet cables

Some network devices are wired; some are wireless.

Computer 1

Computer 2

Computer 3

Game console

On the Job Now

The U.S. military has replaced many of its wired connections with the Wireless Network Defense program, which maintains a wireless network even if one connection is damaged.

Hot Technology Now

You can test the speed of your network connections at speedtest.net. The site tells you how fast you can download and upload data, and can recommend tools for improving your speed.

A WAN can be one large network, or a series of interconnected LANs:

- **A multinational company** would use a WAN to connect all their offices around the world.
- **Governments** might use WANs to facilitate communications between different departments.
- **A national retail chain** could use a WAN to connect store locations to headquarters, so every store can access centralized systems for inventory, personnel, and marketing.

Introducing the Internet

The **Internet** is a collection of personal, local, regional, national, and international computer networks linked together to share data and tasks. It is the largest network in the world. The Internet carries voice, data, video, and graphics.

The **Internet backbone**, the essential infrastructure of the Internet, is owned by several telephone and communications companies around the world; no single entity controls or owns the Internet. Backbone links and routers are maintained by **network service providers (NSPs)**.

An **Internet service provider (ISP)** is a company that offers Internet access to individuals, businesses, and smaller ISPs. The **Web**, a huge collection of interconnected Web pages, is part of the Internet, as are many other data services, including Voice over IP, global positioning systems, and media-delivery services.

Personal Area Networks

A **personal area network (PAN)** connects personal digital devices within a range of about 30 feet (9 meters). Personal area networks work without using wires or cables.

Figure 7-3: WAN using multiple networking technologies

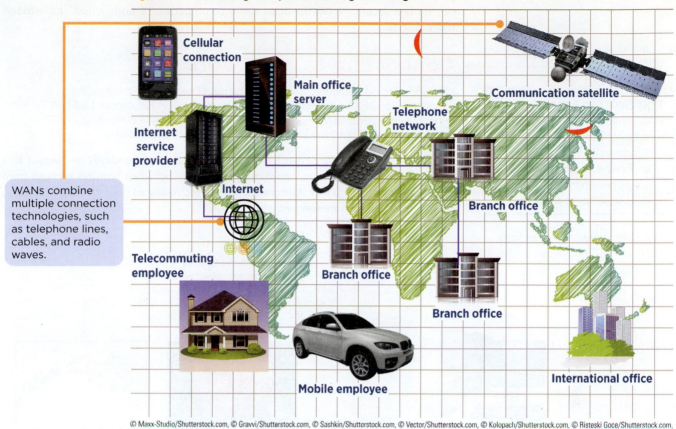

Cellular connection

Main office server

Communication satellite

Internet service provider

Telephone network

Internet

Branch office

WANs combine multiple connection technologies, such as telephone lines, cables, and radio waves.

Telecommuting employee

Branch office

Branch office

Mobile employee

International office

Bluetooth is a type of PAN technology which you can use in the following ways:
- Connect your printer or mouse to your computer.
- Connect your cell phone to a headset or car speakers so you can use the phone hands-free while in the car.
- Transmit data wirelessly from a media player to your computer speakers.

Wired or Wireless

Data in a **wired network** travels from one device to another over cables. Wired networks tend to be more secure and transmit data faster than wireless networks. Data in a **wireless network** travels through the air; usually, it does not require cables. Wireless

By the Numbers Now

The Internet Traffic Report monitors the speed and reliability of Internet traffic around the world. **Figure 7-4** compares Internet connection speeds in Asia, Europe, Australia, North America, and South America. The higher the index value, the faster and more reliable the Internet connection.

Figure 7-4: Internet connection speeds

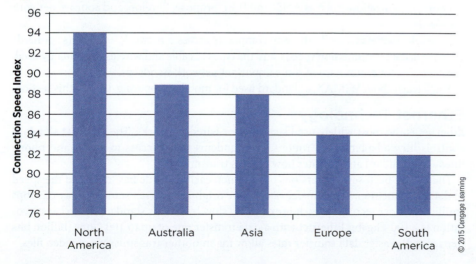

© 2015 Cengage Learning

networks tend to be more convenient and easier to set up than wired networks, but can be less secure. Networks often use a combination of both wired and wireless technologies.

Connecting to a Network

network standard | Ethernet standard | Ethernet | Power over Ethernet (PoE) | Phoneline/HomePNA | Powerline | Wi-Fi (wireless fidelity) | Bluetooth | 3G | 4G | network interface card (NIC) | digital modem | router | mobile computing | Wi-Fi network | WiMAX | hot zone | hotspot | LTE (Long Term Evolution)

Computers need specific network hardware, services, and standards to connect to a LAN or a WAN. In addition, connecting to the Internet often requires services from an Internet service provider. All communication technologies need global standards so they can understand one another.

Figure 7-5: Network connections

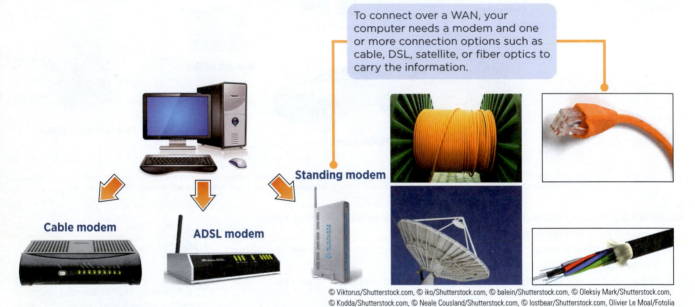

To connect over a WAN, your computer needs a modem and one or more connection options such as cable, DSL, satellite, or fiber optics to carry the information.

Standing modem

Cable modem

ADSL modem

© Viktorus/Shutterstock.com, © iko/Shutterstock.com, © balein/Shutterstock.com, © Oleksiy Mark/Shutterstock.com, © Kodda/Shutterstock.com, © Neale Cousland/Shutterstock.com, © lostbear/Shutterstock.com, Olivier Le Moal/Fotolia

By the Numbers Now

Each month, more than 1.1 billion people update their Facebook accounts, 1 billion people visit YouTube, and 280 million people use Skype.

Network Standards

Computers need a common language to communicate over networks. Network hardware and software must work together, regardless of who made them or where they are located. To ensure that any computer in any part of the world can connect to any network, organizations such as ANSI and IEEE propose, develop, and approve network standards.

Network standards specify the way computers access a network, the type(s) of hardware used, data transmission speeds, and the types of cable and wireless technology used. See **Table 7-3** for a summary of some important network standards.

You'll learn about WiMAX, a standard used for mobile computing, later in this section.

Ethernet Technology

Ethernet is the most widely used standard for wired networks. The **Ethernet standard** controls how adapter cards, routers, and modems share access to cables and phone lines. The standard also dictates how devices transmit data.

There have been several versions of Ethernet; each upgrade has increased the speed of data transmission. The transfer rate for the original Ethernet standard was 10 Mbps (million bits per second), which is extremely slow by today's standards. The latest evolution is a 100-Gigabit Ethernet with a data transfer rate of up to 100 Gbps (billion bits per second). Faster data transfer rates allow for smoother transmission of video files.

By the Numbers Now

3% of Americans still connect to the Internet at home using dial-up connections.

Table 7-3: Network standards and how they are used

Standard	Example devices that use standard	Used for
Ethernet		Establishing wired networks
Power over Ethernet (PoE)		Transferring both power and data via an Ethernet network
Phoneline/HomePNA and **Powerline**		Connecting computers through ordinary telephone wires
Wi-Fi (wireless fidelity)		Creating wireless home and small business networks
Bluetooth		Allowing a wide assortment of devices to communicate wirelessly over short distances
3G, **4G**		Establishing cellular networks

Communications Hardware

Computers need appropriate communications hardware to connect to networks, such as network cards, adapters, modems, routers, hubs, and switches. To connect to a network, your computer might need a **network interface card (NIC)**, which can be wired or wireless. See **Figure 7-6** on the next page.

Most modems today are digital. A **digital modem** sends and receives data and information to and from a digital line. Three types of digital modems are ISDN (for ISDN lines), DSL (for DSL lines), and cable (for cable TV lines), shown in **Figure 7-7** on the next page. All these modems typically include built-in Wi-Fi connectivity.

Hubs and switches provide a central point for network cables. Hubs transfer all data to all devices and switches transfer data only to specified recipients. Recall that most modern networks use switches rather than hubs. A **router** manages network traffic by evaluating network messages and routing them on the best path to their destination.

Figure 7-6: Wired and wireless NICs

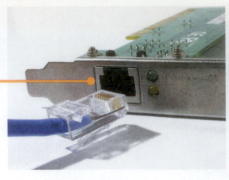

A wired card provides a computer port into which you plug an Ethernet cable.

A wireless card provides an antenna for sending and receiving wireless signals.

Wired

Wireless

© Pixel 4 Images/Shutterstock.com, © skaljac/Shutterstock.com

Hot Technology Now

Check out the app stores of Android at play.google.com, Apple at store.apple.com and Microsoft at microsoftstore.com. You can use your portable device to search the Internet, download movies and music, or send and receive email and text messages anywhere you can get a signal.

By the Numbers Now

A recent survey found that 91% of the adult population owns a mobile phone. Over half of Americans now use mobile phones instead of landlines.

Internet Service Providers

Once you have connected to your local network, you need a way to connect to the Internet, which you do through an Internet service provider (ISP). ISPs use specialized equipment to connect you, for a fee, to the Internet backbone. These connections are made using satellites, cable, phone, or fiber-optic lines.

Most ISPs today offer broadband connectivity capable of transmitting large amounts of data at high speeds. Service areas vary; some ISPs offer service nationwide, while others service a smaller area.

In the past, you had to dial up to reconnect to the Internet after every session. Most connections today are always-on connections, meaning your computer remains connected to the Internet at all times.

Mobile Computing

Smartphones, laptops, tablets, and other handheld devices can connect wirelessly to networks to share data and services, which is known as **mobile computing**.

Wireless LANs and public hotspots use the Wi-Fi standard to connect to the Internet. **Wi-Fi networks** use radio signals to provide high-speed Internet connections to compatible wireless computers and devices. Wi-Fi adapters are often built into portable computers. You can also connect to Wi-Fi networks using a wireless modem.

WiMAX is a standard for longer-range wireless network connections, up to 30 miles. WiMAX is used by cities and cellular networks to provide high-speed Internet access. WiMAX provides network access from fixed locations called **hot zones** or **hotspots**.

Smartphones use Wi-Fi in addition to 3G (3rd generation) and 4G (4th generation) cellular networks. Bluetooth can connect mobile devices at short distances, such as to broadcast your smartphone calls over the GPS receiver in your car.

Figure 7-7: Types of modems

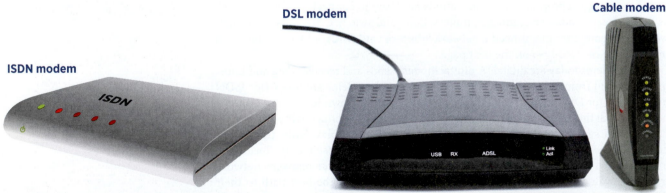

DSL modem

Cable modem

ISDN modem

© Artgraphixel/Shutterstock.com, Petr Malyshev/Fotolia, © Norman Chan/Shutterstock.com

Cellular Standards

Mobile phone standards have evolved to meet the ever-increasing demands of consumers, who want data as well as voice communication on their phones. Cellular companies constantly upgrade their networks and standards for faster, better data transmission. While 3G cellular networks offer Internet services virtually anywhere cellular phone service is used, 4G networks offer high-speed Internet service. It is less widely available, but is expanding rapidly, and should be the dominant cellular standard by 2017.

Many 4G Internet connections can be as fast, or faster, than cable modem or DSL connections. **LTE (Long Term Evolution)** and WiMAX are competing 4G standards offered by different cellular providers.

#ConnectingNow

To save on a smartphone data plan on a 3G or 4G network, connect to a wireless network instead of a cellular network on campus, in a coffee shop, or at home.

How Networks Work

resource | data | network hardware | protocol | domain-based network | domain controller | wireless network | wireless router | Wi-Fi network | Wi-Fi hotspot | tether | personal mobile hotspot | personal hotspot | data encryption | cable | port | RJ-11 port | modem | cable modem | DSL modem | wireless modem | protocol | TCP/IP | IPv4 protocol | IPv6 protocol | bandwidth | broadband | narrowband

Networks connect computers and digital devices to share **resources** (such as storage devices, printers, servers, and communications hardware) and **data** (programs and information).

The Bottom Line
- Networks need hardware to transmit data.
- Networks let you share resources and data to get your work done.

Figure 7-8: Sharing resources and data

Working together, these components create a network.

Network hardware includes clients, servers, modems, network interface cards, hubs, switches, cables, and routers. In order for these components to communicate, they must adhere to common network **protocols**, or rules.

Domain vs. Peer

Networks can be domain-based or peer-to-peer. **Domain-based networks** have a domain controller that acts as a gateway to the network and its resources. A **domain controller** is a hardware device, such as a server, that regulates access to the network. In a domain-based network, computers are not "equal," because they don't all have the same access to network resources.

To log onto a typical domain-based network, you need a username and password; the network is controlled by a network administrator. A peer-to-peer network does not require a controller or a network administrator, because each computer or device is equal on the network and controls access to its own resources, including files and devices.

Wireless Networks

In addition to domain vs. peer-to-peer, networks can be wired or wireless. **Wireless networks** communicate via signals through the air, connecting devices without the use of cables. Mobile computing, which includes tablet computers and smartphones, is a completely wireless technology. Wireless devices include the following:

- Computers
- Printers
- Scanners
- Cameras
- Mobile devices

Wireless routers allow computers to connect wirelessly to a local network or to the Internet. Even though a wireless device transmits signals wirelessly, unless it is using a battery, the device might still be plugged into a wall outlet for power.

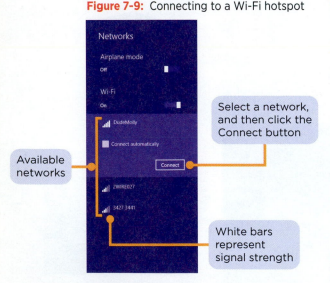

Figure 7-9: Connecting to a Wi-Fi hotspot

Select a network, and then click the Connect button

Available networks

White bars represent signal strength

Wi-Fi Hotspot

A **Wi-Fi (wireless fidelity) network** uses radio signals to connect computers and devices. **Wi-Fi hotspots** let you connect your Wi-Fi-enabled laptop, tablet, or smartphone to the Internet in a public space such as a coffee shop or library.

To connect to a Wi-Fi hotspot:

1. Click the network icon on your Wi-Fi enabled device. (On a Windows computer, the icon is typically located on the taskbar or desktop.) A window opens showing available networks. See **Figure 7-9**.

2. Some networks display a browser window to ask you to agree to their terms.

3. If you are connecting to a private network, you are asked for a username and password.

Tethering and Mobile Hotspots

If you are using your tablet, desktop, or laptop computer in an area with no available Wi-Fi networks, you can still connect it to the Internet if you have a mobile phone. You **tether** (connect) your mobile phone to your computer, using a USB cable or Bluetooth, and then turn on your mobile phone's tethering feature. Your computer can then connect to the Internet using the mobile phone's Internet connection.

To connect more than one computer to the Internet using your mobile phone, you can use the phone as a wireless access point (see **Figure 7-10**), called a **personal mobile hotspot**. Turn on your phone's mobile hotspot (also called a **personal hotspot** in Apple iOS) feature. The devices connect to the Internet using Wi-Fi. Some mobile phones limit the number of devices you can connect to the mobile hotspot.

#ConnectingNow

Place the access point or router in a central location in your home away from physical obstructions such as plaster or brick walls that weaken the signal.

Hot Technology Now

To locate free Wi-Fi hotspots in your town or city, search for your location at openwifispots.com.

Mobile phone carriers charge extra for tethering and mobile hotspot service, and you will need to add this feature to your data service package. Also, check with your mobile carrier to make sure your phone supports tethering and mobile hotspots.

Mobile networks need protection from unethical users who might try to capture your data as it's transmitted through the airwaves. To guard against data theft, most cell networks use **data encryption**, which scrambles and unscrambles data so that it is not usable en route. If you use tethering or mobile hotspots, verify that your carrier encrypts data.

Figure 7-10: Using a phone as a mobile hotspot

Cables, Connectors, Ports

Wired networks have **cables** that connect network devices through **ports** (outlets), using connectors that match each type of port opening. See **Figure 7-11**. Some networks use telephone cables, which connect through telephone **(RJ-11) ports**.

Depending on data transfer requirements, networks use one of the following types of cables:

- Twisted pair, which has the slowest rate of data transfer
- Coaxial
- Fiber optic, which has the fastest rate of data transfer

Modems

A **modem** is a communications device that connects a communications channel such as the Internet to a sending or receiving device such as a computer. Dial-up modems convert digital data into analog data and back, so networks can transmit and receive data via analog telephone lines.

- **Cable modems** send and receive digital data over a cable TV connection. In some cases, the cable modem can be part of a set-top cable box.
- **DSL modems** are external devices that use existing standard copper telephone wiring to send and receive digital data.
- **Wireless modems** are often built into laptop and tablet computers, or they attach via a USB port. A cell phone can work as a modem, too.

By the Numbers Now

A small business or home wireless network can be set up for under $50. Often ISPs provide a free wireless router with a service contract.

Figure 7-11: Connectors and ports

Wired network cables, or Ethernet cables, connect through Ethernet ports using RJ-45 connectors.

Ethernet port and connector

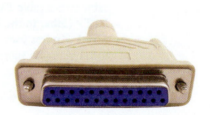

Parallel port connector

Serial port and connector

USB port and connector

USB (Universal Serial Bus) ports connect devices that are wired for USB using USB connectors.

By the Numbers Now

The normal range of a residential wireless modem (a modem with a built-in wireless router) is 150 feet.

Hubs, Switches, Routers

A **hub** or **switch** is a central point of connection for network cables. A **node** is any device connected to a network. Hubs and switches allow different nodes to communicate with each other. Switches are more efficient than hubs because hubs transfer data to all devices, while switches send data only to the intended recipient.

Routers allow different networks to communicate with each other. Routers can also connect networked computers to the Internet, so multiple users can share a connection. Most routers are also switches that contain ports for connecting computers.

Protocols

For network devices to communicate with each other, they must follow a common set of rules, or **protocols**.

All computers on the Internet follow **TCP/IP** (Transmission Control Protocol/Internet Protocol), a network protocol that defines how messages (data) are routed through a network. Part of TCP/IP is IP, or Internet Protocol. Each computer on a network has a unique IP address.

There are two versions of IP addresses: **IPv4** (Internet Protocol Version 4) and **IPv6** (Internet Protocol Version 6). IPv4 was the standard protocol until recently, but the growing number of Internet-connected devices requires more IP addresses than IPv4 can provide. The newer IPv6 addresses use 128 bits, in contrast to IPv4's 32 bits, vastly expanding the possible number of IP addresses, which should be sufficient for the foreseeable future.

Bandwidth

Networks transmit data using the information "roads" and "highways." Smaller roads carry less information than the larger highways.

A common term used to describe information-carrying capacity is **bandwidth**; the higher the bandwidth, the more information the channel can transmit. **Broadband** refers to high-capacity channels, while **narrowband** refers to slower channels with less capacity.

Internet connections vary in bandwidth. Dial-up is a slow narrowband service, while DSL, satellite, cable, and FTTP are considered broadband. If you want to watch movies or use the Internet for video, you need a high bandwidth option.

- **DSL (digital subscriber line)** uses a regular telephone line connection, while cable uses a cable TV connection.
- **FTTP (Fiber to the Premises)** uses fiber-optic cable.
- **Fixed wireless** uses a dish-shaped antenna on a building to communicate with a tower via radio signals.

Types of Networks

topology | network architecture | network topology | tree topology | full mesh topology | partial mesh topology | wired network | wireless network | server | client | star network | bus network | ring network | mesh network | network server | file server | print server | database server | Web server | peer-to-peer (P2P) network | Internet peer-to-peer (Internet P2P) networking | file sharing | BitTorrent | personal area network (PAN) | local area network (LAN) | neighborhood area network (NAN) | metropolitan area network (MAN) | wide area network (WAN) | intranet | extranet | virtual private network (VPN)

A network can be defined by its **topology**—or how computers and devices are physically arranged within it. **Network architecture**, like building architecture, determines the logical design of computers, devices, and media within a network. The two main types of network architectures are client/server and peer-to-peer (P2P). See **Figure 7-12**.

Network Topologies

Network topology defines the physical layout of, and relationship between, network devices. **Table 7-4** on page 7-14 describes several types of network topologies.

The Bottom Line

- Network topologies include star, bus, ring, and mesh networks, as well as combination topologies.
- Network architecture includes client/server and peer-to-peer (P2P).
- File, print, database, and Web servers are powerful computers that manage network traffic and give people access to network resources.

Figure 7-12: Network architecture and topology

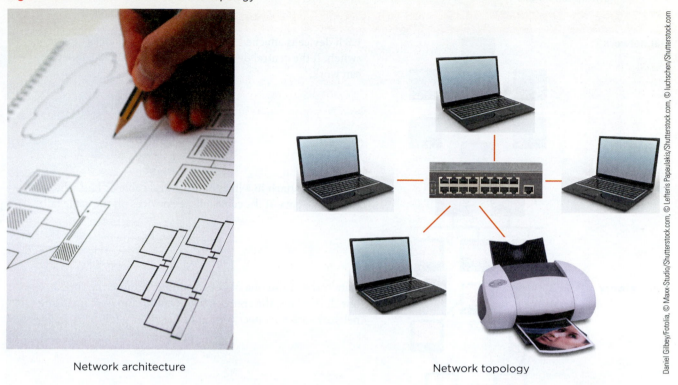

Network architecture

Network topology

Combination Topologies

Some networks combine topologies to connect smaller networks and form one larger network. For example:

- Two star networks may be joined together using a bus to form a network with a **tree topology**. Trees are easily expanded. School and business networks are often based on tree topologies. See **Figure 7-13**.
- In a **full mesh topology**, each device on the network is connected to every other device on the network.
- With a **partial mesh topology**, some devices are connected to all other devices, while others are connected only to those devices with which they exchange the most data.

Wired or Wireless

Devices on a network can connect to each other in one of two ways: with or without wires.

- **Wired networks** send signals and data through wires, which may have to travel through floors and walls to connect to other network devices.
- **Wireless networks** send signals through the airwaves.

Most networks use a combination of wired and wireless connections. Wired networks are generally faster and more secure than wireless networks. Wireless networks make it possible to connect devices in locations where physical wiring is not possible or is difficult.

Client/Server Networks

On a client/server network, one or more computers acts as a **server**, a computer on a network that controls access to hardware, software, and other resources. The other computers on the network request services from the server. Some servers provide centralized storage for programs, data, and information. The **clients** are other computers and mobile devices on the network that rely on the server for their resources. Most client/server networks require a person to serve as a network administrator.

Figure 7-13: Example of a tree topology

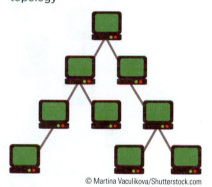

© Martina Vaculikova/Shutterstock.com

 **#ConnectingNow**

Schools typically have a campus network that provides access to servers so students can access class files using connected devices.

Table 7-4: Network topologies

Topology	How the network is arranged	Details
Star network		Each device is attached to the central device such as a server or switch. If the central device fails, none of the attached devices can work.
Bus network		All devices attach in a line to the central cable or bus, which carries the data. If the cable fails, all devices on the cable fail.
Ring network		Data travels from one device to another around the ring. If one device fails, the entire network could stop working. Ring networks are no longer common.
Mesh network		All devices interconnect with each other. Used most often with wireless networks. No single device keeps the network working. If one device fails, the network will keep working if the data can use an alternate path.

© 2015 Cengage Learning. © Martina Vaculikova/Shutterstock.com

Figure 7-14: Network server

© dotshock/Shutterstock.com

Types of Servers

Networks can have many types of servers, each performing different tasks. Servers are typically powerful computers with lots of memory and very large hard drives for storage.

A **network server** works to manage network traffic. It provides access to software, files, and other resources that are being shared via the network. For example, cloud computing requires network servers. See **Figure 7-14**.

Table 7-5 describes common servers and their purposes.

Table 7-5: Types of servers and their purposes

Server type	Purpose
File server	Stores and manages files
Print server	Manages printers and documents being printed on a network
Database server	Stores and provides access to a database
Web server	Delivers Web pages to computers that request pages through a browser

© 2015 Cengage Learning

Peer-to-Peer

Peer-to-peer (P2P) networks are networks of equals (peers), and typically have fewer than 10 computers. They are less expensive and easier to set up than client/server networks because they have no dedicated servers (servers that only serve the network, and are not shared).

P2P networks do not use a central network server. Each peer maintains its own operating system, application software, and data files. Peers can share files and peripheral devices such as printers with peers.

Internet peer-to-peer (Internet P2P) networking is a specific type of P2P networking where files are shared over the Internet directly between individual users. Also called **file sharing**, Internet P2P is commonly used to exchange music and video. However, copyright law and ethics are an issue with Internet P2P. File sharing is illegal if the content is copyright-protected and the exchange is unauthorized.

BitTorrent is a P2P file-sharing protocol that speeds up the download process by dividing files into smaller units, spreading them across multiple networked computers, and downloading from multiple sources at once. BitTorrent is used for distributing music and movies over the Internet.

Other Networks

Networks can also be defined by their geographic coverage. Networks can encompass a very small area or be worldwide in scope.

- A **personal area network (PAN)** is a network of personal devices in a very limited area. A PAN can connect portable devices such as a smartphone with a computer to sync data files.
- A **local area network (LAN)** is a network that connects devices within a small area such as a home or small office building.
- A **neighborhood area network (NAN)** connects devices within a limited geographical area, usually including several buildings such as coffee shops or book stores that offer free Wi-Fi.
- A **metropolitan area network (MAN)** is a public, high-speed network owned and operated by a city or county.
- A **wide area network (WAN)** is a network that connects devices in two or more LANs located in a large geographical area. The Internet is classified as a WAN.

Intranets, Extranets, VPNs

An **intranet** is a private corporate network for use by authorized employees. Intranets are used to coordinate internal email and communications. An intranet typically works like the Internet by allowing employees to use a Web browser to access data posted on Web pages. A company may also set up an **extranet** that allows outsiders, such as customers or suppliers, to access part of its intranet.

A **virtual private network (VPN)** is a private, secure path across a public network (usually the Internet) that allows authorized users secure access to the company network. A VPN can allow an employee located at a satellite office or public wireless hotspot to connect securely to the company network via the Internet. VPNs use encryption and other technologies to secure data transmitted along the path.

The Internet

The **Internet** is the largest network in the world, consisting of millions of computers connected through millions of networks spanning the globe. See **Figure 7-15** on the next page.

Large, powerful computers use the Internet to exchange the information and data needed for shared processing tasks and services. For both personal and business reasons, many people store files and access applications over the Internet, a practice referred to as **cloud computing**.

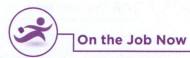

On the Job Now

Digital media producers in the film and television industry use bittorrent.com to post large video files for their customers.

On the Job Now

Commercial pilots traditionally carried heavy flight bags containing all the printed manuals they needed to safely fly the aircraft, but many airlines have issued tablets that contain thousands of electronic documents, charts, navigational aids, checklists, and other key reference materials for the cockpit. Wi-Fi is provided to the pilots to track weather conditions.

The Bottom Line

- People use the Internet every day for tasks such as visiting Web sites to listen to music, do their banking, and stay in touch with family and friends.
- Although many people think the Web is the same thing as the Internet, in fact, the Web is only part of the Internet.

Figure 7-15: Connecting to the Internet

The Internet is a vast source of information and data available as text, audio, video, and graphics.

The Internet provides a way for people around the world to communicate using text, voice, video, and images.

You can connect to the Internet through desktop and laptop computers, tablets, and smartphones.

© nmedia/Shutterstock.com

On the Job Now

A Web graphics designer creates visual concepts by hand or using computer software to communicate ideas that inspire, inform, or captivate consumers.

World Wide Web

The World Wide Web, or **Web**, is one part of the Internet, a worldwide resource for information, commerce, networking, and communications. The Web consists of **Web pages**, documents connected through **links** that include text, graphics, sound, and video. You click the links to go from one Web page to another. Web pages are organized into **Web sites** according to their function, business, organization, or interest. The first page that a Web site displays is called its **home page**, which contains links to other Web pages that can be within or outside of the Web site. **Web browsers** such as Internet Explorer and Google Chrome make it possible for you to view and link to Web pages. See **Figure 7-16**.

Figure 7-16: Library of Congress home page

The Internet address identifies this Web page.

Click text or graphic links to open other Web pages in this Library of Congress Web site.

You access Web sites by using a Web browser, which is an application that allows you to search for and navigate to Web pages.

Library of Congress Prints and Photographs Division

#ConnectingNow

Using Google Wallet, you can tap your phone to pay for purchases in retail stores and redeem offers.

E-commerce

E-commerce, or **electronic commerce**, refers to buying and selling products using the Internet. You pay for your e-commerce transactions electronically using credit cards or online payment services such as PayPal. Other examples of e-commerce include the following:

- **Most banks** have Web sites where customers can manage their money. Customers can check balances and perform other banking transactions. See **Figure 7-17**.

Figure 7-17: Online banking

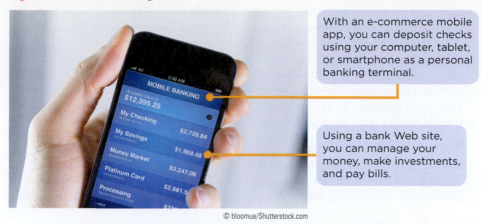

With an e-commerce mobile app, you can deposit checks using your computer, tablet, or smartphone as a personal banking terminal.

Using a bank Web site, you can manage your money, make investments, and pay bills.

© bloomua/Shutterstock.com

- **Internet-only stores and many brick-and-mortar retailers** maintain Web sites to sell products and services. You can view a picture or video of a product, read a description, pay for the product, and arrange to have it delivered without leaving your home.
- **Most schools** use the Web to interact with students and process transactions related to student accounts. Students can register for classes, pay tuition, and take online courses through the Web. Many students, at all levels, submit assignments and work with other classmates on group projects using the schools' Web sites.
- **Airlines and travel agencies** use the Web to sell tickets and make hotel and travel arrangements. Once ticketed, travelers use the Web to manage travel arrangements. Most airlines provide mobile services to check in for flights, track arrivals and departures, and announce delays.

Voice Over IP

Voice over Internet Protocol (VoIP) refers to voice communications over the Internet, and is sometimes called **Internet telephony**. In the past, voice communications travelled only along phone lines, and communications or telephone companies charged for phone calls. With the Internet, voice can travel through the same network lines that carry Web pages and other Internet services. Just as you pay for email services, not each message you send, you also pay for VoIP services, not each phone call you make. In fact, many Internet service providers (ISPs) now offer phone services; if you have a phone number through your ISP, you are using VoIP.

- VoIP providers include Vonage, Skype, Tango, and Google. Often calls from one country to another are included in your monthly Internet fee.
- VoIP allows you to receive calls on your computer from landline or cell phones and to place calls from your computer to these phones.
- You can use different devices to make VoIP calls as long as the device has a speaker and a microphone. Devices can include landline phones, smartphones, laptops, tablets, and even desktop computers.
- If you have a Web cam, VoIP technology lets you include video in your calls.

Email

Email, or **electronic mail**, is the communication tool that lets you send and receive messages through the Internet. Email messages can include attached files that contain sound, video, text, or graphics.

Email uses **store-and-forward technology**. When you send an email message, it travels to a server that stores and then forwards the message along to the recipient.

Similar to traditional mail services, you need an **email address** to send and receive email. See **Figure 7-18**. The username identifies you as the owner of the email address. The domain name identifies the email provider, which can be Web-based (such as Gmail), or your school, business or ISP.

Figure 7-18: Email address format

myname@address.com

User name   at symbol   Domain name

© 2015 Cengage Learning

You create email messages using email client software, which sends email messages from one email address to one or more other addresses. Microsoft Outlook is one example of email client software. If you use a Web-based email provider, you can create, send, and receive messages directly through the provider's Web site.

No matter what type of email client software you use, you can send messages to several people at one time and include formatted text and graphics. Messages typically contain a descriptive subject line to help you organize all your messages. You receive your email messages when you log onto your email account through your computer, smartphone, or other electronic device.

Messaging and Chat

Other Internet messaging services include text messaging, video messaging, and chatting (also called instant messaging). Each has particular benefits; see **Table 7-6**. Depending on the service, messages can include text, links, photos, graphics, and video.

Table 7-6: Communicating through messaging and chatting

Service	Purpose	Benefits
Text messaging	Send short text messages, usually over cellular networks using mobile phones. You can also send text messages through the Web using a desktop or mobile computer.	Send messages to a person or groups quickly.
Chatting	Real-time communication through the Internet between two or more people who are online at the same time.	Have a conversation in real time without using voice.
Multimedia messaging	Send photos, video, or links to Web sites with your messages using desktop or mobile computers.	If your computer or mobile device has a camera, you can send images and video directly from that device.

© 2015 Cengage Learning

Web 2.0

When the Web first became available to the general public, people used it mostly to search for information. Quickly, the Web became a place where people not only viewed Web sites, but contributed to them by posting comments. As fast Internet connections became more common, people also posted graphics, photos, audio files, and videos, which dramatically increased Internet traffic. For example, people posted personal videos on sites such as YouTube.

Web 2.0 uses the same Internet communications infrastructure as the "old" Web; the new name refers to people contributing content in addition to using the Web to find content.

Social Networking

Social-networking Web sites have changed the way people interact, form and maintain relationships, find jobs, promote careers, and communicate with each other. Through Facebook, Twitter, LinkedIn, Google+, and other sites, people communicate by sharing ideas, photos, videos, and links to other Web sites.

To use social networking:

1. Join a site and create a profile.

2. Use the site's privacy settings to determine how much personal information you want to share and with whom.

3. Create a network by inviting people to "be your Friend" or "join your network or circle."

Social networking does pose privacy threats. You reveal personal information when you join and use a site, and your site activity may be tracked or used by people seeking to advertise or do harm.

Social Media

While social networking is a way for people to interact with each other over common interests, **social media** is content provided by network users to other users. On social media sites, users create and share media including video, text, audio, and graphics. Although social media sites such as Flickr and YouTube were originally designed only to share content, users now visit these sites also to exchange opinions, comments, messages, links, and other information, making them similar to social networking sites. In fact, the distinction between social networking and social media is no longer clear, so the terms are used interchangeably.

You might use a social media site to share photos and videos of a family gathering, post a short restaurant review, list links to your favorite places to buy chocolate, or comment on a recent event. Organizations use social media sites to attract and reach customers or members, introduce products and services, and educate people about issues and causes.

Social media used with mobile devices is called **mobile social media**, which can take advantage of location technology such as GPS and time-sensitive data on the mobile device. For example, if you're walking along a city street, you can use a mobile device to visit a social media site that shares reviews for nearby restaurants. When you visit the Web site of a restaurant that interests you, the site can detect whether you are using a mobile device and send it a digital coupon good for the next few hours.

Internet2

As the Internet continues to grow, new technologies develop. **Internet2** is a not-for-profit project founded in 1996 to develop and test advanced network technologies for use in the near future.

Originally, the Internet was used mainly to transmit text, which requires little bandwidth. Millions of people now access the Internet each day, increasing demands for bandwidth. Because they often use the Internet for data-intensive applications such as high-definition television and video communications, the potential for Internet traffic jams is growing.

The Internet2 initiative is working to ensure that Internet technology keeps pace with growing demand.

Net Neutrality

When you use the Internet to research information, buy a product, or use social media, ideally all Web sites have an equal chance of providing services to you. This concept is **net neutrality**—one Web site has the same value or priority as other Web sites. Net neutrality supports the Internet's core principle that its networks should be neutral.

However, companies that provide Internet services want to distribute or charge for bandwidth depending on location, content, or provider of the Web site. For example, they might want to charge more for high-bandwidth services, such as online movies, or provide certain services at different speeds, such as slow download speeds for sites that allow illegal media sharing.

Currently, ISPs in the U.S. are legally prohibited from providing better service or changing bandwidth for any content, even their own.

Companies that oppose net neutrality do not want the government to control or influence the flow of data on the Internet. Those in favor of net neutrality believe it is the government's role to ensure that all traffic on the Internet is treated equally.

Net neutrality is a complex issue because the Internet is a global entity. If it can be regulated, who will do the regulating? Should mobile broadband access be included in legislation involving net neutrality? In the U.S., the Federal Communications Commission will continue to release rules and the courts will continue to decide cases that affect Internet access for years to come.

The Networked World

infrared technology | groupware | network attached storage (NAS) | remote storage | cloud computing | synchronous communication | asynchronous communication | one-to-one instant messaging | group instant messaging | text messaging | video chat | Webcast

Networks connect you to friends, neighbors, and other people all over the world. Email, text messaging, VoIP, and Web browsing are all possible because of networks.

Figure 7-19: Networked world

You can use networks to share hardware and software resources and to centralize file storage.

Mobile devices using wireless technologies have expanded network access so you can communicate and share resources from remote locations virtually anywhere in the world.

Using a network, you can play multiplayer computer games or participate in online conferences from a satellite office.

© bannosuke/Shutterstock.com, © Andrey_Popov/Shutterstock.com, © Dragon Images/Shutterstock.com

Sharing Hardware Resources

Computer networks make it possible to share hardware devices among users. See **Figure 7-20**. Colleagues in a small office can use the same printer, fax machine, scanner, or other device. Sharing hardware saves money.

Figure 7-20: Sharing hardware in a network

Shared network devices use either wired or wireless technology. You can wirelessly sync your smartphone to your laptop computer.

Bluetooth and Wi-Fi devices use radio waves to transmit signals. For example, you could transfer information from your smartphone to your computer if both were Bluetooth-enabled.

Devices with **infrared technology**, such as this mouse, communicate with direct light beams between infrared (IrDA) ports on the devices.

© Christos Georghiou/Shutterstock.com, © vetkit/Shutterstock.com, © Dean Drobot/Shutterstock.com

Sharing Software Resources

Shared software resources can save businesses a significant amount of money with licensed software agreements. Coworkers can share software and hardware if the network uses a central server.

When companies install software on a central server only, troubleshooting problems and running software updates are greatly simplified because the work is limited to a single installation.

With **groupware**, several colleagues can work together on a single document at the same time. Group members can communicate to manage projects, create documents, schedule meetings, and make group decisions. Sharing software and hardware resources through network technology lets organizations and people work together more effectively and more efficiently than ever before.

Storage

Organizations use network storage in their corporate networks and individuals use them in home networks. Some storage devices, called **network attached storage (NAS)**, connect directly to a network. NAS servers provide a centralized location for storing programs and data on large and small networks. Depending on its size and processor configuration, an NAS server can support from two to several thousand connected computers.

Servers accessed via the Internet provide remote, or online, storage. Online storage is used in cloud computing, which is the delivery of computing services via the Internet.

Remote storage is also a service provided by several commercial providers. These sites include Google Drive (for email, Google applications, and files), Flickr (for photos), OneDrive (for Microsoft Office applications and files), iCloud, and Dropbox. **Table 7-7** compares the three major online storage providers for personal files.

#ConnectingNow

A direct line of sight is required between infrared devices, with no obstructions such as a wall or a table between them. Radio waves from Bluetooth or Wi-Fi devices, however, can travel through walls.

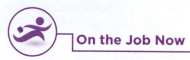

On the Job Now

If your job requires travel, most major airlines provide Internet access for a fee after the plane reaches 10,000 feet.

Table 7-7: Personal online storage providers

Feature	Apple iCloud	Google Drive	Microsoft OneDrive
Web address	icloud.com	google.com/drive	OneDrive.com
Storage capacity	5 GB free storage	15 GB free storage	7 GB free storage
Extras	Store iTunes purchases such as music and TV shows without affecting your storage quota.	Share and collaborate on files including documents, music, images, and videos.	Save Office files directly to OneDrive.

© 2015 Cengage Learning

Cloud Computing

Cloud computing is Internet-based delivery of computing services, including data storage and application software. See **Figure 7-21** on the next page.

Along with its benefits, cloud computing has some drawbacks. Internet-based computing poses security and privacy risks. If you lose your Internet connection, you lose your ability to access the cloud, and everything you store on it, until your connection is restored.

Asynchronous vs. Synchronous

Communication can take place instantly (in real time), or it can be delayed. When you make a phone call and another person answers, you have a real-time conversation. If the person is not there, you leave a message. Communication is delayed until you reconnect. Networking provides services to address each situation. **Table 7-8** on the next page defines the terms asynchronous and synchronous.

Email Uses

Computer networks enable people to communicate by email, or electronic mail. Email is a standard for business communication. Email software gives you the ability to manage and organize messages and send file attachments.

#ConnectingNow

Office 365 allows you to access the Microsoft cloud storage service seamlessly while using the Office suite.

Figure 7-21: Cloud computing

By storing data such as photos and documents, people can better manage storage space on their own devices.

Cloud computing depends on a grid of servers and storage devices. Large corporations and governments use cloud computing for complex data processing and storage.

Photos and music from tablets and smartphones are saved to the cloud automatically.

People use cloud computing to access application software and to store data from multiple computing devices in a single secure location.

© Albachiaraa/Shutterstock.com

Table 7-8: Comparing communication types

Communication type	Requirements	Benefits	Examples
Synchronous communication	Participants must be online at the same time.	Takes place in real time, similar to a phone conversation.	Chat groups, Web conferencing, and VoIP
Asynchronous communication	Does not require participants to be online at the same time.	One person can post a message that can later be accessed by one or more recipients.	Email, social networking posts, and text messaging

© 2015 Cengage Learning

You can send email through the Internet or through a local area network (LAN). People use email in the following ways and more:

- Online vendors rely on email to confirm orders and shipping.
- Schools and universities use email to communicate with staff, teachers, and students.
- Employees use email to communicate with one another.
- Citizens contact their representatives via email.

Text Communication

In addition to email, networks enable people to communicate by instant messaging and text messaging. Some messaging services are available through the Web on social networking sites such as Facebook or LinkedIn.

- **One-to-one instant messaging** occurs in a computer window and in real time.
- **Group instant messaging,** or chat, also occurs in real time in an online chat room.
- **Text messaging** is based on SMS (short message service) and sends a short message, typically less than 300 characters, to or from a mobile device or smartphone. Text messaging can also include pictures and videos up to about 30 seconds.

Text messages can travel on the Internet or over cellular networks. Options for sending and receiving text messages are mobile to mobile, mobile to email, and Web to mobile.

Video Chat

With the expansion of broadband capabilities, many networks have sufficient bandwidth to carry video data as well as voice.

Video chat is used in businesses and education for **Webcasts** (video broadcasts of an event transmitted across the Internet). It is also a popular way for people to stay in touch with friends and relatives who live far away.

Hot Technology Now

Snapchat is a messaging app that lets users send photos and videos (called snaps) to other people and set a time limit for how long recipients can view the snaps.

#ConnectingNow

Office 365 for business or schools includes a video conferencing tool named Lync that provides screen sharing, polling capabilities, and recording.

To use video chat, you need all the components you use for voice communication over the Internet (VoIP), as well as a Web cam and a display device. You cannot have a video chat over a standard phone. Video chatting software lets you control the images that appear onscreen, voice and sound volume, and other features.

You can use smartphones for video chatting as well as desktop, laptop, and tablet computers. See **Figure 7-22**. For example, Facetime is a video chat service provided by Apple for iPhones. You can also video chat through the Internet with services such as Skype, Tango, and Google. Chatters without a Web cam can participate in the chat, but won't be seen on screen by other chatters.

Figure 7-22: Video chatting on a smartphone

© LDprod/Shutterstock.com

Network Risks

online security risk | hacker | cracker | malware | zombie | computer crime | cybercrime | identity theft | theft by computer | war driver | cookie | virus | worm | Trojan horse | spyware | adware | phishing | zombie | bot | botnet | denial of service (DoS)

Networks connect you to other people and resources, but they also expose you to **online security risks**, which are actions that can damage or misuse your computer and data when you are connected to a network. Online security risks include unauthorized use of your computer and access to your data, exposure to malware, and network attacks.

Figure 7-23: Network risks

A **hacker** uses computers to access data without authorization, often illegally. **Crackers** use computers to destroy data, steal information, and commit other malicious crimes.

Malware (malicious software) and spyware can hijack parts of your computer, turning it into a **zombie**.

Computer crimes are illegal acts committed using a computer. **Cybercrimes** are illegal acts committed using a computer on a network or over the Internet.

Data transmitted across networks is vulnerable to interception. In an **identity theft**, hackers steal your personal information, such as credit card numbers.

After hackers access your personal information, they can transfer funds or purchase goods and services using your bank accounts, which is called **theft by computer**.

Username: Username
Password: •••••••
☐ Remember Password
Login   Cancel

© zimmytws/Shutterstock.com, © tommaso79/Shutterstock.com, © Juergen Faelchle/Shutterstock.com, © sixninepixels/Shutterstock.com, © Dusit/Shutterstock.com

Figure 7-24: War driver

On the Job Now

Many financial institutions and retail chains hire risk operations analysts to prevent fraudulent transactions.

#ConnectingNow

Windows Defender is a free antivirus and antispyware program provided with Windows 8.

#ConnectingNow

All platforms can be infected with malware. Almost 700,000 new malware threats for the Android platform were detected in the past year.

Unauthorized Computer Use

Hackers use computers and networks without authorization so they can access valuable data and services without being detected. To bypass basic security measures on computers and networks, hackers detect, guess, or steal passwords and usernames. They also take advantage of wireless networks in public places, which have little or no security, and home computers that have always-on Internet connections.

Besides hackers, unauthorized users can be **war drivers**, people who drive around and connect to wireless networks to gain free Internet access. See **Figure 7-24**.

Privacy Loss

Much of your personal information is readily available to the general public. When you purchase an item over the Internet, your purchase information is available to others. If you register on a Web site, post a photo, or log a comment, this information can also be available to the general public.

Information about you on private networks can also be viewed without authorization. For example, large hospital networks have been known to leak sensitive medical information about patients when their network security was breached.

You need to protect your privacy when online, which you can do in the following ways:

- Give out as little information as possible.
- Manage and monitor your privacy settings on social networking sites.
- Be thoughtful when sending email and text messages. You can never be sure who is reading your message, so private information should be sent with discretion.

Cookies, Spyware, Adware

Commercial Web site vendors employ cookies to identify users and customize Web pages. **Cookies** are ordinary text files that contain personal data such as your username, viewing preferences, and browsing history. Some Web sites provide cookies to other Web sites without your consent to display ads based on your browsing history, for example. Security experts warn that these types of cookies violate user privacy.

Spyware is a form of malware secretly installed on networked computers. Spyware tracks and transmits personal data, such as financial information or browsing habits, without your knowledge or permission. Surreptitiously tracking and transmitting data uses a lot of computer resources. If you notice slowdowns such as a lag between typing text on the keyboard and viewing it on the screen, spyware might be installed on your computer.

Adware displays unwanted advertisements in banners or pop-up windows on your computer, even when you are not visiting a Web site. While most adware itself is more annoying than dangerous, some adware comes with spyware attached.

Identity Theft

When hackers access personal information such as your name, Social Security number, or bank account numbers, they can use it to assume your identity to open lines of credit in your name, order goods and services online, and then pay for them using your funds. Besides stealing your money, identity thieves damage your credit score and integrity.

Phishing scams use email to try to trick you into revealing personal information on the pretense of being your bank or other legitimate institution. See **Figure 7-25**.

Malware

Malware is software written with malicious intent that installs itself without permission and can damage data and programs. **Table 7-9** describes common forms of malware.

Malware installs itself on your computer when you download an infected file from a Web site or open one attached to an email message. To spread, viruses and worms might send copies of themselves to contacts in your computer's address book. Each message appears as though it came from you, when it was actually generated by malware in your network.

Figure 7-25: Phishing examples and characteristics

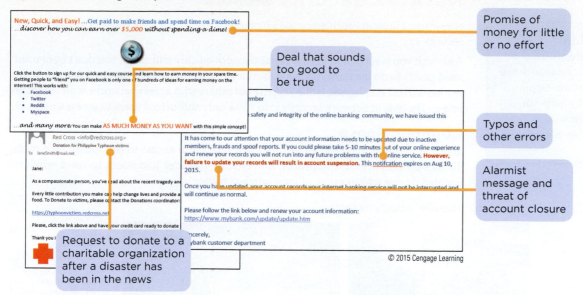

Promise of money for little or no effort

Deal that sounds too good to be true

Typos and other errors

Alarmist message and threat of account closure

Request to donate to a charitable organization after a disaster has been in the news

© 2015 Cengage Learning

Table 7-9: Common forms of malware

Type	Description
Virus	Damages data or changes computer settings without your knowledge
Worm	Copies itself repeatedly, using up computer and network resources
Trojan horse	Hides in or disguises itself as a legitimate program until it is installed on a computer, and then damages files
Spyware	Tracks and transmits personal data without your knowledge or permission

© 2015 Cengage Learning

Bots and Zombies

If hackers gain unauthorized access to networked computers, they can take over the computers and turn them into **zombies**, which are computers controlled by outsiders without the owners' knowledge. After creating a zombie, a hacker can install a **bot**, a program that performs a repetitive task such as sending phishing email messages. The hacker can also group these zombies together to form a **botnet**, which would send out massive amounts of phishing messages, for example.

Botnet attacks often go unnoticed by the victim. The only symptom is a slowing down of your computer as the processor is hijacked for illegal activities.

Denial of Service

Hackers often use a botnet to launch a **denial of service (DoS) attack**, a bombardment of network traffic or messages designed to overload a server. The purpose of a DoS attack is to disrupt network services, such as Internet access.

By overwhelming the server, a DoS attack can also stop all communications and services for a company or Web site. While recovering from a DoS attack, organizations can forfeit significant revenue from customers and advertisers.

Theft by Computer

Theft by computer is a growing problem in the networked world. For a thief to steal cash from a bank or goods from a store, they have to physically walk into the store. To steal using networked computers, a thief can be seated thousands of miles away.

Computer theft occurs when unauthorized users transfer money from one account to another or purchase goods and services with stolen credit card numbers or through other illegal means.

Theft by computer is a growing problem because so much of our commerce is increasingly taking place over the Internet and other networked computers.

On the Job Now

Companies hire forensic scientists who specialize in network traffic to analyze networks and search for botnets.

By the Numbers Now

DoS attacks have increased 256% in the past year.

#ConnectingNow

A virtual currency called Bitcoin has been used to launder profits of both online and offline criminal activity.

Network Security Basics

encryption | firewall | authentication | biometric device | wireless network key | network security key

The Bottom Line
- Protecting a network involves a combination of common sense and complex technology.
- Network security methods include authentication, biometric devices, encryption, and firewalls.

Although you want to access your home network quickly and easily, you don't want uninvited guests to do the same. Likewise, businesses need to provide easy access to their networks for their employees, while keeping out others who access networks with malicious intent. The goal of network security is to allow only authorized users to access a network.

Common Sense

To access a wired network, an intruder needs physical access to the router via a cable. To access many wireless networks, however, an intruder just needs to use a wireless-enabled device within range of your wireless router.

Figure 7-26: Network security methods

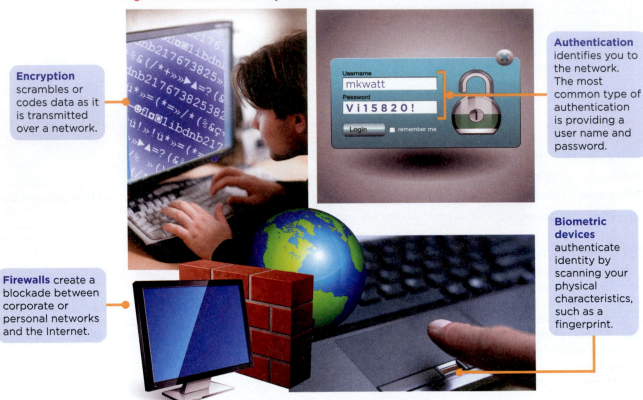

Encryption scrambles or codes data as it is transmitted over a network.

Authentication identifies you to the network. The most common type of authentication is providing a user name and password.

Username
mkwatt

Password
Vi15820!

Login   remember me

Biometric devices authenticate identity by scanning your physical characteristics, such as a fingerprint.

Firewalls create a blockade between corporate or personal networks and the Internet.

© chaoss/Shutterstock.com, © bofotolux/Shutterstock.com, © Nelia Sapronova/Shutterstock.com, © beboy/Shutterstock.com, lightpoet/Fotolia

#ConnectingNow

On your home wireless router, change the Service Set Identifier (SSID) from its default to a unique name that is difficult for others to guess.

Hot Technology Now

PC and Mac users in 71 countries rely on a reputable freeware tool called LastPass (lastpass.com) to remember multiple passwords.

If your network carries sensitive data, use common sense to make sure it's secure.
- **Create strong passwords** for your home network. Include at least eight characters, numbers, letters, or symbols that are not easy to figure out.
- **Set permissions** to determine who can access which resources. Limit access as much as you can.
- **Do not write usernames and passwords** in places where they can be found by others.
- **Enable the highest level of encryption**, such as WPA2 or WPA-TKIP, for a wireless router, and change the router's default administrator password.

Authentication

Identification and authentication methods can be used to verify identity on a computer or network. See **Table 7-10**.

Biometric Devices

Biometric devices add a layer of protection by restricting access on the basis of who you are. For example, if intruders steal a network password, you can still block them from accessing your network using biometric technology.

Table 7-10: Authentication methods

Method	Description
Username	A unique name you create to identify yourself to a computer system
Password	Combination of characters; often used with passwords to create a unique passcode
CAPTCHA	System requiring you to type characters that match a series of distorted characters on the screen; used to verify that your entry is not computer-generated
Physical object	An object such as a room key or ID card with barcodes that verifies your identity when trying to enter a building, office, or other restricted space

Biometric devices authenticate identity by scanning a person's physical characteristics, such as fingerprints, face, eyes, handprint, voice, or even signature. They are most often used by organizations and large corporations with sensitive data.

Fingerprint readers are the most common biometric device in use today. See **Figure 7-27**. You might see one at a bank, on an ATM, or even attached to a PC.

Encryption

As shown in **Figure 7-26**, encryption scrambles or codes data as it is transmitted over a network. If intruders intercept a file in transit, they cannot make sense of the data they find.

You use a **wireless network key** (also called a **network security key**) to scramble and unscramble the data being transmitted between wireless devices.

You can activate encryption for your network through the router. Open the router software using a browser, and then use the router configuration software to set up an encryption protocol and create a wireless network key.

Many wireless networks in coffee shops, hotels, and airports are not encrypted, so they are open to the public. Do not transmit private information on public networks.

Firewalls

Firewalls are designed to block intruders from accessing corporate or personal networks. If you have an always-on connection to the Internet, you can be vulnerable to intrusions. Personal firewalls constantly monitor all network traffic to keep your network secure.

Firewalls are often built into operating systems, such as Windows Firewall for Windows computers. See **Figure 7-28**. Firewalls are also built into the router software of many routers.

You can also install third-party personal firewall programs on your computer to detect and protect your computer from unauthorized intrusions.

Figure 7-27: Fingerprint reader

© Gary James Calder/Shutterstock.com

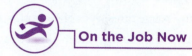

On the Job Now

With additional immigration and healthcare laws, many government and healthcare positions are opening in the field of biometrics engineering.

#ConnectingNow

The iPhone5s was the first phone to include fingerprint biometric scanner technology.

Figure 7-28: Windows Firewall

Purpose of the firewall

Description of what the firewall does

#ConnectingNow

Go to twitter.com, search for **@SAMTechNow**, the book's Twitter account, and then follow @SAMTechNow to get tweets on your home page.

Chapter Review

Introduction to Networks

1. What are the two main types of network architecture? Briefly describe each one.

2. What do you call a network that spans long distances? Give two examples of areas where such a network would be appropriate.

3. What type of network connects digital devices within about 30 feet of each other? Give one example.

Connecting to a Network

4. Give three examples of network standards, and state how each one might be used.

5. What piece of hardware lets your computer connect to networks?

6. What do you call a company that connects you to the Internet?

How Networks Work

7. What lets your laptop, tablet, or smartphone connect to the Internet in a coffee shop?

8. What is a modem? Name three types of modems.

9. Describe the purpose of a network protocol and give an example.

Types of Networks

10. Name three types of network topologies and briefly describe the layout of each one.

11. Describe why one might need a combination topology, and give an example.

12. How does a client/server network differ from a peer-to-peer network?

The Internet

13. Name three services available over the Internet. How might you use each service in your daily life? Which of the services do you use most often and why?

14. Describe three Internet services you can use to communicate with colleagues or friends. What are the key benefits of each service? How are the three services different from each other?

The Networked World

15. Why would you use the following types of communication? Give a brief example of a good use of each: email, Web conference, VoIP, text messaging, chatting, and multimedia messaging.

16. Briefly define social networking. How might a recent college graduate use social networking after taking a job 100 miles from her school? How might a family with grown children living 100 miles apart might use social networking to keep in touch?

Network Risks

17. What is the difference between hackers and crackers? How do hackers and crackers gain unauthorized access to a computer?

18. What are the common forms of malware and how does it infect a computer?

Network Security Basics

19. What are three common-sense strategies for securing a home network?

20. How do encryption and firewalls protect network data?

Test Your Knowledge Now

1. A circuit board with special electronic circuits that connects a computer to a network is called a:
   a. router.
   b. hub.
   c. network interface card (NIC).
   d. switch.

2. A network architecture in which all computers are equal in capability and responsibility is called a:
   a. peer-to-peer network.
   b. client/server network.
   c. wireless access point.
   d. wide area network.

3. A company that offers Internet access to individuals and businesses is a(n):
   a. network service provider.
   b. Internet backbone.
   c. Internet service provider.
   d. wide area network.

4. The most common networking standard for wired networks is:
   a. Wi-Fi.
   b. Ethernet.
   c. Bluetooth.
   d. 4G.

5. The hardware that sends and receives data and information to and from a digital line is a(n):
   a. digital modem.
   b. network interface card.
   c. Internet service provider.
   d. Wi-Fi hotspot.

6. Which network standard lets devices communicate wirelessly over short distances?
   a. Ethernet
   b. Bluetooth
   c. Phoneline
   d. 4G

7. Which of the following network types uses radio signals to connect computers and devices?
   a. Wi-Fi
   b. Ethernet
   c. modem
   d. DSL modem

8. RJ-11, RJ-45, and USB are all examples of:
   a. connectors.
   b. cables.
   c. domain controllers.
   d. ports.

9. What type of network has all devices attached in a line to a central cable?
   a. ring
   b. star
   c. bus
   d. mesh

10. A networked computer that controls access to hardware, software, and other network resources is called a:
    a. client.
    b. server.
    c. router.
    d. modem.

11. You click a(n) _____ to go from one Web page to another.
    a. link
    b. URL
    c. window
    d. app

12. You use _____ when your telephone calls travel over the Internet instead of using traditional phone systems.
    a. cell towers
    b. VoIP
    c. Wi-Fi
    d. cloud computing

13. With _____ computing, you can access files and applications over the Internet.
    a. cellular
    b. VoIP
    c. Wi-Fi
    d. cloud

14. Chat groups, Web conferencing, and VoIP are examples of _____ communication.
    a. asynchronous
    b. synchronous
    c. VoIP
    d. Web 2.0

15. Text messaging is based on _____ technology.
    a. URL
    b. SMS
    c. NAS
    d. ISP

16. A(n) _____ is a type of cybercrime in which hackers steal your personal information, such as bank account numbers.
    a. botnet
    b. identity theft
    c. Trojan horse
    d. denial of service attack

17. The type of malware that copies itself repeatedly, using up computer and network resources, is called a _____.
    a. virus
    b. cookie
    c. Trojan horse
    d. worm

18. Which one of the following is *not* a network authentication method?
    a. password
    b. CAPTCHA system
    c. fingerprint reader
    d. firewall

19. You use a(n) _____ to scramble and unscramble the data being transmitted between wireless devices.
    a. wireless network key
    b. biometric device
    c. ID card with a barcode
    d. wireless router

20. _____ constantly monitor all network traffic to keep your network secure.
    a. Modems
    b. Firewalls
    c. Biometric scanners
    d. Spyware programs

21. In the space next to each image below, write the letter of the phrase that describes it:
    a. Central point for cables in a network
    b. Directs the flow of information along a network
    c. Connects a device to an Ethernet network
    d. Device that sends and receives data to and from a digital line
    e. Card that connects a computer to a network

Try This Now

1: Test Your Home and School Network's Performance

Your local Internet service provider offers different connection options. You should test your network connection to confirm it uses the speed you purchased. Test the speed of your wireless or wired network at your home, workplace, or local coffee shop and compare it to the speed of your school's network.

Open your browser on any computer and then visit the speedtest.net Web site. Tap or click the Begin Test button to test the performance of each network. The test may take up to a minute to complete.

    a. How did the speed of your home, workplace, or local coffee shop compare with the speed of your school's network? Share the download and upload speeds of each location.

    b. Describe three Internet activities that would be best on the faster network speed.

2: Locate Local Free Wi-Fi Hotspots

Knowing the location of a free Wi-Fi connection in your local area can assist you if you ever lose Internet connectivity in your home or dorm. Open your browser on any computer and then visit the openwifispots.com Web site. Enter the name of your closest populated town or city to locate free Wi-Fi hotspots. Try another city if you do not find a listing of hotspots.

    a. What is the name of the town or city that you researched?

    b. How many free Wi-Fi hotspots did you find?

    c. Copy and paste the listing of free Wi-Fi hotspots from the Web site into a word-processing document.

3: Create a Free Video Email

Note: This assignment requires a mobile device with a camera or a computer with a Web cam.

Connecting through a video email message adds a personal and professional touch within the business environment. Eyejot is an easy way to send and receive video email from your computer (PC or Mac) or mobile device, such as an Apple iPhone, iPod Touch, or Android smartphone. Open the browser on any computer and visit the eyejot.com Web site or install the free Eyejot app on your smartphone. Create a free Eyejot account. Record a one-minute video to your instructor using Eyejot about the interesting facts you learned about the connected computer. Send the video email to your instructor.

© iStockphoto.com/xavierarnau

Video Email

    a. Write a paragraph describing an example of how you could use video email in a business setting.

    b. Which device did you use to create your video email? What was your experience?

Critical Thinking Now

1: Thinking Through Your Home Network

After moving to a new apartment complex, you are faced with setting up a wireless home network for your iPad, Windows ultrabook, and your Android phone. Your local neighborhood has DSL available. You are on an electronics retailer's Web site looking for the equipment that you will need to set up your home wireless network. Create a shopping list with the items necessary to create your wireless home network, the retail price, and the steps that you would follow to connect your devices to the wireless network.

2: Protecting Your Wireless Home Network

After reading this chapter, you realize that the wireless network in your home is not secure. Unauthorized users could sit outside your home and perform illegal activities on your home network in your name. In addition, they may be able to view your personal files and slow down your network speed considerably. Write a paragraph including at least four steps that will secure your home wireless network.

3: World Cup Biometric Security

The FIFA World Cup Football Tournament is investigating ways to confirm the identity of the ticket holders. FIFA is warning soccer fans to beware of fraudulent online ticket sales for the next World Cup as it works with international agencies to use biometric security to address the problem. Write a three-paragraph proposal, with each paragraph describing one of three biometric security technologies that could be used to determine ticket holder authentication. Research the pros and cons of each of these biometric technologies.

Ethical Issues Now

Today is the day you move into your new apartment. As soon as you find your tablet among your moving boxes, you power it up to check the available balance at your online bank before you accidentally overdraw your account. You realize that you have not contacted a local Internet service provider to set up service. Out of curiosity, you check to see if any unsecure wireless networks are available in your apartment building. The very strongest wireless network is named ThirdFloorBen and it is not secure.

a. How should you handle this ethical dilemma?
b. What might happen if you use the unsecured network?
c. If your neighbor Ben introduces himself later in the day in the third floor hallway, how would you handle the issue of his open wireless network?

Team Up Now – Identity Rip Off

Zoe Chambers, a college freshman, is a victim of identity theft. No one ever plans to have their identity stolen, but ignorance can unfortunately lead to years of credit score recovery and legal tape. Cassidy Collins, a friend of Zoe's roommate, stayed for the weekend last month in their dorm. Cassidy used Zoe's tablet several times over the weekend with Zoe's permission. Days later, Zoe realized that her online bank balance was much lower than expected. In addition, Zoe received three separate email messages from different credit card companies saying that she had been approved and the new credit cards had been mailed to an unknown address. (Later, she discovered this was Cassidy's home address.)

a. Each member of the team should develop a hypothesis of how it was possible for Cassidy to steal Zoe's identity. Create a combined document of the individual hypotheses.
b. Research what Zoe should do now. Name at least four steps that Zoe should take to investigate this crime.
c. What are several action items that Zoe should do each month to monitor her credit?
d. Research and summarize five signs that you may be a victim of identity theft.
e. Identify a YouTube video that would be best to share at Zoe's dorm for others not to fall victim to the same risk.

Key Terms

3G	denial of service (DoS)	Internet backbone
4G	digital modem	Internet peer-to-peer (Internet P2P)
adware	domain-based network	networking
asynchronous communication	domain controller	Internet service provider (ISP)
authentication	DSL modem	Internet telephony
bandwidth	electronic commerce (e-commerce)	intranet
biometric device	electronic mail (email)	IPv4 protocol
BitTorrent	email address	IPv6 protocol
Bluetooth	encryption	link
bot	Ethernet	local area network (LAN)
botnet	Ethernet standard	LTE (Long Term Evolution)
broadband	extranet	malware
broadband modem	file server	mesh network
bus network	file sharing	metropolitan area network (MAN)
cable	firewall	mobile computing
cable modem	full mesh topology	mobile social media
chatting	group instant messaging	modem
client	groupware	multimedia messaging
client/server network	hacker	narrowband
cloud computing	home page	neighborhood area network (NAN)
computer crime	hot zone	net neutrality
cookie	hotspot	network
cracker	hub	network architecture
cybercrime	identity theft	network attached storage (NAS)
data	infrared technology	network hardware
data encryption	Internet	network interface card (NIC)
database server	Internet2	network security key

network server
network service provider (NSP)
network standard
network topology
node
one-to-one instant messaging
online security risk
partial mesh topology
peer-to-peer (P2P) network
personal area network (PAN)
personal hotspot
personal mobile hotspot
phishing
Phoneline/HomePNA
port
Power over Ethernet (PoE)
Powerline
print server
protocol
remote storage

resource
ring network
RJ-11 port
router
server
social media
spyware
star network
store-and-forward technology
switch
synchronous communication
TCP/IP (Transmission Control Protocol/
    Internet Protocol)
tether
text messaging
theft by computer
topology
tree topology
video chat
virtual private network (VPN)

Voice over Internet Protocol (VoIP)
war driver
Web
Web browser
Web server
Web page
Web site
Webcast
wide area network (WAN)
Wi-Fi (wireless fidelity)
Wi-Fi hotspot
Wi-Fi network
WiMAX
wired network
wireless access point
wireless modem
wireless network
wireless network key
wireless router
zombie

Safety and Security

You don't need a stability ball like Daniel's for proper ergonomics, but finding the best sitting position relieves aches and pains in his neck, shoulders, and back. It also makes him more productive.

Daniel is aware of the digital footprint that he leaves as he posts to his social media profile.

With smaller tablets, higher-resolution screens provide clarity, but the smaller fonts force your eyes to work harder.

© Marcin Balcerzak/Shutterstock.com

Daniel Kohl loves his new tablet. He can either use the tablet on his lap or stand it on a table or another flat surface for angled viewing. Placing the tablet on a table allows for a more relaxed and natural posture, alleviating the strain caused by tablet lap viewing. In addition to caring for his physical safety, Daniel is creating a positive online persona, realizing that future employers will have access to every social media posting.

Microsoft® product screenshots used with permission from Microsoft® Corporation.

Personal Health Risks

repetitive strain injury (RSI) | carpal tunnel syndrome | computer vision syndrome | Internet addiction | ergonomics

As we work, study, communicate, and play, we spend long hours using a screen or keyboard. While we enjoy the benefits of electronic devices, we also have to consider their effects, including stress on both our bodies and minds. Learning about and addressing the negative effects of constant electronic device use can help us remain productive.

The Bottom Line

- When you use a computer or tablet, repetitive movements, such as frequent clicking, tapping, and mouse movements, can cause injuries; eye strain can cause headaches and other problems.
- Frequent computer users may risk social disorders and computer addiction.
- Ergonomically designed workstations can prevent or reduce injury.

Repetitive Strain Injuries

As we use computers, one personal health risk that we may face is **repetitive strain injuries**, or **RSIs**, which are caused by performing the same movement over and over again. The use of computers, tablets, smartphones, and other electronic devices is a leading cause of RSIs. **Carpal tunnel syndrome** is an RSI that affects in the wrist, hand, and arm, and is aggravated by prolonged keyboarding or gesturing on tablets. Symptoms of RSIs include pain, tingling, and numbness as well as difficulty in performing simple movements. RSIs are also caused by performing an action while in an awkward or stressful position. For example, cradling a cell phone or tablet that's too wide or heavy to hold comfortably while you tap, swipe, rotate, or pinch can lead to RSIs.

Figure 8-1: Be aware of personal health risks while using computers

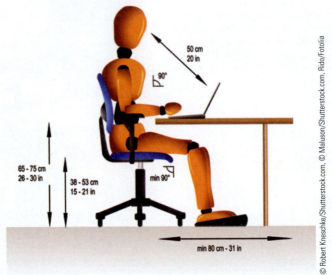

Neck and Eye Strain

Any prolonged digital viewing can cause eye and neck strain. Your eyes can become dry and strained when you look at computer monitors and screens because you blink less. Looking at characters on a screen also makes it harder for our eye muscles to maintain focus. Some people develop **computer vision syndrome**, which can result in eyestrain, headaches, dry eyes, blurry vision, or even double vision. Its effects are not limited to discomfort—you may be less productive at work or school. For some, "I have a pain-in-the-neck at work" is not just a saying. Craning your neck to get in the right position to see clearly, reading through glare, or finding a comfortable place to hold a device can give you a stiff neck that can quickly develop into a distracting headache.

Addiction and Social Disconnect

Most of us enjoy connecting with friends and family on the Internet, surfing the Web, and shopping or playing games online. However, for some people, spending too much time online can lead to a feeling of disconnectedness in other areas of their lives and to feeling out of control due to technology overload and compulsion.

Internet addiction is the excessive use of the Internet for gaming, video, Web surfing, texting, blogging, social networking, or shopping. Some people can't stop using the Internet

By the Numbers Now

People who use computers regularly may perform over 100,000 keystrokes every day. Regular users should pay attention to correct posture and follow ergonomic guidelines (see **Figure 8-1**) to avoid damage to muscles, nerves, and tendons.

#security

If you are under 25, you are considered a part of "Generation Text" and may experience thumb and wrist injuries.

without feeling ill at ease or anxious, which interferes with other aspects of their lives. Internet addictions can cause neglect of face-to-face interactions and isolation from the real world. Or worse, Internet encounters can prompt face-to-face meetings that lead to dangerous situations. Online predators are skilled in assuming an alluring online persona.

If you suspect your computer and Internet use are obsessive and beyond normal, therapists and support groups can help. Balance your technology use with healthy activities, and stay connected to the offline world.

Ergonomic Workstations

The best ways to prevent RSIs and eye and neck strain from using digital devices are to maintain proper posture and to configure your work area ergonomically. **Ergonomics** is the study of safe and efficient working environments.

Some helpful tips for working safely and avoiding injury include the following:
- When sitting at a desktop computer, adjust the height of your chair so that your arms and knees form right angles and your eyes are even with the top third of the monitor.
- Position the keyboard so that your wrists are straight while typing.
- When using laptops and tablets, use a stand or hard binder to raise the device so that you work with the keyboard or tablet screen at an angle. See **Figure 8-2**.

Figure 8-2: Set up workspaces with ergonomics in mind

© Discovod/Shutterstock.com, © iStockphoto.com/angelhell

Most important, whenever possible, break up your workflow—blink often, take breaks to refocus your eyes, get up and move around, and download apps to schedule break reminders.

Data Risks

solid state hard drive | magnetic hard drive | Blue Screen of Death | hacker | cybercrime | hacktivist | white hat | black hat | cloud storage system | cyberterrorism | cyberterrorist | virus | worm | cyberattack | uninterruptible power supply

If you use technology, you're sure to create and acquire a great deal of data stored in files. If you are unable to access files, whether they are lost or corrupted, you can lose hours of work and valuable information, causing a crisis. You can lose documents, photos, journals, projects, personal histories, and even your identity. There are several smart strategies you can follow to protect your data.

Hardware Failure

If the screen or pointing device on your computer or mobile device fails, or some other peripheral device breaks, your data is still intact. However, you store your data—music, photos, video, documents, and messages—on storage devices that can fail or be damaged, leading to data loss.

Although **solid state hard drives** that have no moving parts are relatively stable, **magnetic hard drives** are especially prone to failure. Sometimes a hard drive just dies quietly, but it might show symptoms first. The warning signs of an imminent hard drive failure are frequent slowdowns or freezes and a screeching, grinding, or repetitive clicking sound. Optical storage media like CDs and DVDs can also fail if they become dirty or scratched. Almost any storage device, such as your mobile phone, will fail if it gets wet or damaged.

#security

When using a tablet, some people use their laps as tables, which can cause excessive strain on the neck, shoulders, fingers, wrists, and forearms.

On the Job Now

The number-one job skill necessary in the top 60 growth job fields, according to an IDC study, is oral and written communication.

On the Job Now

Some companies offer their employees standing desks. Using a standing desk can benefit your health. When sitting for long hours, you can suffer from metabolic problems and circulatory issues.

The Bottom Line
- Possible causes of data loss include the following: a personal computer hard drive crash, natural disasters destroying devices, physical damage to devices as a result of water or exposure to extreme climates, theft or loss of devices, and insecure cloud storage.
- If hackers steal your data, identity theft or monetary loss can result.

Figure 8-3: Sign of hard drive crash

Jens Ochlich/Fotolia

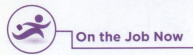

On the Job Now

When an employee connects a personal smartphone to his or her company's wireless network, that person's email and Web site activity can be logged while on company property.

Hot Technology Now

With the new technology called the Internet of Things, consumers may invite a new wave of cyberattack risks into their home thermostats, TVs, and refrigerators.

When a hard drive fails, Windows users see what is commonly called the **Blue Screen of Death**, or BSoD. See **Figure 8-3**. Mac users see the "Marble of Doom," also called "Spinning Beach Ball of Death," or simply the spinning wait cursor that remains on the screen for a long time. These symptoms indicate a serious problem.

Attacks and Hacks

Besides hardware failure, your data is at risk from **hackers**—people who break into computers and computer networks, often by exploiting weaknesses and preventable flaws. The crime of hacking into and attacking networks is known as **cybercrime**.

Some hackers just want to show off their skills and don't intend to do any serious damage. Others have political motivations and may attempt to suppress free speech. Many hackers call themselves **hacktivists** and have a social goal or impact. The hacker community includes **white hat** (nondestructive) and **black hat** (very destructive) hackers. Black hat hackers can do real harm through espionage, theft, or disruption of the network. Hackers can target individual computer users, but they are more likely to target major corporations and divisions of government.

Loss and Theft

You only need to experience one serious data loss to understand its consequences. For both companies and individuals, hardware failure and human error are the most common causes of data loss. Some simple practices can help prevent loss or theft:

- Portable devices and portable media, such as flash drives, DVDs, or CDs, can easily be misplaced or stolen, so it is good practice to have organized storage cabinets in accessible places. Keep devices and media safely stored in locked boxes or rooms, if possible.
- Account numbers and passwords are vulnerable and are prime targets for theft. It is important that you create strong passwords and do not share sensitive data with unauthorized users. Never write passwords down and keep them near a device.

Loss and theft can be expensive. Businesses must calculate the expense of rebuilding a secure environment that was compromised, fund crisis and media management, and pay legal fees. Companies may also face state and federal fines and customers that sue for damages. Furthermore, the harm to a company's reputation may be irreparable and result in a smaller customer base, which means lost revenue.

Natural Disasters

Every year, natural disasters remind us of the vulnerability of our business, academic, or personal records to catastrophic data loss. Hurricanes and storms account for almost half of total losses. Fires, floods, hurricanes, lightning, tornadoes, and earthquakes can strike electronics unexpectedly and destroy all your data. Floodwaters are particularly damaging because of debris, sediment, and contamination.

Make sure you have a data recovery plan before a disaster strikes, such as storing backups in a different location or online. **Cloud storage systems** have backups at various online locations that provide additional protection. By storing data in the cloud, you provide additional protection for your data.

Cyberterrorism

Cyberterrorism is the premeditated disruption of computers and networks. An attack centers on areas that will affect the most people: telecommunications, utility storage and delivery, water supply, emergency services, and banking and financial services. Cyberterrorism is a low-cost action with a high-cost impact. **Cyberterrorists** use automated attack tools such as viruses and worms to wreak their havoc. **Viruses** and **worms** are software that travels through networks to harm computer programs. Cyberterrorists can be politically motivated, taking time to plan an elaborate attack and ensuring they get publicity. A cyberterrorist also can be an angry employee or someone seeking revenge or justice for a perceived wrong.

The effects of a **cyberattack** can include physical damage and a general disruption of regular activities. Lowered public confidence creates a climate of fear and mistrust.

Data in the Cloud

Storing data on servers over the Internet, or in "the cloud," is a popular and economical way to store data. See **Figure 8-4**. However, cloud storage has its drawbacks:

- Moving data across the Internet increases opportunities for theft or manipulation.
- The shift to cloud computing has also increased the demand on servers, storage devices, and networks, and increases our dependence on technology we don't own or control.
- If the Internet is inaccessible as a result of a power outage or another problem, or if your cloud storage provider has technical problems, your data could become unavailable.

Figure 8-4: Cloud computing

Government agencies, corporations, and millions of people have migrated to cloud storage.

© Fenton one/Shutterstock.com

Data Protection

Disasters of every type are bound to happen. Investing in prevention is better than trying to rebuild. The three most important steps you can take to protect your data are back up, back up, and back up! Other steps you can follow:

- Schedule regular backups, whether online or to a device that is protected against whatever might damage your primary device.
- Store backups in more than one location where they are safe from flooding, from other weather elements, and from theft.
- Install an **uninterruptible power supply** to provide battery backup for a short period.
- Educate classmates or colleagues about updating software and about updating and following security protocols. A knowledgeable team is less likely to jeopardize data security.
- Make sure your cloud provider uses strong encryption-based security and has a secure physical environment.
- Never share personal and sensitive information such as Social Security numbers, birth dates, maiden names, or address information unless you are sure whom you are giving it to.

Email and Internet Risks

spam | malware | virus | worm | Trojan horse | rootkit | spyware | phishing | hoax | hotspot | Wi-Fi piggybacking | war driving | firewall | antivirus | antispyware | service pack | wireless router | encryption

The only way to eliminate all risk on the Internet is never to go online—not a practical solution in our current society. See **Figure 8-5** on the next page. Your best bet is to develop some habits that protect you and your data from malware, phishing, hoaxes, spam, and other tools designed to wreck your system or steal your money.

Spam

Junk email, known as **spam**, can be annoying or even dangerous. The goal of a person sending spam is to have you click a link in a message; therefore spam subject lines appeal to emotions such as compassion, trust, or curiosity. Some spam messages try to convince you that your computer already has a virus and instruct you to fix the problem by downloading software or clicking a link. That's when your computer gets infected.

Your Internet service provider and other businesses invest considerable resources to block spam, although junk email does inevitably sneak through. Spam makes up an estimated 85 percent of all email. Spam clogs the Internet and costs consumers an estimated $10 billion a year.

The Bottom Line

- Smartphones and tablets, as well as personal computers, are prime targets for attacks by malware such as viruses, worms, and Trojan horses. Opening an email attachment or going to an unsecure Web site can infect your computer.
- Once your system is infected, your normal computer activities and security are severely compromised.

Hot Technology Now

The Web site snopes.com provides warnings about hoaxes on Facebook and on spam emails. Before you pass on an email stating questionable events, facts, threats, or cures, check it on snopes.com.

Figure 8-5: Threats on the Internet

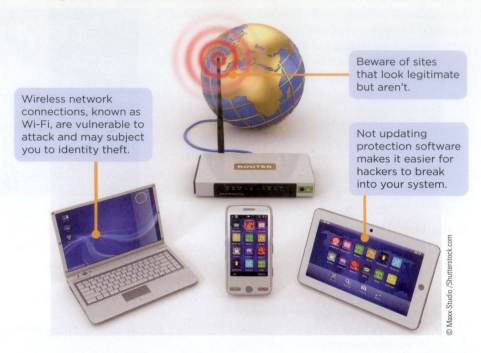

Malware, Viruses, Spyware

The term **malware** refers to viruses, worms, Trojan horses (or Trojans), and other software designed to disrupt a system or exploit data. See **Table 8-1**.

Table 8-1: Malware

Type of malware	Description
Viruses	Can lurk undetected in your system, infect it, and spread when you distribute infected files—especially as email attachments
Worms	Spread by automatically sending themselves to everyone in your address book
Trojan horse and **rootkits**	Disguise themselves as useful programs or apps, but do damage when you run them; allow others to access your system or track and monitor your keystrokes
Spyware	Collects bits of data, such as your surfing habits; can also scan your hard drive and change your default home page because it takes partial control of your system

Phishing and Hoaxes

Just as the name implies, **phishing** involves throwing out "bait" in the form of an email or social media post, in the hopes that a few users will respond, even if the vast majority ignore it. A phishing email or social media post looks genuine, but falsely claims that you must take immediate action. When you click a link in a phishing email and visit the fake site, it asks for your username and password sign-in or account information. After you fill in the form, thieves can access your account and use the data to obtain false accounts in your name.

A **hoax** can be a fake coupon for a brand name store or item or an email that warns about a nonexistent virus in order to get you to click a link that installs malware.

#security

One recent virus blocked users from viewing their own data files until they paid a ransom to unlock their information.

Unsafe Sites

Regardless of how you reach a site, whether by typing a URL or by clicking a link on another page or in search engine results, you cannot assume that all Web sites are safe. Some Web sites "hook" you by falsely reporting that a Web site is unsafe. In reality, it is misleading you into clicking through a series of windows so you activate a scam antivirus program, which is really malware.

If you participate in social media sites such as Facebook, YouTube, or Twitter, malicious users can easily hide malware in posts and links. Online gaming sites and online surveys can also hide malicious software. When you see a deal that seems too good to be true, it usually is.

If your browser and/or computer lacks security software—or if you haven't turned it on or updated it—you might never know that the site you're about to visit is dangerous.

Figure 8-6: Updating software

Software Vulnerability

Hackers and scammers spend time finding and exploiting weaknesses in computers, devices, or Web software. To protect yourself, your system, and your data, you must keep your security software up to date. Software updates often fix security issues, but if you don't install the updates, your computer continues to be vulnerable. Without updated software, smartphones can freeze up, prevent access to new features and functionality, and put your data at risk. See **Figure 8-6**.

Wireless Connections

While a wireless network can extend your reach online, the network and your computer are unprotected if the network is unsecured. **Hotspots**—areas in a wireless network where you can access the Internet—include coffee shops, airports, hotels, libraries, and other public places. Most hotspots (see **Figure 8-7**) are unsecured. Avoid passing sensitive data over unsecured networks. For example, do not do your online banking from a coffee shop's network.

A neighbor—or a stranger—can access your computer or device just by being in range of your unsecured Wi-Fi signal. **Wi-Fi piggybacking** occurs when someone taps into your unprotected Wi-Fi network. At a minimum, piggybacking can slow down your wireless connection.

Another way a hacker can gain access to your Wi-Fi network is by **war driving**, a practice in which someone searches for and maps unsecured Wi-Fi networks from a vehicle. After gaining access to your system, the hacker can pose as you online and download illegal content in your name.

Figure 8-7: Hotspots can be unsecure

Protection Practices

To protect your devices and data, use the same smart practices for every device or computer that connects to the Internet. You can take some simple steps to control unsafe messages:

- Never open an attachment or click a link in an email or text from an unknown source.
- Don't install downloaded software that you have not first checked for malware.
- Keep your passwords in a safe and secure place. If you wrote them on paper, don't post the paper on your monitor or underneath your keyboard or desk.
- If passwords are in a file, add password protection to that file.
- Never enter private information, such as your Social Security number, password, or account information, in a message or site you're not familiar with.
- If you are concerned that you system may have been compromised, close the browser window immediately and run a scan using your security software.
- When in public, if you sign in to a Wi-Fi network that doesn't require a password, don't use the network for private or sensitive information.

 **#security**

Back up your smartphone periodically to a mobile cloud-based service such as iCloud for iPhones.

Software Protection

Cybercriminals are creative and often successful in exploiting software and system weaknesses. To guard against cybercriminals, first make sure that you have installed firewall, antivirus, and antispyware programs. **Firewall** programs protect your system from intruders. See **Figure 8-8** on the next page. **Antivirus** software identifies malware that tries to install on your computer or device. **Antispyware** guards against spyware that attempts to install and then collect and transmit personal data from your system or device.

Figure 8-8: Windows Firewall protection

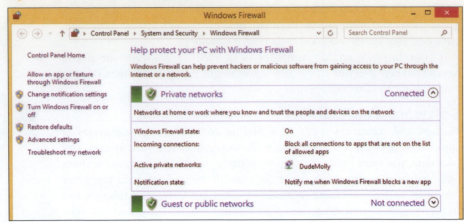

In addition, be sure to install updates and service packs for your operating systems, application software, browser add-ons, and smartphone and tablet apps. **Service packs** are software patches provided by the software publisher to fix bugs and enhance performance. Also, uninstall software that you don't use.

Lastly, make sure your **wireless router**, the device that sends the signal to connect your wireless devices to the Internet, has encryption turned on. **Encryption** ensures that your data is scrambled as it travels between you and its Internet destination, so if a hacker were to intercept your message, he or she would see nothing but scrambled letters. Although no security is 100% safe, encryption can help.

Financial Risks

electronic wallet | PayPal

When you shop, bank, or conduct any type of financial transaction online, you take the risk that your credit card number or other financial information could be stolen. Cybercriminals can steal sensitive data by intercepting it during transmission or by exploiting a weakness in the system. Update your defenses frequently, ensuring that your firewall and antivirus software are always up to date.

Unsecure Web Sites

Some Web sites are not what they appear to be. It's easy to be fooled into thinking you're visiting a secure site when in reality you've fallen victim to a site that only pretends to be legitimate. To ensure that you are using a secure Web site, look for https:// at the beginning of the URL or a padlock icon in the address bar. See **Figure 8-9**. If computer or network protection is weak, hackers can steal sensitive account information by intercepting transaction data when it's transmitted or stored.

Figure 8-9: Unsecure v. secure Web sites

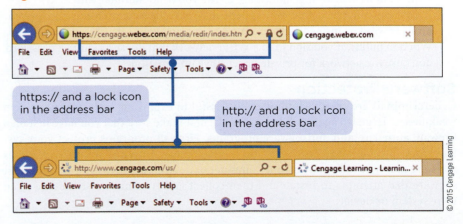

#security

Password-protect your home wireless router to protect from WiFi piggybacking.

The Bottom Line
- If your financial transactions are not secure from hackers, phishing sites, and other online frauds, you can experience significant financial losses.
- Always make sure you're using a secure Web site whenever you conduct any online transaction; use smart practices for every computer or device you use.

© 2015 Cengage Learning

To help ensure safety when using the Web, do the following:
- Be wary of any site that asks for your Social Security number or birth date before you can do business with it.
- Avoid shopping or conducting financial transactions on sites that look real but do not have https:// and a lock icon in the address bar.
- Check the spelling of a site; misspelled sites (for example, if the site URL reads "bankofamerika") are often fraudulent.

Online Banking

Cybercriminals can take advantage of flaws in your security system and steal your banking and financial information. No matter which device you use to access the Internet, there are some simple rules you can follow to protect your data and information.
- Avoid typing sensitive personal or financial information when using a public wireless network.
- Do not enter sensitive or personal information in an email or after clicking a link in an email. Convincing phishing emails can appear to come from your bank or credit card company. No legitimate company will ask you for email sign-in or personal information.
- Delete suspect email that you receive, and call or email your bank if you have any questions.
- Do not unzip or open any unsolicited email or text messages. These can also contain fake forms, phony bills, or vouchers that can release malware on your device once you unzip or open them.
- Update your operating system, Web browser software, and antivirus software when prompted.

Online Shopping

Cybercriminals can take advantage of flaws in shopping sites and wireless networks. Any choices you make or information you provide can be vulnerable to nearby hackers. No matter which device you use to access the Internet, there are some simple rules you can follow to protect your data and information when shopping online.
- Avoid shopping at sites that don't have secure checkout procedures and clear privacy and return policies—or sites that lack contact information.
- Avoid making online purchases while using a public wireless network.
- Beware of Web addresses that are spelled incorrectly or have extra words or numbers in them.
- Don't pay for online items with money transfers. Cybercriminals may offer a better deal if you pay for items with a money transfer. Almost certainly, you'll never receive the item you paid for.
- Use a credit card, **electronic wallet** (software that processes information for secure online purchases), or a **PayPal** account that you can track to trace a problem when you make an online purchase at a secure site. PayPal is a service in which buyers and sellers set up an account that manages and secures online financial transactions.

Mobile Devices

Because mobile devices are easily lost or stolen, leaving a mobile device unlocked instantly exposes your data. It may be tempting to download inexpensive, even legitimate-looking apps from unknown or third-party stores, but the apps often come loaded with malware.

Mobile payment apps transmit payment information from a smartphone to a nearby cashier reader. For security, use apps from a reputable source, such as your bank, credit card company, or retailer. See **Figure 8-10** on the next page.

#security

Keep an eye on your credit card accounts online instead of waiting for your monthly statement to check for fraud.

#security

Set up text or email notifications with your online bank account to notify you of suspicious purchases, significant withdrawals, or a low balance.

By the Numbers Now

According to Amazon, the most popular online shopping days include Cyber Monday, followed by Green Monday (second Monday of December), and Black Friday.

By the Numbers Now

Some "free" apps require in-app purchases—for example, a children's game may ask the child to purchase "more lives." Apple refunded $32.5 million to parents for in-app purchases after losing a lawsuit.

Figure 8-10: Paying with a smartphone

Tyler Olson/Fotolia

Protection Practices

To protect yourself while using the Internet, be smart and be careful. By following these protection practices, you can greatly reduce the chances of losing your financial data to fraudulent activities:

- In addition to making sure your favorite shopping Web sites use https:// or lock icons, also make sure they are members of Web security organizations such as TRUSTe, VeriSign, or the Better Business Bureau.
- Download electronic wallet software and security apps to use when you purchase items. You can also set up software that remotely erases information stored on a mobile device if it's lost or stolen.
- Get in the habit of logging out of your accounts, clearing the history in the Web browser on all your devices daily, and keeping your operating system, browser, and security software up to date.
- Create multiple passwords and be sure that they are strong. The strongest passwords contain uppercase and lowercase letters, symbols, and numbers.
- Check your bank and credit card statements frequently for activity.
- Lock your mobile device and use the highest security settings on your home wireless network.

Privacy Risks

cyberbullying | cyberstalking | identity thief | credit score | credit report | netiquette | online identity | online profile | Incognito mode | InPrivate mode

Identity theft is the nation's fastest-growing crime. Unfortunately, its victims often don't find out about it until they have become victims of fraud. Your online profile on social media (see **Figure 8-11**) gives you many new ways to connect with others—and just as many ways to put yourself in potentially dangerous situations. In addition, Web sites track your browsing history, your identity, and other data. Use protection practices to help shield yourself from misuse of your information and to avoid putting yourself in harm's way.

Identity Theft

An **identity thief** obtains personal information from various online and real-world sources. Thieves might use online phishing messages or physical devices that read credit card or ATM numbers. They target your Social Security number, credit card and debit card numbers, PINs, passwords, and other personal information. An identity thief may steal from you directly, but the ultimate goal is to gain enough information to impersonate you without your knowledge.

With your Social Security number, an identity thief can order a replacement birth certificate or driver's license. Even though this happens without your knowledge or

Figure 8-11: Your online profile

Your online profile is compiled from many of your actions, including comments, postings, likes and shares, as well as the online coupons you use.

© Annette Shaff/Shutterstock.com

permission, you will be responsible for every unpaid bill and financial crime committed in your name. It can be time consuming and expensive to repair your credit rating and reputation when recovering from identity theft.

Fraud

After identity thieves assume your identity, they can then commit various kinds of fraud. For example, an identity thief can easily impersonate you to employers, financial institutions, and even the police if he or she commits a crime in your name. Credit card fraud is also common. Thieves spend all the credit available on the fraudulent cards immediately and, of course, never pay the bills.

This kind of fraud has an instant and long-lasting effect on your **credit score**, the numeric score that affects your future ability to obtain credit. Having a damaged credit score causes problems in many aspects of your life. Education loans, car loans, and home loans become difficult to get, and job or rental applications are denied based on a bad **credit report**. Repairing your credit report after it has been damaged by fraud is a long and grueling process. Even though you did nothing wrong, you may still lose money.

Cyberbullying

Children and young adults are immersed in the Web long before they develop a sense of how to conduct themselves appropriately. **Netiquette** is a set of online communication practices and rules. One netiquette guideline is to treat others online as you would like to be treated.

Instead of following this guideline, cyberbullies badger, humiliate, and torment others. **Cyberbullying** involves humiliation, rumors, lies, taunts, or threats. Some of the cruelest cyberbullies have been preteen or teenage girls, but immaturity is no excuse. Make sure you and your family know how to recognize cyberbullying. See **Figure 8-12**.

People express themselves more boldly online knowing that posts or other communications can be anonymous. School districts often develop policies and guidelines that address cyberbullying. Some states have extended a school's jurisdiction to act in cases that take place off campus or online.

Cyberstalking

Cyberstalkers might harass and threaten coworkers, bosses, former love interests, or someone they disagreed with online. The FBI estimates that 80 percent of all stalking victims are female. **Cyberstalking** often involves the same dynamics as other forms of violence—threats, power, intimidation, and control—and can escalate into real-world violence. To help protect yourself from stalkers, limit how much personal information you share online.

Social Media Sharing

The numerous positive experiences you have interacting in social media and networking communities can be offset by privacy concerns if someone gains access to your information. It's easy to overshare with people you think you can trust, and that's where problems begin. Someone can repost private details about you, including images and video, and within minutes, that information can be shared with people across the country and around the world.

Younger users may not know or care that they're divulging too much information to a predator, placing them in danger. Therefore, it's important for parents and peers to talk about what's appropriate to share. Content stays and is available on the Internet long after you might think it's been deleted or removed. Think about your posts, tweets, messages, photos, videos, comments, and status updates. Consider that in an instant, you've shared something about yourself or someone else that you can never take back.

Figure 8-12: Be aware of cyberbullying

© karen roach/Shutterstock.com

Figure 8-13: Social networks require online profiles

© Gil C/Shutterstock.com

#security

There are two types of cookies. Temporary cookies are session cookies that are stored for a short time and then removed when the browser is closed. Permanent cookies are stored for a long time on your hard drive.

On the Job Now

Do not use your business email address for personal Internet usage. Set up a separate email for shopping online and using personal social media sites.

The Bottom Line
- Personal information is very important to each person and should be safeguarded.
- Vast amounts of personal information are passed among people, employers, and agencies in a flash through computers and the Internet, so it is possible for this information to land in the wrong hands.
- When you conduct business on the Internet that requires you to enter personal information, you can use settings in your browser and your home network router to safeguard your information.

Online Profile

Your **online identity**, also called your **online profile**, consists of your photos, videos, purchases, public posts, comments, and information forwarded and reposted by your friends and by strangers. See **Figure 8-13**. When you click Share on Facebook, post a status, comment or update your LinkedIn profile, or post a photo on Instagram, you lose control of what goes online or shows up in search results.

Employers and other important decision-makers such as school admissions officers can and do check out your Internet "footprint." What you might consider a zealous response to a news story or just sharing a fun party photo can set off red flags if a potential employer or college admissions officer sees it. If you want to post more freely, you can consider creating a personal profile and a public profile on each of the social network sites. Employers screen applicants using social media, and they reject candidates that have lied about experience or qualifications, posted inappropriate content, or made negative comments about previous employers.

Cookies

Just about every site you visit stores a cookie in your computer's browser. Cookies save your user preferences and identify you when you next sign in or visit. Cookies also can monitor your movements on a site and then send that information back to the Web site. A Web site can host ads from a third-party advertiser who then places its cookie on your computer.

Unless you read the Privacy and Terms of Use statements on a Web site, you don't know how a business uses your history. Businesses also collect and track your personal information when you use something as simple as an online coupon. Advertisers combine details about your online and in-store shopping behaviors with other tracking data to form a personalized shopping profile.

If you want to avoid being tracked through your browser when shopping online, you can use your browser's **Incognito mode** or **InPrivate mode.** By selecting these modes, your browser will not save your browsing history, temporary Internet files, form data, cookies, usernames or passwords.

Protection Practices

To help deter identity theft, shred financial documents, monitor your accounts, and protect personal information—and be wary if asked to provide it. These are some helpful guidelines you can follow:

- If you are a victim of identity theft, disconnect from the Internet, close suspect accounts, place a fraud alert on your credit reports, and file a police report and a complaint with the Federal Trade Commission at www.ftc.gov.
- If you're being harassed, bullied, or threatened online, report the abuse quickly.
- Reduce your Internet footprint by deleting old online accounts and increasing the privacy settings on your social network accounts.
- Don't share information via social media that would make you vulnerable. Pay particular attention to the images you share on any device.
- Learn how to configure your browser to block third-party cookies from certain sites and opt out of receiving emails or updates.

Personal Information Security

Social Security number | username | password | PIN (personal identification number) | strong password | authentication | biometrics | two-factor authentication | two-step authentication | two-factor verification | incognito browsing | pharming | phishing | router

What defines who you are to your bank? School? Credit card company? Employer? It's your personal information—facts about you that make you unique, such as your name, birthdate, place of birth, parents' last names, and Social Security number. Your name alone might not be unique, but combined, these facts make it possible for you to carry out activities such as conducting business, getting loans, and applying for jobs. If your personal information is not secure, you could find yourself unable to accomplish these essential tasks.

Figure 8-14: Protecting your identity and data

Many countries in the world assign unique ID numbers to their residents and citizens.

A **Social Security number** is a unique nine-digit number assigned to each individual in the United States. It is used for tracking Social Security benefits, identification purposes, and income tax filing.

Different sites and companies have different requirements for user names, such as number of characters or letters or if capital letters are required.

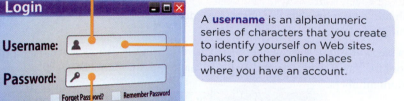

A **username** is an alphanumeric series of characters that you create to identify yourself on Web sites, banks, or other online places where you have an account.

A **password** is a unique combination of characters or letters that you specify. When used in combination with your username, it grants you access to your account or Web site.

A username can be entered on a mobile device. You can click a Remember me box if only you will be using the device.

© zimmytws/Shutterstock.com, © bannosuke/Shutterstock.com, © Oleksiy Mark/Shutterstock.com

Why Personal Information Security Matters

Because cyberterrorists, hackers, and spammers can pose significant threats to your physical, employment, and financial security, it is important to use verification processes and password protection systems to help protect your personal information.

Often, banks and credit card companies will compensate you for losses if you report fraudulent activity in a timely fashion. But, unfortunately, there are groups that illegally gather the information of people who have worked hard to keep their credit scores and reputation in good standing and sell these identities to others for profit. Once someone assumes your identity, it can take years of legal hearings to prove who you really are and straighten out the mess. The best defense is a good offense, so you should follow simple strategies to protect your identity and bank and credit card numbers.

Choosing a Strong Password

Your username and password are often the key to your account information. Unlike most of your personal information and data, such as your bank and credit card numbers and Social Security number, you choose your **username** and **password** to create accounts at Web sites, banks, or wherever such information is needed. Often the combination of username and password is required to get into your account. If you forget your password or username, sites often can mail you a link that lets you set a new one to your email address on record. A password is not a **PIN (personal identification number)**. A PIN typically is a three- to four-digit number that is either assigned by a bank or financial institution or selected by a user to get into accounts through ATM.

Many people select usernames that are familiar and easy to remember. Since it is the combination of username and password that is the key to the information,

By the Numbers Now

The first three digits of your Social Security number identify your geographical location when you applied for the number. The numbers with lowest digits were issued in the northeast, and the highest were issued on the West Coast.

you should create **strong passwords**, which are passwords not easily guessed by another person who wants to access your accounts. So, you should follow some rules to ensure that your accounts are protected.

Passwords can be difficult to remember, but you do not want to reuse the same password at several sites in case there is a breach. You can create similar passwords for several sites that do not have sensitive data, such as a photo site, but you should create a unique password that is strong for your banking. See **Table 8-2**.

Table 8-2: Rules for creating strong passwords

Rule	Bad examples	Better examples
Passwords should have more than five characters; mix letters, numbers, and symbols as well as uppercase letters.	password1 12345	Mtwtf13579# DumFDP076
Do not use a password someone can guess, such as your name, pet's name, or birthday. If using a birthday or pet's name, include random numbers.	JenniferMarch1st1978 EmilyMay1998	Gatsby1129#45 123RoverDog456
Financial institution passwords should be especially strong; if using a common word, mix up letter case and numbers.	poplar789 mybank123	PoPlAr345St789 Shekels5151$

© 2015 Cengage Learning

#security

As visitors from other countries enter the United States, U.S. Customs and Border Protection collects biometric data including fingerprints and photos, which are checked against databases that track terrorists and illegal immigrants.

Two-Step Verification

How does a computer know who you are? If you meet someone face-to-face, or even on a video conference, that person can see that you are you. But if you log into a computer from a remote location, the system needs a way of verifying your identity before granting access to sensitive information. The process of **authentication** is used to verify a user. There are three ways to verify your identity: 1) showing or swiping something you carry, such as a photo ID card; 2) entering information, such as a username, PIN, or a password; and 3) using a personal feature such as a fingerprint.

Biometrics is the use of personal features to identify a person. Biometric systems include fingerprint scanners, facial recognition technology, and retinal scans. Beginning with the iPhone 5s, and now a feature on many smartphones, a fingerprint ID system is available to unlock a phone. See **Figure 8-15**.

Figure 8-15: Fingerprint to unlock a smartphone

A biometric device unlocks the phone only with the thumbprint of the authorized user.

© Alexey Boldin/Shutterstock.com

Two-factor authentication, also called **two-factor verification** or **two-step authentication**, provides added security by requiring two distinct items for verification. These items can be a username and password, an ATM or debit card and a PIN, or a fingerprint and password. Some systems will let you access an account only after you verify a code that is sent as a text message to your cell phone number on record with the account. This code must then be entered into the site or sign-in screen and is good only for one-time use. Once verified, a user is authenticated or authorized to enter or have access to the device, place, or data.

Adjusting Your Browser Settings

When browsing the Internet, you can take advantage of the security built into your browser to help keep your data and identity secure. Most browsers offer **incognito browsing** as a way to surf the internet without leaving a trace on the computer you used. This is helpful when you browse in a public space such as a library. There is nothing left in the History file and cookies are deleted when you close the window.

Check the security settings on your browser to be sure you have a level of security that meets your needs. There are safe site settings, phishing and pharming filters, and other features, such as the Smart Screen Filter in Internet Explorer, that will help keep you safe. **Figure 8-16** shows several options available through the Safety menu in Internet Explorer. Google Chrome also provides many options.

Pharming is an illicit activity in which you are directed to a fake site to enter personal information. Once entered, the information is sold or transferred for illegal activity. **Phishing** is the gathering of information through fake email. You should never click any links that arrive in email claiming to come from your bank. Sure signs of a phishing email include misspellings and dire warnings that inaction will lead to some catastrophe.

If you are unsure whether an email that appears to be from your bank, school, government, or employer is legitimate, call the apparent sender to confirm its authenticity.

Home Network Security

If you have a home network, you should keep it safe and secure. The best way to secure a network is to set up passwords. More often than not, routers are provided by your Internet Service Provider (ISP) as part of your contract. The **router** connects you to the Internet.

When you get a wireless router from an ISP, it comes with a factory default setting. It is important that you follow the specific steps, often provided in the material from the ISP, to set up the router. One of the steps is to specify a password. Create a strong password, because anyone who has it will gain access to your network. If you have a wireless device, such as a tablet or smartphone with Internet access, the password will also let you access the network through that device.

Assigning a strong password to your wireless home network will help ensure the security of your computer information and guard against war driving. Your best defense is a strong password.

Electronics and the Environment

electronic trash | e-trash | e-waste | green computing

Our lives today are full of electronic gadgets, and every year we get new ones and discard old ones. Because we're so used to electronic hardware, we don't usually think about what it takes to produce the device or what happens after we dispose of it. The process of gathering valuable metals from junked electronics is hazardous and profoundly pollutes the environment.

Electronic Trash

Electronic trash, **e-trash** or **e-waste**, consists of discarded computers, cell phones, televisions, stereos, and the electronics from automobiles and appliances. Regardless of the source of e-waste, most experts agree that manufacturers and consumers need to work together to address this growing problem.

Figure 8-16: Internet Explorer Safety menu

#security

Just like phishing, "smishing" uses smartphone text messages as a scam. The text message may contain a link directing you to download a mobile app designed to steal your personal information or your digital wallet to drain your bank account.

The Bottom Line

- Green, or environmentally friendly, computing and recycling can reduce the environmental impact of electronic waste and ultimately reduce costs.
- Electronic waste and disposal is a global issue.

Figure 8-17: Discarding electronics

© dwphotos/Shutterstock.com

On the Job Now

Data destruction of private and confidential information is vital to corporations and small businesses. Information such as Social Security numbers, credit card information, and medical records must be fully destroyed at the end-of-life of all equipment.

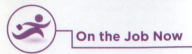

#security

Go to twitter.com, search for @SAMTechNow, the book's Twitter account, and then follow @SAMTechNow to get tweets on your home page.

According to the U.S. Environmental Protection Agency, Americans generate over 2.5 million tons of electronic waste each year. Some school districts, colleges, and universities have an e-waste recycling program. A large university can generate 350 tons of e-waste each year. See **Figure 8-17**.

Toxic Electronic Parts

Although e-waste makes up only 1 percent of what ends up in a landfill, that 1 percent contains 70 percent of the total hazardous material found in landfills. Many communities have passed legislation making it illegal to dispose of e-waste with the general trash.

You may not realize that the chips, circuit boards, disk drives, and plastics in your favorite products are toxic. They contain flame retardants and heavy metals such as lead, mercury, hexavalent chromium, and cadmium phosphors. The e-waste is burned or melted to extract heavy metals like copper, iron, silicon, nickel, and gold. When e-waste is burned or left in a landfill, harmful chemicals are released into the air or groundwater and soil, presenting a risk that people will develop serious health problems by coming into contact with these toxins.

Toxic Trade

The United States exports about 90 percent of its e-waste to countries such as China, India, Nigeria, and Ghana, where environmental and worker safety laws are weak or not enforced. Countries in West Africa, like Ghana, also receive approximately 75 percent of European e-waste.

Only recently have the nations that generate e-waste begun to construct agreements not to ship toxic waste to developing countries unless the countries have adequate waste management facilities. Whether these laws will be successful is still a question. Countries often allow illegal exports of toxic e-waste and ignore guidelines to recycle and reuse locally. Shipping to far-off countries puts e-waste out of sight, but it eventually affects everyone.

Green Computing and Recycling

Green computing is designing, manufacturing, using, and disposing of electronic products in ways that are friendly to both people and the environment. See **Figure 8-18**.

- Look for products that have the Energy Star logo, indicating that the product was built using energy-efficient systems and reduced hazardous materials.
- Donate devices you don't want, rather than discarding them.
- Buy from manufacturers that accept and recycle their used products; then recycle your used electronics.

Being recognized as an e-Stewards recycler is the maximum certification a company or recycling business can receive from the international non-profit environmental watchdog, Basel Action Network. Recycle responsibly to practice green computing.

Figure 8-18: Recycle your electronics

© Blulz60/Shutterstock.com

Chapter Review

Personal Health Risks

1. Define "ergonomics" and give one example.

2. List three problems you might have if your computer screen is not adjusted properly.

3. Explain how a person might get repetitive strain injuries, or RSIs.

Data Risks

4. Name three potential data risks and explain why it is important to have backups of your data.

5. Define the term "hacker" and explain how a hacker might compromise your data.

6. Explain three ways you can safeguard your data.

Email and Internet Risks

7. What are two risks that you need to look out for when using the Internet?

8. Define "pharming," define "phishing," and give an example of how you can protect yourself from both.

9. Explain how malware can damage your data. Define the terms "virus" and "worm."

Financial Risks

10. What should you look for in a bank's Web site before conducting any business on that site?

11. Define two methods for paying for goods or services on the Internet.

Privacy Risks

12. Define "identity theft" and explain why it can be so damaging.

13. What personal information can a thief use to steal your identity?

14. What are the risks of participating in social networking, and how can you protect yourself from those risks?

15. Define the terms "cyberstalking" and "cyberbullying."

Personal Information Security

16. What is biometrics? Give two examples.

17. What is a strong password? Give an example of a password that would be a good choice for a bank account.

18. Explain the difference between a username, a password, and a PIN.

Electronics and the Environment

19. Why is it bad for the environment to dispose of electronics in landfills?

20. Define the term "e-waste."

Test Your Knowledge Now

1. An RSI that affects the wrist, hand, and arm is called _____ syndrome.
   a. Web-based
   b. carpal tunnel
   c. social addiction
   d. computer vision

2. _____ includes excessive use of online games, Web surfing, texting, blogging, and shopping.
   a. E-commerce
   b. Web addiction
   c. Internet addiction
   d. Social networking

3. _____ is the study of safe and efficient working environments.
   a. Phishing
   b. Cybervision
   c. Pharming
   d. Ergonomics

4. Solid state hard drives are more stable than older magnetic hard drives, which are subject to _____, resulting in lost data.
   a. cyberterrorism
   b. crashing
   c. spam
   d. phishing

5. People who break into computers and computer networks—often by exploiting weaknesses and preventable flaws—are called _____.
   a. hackers
   b. white hats
   c. cyberstalkers
   d. Internet addicts

6. _____ is the premeditated disruption of computers and networks.
   a. E-commerce
   b. Cyberbullying
   c. Cyberterrorism
   d. Social networking

7. Systems that have backups at various locations on the Internet, such as OneDrive, are called _____ storage systems.
   a. cloud
   b. sky
   c. Internet
   d. Web

8. _____ is also known as junk email.
   a. Spyware
   b. Spam
   c. Phishing
   d. Piggybacking

9. A type of malware known as _____ travels through computer networks, leaving harmful programs in its wake.
   a. spyware
   b. spam
   c. e-waste
   d. a worm

10. A type of malware known as _____ collects bits of data such as your surfing habits, changes your default home page, and takes partial control of your system.
    a. spyware
    b. spam
    c. e-waste
    d. a worm

11. An email threat known as _____ sends you fake email so that you will click a link and submit your personal data on an illicit Web site.
    a. spamming
    b. pharming
    c. worming
    d. phishing

12. A(n) _____ is an area, often a public place, where you can access the Internet for free on your mobile device.
    a. Wi-Fi
    b. hotspot
    c. Internet zone
    d. router

13. A risk to having an unsecured network in your home is called _____, in which someone can get on your network and use it without your knowledge.
    a. identify theft
    b. cyberbullying
    c. Wi-Fi piggybacking
    d. cyberstalking

14. Which of the following should you install to protect your home network?
    a. firewall
    b. browser
    c. router
    d. spyware

15. You should always install _____ software to protect your computer from malware.
    a. email
    b. browser
    c. anti-virus
    d. spyware

16. _____ is a set of online communication practices and rules.
    a. Phishing
    b. Incognitos
    c. Biometrics
    d. Netiquette

17. _____ is the use of personal features, such as a fingerprint, to identify a person.
    a. Phishing
    b. Incognitos
    c. Biometrics
    d. Netiquette

18. Which of the following is commonly used for authentication at a banking Web site?
    a. username and password
    b. username
    c. birth date
    d. Social Security number and birthdate

19. _____ computing is designing, manufacturing, using, and disposing of electronic products in ways that are friendly to both people and the environment.
    a. Electronic
    b. E-trash
    c. Green
    d. Cyber

20. Electronic trash, or _____, consists of discarded computers, cell phones, televisions, stereos, and the electronics from automobiles and appliances.
    a. e-waste
    b. green waste
    c. cyber trash
    d. spyware

21. In the space next to each image below, write the letter of the phrase that describes it.
    a. secure Web site
    b. biometric device
    c. BSoD
    d. a way to protect online data
    e. form of ID

© zimmytws/Shutterstock.com

© bannosuke/Shutterstock.com

© 2015 Cengage Learning

© Alexey Boldin/Shutterstock.com

Jens Ochlich/Fotolia

Try This Now

1: Proper Ergonomics

Note: This assignment requires a smartphone with a digital camera, or any digital camera.

With iPads, Android tablets, and Windows tablets being commonplace in our world today, researchers are examining the ergonomic impact of these devices. Whether you are using a desktop computer, laptop, or tablet, you can place considerable strain on your body.

a. Research the proper ergonomics of using a desktop computer, laptop, or tablet. Write a list of seven ergonomic guidelines that you should consider when interacting with a computer.

b. Sitting in front of any computer device, use what you have learned and have someone take a picture of you sitting properly in front of the device. Insert the image in the same document as the list of guidelines.

c. Submit the document to your instructor.

2: Internet Hoaxes

Internet hoaxes, such as email scams with get-rich-quick scams or Facebook postings containing misinformation about medical facts, are common. The Web site snopes.com is a source for debunking these false rumors and urban legends.

a. Open a browser and open the site snopes.com.

b. Tap or click the Fraud & Scams link. (If that link is not available, click a similar link.) Next select Identity Theft or a similar topic.

c. Open the links and read about three recent identity theft scams. Write three paragraphs providing an overview in your own words of each of these scams.

d. Submit the document to your instructor.

3: Private Browsing

Note: This assignment requires a browser that has been updated in the last year.

Modern browsers provide private browsing capabilities called InPrivate Browsing in Internet Explorer, Incognito Mode in Chrome, Private Windows in Mozilla Firefox, and Private Browsing in Safari.

a. Write a paragraph about the purpose of private browsing.

b. Research the use of private browsing capabilities within your favorite browser. Open the private browsing feature in any browser. Open three tabs, each containing your favorite Web sites, and take a screen shot. Place the screen shot in the same document as the paragraph written in step a.

c. Submit the document to your instructor.

Critical Thinking Now

1: Business Digital Security Attacks

Each week, headlines are filled with news of hacking attacks resulting in loss of data at large international companies. Research a well-known company that was hacked in the last calendar year. Write at least 150 words about the security infringement. Be sure to mention whether consumers were personally affected by the hacking incident.

2: How Safe Is Snapchat?

Snapchat is a phone app that sends photos such as selfies (photos taken by people of themselves with their own smartphones) to friends, and the images then quickly disappear. Although Snapchat messages are designed to disappear within one to ten seconds, there is no guarantee that the recipient will not take a picture of the message using the screenshot feature of his or her phone. In addition, the friend could take a picture of the sent image message.

Research the privacy policy of Snapchat at snapchat.com and write at least 100 words summarizing the policy in your own words. Do you think Snapchat provides a false sense of security by reporting if the recipient takes a screenshot? Would you be comfortable sending friends images with Snapchat? Why or why not?

Photo Sharing

©william casey/Shutterstock.com

3: Recycling Computers

In the back of your closet, you locate an old "beige" computer. It probably belonged to someone in your family many years ago. After reading this chapter, you are aware that throwing it away in your household garbage could be illegal as well as unethical.

a. Research green computing and proper disposal of a computer.
b. Write a paragraph about steps that should be taken before disposing of a computer's hard drive.
c. Write another paragraph of general locations that can assist you in disposing of your computer.

Green Computing

©Dudarev Mikhail/Shutterstock.com

Ethical Issues Now

Facebook provides a social community that connects over a billion members around the world. When it comes to posting on Facebook, it seems anyone is susceptible to oversharing. Oversharing can include what your roommate consumed at every meal this month or your cousin's ranting about his boss.

a. Research the topic of oversharing on social media. In your own words, write a total of ten comments summarizing dos and don'ts about sharing on Facebook.
b. Research why people overshare on Facebook. Write at least 100 words about why people feel compelled to share with the world topics that they would never share in a room filled with their peers.

Team Up Now – Your Digital Footprint

From the day that you compose your first text message or sign in to a social network, your digital footprint begins a data trail of interactions. Using a free website called Diigo—a social bookmarking site that assists in researching, annotating, and sharing information—search digital material about the guidelines for creating your digital footprint.

a. Each team member should open a browser and go to the site diigo.com. Each member should create an individual account. The site contains videos to assist you in using Diigo.
b. Invite each of your team members to share your annotated pages to build a personal learning network for this team project.
c. Search for sites using the search term "Digital Footprint." Each team member should select five of the most informative sites and use Diigo to annotate a few sentences on each site that provides the best information for your team. Each team member will automatically receive an email from Diigo about what you have shared with your group.
d. Share the sites with your team using Diigo. The site creates a single page listing of the annotated information contributed by your group. In this way, group bookmarks become a repository of collective research.
e. Share this full listing as a bookmark with your instructor.

Key Terms

antispyware	e-waste	repetitive strain injury (RSI)
antivirus	firewall	rootkit
authentication	green computing	router
biometrics	hacker	service pack
black hat	hacktivist	Social Security number
Blue Screen of Death	hoax	solid state hard drive
carpal tunnel syndrome	hotspot	spam
cloud storage system	identity thief	spyware
computer vision syndrome	incognito browsing	strong password
credit report	Incognito mode	Trojan horse
credit score	InPrivate mode	two-factor authentication
cyberattack	Internet addiction	two-factor verification
cyberbullying	magnetic hard drive	two-step authentication
cybercrime	malware	uninterruptible power supply
cyberstalking	netiquette	username
cyberterrorism	online identity	virus
cyberterrorist	online profile	war driving
electronic trash	password	white hat
electronic wallet	PayPal	Wi-Fi piggybacking
encryption	pharming	wireless router
ergonomics	phishing	worm
e-trash	PIN (personal identification number)	

Communication

Chloe is studying abroad in a 10-week summer program in Greece. She loves sharing her experiences with her friends and family back home via her blog.

Communicating through Skype, Facebook, Twitter, Instagram, and email has dramatically shortened the distance between Chloe and her friends and family.

© iStockphoto.com/elemi

For her first study abroad experience, Chloe is studying in Santorini, Greece. Checking in with her academic advisor, parents, and friends back home allows her to share what she is learning in her classes and in her new routine. Her notebook computer has software, an internal microphone, and a camera. She can connect face-to-face with her friends and family online, all with a single tap on her touch screen.

Digital Communication

Webinar | digital communications | podcast | blog | wiki | online social network | communications system | protocol | TCP/IP | wireless fidelity (Wi-Fi) | WiMAX | 802.16 standard | communications software

The Bottom Line

- Digital communications require a communications system and standards.
- To take advantage of digital communications, you also use communications software installed on your digital device, including text messaging and email applications.

When you send a photo and short message to a friend from your smartphone, post a description of a restaurant meal on a blog, or learn how to edit a video while attending a **Webinar** (an online educational Web conference), you are using **digital communications**, which involve transmitting information from one computer or mobile device to another.

Figure 9-1: Using digital communications

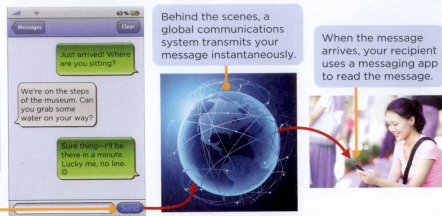

From your point of view, digital communications seem simple: you type a text message, press Send, and you're done.

Behind the scenes, a global communications system transmits your message instantaneously.

When the message arrives, your recipient uses a messaging app to read the message.

© blojfo/Shutterstock.com, © dgbomb/Shutterstock.com, © lzf/Shutterstock.com

#communication

Smartphones use Wi-Fi in addition to 3G (3rd generation) and 4G (4th generation) cellular networks.

By the Numbers Now

The newest Wi-Fi standard is 802.11ac, which can reach the speed of 1 gigabit per second.

#communication

Many cities around the world, such as New York, Detroit, Vancouver, Tokyo, Amman, Nairobi, and Malaga, have business WiMAX networks.

Types of Digital Communication

To connect with other people, you probably use some type of digital communication. Suppose you're planning a trip to Denmark. You might use different types of digital communication.

- Use email, instant messages, or text messages to send and receive digital messages while preparing for your trip.
- To listen to travel tales from other visitors to Denmark, you could download **podcasts** (audio files distributed on the Web) to your smartphone or media player, or you could visit a blog about Denmark. A **blog** (Web log) is an informal Web site of time-stamped articles written in a journal format.
- If you plan to travel with a group, you could contribute to a **wiki**, a collaborative Web site where group members can communicate with each other.
- During your trip, you can update friends back home using an **online social network**, a Web site where members share information.

Communications Systems

If you want to send a message to someone, you use a **communications system**, which sends electronic data from a source to a destination. Along the way, the data can pass through devices that convert it to electrical, sound, light, or radio signals. See **Figure 9-2**.

Communications Standards

To make sure that devices can communicate with each other, they follow communications standards, or **protocols**. These protocols specify the method and speed that devices use to transmit data. **TCP/IP** is a network protocol that defines how to route data across a network. TCP/IP stands for Transmission Control Protocol (TCP) and Internet Protocol (IP). Because all servers on the Internet follow TCP/IP rules, TCP/IP is currently the most widely used communications protocol.

Computers and devices that communicate using radio waves across a medium distance of 100 to 900 feet use **wireless fidelity (Wi-Fi)**. Most Wi-Fi devices today use

Figure 9-2: Using a communications system

Modem converts the message to electronic signals.

Communications channel, such as a cable TV line or fiber optic cable, transmits the signals.

Receiving device, such as another modem, converts the signals into an email message.

Destination device, such as a server, accepts the message.

Your computer or mobile device is the communication source.

Server repeats the process to send the message to your classmate's computer or mobile device.

the 802.11n standard. A laptop might use Wi-Fi to connect to a wireless router and TCP/IP to communicate over the Internet.

To communicate across longer distances, devices can use **WiMAX**, also known as the **802.16 standard**. Computers and devices transmit signals to a WiMAX tower, which can cover up to a 30-mile radius. The tower connects to the Internet or another WiMAX tower.

Communications Software

Communications software helps your computer connect to a network and then work with communications standards to manage transmitting and receiving data. One type of communications software is usually part of a computer's or mobile device's operating system or is provided with networking devices you purchase. See **Figure 9-3**.

Besides communications software built into an operating system, some application software lets users communicate with each other. For example, you can use email software to send and receive email messages, use messaging software on your smartphone, or use Web-based software for a Webinar. The software varies depending on your task.

Communications software works with communication protocols and devices so that all you have to do is enter a message on a computer or mobile device and select a Send command to communicate with people around the world.

Electronic Mail

email message | email system | email service | email server | email client | router | email account | email provider | local email client | Post Office Protocol (POP) | Webmail | Internet Message Access Protocol (IMAP) | Simple Mail Transfer Protocol (SMTP) | email address | domain name | email attachment | spam | spam filter | phishing email

To keep in touch with a friend while you're on the go, communicate with your instructor, or send messages to family members, you can use electronic mail, or email.

#communication

To save money on your smartphone data plan, connect to a Wi-Fi network and make free voice calls on Google Voice (google.com/voice).

Figure 9-3: Communications software

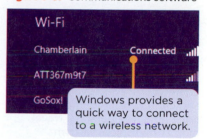

Windows provides a quick way to connect to a wireless network.

The Bottom Line
- When people say "email," they usually mean an email message, which is an electronic document transmitted on a computer network.
- To use email, you need an email account, email software, and a connection to a network such as the Internet.

Figure 9-4: Email requirements

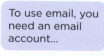

To use email, you need an email account...

...an email application (also called an email client)...

...and a connection to a network such as the Internet.

Email Basics

Any computer or mobile device that can access the Internet can connect with an **email system**, which consists of the computers and software that provide **email services**. The main computer in an email system is an **email server**, which routes **email messages** through the Internet or a private network. See **Figure 9-5**.

Figure 9-5: Using email services

1. Set up an account on an email server, which provides an electronic mailbox for you.

2. The email server retrieves your incoming messages and places them in your mailbox.

3. You use email software to send and receive messages.

4. The email server uses the Internet to send outgoing mail to other email servers.

© indigolotos/Shutterstock.com, © nmedia/Shutterstock.com, © EDHAR/Shutterstock.com

You use email software to send and receive messages. Popular email software includes Gmail, Yahoo! Mail, Outlook, and private services, such as your school's email services.

Communication Process

If someone asked you how to send an email message, you'd probably tell them to use an email program (also called an **email client**) to compose a message and then select the Send button or menu option. But what happens after you select Send?

1. Your email program uses your Internet or network connection to send the message to your email server.

2. Depending on the destination, the email server determines the best route for the message, which often involves sending the message to a series of network devices called **routers**.

3. The last router in the series sends the message to your friend's email server.

4. That email server stores the message in your friend's mailbox.

5. When your friend checks for messages, the email server transfers the message to an email program so it can display the message on your friend's computer.

Email Accounts

If you want to send and receive email, you need an **email account**. To sign up for an email account, you contact an **email provider**, which might be your Internet service provider, a school, an employer, or a Web site such as Yahoo! Mail or Google.

If you sign up with an ISP, your employer, or your school, you can use a **local email client**, which is installed on your computer or mobile device, to send and receive email. This type of email uses **Post Office Protocol (POP)**, a protocol that downloads messages from an email server for permanent storage on your computer.

You can also set up an account through an online service such as Gmail, and then access your email using a Web browser, a system known as **Webmail**. This type of email uses **Internet Message Access Protocol (IMAP)**, a protocol that leaves messages on the server and stores them only temporarily on your computer.

POP and IMAP are protocols for receiving email messages. **Simple Mail Transfer Protocol (SMTP)** is the protocol for sending all types of email messages.

Hot Technology Now

Share your travel adventures and capture your memories by creating a free personal travel blog at mytripjournal.com.

Which type of account should you use? Webmail is ideal for people on the go with mobile devices because they can access their accounts from any computer. Local email is stored on your computer, which lets you keep your messages on your computer's hard drive.

Email Addresses

When you sign up for an email account, your email provider assigns you an email address or asks you to create one. An **email address** has three parts, shown in **Figure 9-6**.

- **User ID**: Typically, this is your name or nickname. Every email address must be unique, however, or email servers couldn't route messages correctly. That's why you see user IDs such as BobJohnson738.
- **"At" symbol**: The @ divides the user ID from the name of the email provider, also called the **domain name**.
- **Domain name**: Although you can often select the user ID, you can't select the domain name because it identifies the email server.

An email address reveals information about the owner. For example, EdMason@ gmail.com is probably an address for someone named Ed Mason using a Gmail account. If you're planning to use your email address for job searches or other professional matters, choose a user ID that appears professional.

Email Messages

Email software displays messages in a two-part form, shown in **Figure 9-7**.

- **Message header**: This part includes the email addresses of the recipients, including those who should receive a courtesy copy (cc). It also includes a subject line to describe the message topic. In addition, the message header can include a blind courtesy copy (bcc) line, which you use to send a message to someone without displaying his or her email address.
- **Message body**: Insert a greeting line with the recipient's name such as "Bethany:" followed by a brief message. Keep the message itself short. Provide longer text or supplemental information in a separate file, which you can attach to the message.

Figure 9-6: Parts of an email address

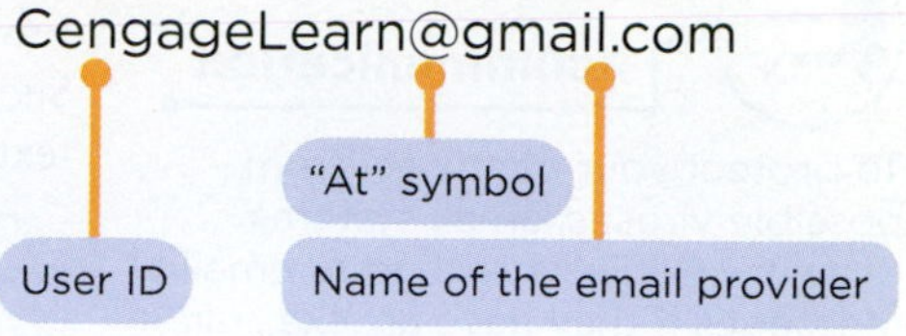

CengageLearn@gmail.com

User ID | "At" symbol | Name of the email provider

© 2015 Cengage Learning

#communication

Email addresses cannot contain spaces.

Figure 9-7: Parts of an email message

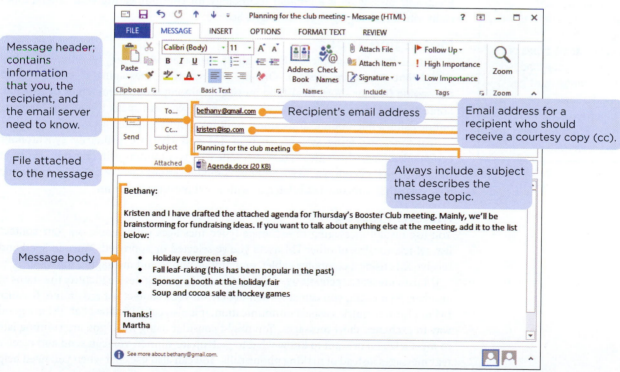

Message header; contains information that you, the recipient, and the email server need to know.

File attached to the message

Message body

Recipient's email address

Email address for a recipient who should receive a courtesy copy (cc).

Always include a subject that describes the message topic.

Bethany:

Kristen and I have drafted the attached agenda for Thursday's Booster Club meeting. Mainly, we'll be brainstorming for fundraising ideas. If you want to talk about anything else at the meeting, add it to the list below:

- Holiday evergreen sale
- Fall leaf-raking (this has been popular in the past)
- Sponsor a booth at the holiday fair
- Soup and cocoa sale at hockey games

Thanks!
Martha

Typical Features

Email software can be located on your computer or on a Web server (for Webmail). Such software provides the form for the message and includes buttons for formatting text, setting a priority for the message, and attaching files.

A file, such as a photo or document, you send with an email message is called an **email attachment**. If you receive a message with an attachment, you can save the attachment on your computer or open it to view its contents.

When you send an email message, your email address is included as the return address so your recipients can respond to your message by using the Reply or Reply All feature. Reply sends a response only to the original sender, while Reply All sends a response to the sender and anyone who received copies.

Email Security

Email is popular and easy to use, but that doesn't mean it's entirely safe. Many email messages you receive can be **spam**, which is electronic junk mail. Spam ranges from offers of goods and services you don't want to messages containing threats such as viruses, which can ruin your data, or keyloggers, which can steal personal information such as passwords.

To guard against spam, use a **spam filter**, which detects unsolicited messages before you open them. Spam filters are often built into email software. If you do receive spam, don't respond to it, even to remove yourself from a mailing list. Your response actually validates your email address.

Another threat is **phishing email**, a fraudulent message designed to trick you into providing confidential information such as your bank account number. To avoid phishing scams, don't click links in messages that appear to come from places such as banks or online merchants. Instead, type the URL of your bank or other legitimate Web site into the Address bar of your browser to go directly to the Web site.

Messaging

real-time messaging system | instant messaging (IM) | chat | synchronous communication | asynchronous communication | contact list | presence technology | online chat | Short Message Service (SMS) | Multimedia Messaging Service (MMS) | chat room | message board | Internet forum | thread | newsgroup

Electronic messaging is a popular technology for communicating with others, especially when exchanging short messages. See **Figure 9-8**.

Messaging Types

A system that lets people exchange short messages while they're online is called a **real-time messaging system**. One-on-one real-time messaging is called **instant messaging (IM)** for short. Real-time messaging among group members is called **chat**. Some systems include voice and video options, so you can speak to and see someone online using a microphone and camera built into your computer.

Real-time messaging systems such as IM and chat are primarily **synchronous communications**, which means that everyone who is communicating must be online at the same time. In contrast, **asynchronous communications** involve one person posting a message that someone reads later, as with a text message or forum.

Instant Messaging

You use instant messaging to exchange typed messages with people on your **contact list**, which consists of other IM users you've selected or approved. You can send and receive IMs using a computer, tablet, or a mobile phone and messaging software.

IM uses **presence technology**, which lets one computing device identify the status of another. As a result, you can see when people on your contact list are online. Because IM is a form of quick, casual communication, it is also called **online chat**. IM is a good way to exchange short messages. You might consider using IM if you are running late to meet a friend or want to know what to pick up for dinner; you can send and receive text messages instead of making phone calls. You can also use chat when you need help

Figure 9-8: Types of electronic messages

A student exchanges instant messages with a friend so they can meet before class.

A consumer joins a chat room where car owners are discussing the pros and cons of a particular car.

A rental agent receives a text message on her smartphone with information about an apartment.

A video game player visits a message board to learn strategies and tips for winning the game.

© Monkey Business Images/Shutterstock.com, © arek_malang/Shutterstock.com, © ArchMan/Shutterstock.com, © aslysun/Shutterstock.com

using software. You usually can visit the software publisher's Web site and find a box labeled "Chat," where you can exchange messages with a technical support expert. For example, if you are having computer problems, use a browser to go to the Geek Squad Web site (www.geeksquad.com), and then click the Chat with an Agent link in the navigation bar to open the Geek Squad chat page. See **Figure 9-9**.

Figure 9-9: Getting help from online chat

Select this option to chat with a Geek Squad expert.

Geek Squad (and other services) ask you to sign in before starting a chat.

Source: Geek Squad

Text Messaging

Text messaging is similar to IM, except that you typically use it on smartphones, not desktop or mobile computers. Text messaging, also called texting or **SMS (Short Message Service)**, is an asynchronous service, which delivers and stores messages until participants decide to view them.

- Most messaging services let you send pictures and short video clips along with text messages. When you do, you are using the **Multimedia Messaging Service (MMS)**, which also allows for longer messages than SMS.
- You can send messages from your mobile device to another mobile device or to an email address.

By the Numbers Now

Although SMS messages are limited to 160 characters, MMS messages have no character limit.

#communication

Text messages are transmitted on your cellular carrier's network, so charges might apply to each text message you send.

Hot Technology Now

Chat instantly with a group of business colleagues or classmates without installing any software using the site simplemeet.me. On a smartphone, you can install WhatsApp to chat without incurring any messaging costs.

- You also can sign up for a Web site to send messages to your mobile device to alert you to breaking news or sports scores, for example.

Chat Rooms

A chat is a real-time typed conversation that you have online. Rather than exchanging messages with one person at a time, you can have a group discussion by using a **chat room**, a location on a server that lets users chat with each other. Anyone in the chat room can participate in the conversation, which is usually about a specific topic. As you type, others in the chat room see what you're typing.

- Some chat rooms allow voice or video chats so that participants can hear or see each other.
- The person who creates a chat room acts as the moderator and monitors the conversation.
- Chat rooms are declining in popularity as more sophisticated online environments, such as social networks and Webinars, are now available.

Message Boards and Forums

A **message board**, also called an **Internet forum**, is an online discussion site where people participate in a conversation by posting messages. Unlike a chat room, a forum temporarily saves messages and often uses a moderator to approve messages before they are posted for others to read. A **thread** or threaded discussion includes the original message and all the replies.

Forums were one of the first technologies for communicating and collaborating online. Another early technology is a **newsgroup**, an online area where users have written discussions on a particular topic. To join a newsgroup discussion, you post a message, called an article, and other users read and reply to it. To participate in a newsgroup, you use a newsreader program, often provided with email software. Web sites that sponsor newsgroups also provide built-in newsreaders.

Podcasts and Online Conferences

podcast | feed | video podcast | streaming audio | Really Simple Syndication (RSS) | Rich Site Summary (RSS) | Web conference | Webinar | video conference

People use communications technology to connect with other people and learn and share information on news and about topics using podcasts, RSS feeds, Web conferences, Webinars, and video conferences.

Figure 9-10: Using podcasts and online conferences

A traveler downloads a podcast to catch up on local news and events while traveling.

A soccer fan subscribes to an RSS feed to keep up with the latest scores and matches.

A business woman uses a Web conference to discuss her company's sales strategy with out-of-town colleagues.

Unable to attend a class in person, a student attends a Webinar instead.

© Dmitrijs Dmitrijevs/Shutterstock.com, © leedsn/Shutterstock.com, © Andrey_Popov/Shutterstock.com, © michaeljung/Shutterstock.com

Podcasts

If you miss a lecture or your favorite comedian's stand-up act, you might be able to catch it on a podcast. A **podcast** is an audio or video file stored online and distributed by downloads or through feeds. A **feed** is basically a service that you subscribe to so you can receive frequently updated Web content. If you subscribe to a feed, you automatically receive downloads of new podcast episodes as they are produced. If you don't subscribe, you can still download podcast episodes, which are usually MP3 files, to your device.

Examples of podcasts include music, radio shows, news stories, classroom lectures, political messages, and comedy routines. **Figure 9-11** shows how to subscribe to an iTunes podcast. A **video podcast** typically is a file in the MP4 format that contains video and audio. After you download an audio or a video podcast, you can listen to it or watch it at any time.

Figure 9-11: Subscribing to an iTunes podcast

2. Select a podcast that interests you, and then select the Subscribe button.

3. Confirm that you want to subscribe, and then wait for the podcast to download to your iTunes library.

1. At the iTunes Store, select the Podcasts button, and then select a category.

Source: Apple

You can download a podcast as a file and listen to it at your convenience or you can stream the audio file. With **streaming audio**, you start listening to the content right away without having to wait for the entire file or broadcast to download to your computer.

RSS Feeds

In addition to podcasts, feeds provide other Web content, such as news stories or blogs, delivered directly to your browser or email software. The technology for feeds is called **Really Simple Syndication** or **Rich Site Summary (RSS)**, a data format for distributing online content.

RSS content is often free, though you need to subscribe to the feed at the Web site offering the content you're interested in. Browsers can detect when a Web page provides a feed. For example, Internet Explorer displays the Feeds button in orange when a feed is available. See **Figure 9-12**.

To subscribe to the feed, click the Feeds button, and then click the Subscribe link on the Web page. When you subscribe to a feed, Internet Explorer lists the feed in the Favorites Center. When a Web site updates the feed, the Favorites Center displays the name in bold. You click the name to read the updated content.

Web Conferences

Suppose you're working on a business project with a team that includes people in different cities. To collaborate on the project, you can have a **Web conference**, a meeting that takes place on the Web.

Web conferences typically are held on computers or mobile phones. Participants use Web conferencing software to sign into the same Web page. One user acts as the host and shares his or her desktop with the group. During the online session, the host can display a document that participants see at the same time. If the host edits the document, everyone sees the changes as they are made.

Figure 9-12: Feeds button

An orange Feeds button on the Internet Explorer Command bar indicates that a feed is available.

© vector illustration/Shutterstock.com

To send typed messages to each other, participants can use a chat window. Finally, participants might also join a conference phone call or use microphones and speakers attached to their computers to speak to each other.

Webinars

A **Webinar**, short for Web-based seminar, is a type of online conference in which a presenter gives a lecture, demonstration, workshop, or other type of instructional activity. Some Webinars involve one-way communication, in which the presenter speaks and demonstrates and the audience listens. Other Webinars are more interactive and collaborative, especially if they allow polling to survey the audience on a topic or if they let participants ask and answer questions.

Webinars and Web conferences often include slide show presentations and videos. Some include electronic whiteboards, where participants can record and save notes, and provide tools for activities such as brainstorming and problem solving.

Video Conferences

Similar to a Web conference, a **video conference** allows people at two or more locations to meet electronically using a network such as the Internet to transmit video and audio data. To participate in a video conference, you need to have a video camera, microphone, and speakers or headphones attached to your computer. Because video conferences let many people from different geographic locations meet electronically, they are different from video phone calls, which connect only two people online. A video conference always allows participants to see and hear each other, while a Web conference does not.

People use video conferences for business meetings, distance education, legal proceedings, and telemedicine. Telemedicine is often the best way to provide medical services to a remote region. By using telemedicine and video conferencing technology, physicians can diagnose and treat patients they cannot examine in person. Recent innovations include extending video conferences to smartphones and tablets, allowing people in hard-to-reach locations to meet and collaborate with colleagues.

Blogs and Wikis

blog | blogger | blogging software | blogosphere | vlog | microblog | wiki | blogware | content management system | post | page | pageview | About page | tag | label

If you like to keep up with the latest social, family, and career news, as well as share information with others, you can take advantage of the power of the Web by using blogs and wikis. See **Figure 9-13**.

Overview of Blogs

Suppose you spend your free time learning how to make desserts. In fact, you're thinking of becoming a pastry chef. How can you tell the world about your experiences? Start a blog. A **blog**, short for Web log, is a Web page listing journal entries with commentary and information, usually about a particular interest. The author of a blog, also called a **blogger**, uses **blogging software**, available at sites such as Blogger.com, to create and publish entries.

Blogs can contain text, photos, video clips, and links to additional information. See **Figure 9-14**. If a blog isn't private, all you need is the Web address to access it. Otherwise, you need permission from the blogger to read entries. Because a blogger can post at any time and doesn't need to be online when readers are, a blog is considered asynchronous communication. Visitors can read and comment on the blog entries but cannot change them.

Types of Blogs

In the **blogosphere**, which is the worldwide collection of blogs, blogs vary by media, length, and purpose. Many blog authors post entries consisting of mostly text, though authors of video blogs, or **vlogs**, mainly post video clips, and authors of photo blogs mainly post photos.

Hot Technology Now

Share your screen with up to 10 friends or colleagues during a free collaborative Webinar using the sites join.me and logme.in.

On the Job Now

Using Google Hangouts, small businesses can set up free voice and video conversations for up to 10 people.

The Bottom Line

- People use blogs to read the opinions of others and to comment on topics of interest to them.
- To collaborate with other people online, you can use a wiki.

By the Numbers Now

Blogger.com, owned by Google, allows each user to have up to 100 blogs per account.

Hot Technology Now

The Microsoft Office 365 Blog (blogs.office.com) helps you discover the answers to questions about Microsoft Office 365.

A **microblog** allows users to publish short messages, usually between 100 and 200 characters, for others to read. For example, Twitter allows messages up to 140 characters.

- Businesses create blogs to communicate with employees, customers, and vendors.
- Personal blogs often focus on family life, social life, or a personal interest or project, such as building a house or planting a garden.
- Other blogs can include commentary on news and politics and are an outlet for citizen journalists, members of the public who report on current events.

Figure 9-13: Using blogs and wikis

A sales clerk at an electronics store loves gadgets, so he starts a blog to let his friends know about the latest smartphones and tablets.

Figure 9-14: Reading and contributing to a blog

Blog posts are dated and then listed in reverse-chronological order on the site.

Blogs can contain text, photos, and links to additional information.

The Roaming Kitchen blogger posted this entry about making hot chocolate.

Click the Read More link to continue reading this post.

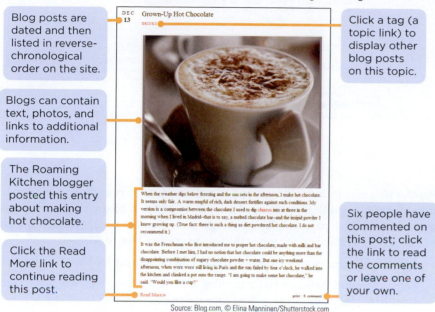

Click a tag (a topic link) to display other blog posts on this topic.

Six people have commented on this post; click the link to read the comments or leave one of your own.

Source: Blog.com, © Elina Manninen/Shutterstock.com

A recent graduate is moving across the country for a new job and is recording her experiences in a video blog.

Overview of Wikis

A **wiki** is a collaborative Web site that members of a group can access and edit using a Web browser. If you want to change something posted on the wiki, you typically select an Edit button or link and then make the change so other users can see it. All group members can make changes to the wiki, which is one thing that makes a wiki different from a blog: readers of a blog can comment on, but not modify, a blogger's posts.

Types of Wikis

If you've ever used a search engine to look up a definition of a term or the meaning of a phrase, you've probably visited Wikipedia, one of the largest wikis on the Web. Wikipedia is a free online encyclopedia with millions of articles. About 75,000 users contribute to Wikipedia by writing, editing, and reviewing articles. You can edit articles by creating a Wikipedia account and then signing in. See **Figure 9-15** on the next page.

Wikipedia is open to the public, but some wikis restrict access to members only. For example, students and teachers often use private educational wikis to collaborate on projects. Researchers use wikis to share findings, offer and receive suggestions, and test their work. Businesses also use wikis, especially when employees are not all in the same physical location. As with blogs, people use wikis to share their knowledge, experience, and point of view.

Blog and Wiki Tools

To create, edit, and maintain a blog, you use blogging software, also known as **blogware**. This type of software is classified as a **content management system**, software that lets a group of users maintain and publish content of all kinds, but especially for Web sites. Blogware provides graphics, photos, standard text, and tools for Web publication and comment posting and moderation.

Another student is using a microblog to exchange information with future graduates about careers and employers.

Figure 9-15: Reading and contributing to a wiki

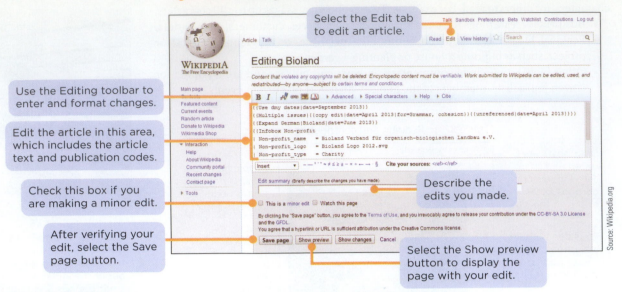

Select the Edit tab to edit an article.

Use the Editing toolbar to enter and format changes.

Edit the article in this area, which includes the article text and publication codes.

Check this box if you are making a minor edit.

After verifying your edit, select the Save page button.

Describe the edits you made.

Select the Show preview button to display the page with your edit.

Source: Wikipedia.org

#communication

Wikis get their name from the Hawaiian phrase "wiki wiki," meaning "quick," because wikis let you collaborate online quickly and easily.

Hot Technology Now

Wikispaces Classroom (wikispaces.com) is designed as an online workspace where students can communicate and work as teams.

The Bottom Line

- You join a social network to share your interests, experiences, contacts, and files with other members of the social network site.
- Social networks are available for a wide range of interests, and can involve sharing media such as photos and videos.

By the Numbers Now

To view the 1.3 billion faces of Facebook, use the Chrome browser to go to app.thefacesoffacebook.com.

Popular blogware includes Blogger and WordPress. Google runs Blogger as a service that publishes blogs with time-stamped articles, or **posts**. A blog consists of separate **pages**, which are Web pages displaying a single post. Your home page lists many posts with the most recent ones at the top of the list. To create a blog in Blogger:

1. Sign into Blogger using a Google account, and then select the New Blog button.

2. Enter a title and Web address for the blog, and then select a template, which provides basic design elements such as colors, fonts, and graphics.

3. Use Blogger's tools to write and publish a post, add images and videos, customize the design, and view the activity on your blog, such as the number of **pageviews**, which indicates the number of times your blog has been viewed in a browser.

After creating a home page, you should create an **About page**, which is where you describe yourself and insert a photo and display name. If you assign your blog to one or more categories, which characterize your content in general, the category list appears on the About page. Anyone on the Web can learn more about you and your blog by visiting your About page.

To attract an audience to your blog, you include tags and links to other Web pages. A **tag** (also called a **label**) is a key term associated with a post. For example, if you publish a post on how to decorate a cake, one tag might be "cake decoration," so that people looking for steps for decorating a cake can find your blog post.

Social Networks

social network | profile | clip | group | Timeline | Wall | friend

If you're like hundreds of millions of people around the world, you use a social network such as Facebook, Google+, or LinkedIn to connect with other people and organizations.

Social Network Basics

Unless you haven't been on the Internet for the past few years, you already know about social networks such as Facebook. But what exactly is a social network? A **social network** is a Web site that links people via the Internet to form an online community. To join a social network, you provide a name and password and complete an online form to create a virtual identity, or **profile**, which includes information you choose to describe yourself.

You can expand your profile to describe your interests and activities and invite friends to visit your pages. Friends can leave messages for you, and you can keep in touch with them by including links to your blog or wiki and by sharing media such as photos.

Figure 9-16: Social networks

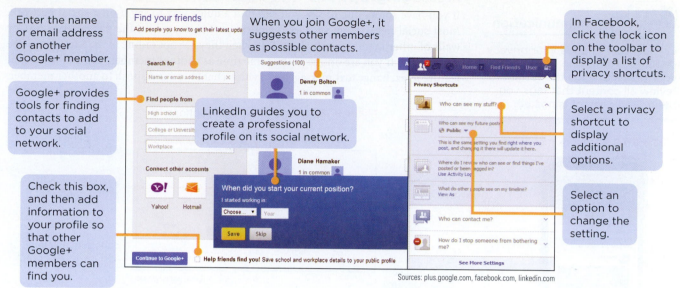

Enter the name or email address of another Google+ member.

Google+ provides tools for finding contacts to add to your social network.

When you join Google+, it suggests other members as possible contacts.

LinkedIn guides you to create a professional profile on its social network.

Check this box, and then add information to your profile so that other Google+ members can find you.

In Facebook, click the lock icon on the toolbar to display a list of privacy shortcuts.

Select a privacy shortcut to display additional options.

Select an option to change the setting.

Sources: plus.google.com, facebook.com, linkedin.com

Social Network Types

Posting messages and finding friends on Facebook is perfect for some people, but what if your main interest is sharing photos or videos? There's a social network for that. On photo-sharing sites such as Flickr, Shutterfly, Instagram, Pinterest, and Snapchat, you can post digital photos and then organize them into albums, add tags, and invite comments.

Video-sharing sites such as YouTube and Vimeo are similar. They provide a place to post short videos called **clips**. You can set up a post so that anyone, or only people you invite, can view your clip.

Other social networks focus on the types of connections you can expect to make on the site. For example, on a professional networking site such as LinkedIn, you keep in touch with colleagues, clients, employers, and other work-related or business contacts.

Social Network Components

One reason everyone seems to belong to a social network is that joining is so easy. All you need is a Web browser and a computer or other device connected to the Internet. See **Figure 9-17** on the next page.

Social networking sites usually provide tools described in **Table 9-1**.

On the Job Now

If you are considering a job in education, visit teachertube.com to find educational resources including videos and presentations.

Table 9-1: Social networking tools

Tool	Description
Edit Profile	Personalize your posts and comments, such as by adding a photo to your profile.
Find Friends	Search for members who share your interests and compile a list of contacts from other sources such as your email address book.
Create Group	Form a **group**, which is a collection of people who share a particular background or interest. Groups can be public (open to anyone), or private (restricted viewing and access, where you have to accept a request to join).
Timeline	Display personalized content from your profile and posts. In Facebook, the **Timeline** (originally known as the **Wall**) lists posts with the most recent content at the top of the list.
Friends or Contacts	On Facebook, contacts are called **friends**; you can display a list of friends by selecting the Search box, and then selecting My Friends. You can also designate some friends specifically as family or as close friends—these are the contacts you keep in touch with the most.
News Feed or Network	Read about the activities of your contacts. On Facebook, this feature is called News Feed; on LinkedIn, it's called Network.

Figure 9-17: Facebook mobile app

On a smartphone, you can install a dedicated app that connects you directly to a social network.

© Denys Prykhodov/Shutterstock.com, Source: facebook.com

Messaging Options

If you have something to say, you can find a quick way to say it on a social network. Most social networking sites let members post messages on the pages, timelines, or walls of other members, which is ideal when they are not online at the same time. See **Figure 9-18**. If you are online at the same time as another member, you can use a chat feature to exchange text messages or a video chat to see and speak to another member.

Figure 9-18: Google+ messaging options

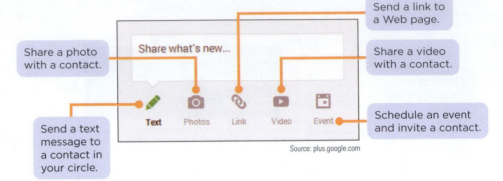

Share a photo with a contact.

Send a link to a Web page.

Share a video with a contact.

Send a text message to a contact in your circle.

Schedule an event and invite a contact.

Source: plus.google.com

Some social networks let you broadcast text, photos, video, and other content as you post it. For example, you can use Facebook's Live Feed tool to let the public or selected members know what you're thinking and doing.

Businesses participate in social networks to encourage consumers to connect to their company by posting messages with questions, comments, and ratings.

Security and Privacy

In general, the security tools you use to keep your computer safe, such as antivirus software, protect your system while you're participating in a social network. The main safety concern is privacy. Once your content is posted, you lose control of it; for example, a photo or comment can make its way across the world and be replicated millions of times in a flash. A big part of social networks is sharing personal details, but remember that those details could be available to other audiences you may not have intended, including current and future employers.

- Write and act professionally on social networks, and post only comments and images that are appropriate for a full range of contacts, from friends to employers.
- Consider how much information you're willing to share online, and adjust your privacy settings accordingly.
- All social networks have privacy policies. Read each policy so you know how the site itself uses your personal information.

Internet Etiquette

etiquette | netiquette | emoticon | flaming | cyberbullying | cyberstalking | online reputation

When you're meeting friends, interacting with family, and working with colleagues, you're guided by rules for acceptable behavior, or **etiquette**. Even if much of your communication is now online, you still need to follow similar dos and don'ts that help make your online interactions civil and productive.

Netiquette

Have you ever received an electronic message that looked like the one in **Figure 9-19**? When you read it, did you feel as if someone were yelling at you?

The author of this message wasn't abiding by the rules of **netiquette**, short for Internet etiquette. Netiquette is a set of guidelines for acceptable online communication:

Figure 9-19: Message in all capital letters

Figure 9-20: Avoid offensive text messages

© bloomua/Shutterstock.com

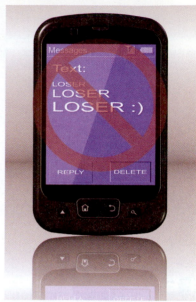

© eteimaging/Shutterstock.com

- Treat others as you want them to treat you. For example, don't use all capital letters in an email message or other communication, because it can seem like rude shouting.
- Be polite in your online communications. Avoid wording that might seem offensive or argumentative. See **Figure 9-20**. Take care when using humor or sarcasm, which can be misinterpreted easily.
- Read your messages before sending them and correct errors in spelling, grammar, and tone.
- Consider email as public communication, because people might forward your message to others without your knowledge.

IM and Chat

Originally, instant messaging (IM), text messaging, and chat were purely social ways to exchange messages among friends. Because they're now valuable business tools as well, you need to follow the professional guidelines listed in **Table 9-2** when sending IMs at work or participating in company chat rooms.

Blog Guidelines

If you participate in blogs as someone who posts entries or makes comments, you should be aware of blog guidelines for both roles:

- As a blogger, you're publishing information online that others might rely on to make decisions. Make sure the information you post is accurate and up to date.
- Acknowledge any connections you have with companies and people you endorse. If you review travel destinations, for example, and a hotel gives you a free vacation, disclose that information when you post a review of the hotel.

#communication

Rule #1 for netiquette: Remember that a human being is on the other side of your communication.

On the Job Now

Never use shorthand abbreviations such as LOL when writing to a customer or client. Apart from sounding too casual, you risk the possibility of people thinking you are simply too busy to write to them properly.

Table 9-2: Guidelines for professional messaging

Message element	Examples	Guidelines
Abbreviations	TTFN BRB	Abbreviations such as TTFN ("ta ta for now") or BRB ("be right back") are too informal for professional communications.
Emoticons	🙂 🙁	An **emoticon** is a symbol for an emotional gesture, such as a smile or frown, that you create using keyboard characters. Emoticons are very informal, so you should use them only in casual messages.
Personal information	"I've never told anyone this, but I really don't like our boss."	Avoid revealing personal information in chat rooms, which are locations on Internet servers where multiple participants can exchange typed messages. You can't verify the identities of the participants, and you don't know how they might handle personal information.

© 2015 Cengage Learning

- As a commenter, read the commenting guidelines on the blog, which usually encourage you to use good judgment and basic courtesy.
- In particular, don't engage in **flaming**, which is posting hostile or insulting comments about another online participant.

Social Network Guidelines

The fundamentals of netiquette apply to social networks just as they apply in other online communications:

- Respect other participants.
- Introduce yourself and get to know other members before adding them as friends. Show consideration for their time by keeping your messages short and focused.
- Before posting a comment, ask yourself how readers will react to it. If it might make someone uncomfortable, don't post it.
- Do not post annoying or unwelcome messages or other information that may make other people very uncomfortable, which could be considered harassment, or **cyberbullying**.
- Do not use social networks to monitor or keep track of a member's activities or whereabouts, which could be considered **cyberstalking**.
- Protect your **online reputation**, which is information about you that others can find on the Internet. Make sure your posts won't embarrass you someday.

Social Networks in Business

Businesses are turning to social networks as a productive way for employees to connect with each other and with customers. If you are using a social network on the job, keep in mind the dos and don'ts listed in **Table 9-3** to build professional relationships and convey an image appropriate for your organization.

#communication

Go to twitter.com, search for **@SAMTechNow,** the book's Twitter account, and then follow @SAMTechNow to get tweets on your home page.

Table 9-3: Dos and don'ts for using social networks in business

Do	Don't
Create a profile for your professional connections apart from your personal ones. In the professional profile, use your full name and a photo of yourself (not a pseudonym or photo of your pet, for example).	Invite visitors to play games or join other activities that could waste their time.
Offer information that visitors to your page will find valuable. Understand who visits your page (such as colleagues or clients), and adjust the content for these visitors.	Post anything that you don't want a future or current boss, colleague, client, or other professional contact to read.
Learn about the people who want to follow you or be your friends. Doing so is good business and helps you avoid an embarrassing connection.	Publish posts or comments when you are not yourself, such as when you are tired or angry.
Post photos, messages, and videos that reflect your professional image and appropriate online reputation.	Publish posts or comments about controversial subjects that others might find offensive.

© 2015 Cengage Learning

Chapter Review

Digital Communication

1. Name four types of digital communication.
2. What is a communications system?
3. What are the two types of communications software you need to communicate with another computer user?

Electronic Mail

4. Describe the five steps involved in sending an email message.
5. What is the main difference between the two types of email accounts you can use?
6. Explain the three parts of an email address.

Messaging

7. What is a real-time messaging system? Give an example of such a system.
8. What is presence technology and how is it used in electronic messaging?
9. What is the purpose of the Multimedia Messaging Service (MMS)? How is it different from the Short Message Service (SMS)?

Podcasts and Online Conferences

10. Describe how you might use a podcast and feed.
11. What is the difference between a Web conference and a Webinar?
12. Explain how to subscribe to an RSS feed.

Blogs and Wikis

13. What is a blog and what kind of content does it provide?
14. What is a wiki and what kind of content does it provide?
15. How is a blog different from a wiki?

Social Networks

16. What is important about your profile on a social network?
17. Describe four types of tools a social network typically provides.
18. Describe two ways social network members can exchange messages with each other.

Internet Etiquette

19. What are three rules for Internet etiquette?
20. Name three actions to avoid when participating in a social network for business.

Test Your Knowledge Now

1. A(n) _____ sends electronic data from a source to a destination.
   a. communications system
   c. netiquette
   d. email address
   b. protocol

2. To make sure that devices can communicate with each other, they follow _____.
   a. timelines
   c. protocols
   b. real-time message systems
   d. presence technology

3. Computers and devices that communicate using radio waves across a medium distance of 100 to 900 feet use _____.
   a. Wi-Fi
   c. WiMAX
   b. TCP/IP
   d. radar

4. In an email system, the email _____ routes messages through the Internet or a private network.
   a. account
   c. server
   b. client
   d. network

5. A service that uses the _____ protocol leaves email messages on the server and stores them only temporarily on your computer.
   a. Post Office Protocol (POP)
   b. Internet Message Access Protocol (IMAP)
   c. Simple Mail Transfer Protocol (SMTP)
   d. Temporary Mail Storage Protocol (TMSP)

6. _____ is the protocol for sending all types of email messages.
   a. Post Office Protocol (POP)
   b. Internet Message Access Protocol (IMAP)
   c. Simple Mail Transfer Protocol (SMTP)
   d. Sending Email Protocol (SEP)

7. Instant messaging uses _____, which lets you see when people on your contact list are online.
   a. presence technology
   b. asynchronous communication
   c. profile technology
   d. Post Office Protocol (POP)

8. Real-time messaging among group members is called _____.
   a. an Internet forum   c. instant messaging
   b. a wiki   d. chat

9. _____ communication involves one person posting a message that someone reads later, as with a text message or forum.
   a. Synchronous   c. Atypical
   b. Asynchronous   d. Instant

10. A _____ is an audio or video file stored online and distributed by downloads or through feeds.
    a. podcast   c. Webinar
    b. blog post   d. protocol

11. A _____ allows participants to see and hear each other through the Internet, while a Web conference does not.
    a. Webinar   c. wiki
    b. video conference   d. video podcast

12. With _____ audio, you starting listening to the content right away without having to wait for the entire file or broadcast to download to your computer.
    a. synchronous   c. syndicated
    b. streaming   d. flowing

13. A _____ allows users to post short messages, usually between 100 and 200 characters, for others to read.
    a. vlog   c. short blog
    b. microblog   d. wiki

14. You use blogware to publish blogs with time-stamped articles, which are called _____.
    a. feeds   c. posts
    b. comments   d. blognews

15. All group members can make changes to a(n) _____, while readers of a blog can comment on, but not modify, a blogger's posts.
    a. microblog   c. wiki
    b. RSS feed   d. profile

16. A _____ network is a Web site that links people via the Internet to form an online community.
    a. real-time   c. social
    b. messaging   d. blogosphere

17. On a social network, you can change your _____ to limit who can see your posts.
    a. profile   c. privacy settings
    b. Timeline   d. friends

18. "Treat others online as you want them to treat you" is an example of _____.
    a. cyberbullying   c. online reputation
    b. flaming   d. netiquette

19. Using a social network to monitor or keep track of a member's activities or whereabouts is called _____.
    a. social monitoring   c. phishing
    b. posting   d. cyberstalking

20. _____ are very informal ways of expressing a short sentiment or phrase, so you should use them only in casual messages.
    a. Emoticons   c. Vlogs
    b. Flames   d. Social network tools

21. In the space next to each statement below, write the letter of the term that defines it.
    a. Webmail   d. profile
    b. chat   e. feed
    c. blog

    _____ An informal Web site of time-stamped articles written in a journal format

    _____ A service that you subscribe to so you can receive frequently updated Web content

    _____ A system for accessing your email using a Web browser

    _____ A name and password you provide to create a virtual identity

    _____ Real-time messaging among group members

Try This Now

1: Top 100 Blogs

Blogs connect us with current news and personal viewpoints. When you read a blog, keep track of what is opinion and what is fact.

    a. Open a browser and then go to technorati.com. Select the Top 100 link to view the most popular blogs.

    b. Scroll through the top 100 blogs on Technorati and open a blog that interests you. After reading the description about the blog topic, open the site that contains your blog of choice.

    c. Read several articles or postings in the blog that you selected. In a document of at least 150 words, summarize the articles that you read on the blog.

    d. Save the document and submit it to your instructor.

2: Educational Video Site

YouTube has hundreds of thousands of free educational videos at youtube.com/education. As you research a topic for a class project, you can focus your search within the educational portion of YouTube to make sure you are using an academic source.

    a. Open a browser and then visit youtube.com/education.

    b. Watch three featured videos on the youtube.com/education site. Write one or two sentences summarizing each of the three video topics.

    c. Locate the search tool for the education page of YouTube. Search for the term "social media." Examine the sources of the social media videos. In a document of at least 100 words, explain how the sources of the education videos differ from those of traditional YouTube videos.

    d. Save the document and submit it to your instructor.

3: Marketing Plan for Facebook

Marketing a local business on Facebook could make the difference between success and failure. Instead of posting random Facebook comments, your employer has requested that you create a digital Facebook marketing plan.

    a. Research the creation of a marketing plan for Facebook. Create a one-page, double-spaced document written in your own words that serves as a Facebook marketing plan for any small business.

    b. Save the document and submit it to your instructor.

Facebook Plan

© iStockphoto.com/Erikona

Critical Thinking Now

1: Product Support Blogs

Companies want to foster the two-way communication between customers and company representatives. Using product support blogs, customers can find product information quickly on their own or they can ask a direct question. Microsoft has a product support blog for Office 365 located at the site blogs.office.com. Open the site in any browser and navigate through the pages. In a document of at least 150 words, write an overview of what this product support site offers to customers.

2: Massive Open Online Courses (MOOCs)

The term "MOOC" can be defined as an online course aimed at an unlimited audience with open access via the Internet. Some MOOCs provide a social platform that provides the class with a way to communicate and ask the professor questions. Research the topic of MOOCs. In a document of at least 150 of your own words, describe MOOC communications.

3: Business Communication Rules

As you communicate to customers in a business setting through email messages, chat, and formal letters, you should follow protocols of formal communication. Research how formal and informal communication are different in the business setting. Write a list of five dos and five don'ts regarding to how to digitally communicate in a formal business setting.

Ethical Issues Now

You just landed your first position dealing with an international company. Each day you will communicate with international clients using email and video conferences. Your boss has requested that you research international netiquette so you do not offend your colleagues or customers.

Netiquette

© Robert Kneschke/Shutterstock.com

    a. With the realization that your client may not be fluent in your own language, list five netiquette guidelines to follow when emailing an international client.

    b. Considering that most international communication is formal, list five general netiquette rules to follow when creating formal email communications.

    c. Write a paragraph about the netiquette guidelines you should follow when video conferencing with an international customer.

Team Up Now – Sharing Your Desktop with Your Team

Discuss a date and time that you can connect with your team online using join.me, a free technology for teams of up to 10 people. The join.me site provides desktop sharing, voice communication, and online chat on a Windows or Mac platform. Establish one person as the team leader, the person who will share a desktop with the other team members and will begin the session at join.me. Open a browser and then go to join.me. The team leader must first start the free trial meeting and send out an email or text message to the team sharing a nine-digit number. The other team members should type the nine-digit number into the "join meeting" text box to begin viewing their team leaders desktop.

    a. When everyone on the team has arrived in join.me, the team member should search google.com or bing.com for other screen-sharing Web sites and applications. Take a screenshot with all the team members' names listed and display of the search results being shown to the team.

    b. Collaborate to research how screen-sharing tools could be productive in the business place. Create a list of 10 business activities or features of business screen-sharing tools that your team locates during your research using join.me.

    c. Submit the combined screenshot and list to your instructor.

Key Terms

802.16 standard	email system	presence technology
About page	emoticon	profile
asynchronous communication	etiquette	protocol
blog	feed	Really Simple Syndication (RSS)
blogger	flaming	Rich Site Summary (RSS)
blogging software	friend	real-time messaging system
blogosphere	group	router
blogware	instant messaging (IM)	Simple Mail Transfer Protocol (SMTP)
chat	Internet forum	Short Message Service (SMS)
chat room	Internet Message Access Protocol	social network
clip	(IMAP)	spam
communications software	label	spam filter
communications system	local email client	streaming audio
contact list	message board	synchronous communication
content management	microblog	tag
system	Multimedia Messaging	TCP/IP
cyberbullying	Service (MMS)	thread
cyberstalking	netiquette	Timeline
digital communications	newsgroup	video conference
domain name	online chat	video podcast
email account	online reputation	vlog
email address	online social network	Wall
email attachment	page	Web conference
email client	pageview	Webinar
email message	phishing email	Webmail
email provider	podcast	wiki
email server	post	WiMAX
email service	Post Office Protocol (POP)	wireless fidelity (Wi-Fi)

Information Literacy

Shawna is taking a challenging math class. She has a great instructor, but practicing online helps her study for the big math test this Friday.

Using the Internet, Shawna can practice skills at her own pace without embarrassment in any class, actively watch videos, and answer almost any question.

© Creativa/Shutterstock.com

Keeping her "A" average in her math class is important to Shawna. She is discovering how to use the Internet to become a self-directed, curious learner. Using free academic Web sites such as khanacademy.org, Shawna can learn how to solve quadratic equations and other math problems at 2 a.m. or any other time of day.

In this Chapter

Microsoft® product screenshots used with permission from Microsoft® Corporation.

Online Information

open site | Open Web | Free Web | Visible Web | restricted site | Deep Web | Private Web | Invisible Web | database

The Web is a vast library of information contained in many millions of sites. With so many sites, it can be difficult to know if the information you find is reliable. To find what you need on the Web, you should understand the types of information the Web provides.

Open Sites

Suppose you need to give a presentation on green technology for a course you're taking. You would probably start by using Google to search for green technology and then look over the results. The Web sites listed in the results are **open sites**, which are freely available to the public. Taken together, these open sites are known as the **Open Web**, also called the **Free Web** or the **Visible Web**.

Figure 10-1: Finding reliable information on the Web

In ancient Egypt, the Library of Alexandria's goal was to collect all the knowledge in the ancient world.

Today, we are attempting to collect all of the modern world's knowledge on the Web. But the Web is so vast that no one is certain how many sites it contains.

Search tools can help you search the Web to find information. You can then evaluate the information to see if it fills your needs.

© leoks/Shutterstock.com, © jannoon028/Shutterstock.com, © Angela Waye/Shutterstock.com

General search engines such as Google can access nearly eight billion Web pages, which is one of the benefits of the Open Web. However, open Web sites can come and go, so you can't rely on them as permanent sources of information. Furthermore, Open Web content changes frequently and has not been reviewed or evaluated by experts. So you need to know how to determine whether the information you find on the Web is dependable and useful.

Restricted Sites

Suppose you're in your school library and want to gather information for your presentation on green technology. When you use the library's online system to search for green technology, the results are significantly different from Google's. The Web sites in the library's search results are **restricted sites** because they require a subscription or other type of membership. See **Figure 10-2**. For example, your student password is probably required before you can access results from your library search. These sites are part of the **Deep Web**, also called the **Private Web** or the **Invisible Web**.

Search engines can't access some pages on these restricted sites because they're part of **databases** (collections of information) such as library catalogs or article

Figure 10-2: Restricted library site

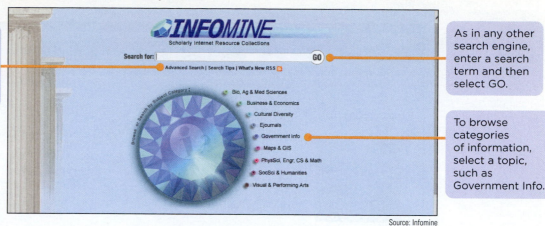

To exclude terms from the search and use other advanced search methods, select Advanced Search.

As in any other search engine, enter a search term and then select GO.

To browse categories of information, select a topic, such as Government Info.

Source: Infomine

collections that require passwords or subscriptions for searching. The number of restricted sites is estimated to be many times larger than the number of sites on the Open Web.

Benefits of the Deep Web are that identified experts develop most of the resources, so they are fairly reliable, and that most resources are part of permanent collections. Publishers and libraries are making agreements with search engines so the public can access their restricted sites, which include many times the number of pages of the Open Web. However, a part of the Deep Web is used for illegal activities.

News Sites

During a major event such as a weather disaster or national election, you can go to news sites and news apps to get quick, often instant, information.

- **Television, radio, and other media** provide up-to-date information on their Web sites, including videos and photos.
- **Print newspapers** and magazines also provide online versions of their articles.
- **New apps** are apps that you can install on your tablet or smartphone; most television and radio stations and print newspapers have news apps.

Sometimes you can view today's content for free but need to subscribe to the site to look at back issues or other special features.

The day of a major event, news sites report facts as they occur, such as the spread of a flood or the number of votes recorded. Information is incomplete because the event is ongoing. Shortly after a major event, news sites report the results and provide details, such as the amount of damage a tropical storm caused.

But while news sites are excellent resources for facts and immediate reactions to current and recent events, they don't typically offer in-depth analysis and perspective, which take more time to develop.

Scholarly Sites

A few weeks after a major event such as an election, news sites stop covering the event because it's no longer new. Instead, scholarly sites provide access to articles and books that analyze the event and place it in historical perspective.

Some scholarly sites are search engines that let you access electronic databases of scholarly publications. For example, ScienceDirect lets subscribers search the full text of thousands of scientific journals.

Other scholarly Web sites are published by professionals for a professional audience. For example, the InTech site (see **Figure 10-3** on the next page) publishes research in science, technology, and medicine.

Scholarly sites include information that's been written and researched thoroughly by experts, double-checked for accuracy, and reviewed by other experts. These sites also have citations, including publication name, date, and author, to help you evaluate them. Therefore, scholarly sites are reliable resources for in-depth, complete information on almost any topic.

By the Numbers Now

The top five most visited news Web sites, in order, include Yahoo! News, Huffington Post, CNN, Google News, and The New York Times.

On the Job Now

According to the U.S. Department of Labor, the median pay for a news reporter, correspondent, or broadcast news analyst is around $37,000 per year.

Hot Technology Now

One of the most popular apps for iOS, Android, and Windows is a news magazine named Flipboard. The free app provides a well-designed magazine format that displays your selection of news sources and social networks in one location.

Hot Technology Now

Popular academic sites include scholar.google.com, wolframalpha.com, and khanacademy.com.

Figure 10-3: Scholarly Web site

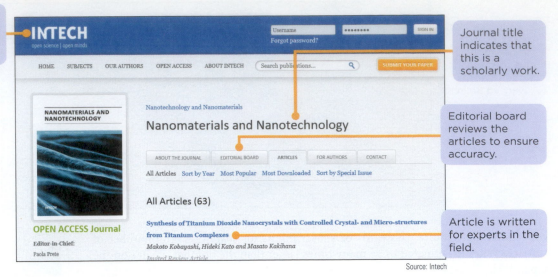

Source: Intech

Searching for Information

word stem | hit | filter | public domain

Just about anyone with a computer knows how to use a search engine to look up information on the Web. But with billions of Web pages available and more being added every day, you need to develop strategies to be search savvy. See **Figure 10-4**.

Search Strategies

Let's say you need to give a presentation on the future of computing and have heard about Internet-connected glasses, which help users navigate and learn about locations and friends who might be nearby. How do you begin researching this technology?

Before you start using a search engine, write down one or more questions you are trying to answer. Next, examine the questions to select a search phrase, which contains key words. The key words you choose should make the search phrase unique and specific. Avoid using a search term that has more than one meaning, such as "glasses" or even "developer glasses."

When you enter a search term in a search engine, it looks for Web pages that contain the key words you specify.

Search Tips

Over 60 million Americans use search engines daily but find what they're looking for only half the time. How can you search more effectively? Start by refining your search term. Use a **word stem** (the base of a word) to broaden a search. **Table 10-1** lists some common search operators you can use to narrow or widen a search.

Many Web sites have tools for searching their pages, but Google can actually search a site more thoroughly. Start the search term with **site:** followed by the site address and

Table 10-1: Common search operators

Use this operator	To indicate	Example
" " (quotation marks)	Pages containing that exact phrase with words in the same order	"computer trends"
+	AND	computer + trends
| (vertical bar)	OR	computer | trends
- (hyphen)	NOT	computer -trends
~ (tilde)	Pages that include synonyms	~computer trends

© 2015 Cengage Learning

Figure 10-4: Searching for information

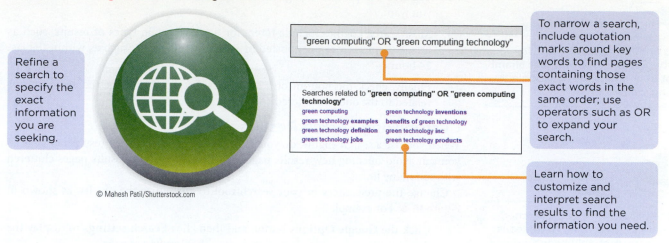

Refine a search to specify the exact information you are seeking.

© Mahesh Patil/Shutterstock.com

"green computing" OR "green computing technology"

Searches related to **"green computing" OR "green computing technology"**

green computing	green technology inventions
green technology examples	benefits of green technology
green technology definition	green technology inc
green technology jobs	green technology products

To narrow a search, include quotation marks around key words to find pages containing those exact words in the same order; use operators such as OR to expand your search.

Learn how to customize and interpret search results to find the information you need.

key words to completely search that Web site. For example, if you wanted to search for information on SAM on the Cengage.com site, you could use the following (with no space after "site:"):

site:www.cengage.com sam

Another Google trick lets you search for related sites. To search for sites related to Flickr, you could type the following (with no space after the colon):

related:flickr.com

Search Results

Suppose you're curious about flexible computer screens on mobile devices, which let you zoom and scroll a page by twisting the device. Enter **flexible computer screen** in a search engine, and the results could include millions of pages.

To find the information you're seeking, learn from your search results, as shown in **Figure 10-5**:

1. Search engines place the most relevant results, or **hits**, on the first few pages. Examine those results for clues about refining your search.

#infoliteracy

If you are using a search engine to find a salsa recipe that does not contain onions, type **salsa recipe −onions**.

#infoliteracy

If you are trying to find related sites to cnn.com, the news network, type **related:cnn.com** to find other international CNN sites.

Figure 10-5: Refining searches with filters and related terms

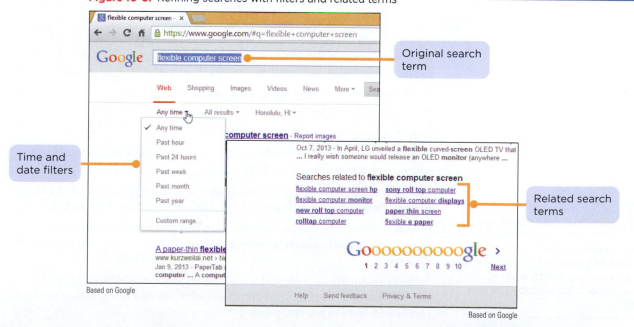

Original search term

Time and date filters

Related search terms

Based on Google

Based on Google

2. You also can preview a page in the results to see if it contains the information you want.

3. Most search engines include **filters** for finding certain types of results, such as images or news, or pages posted in a certain date range, such as within the last 24 hours.

4. Finally, check the bottom of a search results page for suggested search terms related to the one you entered.

Customizing Search Results

When you use a search engine, do you sometimes want to list more results per page so you can avoid opening new results pages? Or do you find the results pages cluttered with too many links?

Change the preferences in your search tool to customize the results, as shown in **Figure 10-6**. For example:

1. Click the **Google Options** button and then click **Search settings** to display the Search settings you can change, including the Results per page.

2. You also can identify your location to search for Web pages relevant to your area.

Figure 10-6: Customizing Google search settings

SafeSearch filters are listed in the Search results category.

Set your geographic location.

Select Never show Instant results and then select the number of results you want to display per page.

Turn on the SafeSearch filter.

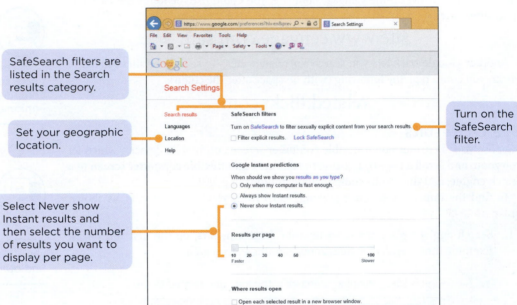

Based on Google.com

3. Some search engines also let you limit the results to personalized content. For example, Google lets you limit the results to pages you have or have not already visited.

4. If offensive content turns up in your results, turn on the SafeSearch filter to remove as much explicit content as possible.

Search Engine Tools

If you're getting stumped in your online searches or want more direct access to basic information, search engine tools can help.

1. Most search engines provide definitions of words and phrases. For example, type **define cybercafe** as a search term to find a quick definition of "cybercafe."

2. In a more direct way, you can calculate numbers and convert measurements. For example, enter **8 kilometers in miles** at Ask.com to figure out if you can walk the distance.

3. If you're researching a topic and want to learn about new articles, blog posts, or other online information as it becomes available, set up a Google Alert to receive emails with links to relevant pages. See **Figure 10-7**.

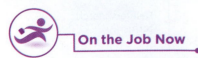

Figure 10-7: Setting a Google alert

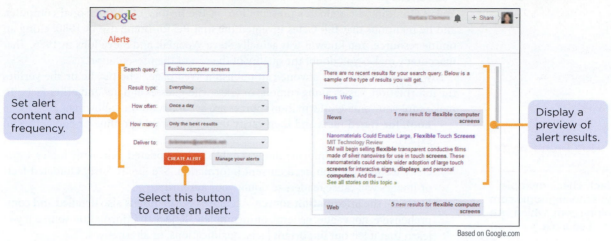

Set alert content and frequency.

Select this button to create an alert.

Display a preview of alert results.

Based on Google.com

To see a sampling of a book's text, use the book's title as your search term in Google, and then click Books in the search bar. If the book is in the **public domain**, which means the copyright has expired or otherwise doesn't apply, you can click Read to read the free e-book.

Evaluating Online Information

CARS checklist | credible | accurate | reasonableness | support | credit line

On the Internet, anyone can publish anything to a Web site, a blog, or a social media site, regardless of whether the information is true. If you use the Internet for research, be skeptical about the information you find online. Evaluate a Web page before you use it as an information source. See **Figure 10-8**.

Credibility

When someone is providing you information face to face, you pay attention to clues such as body language and voice tone to determine whether that information is **credible**, or believable. Obviously, you can't use that same technique to evaluate the credibility of a Web page, so you need another way to establish the page's credibility.

For example, suppose you are researching targeted Web ads and find a page you want to use.

1. **Identify the author**. Look for a link such as About us or Background, and then click it to learn about the person or organization responsible for the Web page.

2. **Check the author's credentials**. Look for a title, such as President or Senior Editor. If you find biographical information, read it to learn whether the author has a degree in a field related to the topic. You also can use a search engine such as Google or the professional networking site LinkedIn to search for the author's name and see whether the information qualifies the author as an expert on the subject.

Figure 10-8: CARS checklist

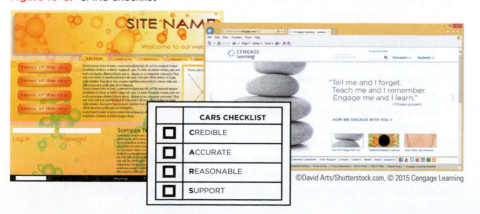

©David Arts/Shutterstock.com, © 2015 Cengage Learning

CARS CHECKLIST	
☐	**C**REDIBLE
☐	**A**CCURATE
☐	**R**EASONABLE
☐	**S**UPPORT

The Bottom Line

- To evaluate online information, apply the **CARS checklist** to ensure that the information is credible, accurate, reasonable, and supported.
- Look at potential online sources critically—a site with errors, a bad design, or an unclear navigational structure may be unprofessional and therefore unreliable.

#infoliteracy

Be careful to distinguish between a Webmaster and an author when citing a Web site as an information source. A Webmaster designs and updates an author's writings but is not the source of the content.

#infoliteracy

Check the domain in a site's URL when you want to use the site as a reference. In some cases, the domain shows where the page originated. For example, a site ending in .de was posted in Germany.

Accuracy

You're attending a classmate's presentation on the history of the personal computer, and he mentions that Bill Gates invented the first PC for home use in 1980, citing an online resource. You know it was actually Steve Wozniak and Steve Jobs in 1976. That inaccuracy makes you doubt the quality of the rest of the presentation.

Always remember that anyone can publish a Web page, whether he or she verifies the information, passes along rumors, or takes wild guesses at dates and other facts. To make sure your online information sources are **accurate**, do the following:

- **Look for stated facts** and then verify them by searching online or contacting an expert.
- **Check the date** the information was published or updated. For many topics, especially technology, you need current information. See **Figure 10-9**. Outdated facts or images will cause readers to doubt your authority.
- **Evaluate the information source**. Accurate information is also detailed and comprehensive, not vague, general, or incomplete. Reject an information source if you learn that it left out important facts, qualifications, or alternatives.

Figure 10-9: Checking the Last Updated date

Recent date helps ensure accuracy.

Reasonableness

Along with credibility and accuracy, consider how reasonable an online information source is. "Reasonable" means fair and sensible, not extreme or excessive. To evaluate **reasonableness**, start by identifying the purpose of the Web page. Is the page designed to provide facts and other information, or to sell a product or service? To express opinions? A page that provides information should do so objectively. Look for the following:

- **More than one point of view**. Evaluate how the author balances them.
- **Emotional or biased language**, which is often a sign that the author is not being fair or moderate. Even opinions should be expressed with a moderate tone.
- **Conflict of interest**. For example, if the page reviews a certain brand of smartphone and the author sells those types of phones, he or she has a conflict of interest.

Support

Suppose you read an intriguing claim on a Web page: a poll found that most people consider computer professionals to be highly ethical. But the page doesn't link to the poll itself or mention other sources that support this claim. Therefore, the page is failing the final criterion in the CARS checklist: **support**.

To evaluate a Web page's support, look for the following:

- **Links or citations** to reputable sources or authorities. Test the links to make sure they work.
- **Other pages and print material on the topic**, to see if they cite the same sources.
- **Quotations** from experts.
- **For photos or other reproduced content**, a **credit line** should appear somewhere on the page that states the source and any necessary copyright information.

An information source that simply states a belief or conclusion without support is basically expressing an opinion, not offering documented information.

Evaluation Tips

When evaluating an online information source, you often can trust your initial reactions to a Web page. For example, if the page contains typos and grammar errors, the author didn't take the time to review, edit, and polish the writing. An authoritative resource usually does.

Consider the design of the Web page itself. If the page is difficult to navigate, search, or read, it's not as useful as a well-designed page. Any graphics, photos, video clips, or animations should enhance the content, not clutter the page. See **Figure 10-10**.

Figure 10-10: Poorly designed Web page

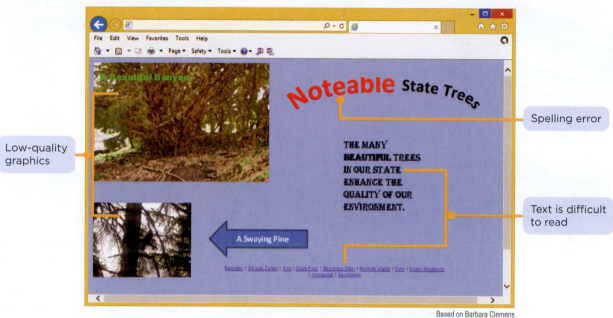

Low-quality graphics

Spelling error

Text is difficult to read

Based on Barbara Clemens

Finally, apply these same evaluation tips and the CARS checklist to your own writing, whether online or not. When you organize the material you've gathered and communicate it to others, you switch from being a consumer to being a producer of information. That means you have a responsibility to make sure the information you provide is credible, accurate, reasonable, and has support.

Search Tools

general search engine | spider | crawler | index | query | metasearch engine | subject directory | specialty search engine | social search tool

Searching the Web for just the right information can be time consuming and tedious—and you may wonder if you're searching in the right places. You can improve your searches by using online search tools. See **Figure 10-11** on the next page.

General Search Engines

You're working on a presentation about Web design and need to know the common navigation patterns for Web sites. How can you find this information quickly?

You'd probably start a **general search engine** such as Google, Bing, or Yahoo! and enter a search term or phrase such as **Web site navigation patterns**. Within seconds, the first page of search results lists a dozen Web pages that might contain the information you need.

You may wonder how a general search engine chooses the results you see. When you perform a search, a general search engine does not search the entire Internet. Instead, it compiles a database of information about Web pages. It uses programs

The Bottom Line
- In your searches, you can use general search engines, such as Google, metasearch engines, and subject directories to find just the information you want.
- Specialty search engines and social media tools can lead you to valuable information sources other than Web sites.

Figure 10-11: Online search tools

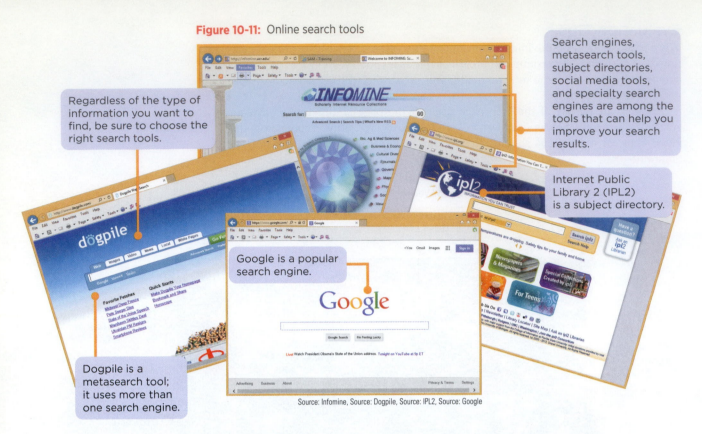

Regardless of the type of information you want to find, be sure to choose the right search tools.

Search engines, metasearch tools, subject directories, social media tools, and specialty search engines are among the tools that can help you improve your search results.

Internet Public Library 2 (IPL2) is a subject directory.

Google is a popular search engine.

Dogpile is a metasearch tool; it uses more than one search engine.

Source: Infomine, Source: Dogpile, Source: IPL2, Source: Google

called **spiders** or **crawlers**, software that combs the Web to find Web pages and add new data about them to the database. These programs build an **index** of terms and their locations.

When you enter a search term, or **query**, a general search engine refers to its database index and then lists pages that match your search term, ranked by how closely they answer your query.

Metasearch Tools

Although it is popular, Google covers only a fraction of the Web. Some pages that Google indexes in its database are different from the ones that Bing, Yahoo!, and other search engines index. To do a thorough search, however, you don't need to enter the same query in each search engine.

Instead, you can use a **metasearch engine**, such as Dogpile or Mamma, which lets you enter a search term once and then sends that query to many search engines at the same time. See **Figure 10-12**.

Figure 10-12: Dogpile metasearch engine

Dogpile shows related search terms to help you find the information you need.

Dogpile eliminates duplicate results and selects only a certain number of pages from each source.

Dogpile shows a list of sites that all search engines found.

Based on Dogpile

Subject Directories

Search engines are great when you already have an idea of what you want to find, such as pages predicting the future of the Web. But what if you want a more narrow view of what's available on the Web, focused on a particular subject? You can use a **subject directory**, which is a catalog of Web pages organized by subject.

Like a catalog in the library, a subject directory is the work of people (usually subject-matter experts) who can evaluate the content of a Web site and classify it. Subject directories offer a limited number of Web pages and help you discover new topics and content.

One of the first comprehensive subject directories was the Open Directory Project (**Figure 10-13**). To use it, you select a general category, such as Computers, and then drill down through the other topics.

Figure 10-13: Open Directory Project

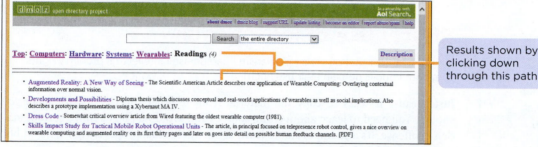

Based on Open Directory Project

Specialty Search Engines

Suppose you're interested in alternative energy and want to research wind power. When you use a general search engine to search for wind alternative energy, the results include millions of Web pages, many for commercial businesses. Where do you go to find academic information for your research? Try using a **specialty search engine**, which lets you search databases, news providers, podcasts, and other online information sources that general search engines do not always access.

A search tool's ability to search databases is important, because much of the information on the Web is stored in databases. To access database information, you need to use a special search form and may need to enter a username and password. For example, Google Scholar searches scholarly literature from many disciplines and includes articles, books, theses, and abstracts.

Other specialty search tools let you find information published on certain types of sites. For example, use Google News or Alltop to find news stories and Podcast Search Service to search podcasts.

Social Media Tools

Like most students, you probably spend time using social media, such as social networks, that let you connect with others. Suppose you had a memorable online discussion about climate change and want to know what others think about the topic. You can use a **social search tool** to search blogs, microblogs, comments, and conversations on social media sites.

Social media search tools are designed for finding subjective content, such as comments, reviews, and opinions. Some social media search tools such as SocialMention let you search one or more social networks, blogs, and other sites at the same time.

General search engines, including Google and Bing, also provide social search tools. For example, when you're signed into Facebook, you can use Bing to ask friends for advice or to see which friends liked an event you attended. Social networks such as Facebook, Foursquare, and Twitter are designing tools for searching data shared by members, including Like button votes for articles, videos, and other Web information.

Hot Technology Now

The site Creative Commons (creativecommons.org) lets you share your music, videos, writing, or code, and lets others search for this content by subject. Creative Commons' licenses provide a flexible range of protections and freedoms for authors, artists, and educators.

Hot Technology Now

To find your local news at Bing, open bing.com/news. Type **local** followed by the name of your city or town, as in **local Toledo**.

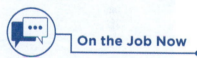

On the Job Now

To create a free, professional online newspaper from sources such as Twitter, Google+, Facebook, YouTube, and RSS feeds, go to the site paper.li. You can customize your topic to tap into the constant flow of information.

Hot Technology Now

To create a custom Twitter experience and manage multiple accounts, use the TwitterDeck app, available for the iPhone and Android platforms.

Other Search Tools

If you've searched for information using a variety of search tools and still can't find what you're looking for, don't despair. Consider using innovative approaches to finding information. Some search sites help you refine research topics, shown in **Table 10-2**.

Table 10-2: Additional search tools

Search tool	What it does
Glean Comparison Search	Compares differing viewpoints on a research topic
Wolfram Alpha	Answers factual questions directly, without listing Web pages that might contain the answer
Blinkx	Finds videos or other multimedia; uses speech recognition to match the audio part of a video with your search term
Ask a Librarian	Connects you to librarians at the Library of Congress and other libraries; allows you to engage in an online chat or submit your question in an online form

© 2015 Cengage Learning

Ethical Use of Information

ethics | citation | citation style | plagiarism | paraphrase | intellectual property rights | copyright | public domain | fair use doctrine

Just because it's easy to copy the material from Internet sources doesn't mean you should. You need to learn about citing sources and avoiding plagiarism, a serious academic offense. It's also important to learn about intellectual property rights, the public domain, and the fair use doctrine.

Ethical Decisions

Because the Internet provides easy access to other people and to information, you should carefully consider how you use that information. When you use the Internet for research, you face ethical decisions. **Ethics** is the set of moral principles that govern people's behavior. Many schools and other organizations post codes of conduct for computer use, which can help you make ethical decisions while using a computer.

Figure 10-14: Ethical use of online information

A copyright is a way of protecting the rights of intellectual property owners.

Know how to cite works or apply fair use guidelines to avoid **plagiarism**, which is using the work or ideas of others and claiming them as your own.

The Internet is full of information, images, videos, music, and other material that you can easily copy using your computer. But you must make ethical decisions about how you can and should use that information.

© Wilm Ihlenfeld/Shutterstock.com, © koya979/Shutterstock.com, © chanpipat/Shutterstock.com

Citing Sources

Ethically and legally, you can use other people's ideas in your research papers and presentations, but you must cite the source for any information that is not common knowledge. A **citation** is a formal reference to a published work.

Thorough research on technology and other topics usually involves books, journals, magazines, and Web sites. Each type of information source uses a different **citation style**. Instructors often direct you to a particular citation style, such as MLA, APA, or Chicago. You can find detailed style guides for each style online. Some software, such as Microsoft Word, helps you create and manage citations and then produce a bibliography, which is an alphabetical collection of citations. See **Figure 10-15**.

By the Numbers Now

If a photographer created a photo after March 1, 1989, it is copyrighted until 70 years after the photographer dies.

Figure 10-15: Citing sources in Microsoft Word

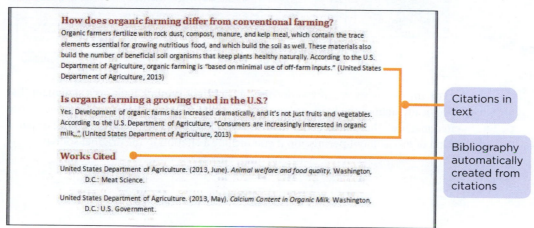

Avoiding Plagiarism

If you use the content from a Wikipedia article but change some of the words, do you have to cite the source for that material? Yes, you do. Otherwise, you are guilty of **plagiarism**, which is using the work or ideas of someone else and claiming them as your own.

To avoid plagiarism, cite your sources for statements that are not common knowledge. Even if you **paraphrase**, which means to restate an idea using words different from those used in the original, you are still trying to claim someone else's idea as your own. Cite sources when you borrow ideas or words to avoid plagiarism.

#infoliteracy

Authors and musicians need protection from digital piracy. In less than 24 hours after the release of Dan Brown's *The Lost Symbol*, over 100,000 pirated digital copies were downloaded.

Intellectual Property Rights

If you copy a photo from the Internet and use it in a report, you might be violating the photographer's **intellectual property rights**, which are legal rights protecting those who create works such as photos, art, writing, inventions, and music.

A **copyright** gives authors and artists the legal right to sell, publish, or distribute an original work; and it goes into effect as soon as the work exists in physical form.

So if you want to use a photo in your report, you need to get permission from the photo's owner. Contact the photographer by email, and explain what you want to use and how you plan to use it. If a copyright holder gives you permission, keep a copy of the message or document for your records. The holder may also tell you how a credit line should appear. Acquiring permission protects you from potential concerns over your usage and also protects the copyright holder's intellectual property rights.

By the Numbers Now

Patents protect intellectual property rights for a certain period, usually 20 years from the original patent date.

Public Domain/Fair Use

Some work is in the **public domain**, which means you can use it freely because it is not subject to copyright. This applies to material for which the copyright has expired and to work that has been explicitly released to the public domain by its owner. Many Web sites provide public domain files free for you to download. Much information on U.S. government sites is in the public domain, although you must attribute the information and be aware that the sites might contain copyrighted information. See **Figure 10-16** on the next page.

Figure 10-16: Copyright information on the U.S. Department of Agriculture site

Based on USDA.gov

#infoliteracy

Go to twitter.com, search for **@SAMTechNow**, the book's Twitter account, and follow @SAMTechNow to get tweets on your home page.

For any online source, if you don't see a copyright symbol, look for a statement that specifically defines the work as being in the public domain. For quotations and other cited material, the United States **fair use doctrine** allows you to use a sentence or paragraph of text without permission if you include a citation to the original source.

Chapter Review

Online Information

1. What are the four major types of Web sites?
2. What do you call a collection of information, such as a library catalog? Why can't general search engines access them?
3. Name one benefit and one disadvantage of the Deep Web.
4. How do scholarly sites differ from news sites?

Searching for Information

5. What do search operators allow you to do? Name three search operators and explain how you would use each one in a search.
6. Name two ways you can customize your search results.
7. What can you find at the bottom of a search results page, and how can they help you?
8. What is public domain material? Give one example.

Evaluating Online Information

9. Briefly describe the CARS checklist and how you would use it in searching the Internet.
10. How might you establish that a Web source is credible?
11. Name two tools you might use to look for a Web site author's credentials.
12. Name three types of support that a Web site might provide.

Search Tools

13. How does a general search engine locate information?
14. What does a Web spider do?
15. What is an advantage of a metasearch engine? Give an example of a metasearch site.
16. What is an advantage of a specialty search engine?
17. Describe a subject directory and give one example.

Ethical Use of Information

18. Define "ethics," and explain how ethical principles can guide you in your use of Internet material.
19. What is a public domain work?
20. Briefly describe the United States fair use doctrine.

Test Your Knowledge Now

1. A Web site that requires a subscription or membership is called a(n) _____.
   a. open site
   b. new site
   c. scholarly site
   d. restricted site

2. Which search operator would you use to locate pages with an exact phrase, in the same order?
   a. +
   b. -
   c. " "
   d. ~

3. When you perform a Web search, what do you call the most relevant results?
   a. hits
   b. citations
   c. filters
   d. queries

4. Which of the following would you use to broaden a search?
   a. a word stem
   b. " "
   c. site:
   d. -

5. Checking a site author's credentials is one way to establish a site's _____.
   a. reasonableness
   b. credibility
   c. accuracy
   d. support

6. Which of the following is *not* part of the CARS checklist?
   a. copyright
   b. accurate
   c. reasonable
   d. support

7. Which of the following is one way to establish a site's accuracy?
   a. Check the site's date.
   b. Identify the author.
   c. Look for just one point of view.
   d. Look for the author's credentials.

8. What part of the Web is used for illegal activities?
   a. news sites
   b. the public domain
   c. the Deep Web
   d. subject directories

9. Which of the following is a metasearch engine?
   a. Google
   b. Mamma
   c. Open Directory Project
   d. Wolfram Alpha

10. Which of the following operators lets you search for pages that include synonyms for your search term?
    a. -
    b. +
    c. " "
    d. ~

11. Which of the following sites specializes in supplying differing viewpoints on a topic?
    a. Wolfram Alpha
    b. Glean Comparison Search
    c. Alltop
    d. Yahoo!

12. A specialty search engine lets you search _____.
    a. multimedia sites
    b. blogs, microblogs, comments, and conversations on social media sites
    c. databases, news providers, and podcasts
    d. a catalog of Web pages organized by subject

13. What do you call a collection of information, such as a library catalog or article collection, that requires passwords or subscriptions for searching?
    a. database
    b. the Deep Web
    c. the public domain
    d. a subject directory

14. Text that is *not* subject to copyright is found in _____.
    a. Wikipedia
    b. citations
    c. ethics
    d. the public domain

15. Which of the following searches lets you find sites that mention either onions or radishes?
    a. onions + radishes
    b. onions ˜ radishes
    c. onions | radishes
    d. "onions + radishes"

16. MLA, APA, and Chicago are examples of _____.
    a. the fair use doctrine
    b. intellectual property rights
    c. copyrights
    d. citation styles

17. Plagiarism is best defined as _____.
    a. using another's work and claiming it as your own
    b. a citation style
    c. moral principles that govern our behavior
    d. the act of citing sources

18. Which of the following helps you find certain types of search results, such as images or news?
    a. Web page filter
    b. search engine alert
    c. the CARS checklist
    d. a citation

19. Which of the following are Web sites that are reliable sources for in-depth, complete information?
    a. open sites
    b. news sites
    c. scholarly sites
    d. search engine sites

20. Which of the following is *not* a way to customize search results?
    a. Identify your location.
    b. Turn on the SafeSearch filter.
    c. Limit results to personalized content.
    d. Use a spider.

21. In the space next to each image below, write the letter of the phrase that describes it.
    a. setting alerts
    b. citation
    c. a method to help ensure source accuracy
    d. setting filters
    e. helps ensure site accuracy

CARS CHECKLIST	
☐	**C**REDIBLE
☐	**A**CCURATE
☐	**R**EASONABLE
☐	**S**UPPORT

© 2015 Cengage Learning

NASA
Page Last Updated: January 15th, 2014
Page Editor: Jim Wilson
NASA Official: Brian Dunbar

Source: Nasa

✓ Any time
Past hour
Past 24 hours
Past week
Past month
Past year
Custom range...

Search query:	container gardening
Result type:	News
How often:	Once a week
How many:	Only the best results

Based on Google

According to the U.S. Department of Agriculture, "Consumers are milk..." (United States Department of Agriculture, 2013)

Try This Now

1: Power Googling

To become a Google power user, practice the following special searches at Google.com. For each search, take a screenshot of the results page. Place the screenshots in a single Word document, and then submit the document to your instructor. (For instructions on taking screenshots, see the "Getting Started" chapter.) Open a browser, open the site google.com, and then use the following search terms:

    a. Type **weather** and the name of your town or city (example: **weather Phoenix**).

    b. Type the stock ticker symbol of a company you know (example: **MSFT**).

    c. Type **time Tokyo**.

    d. Type the name of any major sports team in season now (example: **Miami Dolphins**).

    e. Type **sunrise** and the name of any city (example: **sunrise Boston**).

    f. Type any math problem (example: **4*7 +(sqrt 8)**).

    g. Type **earthquake**.

    h. Type **population** and the name of any state or province (example: **population New Jersey**).

    i. Type **define** followed by any word (example: **define antiestablishment**).

2: Your Career Social Media Newspaper

Note: To complete this assignment, you must have an account with a social media site such as Facebook or Twitter.

You can create an online paper in minutes by selecting custom topics from millions of social media posts and Web articles published each day. Open a browser and then open the site paper.li.

    a. Create a free account at paper.li.

    When you create a paper.li account, you authorize the Web site to access content in your Twitter, Facebook, or other social media account. Paper.li publishes content from these accounts to create an online newspaper. If you do not agree to these terms, return to the paper.li home page, click the Learn more button on the navigation bar, and then read about how paper.li works. Complete steps b and e to take a screenshot of a completed newspaper and paste the image in a Word document. Below the screenshot, write at least 100 words describing how paper.li works.

    b. Tap or click Newsstand to gather ideas for your online newspaper.

    c. Tap or click Create a paper. Create an online paper based on a career field that interests you. Give your paper a unique name and choose to create a weekly edition.

    d. Search for topics within the career field you selected. Use the plus icon to add several sources to your newspaper.

    e. Take a screenshot of your online newspaper. Paste the screenshot in a Word document, and then submit the document to your instructor. (For instructions on taking screenshots, see the "Getting Started" chapter.)

3: Learn for Free at Khan Academy

Learn for free at Khan Academy in subjects such as math, art, computer programming, chemistry, biology, history, and medicine. Open a browser, and then open the site khanacademy.org.

    a. Sign in with your Facebook user name or your email address.

    b. Locate a subject area of your choice and select a level appropriate for you.

    c. Select Activity in the left pane, and then watch three complete Khan Academy videos. Each video provides a box for a Tips & Thanks comment. In this comment box, type a comment describing your impression of each of the three videos.

    d. Take a screenshot of each video with your comments. Paste the three screenshots in a single Word document. (For instructions on taking screenshots, see the "Getting Started" chapter.)

    e. Save the document and submit it to your instructor.

Critical Thinking Now

1: Infographics

Infographics represent complex data or knowledge in a clear graphical display. Open the site infographic.com, and then select the Portfolio link on the navigation bar. Select an infographic, review it, and then click the Next link to view another infographic. Select one interesting infographic, and then take a screenshot of it. Paste the screenshot in a Word document and write a paragraph containing at least 100 of your own words describing the information displayed in the infographic.

2: Search Engine Showdown

Using the right search engine can ultimately save you time and increase your productivity. First determine your search term. Search for information about a famous person of your choice using google.com, scholar.google.com, bing.com, and dogpile.com (a metasearch engine). Take a screenshot of each of the four results pages and paste the screenshots in a Word document. Write at least 150 words explaining how each search engine performed during your search engine showdown.

3: Plagiarism

Because anyone with an Internet connection has unlimited access to online information, schools, publishers, and other organizations must discourage plagiarism by setting clear standards for original work. Check on your school's Web site, read your student handbook, or interview an instructor or administrator at your school to learn about its plagiarism policy. Write a paragraph about your school's plagiarism consequences and submit it to your instructor.

Ethical Issues Now

You were employed at a publishing company that designed a cutting-edge system for delivering e-books online. You contributed ideas that were critical to the development of the project idea. Research the topic of intellectual property.

a. Can you take the design idea with you and use it at another company when you leave the publishing company? Write at least 100 words to substantiate your answer.

b. Would it matter if the design idea were trademarked? Why or why not?

Intellectual Property

© Helder Almeida/Shutterstock.com

Team Up Now – CARS Checklist

Before you can cite a source, you must determine if a Web site is credible, accurate, reasonable, and has the proper support. Using the search engine scholar.google.com, each member of the team should research the topic of "flipping the classroom." Each team member should select a different site that explains the concept of flipping the classroom. Using the CARS checklist, each member must document the Web site URL and answer the following questions:

a. Credible: What evidence was provided to make the argument persuasive? Are there enough details for a reasonable conclusion about the argument?

b. Accurate: What date was the information published? Would any of the content be considered vague?

c. Reasonableness: Based on the author's statements, what was the tone of the article? Would you consider any portion to be slanted or biased?

d. Support: What are the sources of the site? Does the author provide contact information so that you can ask questions?

Share your results with your team and submit the combined information to your instructor.

Key Terms

accuracy	filter	Private Web
CARS checklist	Free Web	public domain
citation	general search engine	query
citation style	hit	reasonableness
copyright	index	restricted site
crawler	intellectual property rights	social search tool
credibility	Invisible Web	specialty search engine
credit line	metasearch engine	spider
database	open site	subject directory
Deep Web	Open Web	support
ethics	paraphrase	Visible Web
fair use doctrine	plagiarism	word stem

Intro to Media

Luke is taking Music Appreciation 101 this semester as an online course. He has been listening to popular genres of American music, including blues, jazz, country, rock, rap, and pop.

Luke also uses YouTube to watch and listen to music videos and premiere performances.

The Music Appreciation instructor posted many samples of music on the course's Web site so students can play them on any computer platform.

© Africa Studio/Shutterstock.com

Luke is surprised by how much he is enjoying an eclectic mix of music from Beethoven to Frank Sinatra, including artists that were never part of his playlist before, such as Conway Twitty, Bread, and Louis Armstrong. Armstrong is right: It *is* a wonderful world! Luke's assignment today is to watch and listen to early jazz musicians on YouTube, such as Scott Joplin and Bessie Smith.

Microsoft® product screenshots used with permission from Microsoft® Corporation.

Graphics

graphic | digital graphic | bitmap | pixel | vector | BMP | GIF | JPEG | PNG | TIF | download | Clip Art gallery | digital camera | graphics tablet | scanner | graphics software | paint software | image-editing software | drawing program | photo-editing software | computer-aided design (CAD) software | 3D CAD software | resolution | resolution dependent | megapixel | compression | lossy compression | lossless compression

A **graphic** is an image or picture. A **digital graphic** is an image you can see, store, and manipulate on a computer, tablet, smartphone, or other digital device. You can obtain graphics from external sources such as the Web, or you can create your own.

Image Types/Formats

The two basic types of digital images are bitmap and vector. **Bitmap** images assign colors to the smallest picture elements, called **pixels**. See **Figure 11-2**.

Figure 11-1: Types of graphics

Graphics can be color or black and white, and may incorporate text.

Illustrations convey concepts and ideas.

Computer-aided design (CAD) software creates highly detailed 3D images.

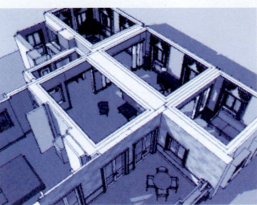

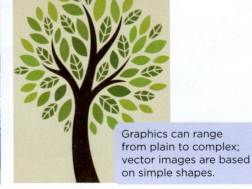

Graphics can range from plain to complex; vector images are based on simple shapes.

Courtesy of Judy Walker Design, Courtesy of Peter Clemens, © miumiu/Shutterstock.com

#intromedia

Android, iOS, and Windows apps on mobile phones typically display .png files, which have small file sizes due to their high compression rate.

Vector images are based on simple objects that can be grouped and layered to create a graphic. Bitmap and vector images are created and stored in a variety of file formats, shown in **Table 11-1**.

Downloading Graphics

If you want to add a picture to your document or presentation to illustrate a key point, you can **download** it, which means to transfer it to your computer. Many software products, including Microsoft Office, come with built-in **Clip Art galleries** containing a variety of illustrations and photos.

The Internet provides a rich source for graphics. Web sites such as Shutterstock and Fotolia maintain large inventories of pictures and other graphics, which you can download for a fee. You can also find free images (and other creative works), at creativecommons.org, which allows creators to supply material for free use by the public under the Creative Commons copyright licenses.

Figure 11-2: Pixels in a bitmap image

When viewed as a whole, the colored pixels create a unified, realistic image.

© Eric Milos/Shutterstock.com

Table 11-1: Common graphics file formats

Graphic file format	File extension	Details
BMP	.bmp	The Windows bitmap format; files can be large
GIF	.gif	A vector format used for simple graphics and short Web animations
JPEG	.jpeg or .jpg	A bitmap format used by many digital cameras; images are high quality, but files can be large
PNG	.png	A bitmap format used for Web graphics; good quality and highly compressed
TIF	.tif or .tiff	A bitmap format used for photos and graphics; files tend to be large

© 2015 Cengage Learning

Search engines such as Google and Bing help you find links to Web sites containing graphics relating to specific topics. However, when you download a graphic from an external source, be sure to follow any copyright restrictions on using the graphic.

Creating Graphics

If the graphic you need is not readily available, why not create it yourself? You can create graphics using hardware devices such as those shown in **Figure 11-3**.

On the Job Now

If you need to purchase the rights to a professional photo to use in a work project, consider using istockphoto.com or gettyimages.com.

Hot Technology Now

Create graphic images for free at sumopaint.com.

Figure 11-3: Creating graphics using hardware devices

Digital camera

Scanner

Graphics tablet

Graphics software

© Dinga/Shutterstock.com, © PRILL/Shutterstock.com, thampapon1/fotolia, © ifong/Shutterstock.com

A **digital camera** creates a digital image of an object, person, or scene. The file format depends on the camera settings.

You can use a **graphics tablet** to create drawings with a pressure-sensitive pen. Architects, mapmakers, designers, and artists use graphics tablets. A **scanner** converts a printed document into a bitmap file by dividing the image into a grid of tiny cells and assigning colors to each cell. Scanners vary in size and shape and include flatbed, sheet-fed, pen, and handheld types.

Graphics Software

In addition to capturing images with hardware devices, you can use a variety of popular **graphics software** to create your own graphics or modify existing ones. You can create images with **paint software** such as Microsoft Paint using brush tools and paint palettes that simulate water colors, pastels, and oil paints. Paint and other **image-editing software** let you modify existing images. For example, you can rotate an image on its axis, change its colors, or modify lines and other shapes.

Drawing programs, such as CorelDRAW, let you create simple cartoon-like images. Some programs let you layer graphics one on top of the other to create collages. You can use **photo-editing software**, such as Adobe Photoshop, to enhance and correct photographs. For example, you can add effects such as reflection or sepia, or even correct problems such as red-eye or poor lighting.

Computer-Aided Design

Some graphics require more sophisticated software. Architects, scientists, designers, engineers, and others use **computer-aided design (CAD) software** to create highly detailed and technically accurate drawings. With CAD software, drawings can be shared, modified, and enhanced with exceptional speed and accuracy. See **Figure 11-4**.

Interior designers use CAD software to model proposed room designs. Clothing designers can experiment with fabrics and patterns. Architects use CAD to design buildings and create floor plans. Engineers and scientists use **3D CAD software** to create wireframe drawings of objects, which they can rotate to view from multiple angles. You can also overlay materials on CAD designs to see the visual and technical impact of different materials.

Lastly, some CAD software even generates material lists for building designers to pass on to the construction teams.

Resolution and Compression

When using graphics in your work, you should be aware of how certain properties affect the way graphics look. **Resolution** refers to the clarity or sharpness of an image: the higher the resolution, the sharper the image. Bitmap graphics are **resolution dependent**, which means image quality deteriorates as size increases. Vector graphics keep the same quality as their size increases.

On a digital camera, resolution is typically measured in **megapixels**, or millions of pixels. The higher the number of megapixels, the higher the resolution of your photos, and the larger the picture files. However, high-resolution photos and other complicated graphics can be difficult to copy, download, or send as email attachments, due to their large file size.

Compression makes graphics files smaller by reducing the number of bits a file contains. JPEG files use **lossy compression**, which means some of the original file data is discarded during compression. Fortunately, the "lost" data is generally not noticeable. TIF, PNG, and GIF files can be compressed using **lossless compression**: when uncompressed, the files contain all of their original data.

Using Graphics

You can use graphics to improve your work as follows:
- Stories and articles become more interesting and memorable with dramatic or informative **photos**.

Figure 11-4: CAD software drawings

© ArchMan/Shutterstock.com, © Kotkoa/Shutterstock.com

- **Illustrations** and **drawings** can convey ideas and concepts better than words alone can.
- **Product photos** are essential on shopping Web sites.
- **Graphic logos** on corporate documents and Web sites help increase brand awareness.
- **Graphical buttons and icons** help to execute commands, display menus, or navigate documents or screens.
- Simple **cartoons** can add humor to your work.

No matter the context, graphics add functionality and fun to documents and Web pages.

Audio

digital audio | VoIP (Voice over IP) | MP3 | AAC | MP4 | RA | WAVE | WAV | AIFF | WMA | voice-over | audio input device | headset | sound recorder software | digitize | analog sound wave | sampling | sampling software | synthesized sound | MIDI (Musical Instrument Digital Interface) | speech synthesizer | phoneme | text-to-speech software | speech recognition software | speech-to-text | speech-to-text software | sound card | audio software | skin | stand-alone player | browser plug-in | audio capture and editing software | music production software | mix

If you listen to music using your computer or mobile device, you are listening to digital audio. **Digital audio** is any type of sound that is recorded and stored as a series of 1s and 0s. Digital audio can enhance any presentation or movie.

The Bottom Line

- Audio hardware and software let you record or synthesize digital sound files in a variety of file formats.
- You can play digitized sound files on your computer, edit them, and use them on Web sites and in presentations.

Figure 11-5: Using digital audio

You can record and play digital audio files using any computer or mobile device.

You can edit sound files using audio editing programs.

When you Skype with far-flung family and friends, you are using **VoIP (Voice over IP)** technology, which enables people to speak to each other over the Internet.

© Andresr/Shutterstock.com, © Maridav/Shutterstock.com, © ArtFamily/Shutterstock.com, © istockphoto.com/track5

Audio File Formats

Audio files can be stored in a variety of formats, each with a specific purpose. You can recognize the different audio file formats by looking at the file extensions. **Table 11-2** summarizes common audio file formats.

Table 11-2: Common audio file formats

File format	File extension	Compressed?	Notes
MP3	.mp3	Yes	Common music format
AAC and **M4P**	.aac and .m4p	Yes	Apple uses this format for iTunes downloads; also copy protected
RA (RealAudio)	.ra	Yes	Supported by RealPlayer; sound quality can be substandard
WAVE or **WAV** (Waveform Audio)	.wav	No	Files are large; good to excellent sound quality
AIFF (Audio Interchange File Format)	.aiff or .aif	No	Files are large; good to excellent sound quality
WMA (Windows Media Audio)	.wma	Yes	Played using Windows Media Player; also copy-protected

© 2015 Cengage Learning

Hot Technology Now

To convert images or audio files from one type to another type, such as from WMA to MP3, use the free site zamzar.com.

Hot Technology Now

One of the most popular programs available for recording sound is called Audacity (audacity.sourceforge.net). Audacity is a free, open source, cross-platform program that works on Macs and Windows and Linux computers.

Recording Sound

You may want to record yourself performing a song or reading a **voice-over**, or voice narration, to add to a slide presentation. You can easily record voice-overs and save the recordings for playback on a computer, but you need the following hardware and software:

1. You need an **audio input device** such as a microphone or headset. A **headset** combines speakers and a microphone into one device.

2. You also need **sound recorder software** to capture the sound from the input device.

3. Finally, you need to **digitize** the captured sound, which means to convert it to a format your computer can read.

Sound is produced when vibrations, such as a drumstick hitting a drum pad, cause pressure changes in the surrounding air, creating **analog** (continuous) **sound waves**. A process called **sampling** converts the analog sound waves into digital sound. **Sampling software** breaks the sound wave into separate segments, or samples, and stores each sample numerically. The more samples taken per second, the higher the sound quality and the larger the file. See **Figure 11-6**.

Once you capture and digitize sound, you can save it as an audio file and then play it back or edit it as you wish.

Synthesized Music

Some digital audio files are recordings of actual sounds; other sounds, known as **synthesized sounds**, are created artificially by computers and special software.

Figure 11-6: Analog, digital, and sampling sound

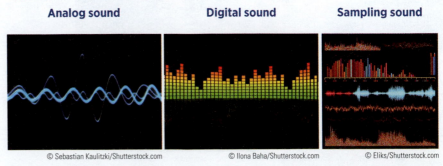

Analog sound © Sebastian Kaulitzki/Shutterstock.com   Digital sound © Ilona Baha/Shutterstock.com   Sampling sound © Eliks/Shutterstock.com

The term **MIDI (Musical Instrument Digital Interface)** refers to a system for creating and storing synthesized music. MIDI files do not contain sound; rather, they contain instructions for generating specific sounds, including pitch, volume, and note duration.

A computer reads these instructions and encodes the resulting MIDI "music." MIDI music files have .mid, .cmf, or .rol file extensions. MIDI files are much more compact than digital audio files; they take up less storage space and are easier to transmit. However, MIDI files do not produce high-quality vocal sounds. They lack the "tonal" qualities associated with real-life, high-quality music, so they can sound artificial to the trained ear.

Synthesized Speech

In addition to music, computers can synthesize speech. **Speech synthesizers** break words into individual sound units, called **phonemes**. Synthesizers string these phonemes together to create words and phrases. **Text-to-speech software** then generates the corresponding sounds from the phoneme sequences to create synthesized speech.

Synthesized speech is widely used in mobile communications and call centers. To make computers accessible to the visually impaired, synthesized speech reads aloud from the screen. Text-to-speech technology also lets you type text into your computer, create a sound file, and then play it back, post it on a Web site as a podcast, or email the sound file.

Speech Recognition

Speech recognition software, or **speech-to-text**, does the reverse of text-to-speech software by translating spoken words into text. **Speech-to-text software** analyzes speech and converts the sounds into phonemes. The phonemes are then matched to words in a digital dictionary and written as text on the screen.

Using speech recognition technology, you can activate computer commands or browse the Web using your voice instead of a keyboard and mouse. If you use this technology with word processing software, you can even create a report by speaking into your computer's microphone.

Playing Sound

Playing sounds on a computer or digital device requires special hardware and software. A **sound card**, shown in **Figure 11-7**, is a circuit board that gives the computer the ability to process sound.

Speakers play sound and can be built-in or attached as peripheral devices to your computer. Add-on speakers, though bulkier, often offer higher-quality sound than built-ins. If you're in an environment such as an office or library, where speakers are not practical, you can use a headset or headphones to keep the sound private.

You also need software to play sound. **Audio software** is included on portable media players such as iPods and smartphones and often offers features such as file-shuffling and volume control; some audio software even has **skins**, visuals to go along with the sounds.

When playing certain types of audio files on a desktop or laptop, including MP3 and RA files, you need a **stand-alone player** or **browser plug-in** such as RealPlayer or QuickTime. For Windows computers, Windows Media Player is a popular application for playing stand-alone audio files such as downloaded songs. Other types of sound files, such as AIFF and WAV, can be streamed over the Web and played in a browser on your computer without additional software.

Editing Sound

You can edit, copy, and share digital audio files using **audio capture and editing software**. You can enhance audio by removing background and other unwanted noises or pauses, deleting or reordering entire sections, and adding special effects.

Music production software such as Apple GarageBand lets you record, compose, **mix** (combine), and edit music and sounds. See **Figure 11-8** on the next page. You can create sounds of multiple instruments, change tempos, add notes, or rearrange a score to produce a unique arrangement.

By the Numbers Now

Audio engineers are paid between $300 and $1500 to digitally mix and master a song. Mixing involves balancing the individual tracks, and mastering involves optimizing the overall level to compete with commercial playback systems.

By the Numbers Now

In 1993, speech recognition systems had a 10 percent accuracy rate. In 1999, the accuracy improved to 81 percent. Today, speech recognition systems are 96 percent accurate.

#intromedia

Using Windows 8.x, type **Windows Speech Recognition** in the Search box to start the built-in speech recognition program, which allows you to control your computer with your voice.

Figure 11-7: Sound card

© DeSerg/Shutterstock.com

Figure 11-8: Editing a sound file in Garage Band

Each sound track appears in the timeline with controls for each one.

Controls for the selected sound track appear in the Audio region.

Waveforms for selected sound.

Software "instruments" are listed in this panel.

Source: Garage Band

While many music production programs are geared toward consumers, full-featured audio software such as Adobe Audition lets professionals edit sound for commercial Web sites, podcasts, presentations, and even TV shows and movies.

Finally, audio-editing programs and features are often integrated into video-editing software because sound tracks are integral to video.

Video

video | digital video | HD (high-definition) video | digital video camera | camcorder | smartphone | Web cam | video card | media player | streaming video | video conferencing | video-editing software | transition | codec | Moving Pictures Experts Group (MPEG) | streaming media | on-demand content | live streaming | plug-in | set-top box | smart TV

You probably use video often for entertainment, school, and work. **Video** combines moving images and sound and can be live or prerecorded. Video can range from home slide shows on your home computer to feature-length high-definition Hollywood movies.

The Bottom Line

- You can create digital videos using a digital video camera, and play them back on a computer or other device with the appropriate hardware and software.
- You can edit a digital video file to adjust its length and appearance, and to add special effects, text, graphics, and audio.

Figure 11-9: Uses for digital video

You can use video to communicate in real time with other people. Businesses often use video conferences to conduct meetings on a network or the Internet.

It's easy to create videos using a video camera or smartphone.

Video is an important way of presenting content on the Web for individuals and companies.

In many programs, you can edit video—even Microsoft PowerPoint lets you make basic changes.

© Blend Images/Shutterstock.com, © 1000 Words/Shutterstock.com, © dolphfyn/Shutterstock.com, PowerPoint video courtesy of Barbara Clemens

Capturing Video

A **digital video** is a series of image frames displayed quickly enough for us to perceive them as continuous motion. Digital videos can come from a digital video camera, video-enabled smartphone, DVD, or digital video recording (DVR) device. DVDs and DVRs are used less frequently as time goes on. Some video today is **HD (high-definition) video**, which produces a much sharper picture than standard definition video.

A **digital video camera**, **camcorder, or smartphone** (see **Figure 11-10**) captures full-motion images and stores the images in a file on the camera or phone. Digital video files are large: when you transfer a video from a digital video camera to your computer or storage media, you could need 1 to 30 GB of storage for each hour of video, with HD video requiring storage space in the upper end of the range.

A **Web cam** is a digital video camera that captures video and sends it directly to a computer. Web cams are often built into laptops, tablets, and smartphones. They can also be attached to any computer through a USB or FireWire port.

You can view desktop videos using popular software such as RealMedia player, Windows Media Player, or Apple QuickTime Player. Many people watch videos using the YouTube app on mobile devices.

Playing Video

To watch video on a computer, you need special hardware and software. The hardware is built into computers, tablets, or smartphones and includes a **video card**—a circuit board that lets your computer process video—screen, and speakers.

You also need software called a **media player**. With a Windows computer, you can use Windows Movie Maker, which lets you edit videos as well as watch them. Most tablets and smartphones also include the software to display video. Video technology changes so quickly that you need to update your media player and related software frequently.

You can enhance a PowerPoint presentation by embedding a video to play during a presentation. The video player software is included with the presentation software. Adobe Flash Player is a popular format for playing Flash videos, and Adobe video-editing software lets you create and edit Flash videos.

Video on the Web

Fast Internet connections have made watching videos on computers and mobile devices almost as popular as watching television. You can watch videos on many Web sites, whether the videos are posted by individuals, by Web developers, or as advertising on Web sites. People use Web sites such as YouTube and Vimeo to share personal videos; you can also watch commercial movies and TV through YouTube.

One way to store and present video on the Web is as individual video files, such as movie clips that you must download completely before playing them. Another method is **streaming video**, which transfers a segment of a video file from the Web to your computer, letting that segment play while the next segment is being sent. You'll learn more about streaming video later in this chapter.

Video conferencing, or face-to-face meetings using computers, is increasingly used on the Web as a way of reducing business travel costs and bringing friends and family together over long distances. Microsoft Lync lets users stay in audio and video contact using Windows computers as well as Windows, iOS, and Android smartphones. With Google Hangouts, you can have group conversations with live video calls using computers as well as Apple and Android devices.

Editing Video

Video-editing software makes it possible for anyone with a home computer to enhance and customize video. You can transfer video files from a camcorder for editing on your computer. You can also shoot and edit video using your smartphone. Most video-editing

Figure 11-10: Digital video camera and smartphone

© Olinchuk Shutterstock.com, © Jaros/Shutterstock.com

#intromedia

Windows 8.x includes the Video app, which lets you download and play Xbox movies and TV shows (for a subscription fee), or play other video files stored on your computer.

By the Numbers Now

Ultra HD (4K) televisions play Ultra HD videos on screens with an ultra-wide ratio of 21 × 9, which display vivid, detailed images that rival those shown in feature-length movies.

#intromedia

The latest versions of Windows include Skype, which you can use to make Internet calls, exchange instant messages, and engage in video chat.

Hot Technology Now

The top educational video sites for students include teachertube.com, youtube.com/schools, discoveryeducation.com, ted.com, and video.nationalgeographic.com.

software shows the video as a timeline with separate tracks for video and sound. Windows Movie Maker (see **Figure 11-11**) and Apple iMovie are popular personal video editing programs.

Figure 11-11: Editing video in Windows Movie Maker

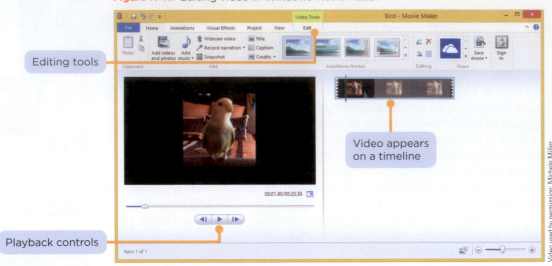

Editing tools

Video appears on a timeline

Playback controls

Video used by permission: Michele Miller.

You can delete unwanted footage or rearrange or copy scenes to produce a professional-looking video. You can also add voice and music over existing scenes to narrate a scene or create a mood.

Transitions are graphics that help a viewer know when one scene ends and another begins. You can use video-editing software to insert transitions such as fades and swipes between scenes.

Videos can consume a lot of storage space—up to 30 GB per hour of video. For this reason, many users save the files in compressed format and store videos on DVDs or external hard drives after editing.

Codecs

When you edit video, it's in an uncompressed, or raw, format. After editing, you use a **codec** (compressor/decompressor) to convert the video into other formats and reduce file size for distribution. **Moving Pictures Experts Group (MPEG)** is a popular video compression standard, with a widely used codec called MPEG-4 or MP4. Other popular codecs include Apple QuickTime, DivX, and Windows Media Video. Video files may use file extensions such as .mkv, .mts, and .mov.

With the variety of digital video media, viewing and editing software, and distribution methods available today, you can create and distribute just the video you want.

Streaming Media

You can access audio and video content on your computer via **streaming media**, which lets you watch or listen to the content as it arrives. For **on-demand content** such as radio or TV shows, the original media file is stored on the media distributor's server, and is sent to your computer for viewing. Because the file is stored, you can watch it many times. Examples of on-demand content include Netflix, Hulu, YouTube, and Pandora Internet Radio. In contrast, with **live streaming**, such as sports events, the content is sent out live, as it happens, and is available only once.

Your computer needs to decode the streamed content to play it. To decode, your computer uses a media player, such as Windows Media Player or Apple Quick-Time, or a **plug-in** (a component added to your Web browser) such as the Adobe Flash Player.

Hot Technology Now

The five most popular mobile apps for editing video on your smartphone include Magisto, Montaj, Viddy, Cute CUT, and Qik Video. Most of the apps have tinting, storyboarding, textures, custom filters, and sharing capabilities.

In addition to viewing streaming media on your computer, you can view it on your television set. You need additional hardware, including a **set-top box** (such as Apple TV, Roku, or Google Chromecast), Blu-Ray player, or game console, which lets you view the Internet content (including social media sites such as Facebook and LinkedIn) on your TV. Increasingly, **smart TVs** are incorporating the Internet abilities of set-top boxes, including streaming media and social media. (You'll learn more about social media later in this chapter.) See **Figure 11-12**.

Figure 11-12: Streaming media to your computer and TV

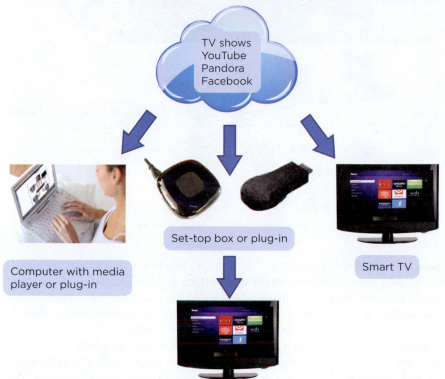

© Goodluz/Shutterstock.com, © irin-k/Shutterstock.com; photos courtesy of Barbara Clemens, © iadams/Shutterstock.com

#intromedia

Many people are cutting the cord to their cable and satellite paid television subscriptions. You can create your own personal entertainment hub with smart TVs, Roku, Apple TV, Chromecast, and Xbox Video to watch your favorite shows, movies, news, and sports.

Animation

animation | simulation | PowerPoint transition | 3D animation | frames per second (fps) | in-betweening | animated GIF | SWF format | HTML5 | wireframe drawing | rendering | animation software

If you have played a video game lately or seen an animation-enhanced film such as *Toy Story*, *Brave*, *Avatar*, or *Frozen*, then you've experienced **animation**, the art of bringing an object to life by giving it the appearance of motion or activity. See **Figure 11-13** on the next page.

The Bottom Line

- Animation is used in films and games, as well as in education, training, and business presentations.
- Three-dimensional animation is common in films and computer games, while 2D and 3D animation appear on the Web.
- You can create animations using animation software.

Animation Uses

Although we commonly think of animation as being used for entertainment in films and games, animation has other uses. For example, animation can teach medical students a procedure. **Simulations** are sophisticated computer animations that are useful for training and teaching in many fields, particularly in areas in which learning can be dangerous or difficult. See **Figure 11-14** on the next page.

A popular use of simple animations is in PowerPoint or Prezi presentations, in which you can animate slide text and objects. **PowerPoint transitions**, the way one slide moves to another, are a type of animation. You can also embed a graph from a spreadsheet program such as Microsoft Excel and animate the bars to emphasize important trends.

Animation in Films

Special effects for movies, as well as entire animated films, are produced using **3D animation**. Digitally animated films, such as *Planes* and the *Shrek* series, are examples

On the Job Now

Mobile game app development is one of the world's fastest-growing occupations. Game developers receive 70 percent of the app's price as payment each time their app is purchased in the various app stores.

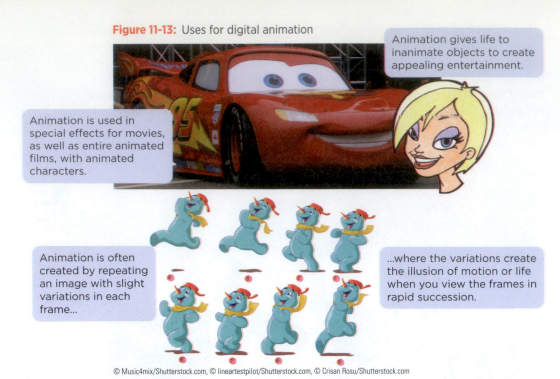

Figure 11-13: Uses for digital animation

Animation gives life to inanimate objects to create appealing entertainment.

Animation is used in special effects for movies, as well as entire animated films, with animated characters.

Animation is often created by repeating an image with slight variations in each frame...

...where the variations create the illusion of motion or life when you view the frames in rapid succession.

© Music4mix/Shutterstock.com, © lineartestpilot/Shutterstock.com, © Crisan Rosu/Shutterstock.com

Figure 11-14: Using simulation for training

flun/Fotolia

Simulation is used to teach pilots new techniques for flying a plane.

Figure 11-15: Real-time animation in 3D computer gaming

One02/fotolia

#intromedia

The glasses-free 3D TV market is growing, meaning you can watch 3D animation movies in your home.

of how sophisticated 3D animation has become. When you're watching animation, you're actually seeing many **frames per second (fps)**, with an image in each frame. For example, television uses 30 fps, many videos use 24 fps, and 3D computer games often display 60 fps. 3D animation in films is done during the production phase, while the film is being shot, and then incorporated into the final footage.

Animation is created using a sequence of bitmap images in which one or more objects are changed slightly between each image. Not surprisingly, this technique is called **in-betweening**. You can create the in-between bitmaps manually or let a computer create them.

Animation in Games

Animated special effects in computer games, such as massive battle scenes, are created using a sequence of bitmap images with objects moved or changed between each rendering. Whereas animation in films is done ahead of time and then incorporated into the rest of the film, 3D computer game animation is produced as you're playing. See **Figure 11-15**.

This real-time animation consumes an incredible amount of computer resources. At 60 frames per second, your computer must handle more than 1 billion bits of information every second just to display a 3D image in 32-bit color. The computer also has to track the movements of each player, using even more resources.

Web Animation

When you view a Web page and objects move, you are viewing animation. Animation is frequently used on Web sites to enhance text as well as images. An **animated GIF** is essentially a series of slightly different bitmap images displayed in sequence to achieve animation effects.

Adobe Flash is used to create static or animated graphics in the **SWF format**, which is designed for Web use. SWF graphics use the .swf extension. Because they are bitmap images, GIF files are larger than most animations created in Adobe Flash. Their larger size makes GIF files less desirable than Flash animations on a Web page because larger files take longer to travel from a server to a browser over the Internet. Also, they are not supported on mobile devices or most modern browsers. Web animations created with **HTML5**, the latest version of the Hypertext Markup Language, are gaining in popularity.

2D vs. 3D

Animation can be 2D or 3D. Three-dimensional animation is more complex than 2D animation because the artist must first create the 3D graphic, and then create 24 to 60 versions of the graphic for each second of animation.

To create a 3D animation, you start with a 2D object and then add shadows and light. Next, you define the texture of each surface of the object, which determines how the object reflects light. One way to create a solid 3D image is to apply highlights and shadows to a **wireframe drawing** (a 3D object composed of individual lines) in a process called **rendering**. See **Figure 11-16**.

Although the process sounds complicated, animation software can make it more manageable.

Figure 11-16: 3D rendering

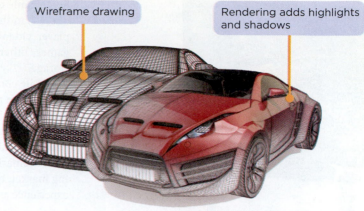

Wireframe drawing

Rendering adds highlights and shadows

© Mikhail Bakunovich/Shutterstock.com

Animation Software

With a personal computer and readily available software, anyone with a little training and some skill can create animations. **Animation software** includes Adobe Illustrator, Adobe After Effects, Adobe Flash, and Microsoft Silverlight. Professional-level animation software such as Autodesk Maya and NewTek LightWave is expensive and has a steep learning curve.

HTML5 includes support for creating and displaying animation and is being used by Apple on its iPhone, iPad, and other products.

Hot Technology Now

To create 3D images with a digital camera, check out the site www.123dapp.com/catch or download the free app 123D Catch for iPads.

Gaming

video console | game console | game controller | force feedback | head-mounted display | OLED (organic light-emitting diode) technology | software development kit (SDK) | virtual world | avatar | motion-sensing game console

Digital electronics and gaming are interactive media that engage players. Today's video games use high-end graphics, sophisticated processors, and the Internet to create environments that rival reality and bring together players from around the world. Games account for most software sales, totaling nearly $100 billion in revenue. Computer and video games include role-playing, action, adventure, education, puzzles, simulations, sports, and strategy/war games.

Hardware

Most games are played on **video consoles** with special controllers. A popular choice for video gaming is a **game console** such as the Xbox, Nintendo Wii, or Sony PlayStation. These use handheld controllers as input devices, a television screen or computer monitor as an output device, a hard drive, and optical discs or memory cards for storage. See **Figure 11-17** on the next page.

On consoles that connect to the Internet, you can play with multiple players online and stream TV or movies. Large-scale multiplayer games such as Halo, EverQuest Next, Guardians of Middle Earth, Titanfall, and World of Warcraft operate on multiple Internet servers, with each server able to handle thousands of players.

However, many games can be played on computers, tablets, or smartphones that use a keyboard, mouse, touchpad, or touchscreen to input commands. Simple games such as card games often come with the operating system of a computer. Hardware for handheld game consoles, tablets, and smartphones is built into the devices. Some devices use cartridges, memory cards, or miniature optical discs to store games.

The Bottom Line

- Most sophisticated video gaming requires video or game consoles, but many others can be played on computers, tablets, and smartphones.
- High-end game controllers take many forms: some use technology that lets users feel resistance in response to actions, and some are motion sensitive.
- Developers can create virtual worlds where participants assume identities and buy and sell items in virtual economies.

Figure 11-17: Gaming hardware

Input devices   Storage device

Mobile Gaming

Some game consoles are self-contained devices that fit in one hand. These handheld consoles are designed for single-player or multi-player video games. See **Figure 11-18**. Some use cartridges to store games; others use a memory card or a miniature optical disc for storage.

Mobile computing and smartphones have put the world of gaming right in the palms of many hands. Phones often come with scaled-down game versions to introduce them. Popular games like Angry Birds can "go viral" and become overnight sensations. Some games, such as Words with Friends, are designed to be played by people with similar smartphones or on social networks. Game apps are a growing market, but many people feel that game apps can't offer the same experience as game consoles.

Game Controllers

Joysticks, wheels, gamepads, and motion-sensing **game controllers** are input devices used to control movement and actions of players or objects in computer games, simulations, and video games. Game controllers take many forms. Depending on the type of video game, the control can look like a steering wheel, a guitar, a TV remote, or many other forms.

Some game controllers also include **force feedback**, a technology that lets the users feel vibration or resistance in response to their actions. Some motion-sensitive consoles allow players to interact using a series of sensors and a camera that track their motion in 3D.

Head-mounted displays give a personal, immersive gaming experience, often in 3D. These devices may use **OLED (organic light-emitting diode) technology** to display the game and respond to motion.

By the Numbers Now

For games and other apps, Apple iOS developers have received more than $15 billion since the introduction of the App Store.

Gaming Graphics

Today's video games feature startlingly real graphics. Gaming graphics are created by graphic artists and technical illustrators, who use advanced software and graphics tablets to generate complex images. Windows, Android, and Mac OS X offer **software development kits (SDKs)** for games, with tools for creating 2D and 3D drawings, as well as game-playing interfaces, multiplayer control, and more.

Although most computer games are viewed on a 2D screen, developers are designing 3D graphics, which appear to have height, width, and depth, making many computer games look surprisingly real.

Figure 11-18: A handheld gaming console

The controls, the screen, and the speakers are built into the device.

The screens are small—3 to 5 inches.

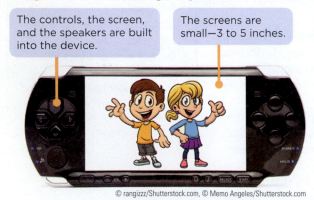

Virtual Worlds

Virtual worlds are communities participating in commerce and daily activities on the Internet. Second Life, shown in **Figure 11-19** is an example of a successful virtual world.

Players are willing to spend a great deal of money to create virtual worlds where "make-believe" assets are exchanged. The currency system in Second Life even has an official market-driven exchange rate, and you can buy and sell virtual assets on eBay and other online marketplaces.

Second Life allows you to assume an imaginary, or virtual, identity called an **avatar** that can role-play with other characters, spend money to build homes, and buy goods such as clothing. A basic account can be free, with other activities requiring a fee. For example, a pair of sneakers for your online avatar might cost 70 cents.

SimCity is a popular series of video games in which participants build a city, complete with power and transportation systems, and deal with disasters such as tornadoes and even train crashes.

Future of Gaming

Game consoles are also being used for activities other than entertainment. For example, doctors can practice their fine motor skills on surgery simulators using **motion-sensing game consoles**. Physical therapists use the Nintendo Wii game system to help arthritis patients build strength and endurance and to increase range of motion. Recreation with Wii or Kinect sports games may help stroke and injury victims recover faster.

One software manufacturer is using gaming concepts to enhance e-commerce by creating a virtual shopping experience with 3D stores. You can browse aisles, view product labels, and even compare products side by side.

Figure 11-19: Second Life virtual world

Source: Second Life

Social Media

social media | social networking | blogging | microblogging | media sharing | content sharing | collaborative project | social bookmarking | social news | file sharing | virtual game world | virtual social world | crowdsourcing | crowdfunding

Since the early days of the Web in the 1990s, computer users have seized on social media as a way to interact with each other using text, pictures, sound, and video. The dawn of tablet computers and mobile devices such as smartphones has only spread the reach and influence of social media. See **Figure 11-20**.

What Is Social Media?

Social media refers to the many ways computer users share information and interact using the Internet. See **Figure 11-21** on the next page. The information they share ranges from stories, photos, news, and opinions to complete diaries, daily life updates, professional networking and job searching, as well as sophisticated games.

Social media differs from other forms of communication because it is:

1. **Immediate**: Traditional forms of personal and business communication take time: Letters have to travel through the mail; newspapers and books have to be published, distributed, and sold. Communication using social media can take place almost immediately: a Facebook update can prompt reactions within seconds.

The Bottom Line

- Social media allows people to share information with others around the world, instantaneously.
- Different types of social media let you network with others, publish your ideas, share media, work collectively, share links, news, and files, and play interactive games in virtual environments.
- While social media has many benefits, it entails some risks; users must decide if, and how, they want to participate.

Figure 11-20: Types of social media

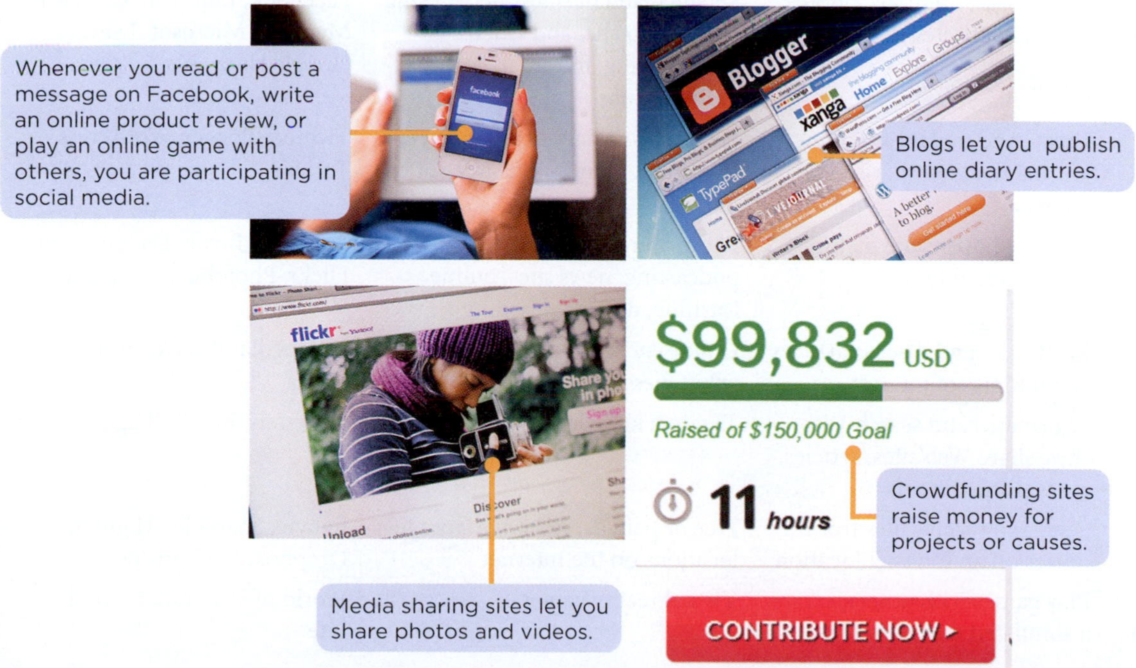

Whenever you read or post a message on Facebook, write an online product review, or play an online game with others, you are participating in social media.

Blogs let you publish online diary entries.

$99,832 USD

Raised of $150,000 Goal

⏱ **11** *hours*

Crowdfunding sites raise money for projects or causes.

Media sharing sites let you share photos and videos.

CONTRIBUTE NOW ▶

© iStockphoto.com/Erikona, © iStockphoto.com/Bfazon1, © iStockphoto.com/william87, Courtesy of Indiegogo.com

Figure 11-21: Using social media

© BigLike Images/Shutterstock.com

2. **Widespread**: Since their beginnings in the 1990s, social media Web sites have exploded in popularity worldwide. According to a recent estimate, one in four people around the world uses social networking—more than 1.7 billion users. In the United States alone, over 70 percent of computer users participate in social networking.

3. **Interactive**: Traditional media outlets such as television, newspaper, and radio are "one-way streets," with little opportunity for users to respond. With social media, interactivity is common and expected. A user posts a photo or a video on a sharing site hoping to get a response from others. In fact, almost all traditional media outlets, such as TV and radio, have social media sites where users can post reactions and contribute content.

Social media helps us form online communities with users with similar interests around the world.

Types of Social Media

Social media has evolved into many forms, which are summarized in Table 11-3. You can choose the types of social media in which to participate, depending on your interests.

While placing Web sites into categories can help organize your thinking about social media, a Web site might span more than one category. For example, you can share YouTube videos on Facebook, and you can post comments on blogs.

Gathering Support with Social Media

Social media has become a major way for individuals and organizations to gather knowledge, support, or contributions from a worldwide audience. Such support might include physical labor, data collection, research, or financing.

Crowdsourcing entails using the Internet and the "intelligence of the crowd" to accomplish a task or solve a problem for the benefit of all. Project leaders put out a public request on the Internet, sometimes called an "open call," and motivated people respond. Examples of crowdsourcing include the following:

- **Community projects**, such as a beach cleanup, or electronic petitions to accomplish a change in a community
- **Creative projects**, in which people contribute ideas such as designing a new public building or a new state license plate

Table 11-3: Types of social media

Type	Lets you	Includes	Examples
Social networking	Share ideas, opinions, photos, videos, Web sites	Personal and business networking, chat, video chat and video conferencing, instant messaging, online dating	Facebook, LinkedIn, Google+, Myspace, Microsoft Lync, Google Hangouts
Blogging and **microblogging**	Create and update an online journal that you share with readers	Personal journals, expert advice, information on special areas of interest	Twitter, Blogger, WordPress, Tumblr
Media sharing and **content sharing**	View and distribute pictures, videos, audio files	Photo and video sharing, podcasting, news sites, online learning, distance learning	YouTube, Break, Dailymotion, Flickr, Photobucket, Picasa
Collaborative projects	Read, add, and discuss articles about topics of interest	Online encyclopedias, forums, wikis, message boards, news groups,	Wikipedia, WikiAnswers, Wikia
Social bookmarking and **social news**	Tag (mark) and search Web sites; share Web sites, articles, news stories, media	Tagging; knowledge management	Delicious, Reddit, Digg
File sharing	Send and receive files from others on an Internet location	Free or paid access to file storage locations on the Internet	Egnyte, ShareFile, Hightail, Dropbox, WeTransfer
Virtual game worlds and **virtual social worlds**	Play games with others; create a simulated environment	Virtual reality games	World of Warcraft, Second Life

© 2015 Cengage Learning

- **Skill-based projects**, in which people donate skills such as editing, translation, scanning, or data transcription to create or improve publicly available data (such as census information, databases, or historic newspapers)
- **Location-based projects**, such as wildlife counts, language use surveys, or a recent NASA project that asks citizen astronomers to help locate asteroids that may pose a threat to earth

A particular type of crowdsourcing is **crowdfunding**, in which individuals come together on the Internet to provide funding that will support others in an endeavor. See **Figure 11-22** for an example of a successful crowdfunding project on Kickstarter.com. Other popular crowdfunding sites include Indiegogo and Crowdfunder.

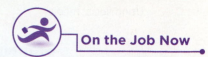

On the Job Now

If a business does not have the talent in house to handle a new project, CrowdSource (crowdsouce.com) provides a managed workforce for hire.

Figure 11-22: A successful Kickstarter campaign

Crowdfunding might benefit startup businesses that need seed money to get started...

...small businesses seeking investments to support expansion...

...or civic organizations that need funding for community projects.

Crowdfunding is used to solicit donations for a cause or charity, such as assisting a family in financial need.

Source: Kickstarter, Inc.

Evaluating Social Media

Opinions of social media vary widely: some people use it regularly and can't imagine life without it; others are suspicious and avoid it completely. So is social media a positive force in our lives, or a negative one? There is support for both sides.

Pros: On the plus side, social media is accessible; it's an inexpensive way for people to reach a wide audience. Communications can be immediate, and they're easy to change. Businesses can communicate easily with customers and hear their reactions. News organizations use social media to post breaking news and to receive contributions of news items from their audience. Social media can help people overcome isolation so they feel informed and connected.

Cons: On the minus side, the quality of social media content can vary widely because it lacks the expert oversight of traditional media (editors or managers, for example). Security and privacy are also important concerns:

- It's not always possible to control who can access personal data posted online.
- New online acquaintances might misrepresent themselves using false identities.
- Users need to exercise care regarding the type of information they post; for example, future employers may form unfavorable opinions of job candidates who have posted unprofessional images and language in the past.
- Some users are uncomfortable that businesses can track our browsing and shopping habits so they can target us with customized advertising.
- Other people become addicted to social media, at the expense of personal relationships.

In the end, it's up to individual users and businesses whether the benefits of social media outweigh the risks. But social media use will likely continue its growth for the foreseeable future.

#intromedia

Go to twitter.com, search for **@SAMTechNow,** the book's Twitter account, and then follow @SAMTechNow to get tweets on your home page.

Chapter Review

Graphics

1. Name three graphic file formats that can produce large file sizes.
2. Name the four main ways you can create a graphic yourself.
3. What kind of software lets scientists and engineers create highly detailed and technically accurate drawings?

Audio

4. What does MIDI stand for? Briefly describe it use.
5. Briefly describe how a speech synthesizer works.
6. What kind of software is Apple GarageBand, and why would you use it?

Video

7. What kind of digital video camera captures video and sends it directly to a computer?
8. What hardware and software does your computer need to play video?
9. Name two kinds of streaming media, and give an example of the kind of program you might view with each one.
10. Name two programs you might use for video conferencing and the type of hardware that is compatible with each one.

Animation

11. What kind of animation is useful for training and teaching, particularly when learning can be dangerous or difficult?
12. Briefly describe in-betweening and how it is used in animation.
13. Name three software products that let you create animations.

Gaming

14. Xbox 360 and Nintendo Wii are examples of what kind of hardware?
15. Name three types of input devices used to control movement and player actions in computer games.
16. In virtual world software, what do you call an imaginary identity you can use for role-playing?

Social Media

17. Name three ways that social media differs from traditional communications, and give examples of each one.
18. On what type of social media site would you maintain a personal journal to share with others?
19. Give two examples of file sharing sites.
20. If you wanted to raise funds online for a new business you plan to start, what type of site would you use?

Test Your Knowledge Now

1. Which of the following is a highly compressed bitmap graphic format used for Web graphics?
   a. PNG
   b. BMP
   c. TIF
   d. GIF

2. _____ is a photo-editing software product you can use to correct red-eye.
   a. Microsoft Paint
   b. Adobe Photoshop
   c. CorelDRAW
   d. Microsoft Office

3. What type of graphic keeps its quality as its size increases?
   a. bitmap
   b. JPEG
   c. BMP
   d. vector

4. Which of the following is a copy-protected audio file format used by Apple iTunes?
   a. WAV
   b. WMA
   c. RA
   d. MP4

5. What converts analog sound waves into digital sound?
   a. sound recorder software
   b. sampling software
   c. a synthesizer
   d. an audio input device

6. Which of the following converts speech into text on a computer screen?
   a. text-to-speech software
   b. speech recognition software
   c. speech synthesizer
   d. MIDI files

7. To edit videos, you can use video-editing software such as
   a. Vimeo.
   b. YouTube.
   c. Apple iMovie.
   d. Apple GarageBand.

8. To convert a video to another format to reduce its file size, you would use a
   a. camcorder.
   b. media player.
   c. plug-in.
   d. codec.

9. A _____ lets you view Internet content on your television.
   a. media player
   b. codec
   c. set-top box
   d. video card

10. A series of image frames displayed quickly enough for us to perceive them as continuous motion is called
    a. digital audio.
    b. skins.
    c. streaming video.
    d. digital video.

11. How many frames per second (fps) does a typical 3D computer game use?
    a. 24
    b. 30
    c. 60
    d. 200

12. Animation in 3D computer games is created
    a. in "real time," as you're playing.
    b. during the production phase.
    c. using PowerPoint transitions.
    d. using simulations.

13. A series of slightly different bitmap images displayed in sequence on the Web is called a(n)
    a. wireframe drawing.
    b. rendering.
    c. animated GIF.
    d. simulation.

14. Which of the following is an example of a game console?
    a. Second Life
    b. Halo
    c. Xbox 360
    d. SDK

15. Which of the following is used to help stroke and injury victims recover faster?
    a. SDKs
    b. Second Life
    c. Nintendo Wii
    d. OLED technology

16. Which of the following is an example of Virtual World software?
    a. Nintendo Wii
    b. Second Life
    c. Angry Birds
    d. EverQuest

17. Which of the following is a large-scale multiplayer game?
    a. Guardians of Middle Earth
    b. Sony PlayStation 4
    c. Avatar
    d. Autodesk Maya

18. Which type of social media site would you use to share ideas, photos, videos, and opinions?
    a. collaborative projects
    b. social bookmarking
    c. file sharing
    d. social networking

19. Which of the following is not a feature of social media?
    a. immediate
    b. interactive
    c. solitary
    d. widespread

20. What type of social media site would you use to gather volunteers for a town cleanup project?
    a. crowdfunding
    b. file sharing
    c. blogging
    d. crowdsourcing

21. In the space next to each image below, write the letter of the phrase that describes it.
    a. Set-top box
    b. Digital sound
    c. Gaming input device
    d. Analog sound
    e. Sound card

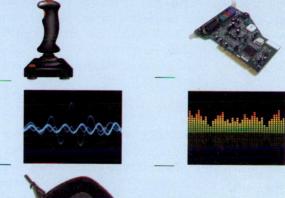

___

___

___

Try This Now

1: Professional Graphics Design Presentation with Canva

Creating a professional-looking document online can be very simple using a Web site named Canva.com. This free site provides designs for Web and print, flyers, Facebook covers, and blog graphics. Open a browser (preferably the free Chrome browser) and then open Canva.com to begin designing a professional presentation.

    a. Create a free account at canva.com so you can save the graphics and documents you create. Next, start a new design based on the Presentation design. Select any layout for your presentation in the left column.

    b. Using the built-in design layout, create a three-page presentation about what you can do with canva.com designs in your personal and business life. *Hint*: To add a new page, select the + Add a new page button.

    c. After adding text and images to your three-page presentation, select Link & Publish. Submit the link of your completed presentation to your instructor.

2: Infographics at Visual.ly

Infographics arrange and organize graphics and text so you can see patterns and trends at a glance. Open a browser and open the site visual.ly. (The .ly is the extension of the Web site.)

    a. Search for a keyword such as Internet, technology, graphics, audio, or social networking in the Search text box (select the magnifying glass icon to open the Search box).

    b. Open and examine three Infographics displayed in the search results.

    c. Copy and paste each of the three Infographics into a Word document that identifies your search term. Write a paragraph to explain what information is explained within each graphic. Submit the document to your instructor.

3: Professional LinkedIn Social Presence

The professional social media site LinkedIn is helpful for career networking. LinkedIn allows you to search for volunteer positions in addition to paid jobs. Open a browser and then open the site linkedIn.com. Create a professional profile to begin making connections with people that can recommend you for a position.

    a. Create a professional profile that includes your career interests. List your education, job experience, skills, and expertise.

    b. After you complete your profile, share it with your instructor by adding a connection.

Critical Thinking Now

1: Professional Design with ColorHunter

Creating a professionally designed color palette can give a polished look to a Web page, Word document, or PowerPoint presentation. Search for a colorful picture online at bing.com or google.com using the image search feature, and then download the image to your local computer. Open the site colorhunter.com and upload the image to create a free color palette based on the hues and tones of the image. In a Word document, display the picture and a screenshot of the palette from Color Hunter. Write a paragraph of at least 100 words on the topic of how a color palette based on a company's logo could be used within professional documents.

2: Most Popular Video Games

Gaming is a massive economic market for both console computer games and mobile game apps. Research current information from the current calendar year to answer the following questions.

    a. What are the five most popular console games? Explain the topic of each game.

    b. What are the five most popular games for the iPhone platform? Explain the topic of each game.

    c. What are the five most popular games for the Android platform? Explain the topic of each game.

© iStockphoto.com/Ranplett

Gaming

3: Social Networking Security Best Practices

In business, creating a social profile with a networking site such as LinkedIn is important to meet and stay in touch with your colleagues. Most businesses rely heavily on effective networking practices to connect with clients and potential employees. Research the best practices for business social networking. In your own words, list the 10 best practices for social networking in the business world.

Ethical Issues Now

YouTube and the Ethics of Copyright

The Digital Millennium Copyright Act covers many of the copyright laws for Internet postings. The most common infraction of this set of laws is the posting of other people's movies and music on sites such as youtube.com.

    a. Research the Digital Millennium Copyright Act. In at least 100 of your own words, briefly explain what this set of laws covers.

    b. Research the Terms of Service for youtube.com. In at least 100 of your own words, briefly explain what the Web site allows when you post a video to YouTube.

    c. If you own copyright to your own video and post it to youtube.com, people can legally watch this video as many times as they want. Would it be legal for your audience to download your YouTube video to watch later if they have a very slow Internet connection in their apartment? What do the YouTube Terms of Service say about this action?

Team Up Now – Record a Podcast (Audio Blog)

Audio Podcast

© iStockphoto.com/enat

Note: This assignment requires the use of a headset or built-in microphone for audio recording.

    Many companies create free audio and video podcasts about new products to post on Web sites or to make available for download. Search YouTube videos about the latest Consumer Electronics Show (CES) in Las Vegas and find a new technology product that interests your team. You may use any audio recording technology for this assignment on a computer or smartphone. If you do not have audio recording software, download a free copy of Audacity for a Windows, Mac, or Linux computer at the site audacity.sourceforge.net.

    a. Before you record a podcast, it is best to write a script. As a team, research a technology product from the latest Consumer Electronics Show (CES), an international trade show featuring innovative electronics and technology. Write a script of at least 250 words about this product.

    b. Split up the script in equal parts by topic and record the audio for your commercial podcast about the new technology product.

    c. Save the audio file in the format requested by your instructor. Submit the script and audio podcast to your instructor.

Key Terms

3D animation
3D CAD software
AAC
AIFF
analog sound wave
animated GIF
animation
animation software
audio capture and editing software
audio input device
audio software
avatar
bitmap
blogging
BMP
browser plug-in
camcorder
Clip Art gallery
codec
collaborative project
compression
computer-aided design (CAD) software
content sharing
crowdfunding

crowdsourcing
digital audio
digital camera
digital graphic
digital video
digital video camera
digitize
download
drawing program
file sharing
force feedback
frames per second (fps)
game console
game controller
GIF
graphic
graphics software
graphics tablet
HD (high-definition) video
head-mounted display
headset
HTML5
image-editing software
in-betweening

JPEG
live streaming
lossless compression
lossy compression
media player
media sharing
megapixel
microblogging
MIDI (Musical Instrument Digital Interface)
mix
motion-sensing game console
Moving Pictures Experts Group (MPEG)
MP3
MP4
music production software
OLED (organic light-emitting diode) technology
on-demand content
paint software
phoneme
photo-editing software
pixel
plug-in

PNG
PowerPoint transition
RA
rendering
resolution
resolution dependent
sampling
sampling software
scanner
set-top box
simulation
skin
smart TV
smartphone
social bookmarking
social media
social networking

social news
software development kit (SDK)
sound card
sound recorder software
speech recognition software
speech synthesizer
speech-to-text
speech-to-text software
stand-alone player
streaming media
streaming video
SWF format
synthesized sound
text-to-speech software
TIF
transition
vector

video
video card
video conferencing
video console
video-editing software
virtual game world
virtual social world
virtual world
voice-over
VoIP (Voice over IP)
WAV
WAVE
Web cam
wireframe drawing
WMA

A Changing World

Leela is learning how to develop mobile apps because companies today connect to their customers through mobile devices.

Leela is especially interested in new mobile apps that are changing daily life, such as those that control the temperature of your home or send texts from your refrigerator when you are running low on groceries.

© iStockphoto.com/ContentWorks

Every new development in technology brings with it new career opportunities, and the field of mobile app development is no exception. Leela Chopra is taking a class on developing Android apps for smartphones and tablets. She is dedicated to creating apps that help everyone avoid stress and lead more fulfilling lives.

In this Chapter

Embedded Computers

embedded computer | adaptive system | telematics | smart card | Internet of Things (IoT) | near field communication (NFC) | radio frequency identification (RFID) tag | home automation | kiosk

The Bottom Line
- An **embedded computer** is a tiny special-purpose computer included as a component in a larger product.
- Embedded computers perform specific tasks in a product. For example, they manage transactions in ATMs and monitor the temperature in programmable home thermostats.

Fifty years ago, people imagined that future inventions would include talking cars that drove on their own and refrigerators that tracked what you ate that day. These futuristic devices are possible now because of embedded computers. See **Figure 12-1**.

Automobiles

Perhaps you've heard about cars that can park themselves. What's next? Cars that can drive on their own. Google is developing a self-driving car that uses embedded computers to control acceleration and braking along with a rooftop sensor and a global positioning system (GPS) to navigate. See **Figure 12-2**.

Figure 12-1: Embedded computers

Cruise control systems use embedded computers to maintain speed.

An embedded computer in a refrigerator can signal when food is no longer fresh.

An embedded computer monitors the temperature in programmable home thermostats.

Riders on mass transit systems can use a smart card with an embedded computer chip instead of tickets or tokens.

© Ye Liew/Shutterstock.com, © Oleksiy Mark/Shutterstock.com, © auremar/Shutterstock.com, © Heymo/Shutterstock.com

Figure 12-2: Google self-driving car

Rooftop sensor and a GPS help to navigate this self-driving car.

Embedded computers control acceleration and braking.

HANDOUT/Reuters/Landov

Although self-driving cars are years from mass production, embedded computers already improve the safety and efficiency of all automobiles manufactured today:
- An embedded computer monitors engine emissions in your car and adjusts settings such as idle speed to keep the emissions as low as possible.
- Cruise control systems use embedded computers to maintain speed.

- **Adaptive systems** can detect if your car is following another car too closely and adjust the speed to maintain a safe distance.
- Airbag sensors can detect the severity of a collision and inflate the airbag accordingly, which reduces airbag injuries.
- Some cars use **telematics**, a wireless communication technology, to provide systems such as dashboard navigation and remote vehicle tracking.

Public Transportation

Americans are using public transit more now than they have in over 50 years. One reason for the move is that embedded computers are helping to make public transportation convenient, efficient, and safe. For example, on smart buses, drivers use touchscreens to check traffic, communicate with people waiting for rides, collect fares, and provide travel information to riders waiting for the bus.

In addition, mass transit systems use smart cards instead of tickets or tokens. About the size of a credit card, a **smart card** contains an embedded computer chip to manage payments and deposits and to provide security.

Public transportation vehicles can communicate with embedded computers in road signs to reduce traffic congestion, display the safest speed limits for the conditions, and transmit warnings to drivers.

Home Appliances

Imagine washing machines that launder clothes using the most efficient amount of electricity and water, and ovens you can turn off from smartphones. Although they sound futuristic, these smart home appliances are available today. They are part of the **Internet of Things (IoT)** and use embedded computers to reduce energy consumption and enhance daily living.

In some home appliances, an embedded computer controls how much energy the appliance is using. You can even set the machine to run when electricity rates are at their lowest. Other appliances can send messages to your mobile device. For example, they can alert you when a dryer's cycle is complete. You also can use a mobile device to control appliances, such as setting an oven's temperature. See **Figure 12-3**.

Finally, appliance technicians can use embedded computers to remotely troubleshoot mechanical problems.

Supermarkets

Embedded computers in appliances such as refrigerators and ovens are only half the story. The other half is embedded technology in supermarkets and other stores.

Near field communication (NFC) is a short-range wireless technology that works with smartphones and **radio frequency identification (RFID) tags**, which are programmable computer chips embedded in paper or plastic. If a grocer includes an RFID tag next to a product on the shelves, you can hold your smartphone near the tag to send a coupon or detailed nutritional information to your phone.

Another shopping technology uses a robot-controlled grocery cart that stores your shopping list, tracks your purchases, and helps you find items anywhere in the store. With these technologies, you can fill a shopping cart from home, pay for the products using a smartphone, and then arrange to have the goods delivered to your door—avoiding the store completely.

Homes

Buyers have always balanced cost, location, and size when searching for a new home. Now they can consider an additional factor: home automation. **Home automation** involves controlling systems such as heating, cooling, and security to increase comfort, quality of life, and even health.

Using sensors and embedded computers, you can set up a home automation network and communicate with it from a control pad or mobile device. For example, you can set music to start playing as party guests arrive, lock or unlock doors remotely, and turn off lights in empty rooms. See **Figure 12-4**.

Figure 12-3: Using a mobile device to control an appliance

Smartphone turns on the oven and sets the temperature.

© Ingrid Balabanova/Shutterstock.com, © vectorlib.com/Shutterstock.com

Figure 12-4: Home automation

Home automation app lets owners control home systems inside or outside the house.

© Denys Prykhodov/Shutterstock.com

Home automation systems are especially valuable for older people who want to live independently. They can coordinate smart refrigerators that track nutrition, smart ovens that simplify cooking tasks, and monitors that detect when someone needs help.

ATMs and Kiosks

Using an automated teller machine (ATM) to withdraw cash from a bank account is nothing new. You insert a card with a magnetic stripe, enter a personal identification number, and then indicate the amount of cash you want to receive. Recent innovations are improving card security: soon, most cards will have an embedded chip instead of a magnetic stripe, which is much more difficult to copy.

New technology also makes the machines more personal. For example, using one type of ATM, you can interact with a bank teller by videoconference.

Banks aren't the only businesses that have automated customer interactions. Machines called **kiosks** enable self-service transactions in busy locations such as airports and hotels, so you don't have to wait in line to check in for a flight or a room. Healthcare providers can also install kiosks or tablets for patients, who can use them to check in and enter information such as insurance numbers.

Connected Homes

online banking | e-learning | asynchronous course | synchronous course | live blogging | on-demand media | electronic retail (e-tail) sales | mobile commerce (m-commerce)

Your grandparents probably spent much of their day outside their home. They managed their finances at their local bank, picked up a paper at a newsstand, went to a theater to see movies, and shopped along a downtown street or in a mall. Now you can perform all of these activities from home using a computer and an Internet connection.

Figure 12-5: Managing daily living tasks

E-learning is formal education in which students connect to instructors, information, and other students online.

Track your bank balances and conduct financial transactions online.

Research products and services online, and then make a purchase from any Internet-connected device.

Find and read news articles and opinions online, in some cases, even as events are happening.

© bloomua/Shutterstock.com, © Andresr/Shutterstock.com, © LDprod/Shutterstock.com, © iStockphoto.com/LdF

Online Finances

Most people use computers in some way to manage their finances. For example, you might use financial software to balance your checkbook and track your income and expenses. Banks and other financial institutions also let you do **online banking**, in which you use a computer connected to the Internet to manage your bank accounts.

At many Web sites, you can plan for retirement, maintain a budget, and calculate mortgage payments. The IRS has a Web site where you can file your federal tax return. If you want to invest in the stock market, you can use online investing tools to buy and sell stocks and bonds without using a broker.

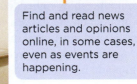

Online Education

Suppose you want to enroll in a career-training program, but your current job or family responsibilities prevent you from enrolling in traditional classes. A popular solution is online education, also called **e-learning**, short for "electronic learning." E-learning involves formal education in which students connect to instructors, information, and other students using a computer and the Internet.

Some courses are **asynchronous courses**, which means that instead of receiving instruction live from a teacher, you connect to educational content such as recorded demonstrations and lectures to participate at your own pace. Others are **synchronous courses**. The instructor holds a class that you and other students attend virtually. The teacher speaks, plays videos, and shows presentations. When you ask a question, you receive an immediate response from the instructor. In both types of online education, you interact with other students using blogs and wikis to hold discussions, collaborate on projects, and brainstorm.

News and Information

Fifteen or twenty years ago, most people learned about world events through television or newspapers. The Web has changed all that in the following ways:

- **Type of information**: The Web has changed the kind of information provided in news reports. TV newscasts feature amateur videos from video-sharing sites to cover events such as weather disasters. Newspapers quote blog members who post eyewitness accounts of events, an activity called **live blogging**.
- **Access to information**: As a news consumer, you can use the Web to access almost every newspaper and magazine in the world. If you run across an article you find important or funny, you can share it with your friends on social networks. In fact, referrals from social networks are the fastest-growing source of traffic for news Web sites.
- **Contribute to information**: On hybrid Web sites that combine news and blogging, you can develop and refine news reports by commenting on them and posting contributions.

Entertainment and Media

As with news and information, the Web has transformed entertainment and media by delivering it online. **On-demand media** is popular because you can view or listen to it at any time rather than according to a set schedule. For example, you can do the following:

- Download digital books and magazines and then use an e-book reader or tablet to read them.
- Acquire, search, and store digital books and magazines more easily than printed copies.
- Play TV shows, movies, and music online, instead of downloading them.
- Subscribe to podcasts of radio programs or other audio content, and then listen to them at your convenience.

The Web is making entertainment more personal in other ways. For example, using an online music service, you can create a personal radio station by listening to songs and then voting for the ones you like or dislike. See **Figure 12-6**.

Shopping

Do you like to research products and services online before you buy them? If so, you are part of the trend in **electronic retail (e-tail) sales**. E-tail Web sites are helpful to consumers looking for bargains. These sites provide product descriptions and reviews and let you compare features and prices of similar products. You can make purchases online or save items in a wish list for you or others to purchase later.

Another shopping trend is **mobile commerce (m-commerce)**, which involves using wireless mobile devices such as smartphones and tablets to make retail purchases. You can use mobile devices to purchase almost any product or service. Instead of carrying cash or even bank cards, you can use your mobile device to scan a graphic code and then authorize a payment from a connected account. See **Figure 12-7**.

Hot Technology Now

Create a custom magazine using the Paper app, which is published by Facebook. The magazine format provides a social networking news feed of posts from your Facebook friends.

Hot Technology Now

Listen to streaming radio stations and create a custom playlist on popular music services at Spotify, Pandora, Xbox Music, iTunes Radio, and ShoutCast.

By the Numbers Now

E-tail accounts for 1 out of every 10 retail dollars spent, and is projected to grow significantly in the immediate future.

Figure 12-6: Online entertainment

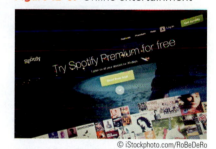

© iStockphoto.com/RoBeDeRo

Figure 12-7: M-commerce

In many places, you can use your smartphone to pay for purchases.

© Tyler Olson/Shutterstock.com

Intelligent Workplaces and Classrooms

enterprise computing | social enterprise | telecommute | BYOD | computer-aided manufacturing (CAM) | machine-to-machine (M2M) | telemedicine | mobile health (mHealth) | digital divide | learning management system (LMS)

Innovations in workplaces and classrooms are making it possible for all types of people to work and learn more productively.

Enterprises

Have you dreamed of starting a career in a major corporation and working your way up to the executive suite? If so, you aspire to be part of an enterprise. Enterprises have special computing needs because they employ hundreds or thousands of people in many locations.

Figure 12-8: Working and learning online

A recent college graduate starts a new job with a major corporation, but spends three days a week working from home.

Following directions from a surgeon on a video conference, a medical team prepares to treat a patient who lives far from a surgical hospital.

A factory foreman supervises robots on the assembly line from the safety of his office as they perform dangerous manufacturing tasks.

Elementary school students use computer simulations to learn how a cold virus develops and spreads.

© spotmatik/Shutterstock.com, © Nataliya Hora/Shutterstock.com, © iStockphoto.com/Blend_Images, © Hurst Photo/Shutterstock.com

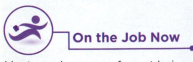

On the Job Now

Most employees prefer not being stuck at their desk with a desktop computer. Mobile computing provides the flexibility employees like and makes telecommuting easy.

Enterprise computing refers to the computer network a business uses to let employees communicate with customers, vendors, and other employees. To make that communication easy and familiar, businesses are developing the **social enterprise**, which uses short blog posts and collaboration tools instead of email and in-person meetings.

Because they can connect to the enterprise network from anywhere, employees who need flexible work schedules can **telecommute**—an arrangement that lets them work from home and conduct business using the phone and the Internet.

When they do come to the office, employees increasingly are bringing their own computing devices, a trend called **BYOD** for "bring your own device." Employees strongly prefer using their own mobile devices to desktop computers issued by the information technology (IT) department of their employer.

Manufacturing

When you think of a factory, you probably imagine a chaotic place full of industrial dangers where people work on an assembly line to produce identical products. That type of manufacturing is becoming a thing of the past. New and future factories are bright centers of innovation, primarily due to **computer-aided manufacturing (CAM)**.

Manufacturers use CAM to streamline production and ship products out the door more quickly. With CAM, robots perform work that is too dangerous, detailed, or monotonous for people. Computers on the shop floor also make it possible to order parts and materials from the warehouse just in time to assemble a custom product according to the customer's specifications. This streamlined approach is called just-in-time manufacturing. See **Figure 12-9**.

Finally, using **machine-to-machine (M2M)** communications, a company's computers can monitor assembly lines and equipment to keep them running safely and efficiently.

Healthcare

Every job in healthcare involves computers, whether patients receive care in a hospital, clinic, or their own homes. Physicians use computers to monitor patients' vital signs and to research symptoms and diagnoses. Surgeons use computer-controlled devices to provide precision during operations such as transplant surgeries.

If you live in a remote area and need to see a specialist, your doctor might use tele-medicine to confer with the specialist. **Telemedicine** involves holding a video conference with another healthcare professional.

Mobile health (mHealth) is a growing trend. Doctors and nurses typically use smart-phones and tablets to access electronic patient records. Patients also can use mHealth devices to monitor their conditions and treatments, reducing their dependence on overburdened healthcare systems. For example, one mHealth application tracks prescription information and reminds patients to take medications by sending text messages to their mobile devices.

Transportation Services

You've heard of the global economy. A product such as a soccer ball is developed in one country, manufactured in another using materials from three other countries, and then sold around the world. The global economy needs high-tech transportation services to run efficiently.

If you work in the transportation industry, you use handheld computers to scan codes on packages or containers full of products before loading them on a vehicle, train, ship, or plane. See **Figure 12-10**. A computer automatically routes the packages to their destinations as efficiently as possible. You can track the progress of a package using almost any computing device.

If you're driving a truck or other vehicle, you use an onboard navigation system with GPS, which communicates with satellites to determine your exact location. The entire transportation industry relies on GPS to navigate from one location to another quickly and safely.

Elementary Education

Imagine a group of fifth graders tracking the path of an electron in a water molecule or solving urban traffic problems. Computer games and simulations in the elementary classroom make such investigations possible, helping students visualize processes that are otherwise hard to see.

Schools also are using special social networking tools designed for education to pro-mote school events, work cooperatively on group projects, and prevent bullying. As the cost of mobile devices declines, schools are adopting them to help close the **digital divide**—the gap between those who can access digital information, especially on the Internet, and those who cannot.

In developing countries, programs such as One Laptop per Child bridge the digital divide by providing mobile computers costing about $200 to school-age children. In developed countries, this initiative is called One-to-One.

Higher Education

Look in the backpack or hand of the average college student and, chances are, you'll find a smartphone or tablet. Besides using these mobile devices for social networking and texting, you can take advantage of recent innovations to further your education. For example, you can visit Web sites such as Academic Earth and connect to resources such as iTunes U to watch video lectures, demonstrations, and performances by world-class professors.

Figure 12-9: Computers on the shop floor

© Monkey Business Images/Shutterstock.com

Hot Technology Now

A free app named ZocDoc finds available appointment times with local doctors based on zip code.

Figure 12-10: Electronic shipping

Handheld computer scans the code on a package.

© Kzenon/Shutterstock.com

Hot Technology Now

The educational site Merlot.org provides free learning content and apps for online courses.

Instructors can use a **learning management system (LMS)** to set up Web-based training sites where students can check their progress in a course, take practice tests, and exchange messages with the instructor and other students. In fact, SAM offers many of these features. See **Figure 12-11**.

Figure 12-11: Learning management system

SAM is a Web-based training site where students can check their progress in online activities and take practice tests.

© 2015 Cengage Learning

Some schools provide these systems in the cloud, which means they are installed on a server so that students can access the systems at any time using their Web browsers. Schools can then enhance the systems more frequently and easily, keeping pace with commercial software.

Artificial Intelligence

artificial intelligence (AI) | conventional AI | computational AI | expert system | heuristic | neural network | data mining | robotics | robot | natural language processing | speech recognition | virtual reality (VR) | augmented reality

It was big news when a computer named Deep Blue beat the reigning world chess champion, and even bigger news when a computer named Watson beat two all-time champions on the television game show Jeopardy! These are only two examples of **artificial intelligence (AI)**, a branch of computer science devoted to increasing the intelligence of machines. See **Figure 12-12**.

AI Basics

Computers with AI can collect information to make decisions, reach conclusions, and combine that information in new ways, which is a form of learning. They also can communicate using language. AI applications fall into two broad categories: conventional AI and computational intelligence, as shown in **Table 12-1**.

The Bottom Line
- AI affects our lives every day with intelligent text completion, video game controls that recognize human motion, and talking smartphones that carry out our requests.
- AI is the technology behind robotics, voice recognition, and software such as expert systems and neural networks.

Figure 12-12: Artificial intelligence

Self-propelled vacuum cleaners are robots that use AI to navigate rooms.

A computer named Watson used AI to beat two all-time champions on Jeopardy!

Smartphones that accept voice input use AI to respond to spoken commands.

Personal investment software uses AI to help investors select stocks and bonds.

© John Kasawa/Shutterstock.com, © bloomua/Shutterstock.com, © iStockphoto.com/theasis, Jeopardy!/Landov

Table 12-1: Categories of AI

Type	Definition	Example
Conventional AI	Takes advantage of a computer's ability to use logic, or statistics and probabilities, to solve a problem	Search engine suggesting a search term after you enter a few letters
Computational AI	Performs cycles of tasks and learns from each cycle	Financial system that helps investors select the best stocks or bonds

AI Software

When you visit the doctor seeking treatment for a skin rash, you trust that the doctor has enough expertise to tell the difference between a common rash and something more serious. To make an accurate diagnosis for more complicated medical problems, your doctor might use an **expert system**—conventional AI software programmed to follow rules specified by an expert in the field.

Expert systems use **heuristics**, or rules of thumb, to solve problems, just as people do. For example, if it's a hot summer day and your rash is red and itchy, an expert system would conclude that you might have a heat rash.

In contrast, software that relies on computational intelligence can learn for itself. **Neural networks**, for instance, use technology to simulate how our brains generate paths from one neuron to another when gaining knowledge. Neural networks are well-suited to recognizing patterns such as those in sounds and symbols, which leads to speech recognition and reading. **Figure 12-13** compares an expert system with a neural network.

#changingworld

You interact with artificial intelligence in your daily life when a site such as amazon.com suggests products that you might like. To make these suggestions, Amazon uses data mining to compare your shopping profile to those of other shoppers.

Figure 12-13: Expert systems and neural networks

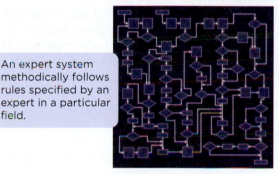

An expert system methodically follows rules specified by an expert in a particular field.

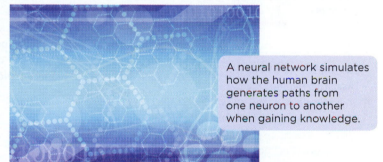

A neural network simulates how the human brain generates paths from one neuron to another when gaining knowledge.

© maxstockphoto/Shutterstock.com, © wongwean/Shutterstock.com

Instead of diagnosing a condition using heuristics, a neural network could use **data mining**, a search technique that organizes and analyzes data in a meaningful way, to quickly analyze a mountain of data and recommend the best treatment.

Robotics

Robots seem to be everywhere: on the factory floor, in the operating room, and even collecting soil samples on Mars. **Robotics** is the area of AI that focuses on practical uses for **robots**, which are machines that can move automatically.

Researchers have designed robots that roll, walk, and glide. Many types of robots have been used on factory floors for decades. Some robots interact with people by recognizing speech and interpreting gestures and facial expressions. See **Figure 12-14**.

For the most part, robots' accomplishments are limited by their programming. A robot vacuum can clean the floor but not learn which rooms need cleaning the most frequently. However, a new generation of robots is being developed that mimics the way people can sense, learn, and adapt as they perform tasks. For example, such robots can serve as receptionists in hospitals, assist the elderly, and clean office buildings.

Figure 12-14: Robotics

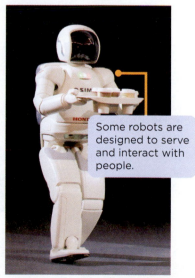

Some robots are designed to serve and interact with people.

© Catwalker/Shutterstock.com

Hot Technology Now

Open YouTube and search for "Double Robotics" to view a robot that provides face-to-face interaction.

Hot Technology Now

The Oculus Rift virtual reality headset provides a truly immersive gaming and entertainment experience. It provides a 3D interactive screen in a head-mounted display that you wear like a pair of goggles.

The Bottom Line
- **Assistive technology (AT)** includes devices and software designed to help people with disabilities.
- AT includes technologies to provide assistance to those with visual, audio, motor, and educational disabilities.

Speech

When you say, "Where can I find lunch around here?" to a smartphone, how does it understand your request? The answer is **natural language processing**, a type of AI that computers can use to understand natural human languages, such as English.

Natural language processing makes speech recognition possible. With **speech recognition**, a computer can understand and react to spoken statements and commands. Using speech recognition tools on a mobile phone, for example, you can say, "Call Nancy Ferguson," and have the phone dial the number for Nancy Ferguson as specified in its contacts list.

Speech recognition software uses AI to gather the sounds of your speech, compare them to a large library of words, phrases, and sentences, and then make a best guess about what you said. To enjoy the full benefits of speech recognition software, you must train it so it understands your speaking style and terms you use often.

Virtual Reality

Have you played a super-realistic online game that lets you explore worlds and interact with digital beings? If so, you have enjoyed immersive virtual reality. **Virtual reality (VR)** is a computer-simulated, 3D environment that you can explore and manipulate. **Augmented reality** is a type of VR that uses an image of an actual place or thing and adds digital information to it. For example, a map that shows the location of nearby transit stops or a football broadcast that shows a first-down marker is using augmented reality.

Although VR developers work mostly with digital graphics and animation, they use artificial intelligence when creating virtual creatures that make decisions and change their behavior based on interactions with others.

Outside of games, science and medicine use VR for training and research. For example, medical students can use VR to practice their emergency medical skills. NASA uses VR to simulate space flight and the environment of other planets. NASA also uses VR along with AI to train a robot that performs repairs, for example. In fact, VR is most helpful exploring outer space, the depths of the oceans, and other hard-to-reach places.

A Helping Hand

assistive technology (AT) | screen reader | personal listening assistant | closed caption | fine motor control | word prediction software | dyslexia | Dyslexie

A student in a wheelchair can take a full load of classes using a tablet computer for course work. A musician with low vision can use the accessibility features on her computer to explore the Web. These people and thousands more like them are productive because of assistive technology.

Figure 12-15: Assistive technology

Assistive technology includes touch-based programs with audio feedback so users with visual impairments can find controls on their own.

Tablets demand less fine motor control than laptop or desktop computers.

Closed captions display the text version of spoken words in online videos for users with hearing impairments.

Visual Assistance

Millions of colors, crisp resolution, rich use of shadows and gradients—these qualities help to make computers engaging and easy to use. But what if you had poor vision or couldn't distinguish certain colors? How could you interact with computers and take advantage of all they offer?

You could use any of a growing number of technologies designed to make computers easier to use if your sight is impaired. For example, computers and mobile devices have speech recognition tools that let you speak commands out loud. See **Figure 12-16**.

Operating systems include settings to increase the size of text and objects or change their color. You also can use a **screen reader**, software that reads onscreen text aloud, especially on Web pages. Another option is a Braille printer, which prints information in Braille.

Audio Assistance

In some classrooms, teachers are actually encouraging students to wear earphones plugged into digital devices. The students aren't using the devices to listen to their iTunes playlists but to help them hear the teacher better. In some cases, these **personal listening assistants** record spoken information such as classroom lectures so students can play it back later.

Other audio aids include **closed captions** in online videos, a move big and small broadcasters alike are adopting. Closed captions display the text version of spoken words in a video or other presentation. Movie theaters can provide personal captioning devices, such as those that attach to cup holders on theater seats.

Limited Mobility

Even if you have difficulty walking or performing other movements, you can still explore the digital world using innovations in computer technology. For example, instead of using a mouse, touchscreen, or keyboard, you can manipulate a trackball attached to table or wheelchair. Some systems recognize gestures such as sign language, lip and facial movements, or even eye motions—so you literally could start playing a video in the blink of an eye.

Using technology straight out of science fiction, people with paralyzed limbs can have a computerized transmitter implanted in their brain so they can control a computer with their thoughts. When combined with robotics, these innovations let people with limited mobility live more independent lives. For example, robots with gesture recognition could turn on the lights, clean the floor, or make dinner in response to a nod, blink, or thought.

Fine Motor Disabilities

When you try to type text or draw an image very quickly, it usually contains many errors because you are giving up fine motor control for speed. **Fine motor control** involves coordinating small muscle movements, usually in the fingers and hands, to accomplish a task.

Tablets are a boon to people with fine motor disabilities because they demand less fine motor control than laptop or desktop computers. Users can touch a tablet's large icons, type using the onscreen keyboard, and navigate Web pages by swiping.

On any kind of computer, **word prediction software** reduces the number of keystrokes you need to make when writing, which makes communicating easier. See **Figure 12-17**. These features are available on popular, mainstream products that people with physical disabilities can use without modifying them, making it easier and less expensive to adopt the technologies.

Figure 12-16: Speech recognition on an iPhone

© iStockphoto.com/yusufsarlar

#changingworld

For general computer use, operating systems let you adjust the volume, change computer sounds, and use text or other visual alternatives to sound cues.

#changingworld

Tobii Technology, a vendor in eye-tracking technology, is teaming up with Beamz, a developer of digital music products, to create products that let users with communication or mobility disabilities play and control songs only with eye movements.

Figure 12-17: Word prediction software

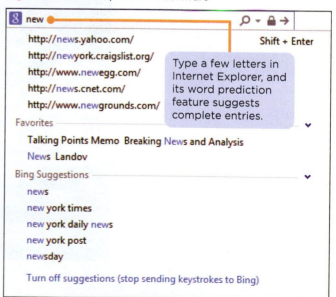

Educational Assistive Technologies

Affordable assistive technology is changing the modern classroom, especially for students with learning disabilities and other cognitive problems. In particular, students are using tablets with AT software designed to improve communication, behavior, and learning. These are some examples:

- Nonverbal students can manipulate pictures on a tablet to communicate.
- Students with **dyslexia**, a difficulty in learning to read and comprehend written words, can display text in **Dyslexie**, a font designed to help them read and write.
- Students with autism generally respond more favorably to images than language, so teachers are using slide shows that teach social skills and appropriate behaviors.

Overall, the recent popularity of tablet computers is spurring significant progress for students with learning impairments.

Green Computing

vampire device | e-reader | e-writer

When you buy a computer, experts tell you to look for one with a large hard drive, lots of memory, and a powerful processor. Considering the high cost of electricity and the global need to conserve resources, you also should look for a computer that saves energy.

The Bottom Line
- Green computing means using computers and mobile devices in environmentally responsible ways.
- Following green computing practices reduces energy consumption and conserves resources.

Figure 12-18: Green computing

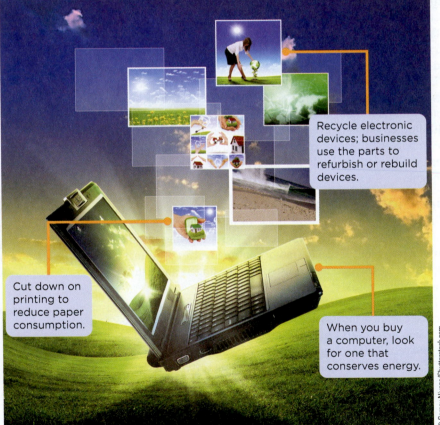

Recycle electronic devices; businesses use the parts to refurbish or rebuild devices.

Cut down on printing to reduce paper consumption.

When you buy a computer, look for one that conserves energy.

© Sergey Nivens/Shutterstock.com

Going Green

If you're concerned about how much energy computers consume and how much waste they contribute to the environment, you're not alone. Companies that create and use computers realize that green computing makes business sense because it saves money and resources.

Manufacturers are making an effort to build energy-efficient computers and use recyclable cases and packaging. They are also reducing the amount of toxic chemicals in components such as monitors to make them easier to recycle.

You can help reduce energy consumption by unplugging **vampire devices**, which are those that draw power even when they are turned off or in standby mode, such as computers, chargers, and home electronics. Conserve resources when you can. For example, reading email messages onscreen instead of printing them can save tons of paper over time.

Recycling Electronics

As a conscientious consumer, you probably take advantage of recycling programs for paper, glass, and plastic. You also can recycle computer equipment, though doing so is more complicated than placing an old monitor in a recycling bin.

- **Recycling centers**: Some community and private recycling centers accept electronic equipment, but many charge a fee because they must safely extract the hazardous materials the equipment contains.
- **Device manufacturers**: The companies that manufacture electronic equipment often collect and recycle their products, and some reclaim parts that they can use to refurbish other products.
- **Creative reuse**: People make mobiles and wind chimes from old CDs, mosaics from keyboard keys, and clocks from hard drives. See **Figure 12-19**.

Recycling Ink and Toner

Laser and inkjet printers that quickly produce high-quality text can benefit businesses and consumers alike. But they also generate an enormous amount of e-waste. In North America, people discard over 350 million ink and toner cartridges per year in landfills. These cartridges can take up to 450 years to decompose.

Instead of throwing away your ink and toner cartridges, recycle them. Most printer manufacturers provide postage-paid shipping boxes so you can return the cartridges for recycling. Manufacturers also refill used cartridges and resell them at reduced rates. Refilling cartridges consumes less energy than manufacturing new ones. If you buy recycled cartridges to begin with, you are reducing e-waste and energy consumption at the same time.

Paperless Society

Has a store clerk recently asked whether you want a printed receipt? Forgoing printed receipts is part of a larger move toward a paperless society, which provides and stores information electronically instead of on paper.

Right now, the United States uses about 71 million tons of paper each year, which is close to one billion trees' worth of paper. Paper mills also contribute significant amounts of pollution to the environment. To combat this, businesses and organizations are cutting down on paper consumption. For example, the U.S. government is phasing out paper checks for Social Security and other benefit programs.

Digital alternatives let you decrease your personal paper use. For example, **e-readers** let you read paperless books, and **e-writers** make it possible to write paperless notes, draw sketches, and even make doodles.

Donating Computer Equipment

Instead of letting a PC collect dust in a back room or leak toxic chemicals into a landfill, donate the computer to a school, church, or community program. Secondhand stores often accept old computer equipment if it's in good working order.

Refurbishers repair newer computer equipment and sell it or distribute it to groups that need it. To aid refurbishers, include the keyboard, mouse, and other peripherals

Figure 12-19: Creative reuse of electronic products

CD is used in a wind chime instead of being discarded.

© chungking/Shutterstock.com

#changingworld

Consumers save paper by paying most of their bills online, sending email instead of handwritten letters, and accepting receipts as instant messages for most transactions.

along with the original documentation or other printed information. Before donating a computer, protect yourself from identity theft by wiping the hard disk to remove all of its data. Deleting files does not thoroughly remove data. Use a special disk-wiping program to make sure the job gets done properly.

Careers

information technology (IT) department | resume | Web portfolio | certification | certification exam

You can take advantage of community and online resources to pursue careers in the computer industry.

Figure 12-20: Technology careers

A recent graduate used his degree to secure a position as a software engineer, one of the fastest-growing occupations in the computer field.

A freelance designer enrolled in a program on Web site design and is now starting her career at a global company.

A former computer technician visited the online job boards until he found an exciting job with an innovative software publisher.

© michaeljung/Shutterstock.com, © wavebreakmedia/Shutterstock.com, © EDHAR/Shutterstock.com

Technology Jobs

Whether you want to work for a major corporation or a small startup business, you can find ample job opportunities in the computer field. Technology jobs include the following:

- **Enterprise**: To manage computer systems and their software, medium and large businesses usually have an **information technology (IT) department**. As a member of an IT department, you might set up computer equipment, design and maintain systems, train and assist other employees, or develop security practices.
- **Manufacturing**: If you work for a company that manufactures computer equipment, your job could range from assembling computer parts to engineering new products.
- **Software**: In the software field, you might write programming code, test programs, design an application, or develop an exciting new computer game.
- **Sales**: If you work for a company that sells computers, you present hardware and software that meets a buyer's needs.

Job Searches

Are you happiest tinkering with a faulty circuit board or sluggish printer? Do you design Web pages or write user guides for your friends? Do you delight in solving computer problems for other people? If you answered yes to any of these questions, you should look for a job in the computer field.

1. Start your job search by learning about specific types of technology jobs that suit your skills. Web sites such as that of the Bureau of Labor Statistics describe hundreds of jobs, including those in the computer field. See **Figure 12-21**.

The Bottom Line
- Careers in technology fields are among the highest paying and in the most demand of all employment fields.
- To prepare for a career in technology, you need training and possibly certification.

On the Job Now

Creating mobile apps for Android, iOS, and Windows is one of the fastest-growing jobs on the market.

By the Numbers Now

Based on a current study by TheLadders, 7 of the top 10 fastest-growing job titles during the last five years are technology positions that require specific technical skills for developing software and mining data.

Figure 12-21: Technology careers

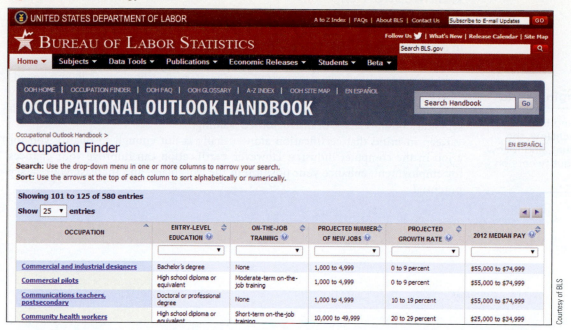

Courtesy of BLS

2. Look in many places for job openings, including local notices, your school's career placement office, and Web resources. Web resources include online newspapers, company Web sites, and job-search sites.

Resume Preparation

After scouring the Web, talking to friends, and reading want ads, you've found a few jobs you're qualified for and maybe even one that looks like your dream job. Now what? Prepare your **resume**, a summary of your education, work experience, skills, and accomplishments. An effective resume is clear, concise, accurate, and easy to read.

Resumes you submit electronically, such as by posting on a Web site or sending as an email attachment, probably will be scanned electronically. That means you need to focus on content, not formatting. Ask friends and career advisors to review your resume and offer suggestions for improvement.

Consider creating a **Web portfolio**, which is a hypertext version of your resume that includes links to samples of your work, such as Web pages you designed or programs you wrote.

Career Education

Perhaps you have a part-time job selling computer devices or training people in how to use applications. This kind of experience can prepare you for a career in the computer industry. Most likely, you need additional formal education.

A technical college, also called a trade school or career college, teaches you specific skills in programming, networking, or security, for example. You generally can complete a technical college program and receive a certificate or an associate's degree within two years of full-time studies.

To earn a bachelor's degree, you can attend a four-year college or university and study computer information systems, computer science, or computer engineering. As in many other fields, the more advanced your degree in a specific field, the better your chance of success.

 **#changingworld**

Consider adding a section to your resume detailing the technology skills and applications that you have mastered, such cloud computing and Microsoft Excel.

 **On the Job Now**

Post your resume on LinkedIn. com to network with your colleagues, classmates, and friends.

 **On the Job Now**

Most businesses consider that MOS (Microsoft Office Specialist) certification demonstrates mastery of the most recent version of Microsoft Office.

Certification

Once you're armed with an associate's, bachelor's, or advanced degree in a computer field, how can you stand out from other job seekers? You can earn **certification** in a particular area, such as software, hardware, operating systems, networking, or databases.

To become certified, you demonstrate your mastery of technology skills and knowledge by taking and passing an exam. A **certification exam** is an objective test offered by an authorized testing company. Most people prepare for a certification exam through self-study, online classes, or instructor-led training.

Keep in mind that certification alone usually is not enough to qualify you for a job in the computer industry. However, certification can improve your chances for employment, enhance your position in the workplace, and increase your salary potential.

#changingworld

Go to twitter.com, and then search for **@SAMTechNow**, the book's Twitter account, and follow @SAMTechNow to get tweets on your home page.

Chapter Review

CHAPTER 12

Embedded Computers

1. What is an embedded computer? Give two examples of embedded computers.
2. Describe a benefit of adaptive systems in an automotive vehicle.
3. How are embedded computers used in home appliances, public transportation, and supermarkets?

Connected Homes

4. What is e-learning? In what circumstances might you use e-learning?
5. How has delivering information online changed the news industry?
6. What is m-commerce and what advantages does it offer?

Intelligent Workplaces and Classrooms

7. What is a social enterprise and why might businesses want to use it?
8. How do manufacturing companies use computer-aided manufacturing (CAM)?
9. How do doctors, nurses, and patients participate in mHealth?

Artificial Intelligence

10. Give an example of conventional AI and of computational AI.
11. What is robotics? Give an example of how robotics is used today.
12. How does speech recognition software use AI?
13. How do science and medicine use VR?

A Helping Hand

14. Name five examples of assistive technology.
15. How do mobile devices with touch screens help people with disabilities?

Green Computing

16. What are vampire devices and how should you deal with them?
17. Describe three ways you can recycle electronic equipment.
18. What should you do before donating a computer to an organization?

Careers

19. What types of responsibilities do employees in IT departments have?
20. What is certification and why might you want to earn it?

Test Your Knowledge Now

1. A(n) _____ monitors engine emissions in your car and adjusts settings such as idle speed to keep the emissions as low as possible.
   a. virtual reality chip
   b. near field communication (NFC) device
   c. automotive robot
   d. embedded computer

2. A washing machine that launders clothes using the most efficient amount of electricity and water and an oven you can turn off from a smartphone are part of the _____.
   a. Web of Things
   b. Internet of Things
   c. Internet of appliances
   d. world of AI

3. Mass transit systems can use _____ instead of tickets or tokens.
   a. ATM cards
   b. smart cards
   c. smart drivers
   d. cash

4. _____ is a short-range wireless technology that works with smartphones so that you can receive detailed nutritional information about products in a supermarket, for example.
   a. Near field communication (NFC)
   b. Computer-aided manufacturing (CAM)
   c. Computer-aided shopping (CAS)
   d. Short-range communication (SRC)

5. When you connect to educational content such as recorded demonstrations and lectures and learn at your own pace, you are participating in _____.
   a. an asynchronous course
   b. telematics
   c. m-learning
   d. artificial intelligence

6. Blog members who post eyewitness accounts of live events are _____.
   a. virtual editors
   b. witness blogging
   c. live blogging
   d. synchronous bloggers

7. _____ is popular because you can view or listen to it at any time rather than according to a set schedule.
   a. Live blogging
   b. The Internet of music
   c. Telemusic
   d. On-demand media

8. Employees who need flexible work schedules can _____, an arrangement that lets them work from home and conduct business using the phone and the Internet.
   a. telecommute
   b. data mine
   c. go on sabbatical
   d. use synchronous learning

9. Using _____ communications, a company's computers can monitor assembly lines and equipment to keep them running safely and efficiently.
   a. robot
   b. asynchronous
   c. machine-to-machine (M2M)
   d. radio frequency identification (RFID)

10. If you live in a remote area and need to see a specialist, your doctor might use _____ to confer with the specialist during a video conference.
    a. telecommuting
    b. mobile medicine (mMedicine)
    c. computer-aided medicine (CAM)
    d. telemedicine

11. The gap between those who can access digital information, especially on the Internet, and those who cannot is called the _____.
    a. Internet gap
    b. digital divide
    c. information rift
    d. vampire portal

12. Video game controls that recognize human motion and talking smartphones that carry out your requests are examples of _____.
    a. learning management systems
    b. artificial intelligence
    c. adaptive systems
    d. smart cards

13. A system that performs cycles of tasks and learns from each cycle is using _____.
    a. conventional AI
    b. computational AI
    c. assistive technology
    d. e-learning

14. Expert systems use heuristics, which are _____, to solve problems.
    a. types of databases
    b. computer-to-computer communications
    c. opinions
    d. rules of thumb

15. _____ language processing is a type of AI that computers can use to understand human languages.
    a. Foreign
    b. English
    c. Machine
    d. Natural

16. _____ includes devices and software designed to help people with disabilities.
    a. Disabled technology
    b. Assistive technology
    c. Help features
    d. Green computing

17. Computers and chargers that draw power even when they are turned off or in standby mode are examples of _____ devices.
    a. vampire
    b. power
    c. neural
    d. green

18. Eliminating printed receipts is part of a larger move toward a(n) _____, which provides and stores information electronically.
    a. social enterprise
    b. electronic revolution
    c. paperless society
    d. refurbished society

19. To manage computer systems and their software, medium and large businesses usually have a(n) _____ department.
    a. enterprise
    b. green computing
    c. social networking
    d. information technology

20. To _____ in a technology field, you take and pass an objective exam offered by an authorized testing company.
    a. create a resume
    b. apply for a job
    c. avoid formal education
    d. earn certification

21. In the space next to each term below, write the letter of the phrase that defines it.
    a. embedded computer
    b. home automation
    c. neural
    d. e-writer
    e. e-learning

    _____ A type of network that controls systems such as heating, cooling, and security to increase comfort, quality of life, and health

    _____ A tiny special-purpose computer included as a component in a larger product

    _____ Formal education that involves students connecting to instructors, information, and other students using a computer and the Internet

    _____ A device that makes it possible to create paperless notes and sketches

    _____ A type of network that uses technology to simulate how our brains generate paths from one neuron to another when gaining knowledge

Try This Now

1: Internet of Things

The Internet of Things is the latest buzzword that describes the embedded sensors and communication technology in everyday devices. The Internet of Things is growing quickly and changing our kitchens, lighting, heating, and other systems in our lives.

a. Search YouTube for a current video about the Nest home thermostat. In a Word document, insert the URL of the video and then write an overview of the video in your own words in paragraph format.

b. Search YouTube for a current video about a smart refrigerator. In the same Word document, insert the URL of the video and then write an overview of the video in your own words in paragraph format.

c. Search YouTube for a current video about smart parking meters. In the same Word document, insert the URL of the video and then write an overview of the video in your own words in paragraph format.

2: Educational Sites

Whether you want to supplement course information or spark your intellectual curiosity, educational sites provide an excellent resource for learning. Open a browser and then open the site academicearth.org.

a. Investigate the Academic Earth site. Name five major universities that contribute lectures to Academic Earth.

b. Name any five online courses that you can view in Academic Earth.

c. Watch one of the video elective or course videos. Create a document that contains the video title and a list of 10 topics discussed within the video.

3: Online Job Search

Years ago, job searches were conducted primarily with the Help Wanted ads in a newspaper. Today, posting your resume online, searching jobs sites, and online networking connects an employee to an employer.

a. Identify five online job search engines. Search each of the five job sites for openings in a position that interests you. Take a screenshot of the search results page from each of the five job sites.

b. Place the screenshots in a single Word document. After each screenshot, write a paragraph about each online job search engine for a total of five paragraphs. Compare the ease of use, results, and layout of the site.

c. Save the document and submit it to your instructor.

Critical Thinking Now

1: Home Automation Apps

With your smartphone and the right app, you can control the lights, appliances, thermostat, audio and video equipment, window coverings, and security cameras in your home. Search for a smartphone app that is designed to automate your home. In a Word document of at least 150 words, discuss the app and the total cost for setting up an automated home, and then submit the document to your instructor.

Home Automation

© Brian A. Jackson/Shutterstock.com

2: Virtual Reality in Real Estate

Virtual reality and augmented reality are becoming the new standards in viewing real estate locations. Open a browser and then open bing.com/videos. Search for "augmented reality real estate" and watch at least five videos on the topic. In a Word document, insert the URLs of the five videos and then write a short paragraph providing an overview for each video.

3: Technology Jobs

Every job uses technology to some extent, but fields that are dedicated to technology are booming. Research the fastest-growing technology jobs. Locate the five technology jobs with the most growth potential and then rank them in a list. Write five paragraphs that explain each job.

Ethical Issues Now

Recently, Moshe Vardi, a computational engineering professor at Rice University, predicted that computer intelligence was growing so quickly that most human jobs would be automated by 2045. Research the topic of artificial intelligence and the workforce.

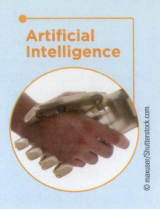

Artificial Intelligence

© maxuser/Shutterstock.com

a. If software could wipe out most of the job market overnight, how would this affect our lives? Write at least 100 words expressing your reaction in a Word document.

b. If artificial intelligence can mimic a text-to-speech engine that replaces most customer service agents, should a company's ethics board consider not using the software because of the effects on the work force? Write at least 100 words expressing your opinion in a Word document.

Team Up Now – Telecommuting Friendly Businesses

Employers that encourage employees to work from home are considered telecommuting friendly. Each team member should use the term "telecommuting friendly companies" in a search engine.

Based on your team's findings, assign each person to research a specific field that has expanded telecommuting opportunities. Each team member should write a paragraph about his or her findings.

As a team, research five positive aspects and five negative aspects of telecommuting. Next, research Marissa Mayer's opinion of telecommuting. Write a paragraph on whether your team agrees or disagrees with Ms. Mayer.

Share your results with your team and submit the combined information to your instructor.

Key Terms

adaptive system
artificial intelligence (AI)
assistive technology (AT)
asynchronous course
augmented reality
BYOD
certification
certification exam
closed caption
computational AI
computer-aided manufacturing (CAM)
conventional AI
data mining
digital divide
dyslexia
Dyslexie
e-learning
electronic retail (e-tail) sales
embedded computer

enterprise computing
e-reader
e-writer
expert system
fine motor control
heuristic
home automation
information technology (IT) department
Internet of Things (IoT)
kiosk
learning management system (LMS)
live blogging
machine-to-machine (M2M)
mobile commerce (m-commerce)
mobile health (mHealth)
natural language processing
near field communication (NFC)
neural network
on-demand media

online banking
personal listening assistant
radio frequency identification
   (RFID) tag
resume
robot
robotics
screen reader
smart card
social enterprise
speech recognition
synchronous course
telecommute
telematics
telemedicine
vampire device
virtual reality (VR)
Web portfolio
word prediction software

Index